# New Keynesian Economics

**MIT Press Readings in Economics**
**edited by Benjamin Friedman and Lawrence Summers**

*New Keynesian Economics*, vol. 1, *Imperfect Competition and Sticky Prices*, edited by N. Gregory Mankiw and David Romer, 1991

*New Keynesian Economics*, vol. 2, *Coordination Failures and Real Rigidities*, edited by N. Gregory Mankiw and David Romer, 1991

# New Keynesian Economics

Volume 1
Imperfect Competition and Sticky Prices

edited by N. Gregory Mankiw and David Romer

The MIT Press
Cambridge, Massachusetts
London, England

© 1991 Massachusetts Institute of Technology

This book was set in Times New Roman by Asco Trade Typesetting Ltd., Hong Kong, and printed and bound in the United States of America.

Library of Congress Cataloging-in-Publication Data

New Keynesian economics/edited by N. Gregory Mankiw and David Romer.
    p.    cm.—(MIT Press readings in economics)
    Includes bibliographical references.
    Contents: v. 1. Imperfect competition and sticky prices—v. 2. Coordination failures and real rigidities.
    ISBN 0-262-13266-4 (v. 1).—ISBN 0-262-63133-4 (pbk.: v. 1).—ISBN 0-262-13267-2 (v. 2).—ISBN 0-262-63134-2 (pbk.: v. 2)
    1. Keynesian economics. 2. Competition, imperfect. 3. Labor market. 4. Credit.
I. Mankiw, N. Gregory. II. Romer, David. III. Series.
HB99.7.N88    1991                                                                    90-6358
330.15′6—dc20                                                                         CIP

# Contents of Volume 1

# Contents of Volume 2

## Series Foreword

Economics, like many scientific disciplines, combines deductions from axiomatic principles and inference from empirical observations. Rigorous, logical thinking about the consequences that follow from specified sets of circumstances constitutes the backbone of the subject. But because the primary object of most economic thinking is to gain an understanding of a particular set of circumstances—those characterizing, in whole or in part, the world in which real men and women live, and work, and consume the fruits of their labors—observations of that world provide a way to distinguish which sets of circumstances and consequences (in economists' common parlance, which "models") merit investigation and perhaps even application. To a large extent, progress in the field has historically reflected just this combination of axiomatic deduction and empirical inference. Visible changes in the economic environment suggest new sets of conditions to be analyzed. The resulting model delivers specific implications. Whether those implications do or do not jibe with observed economic phenomena steers researchers either to build on the underlying model—to extend or refine it, or apply it to more specialized situations—or to search for a new model potentially more consistent with observed reality. And so, thinking in economics continues to evolve.

One result of this continuing evolution is that the study of economics, especially at the graduate level, is problematic. What economists "know" depends on when they are supposed to know it. Although the basic principles governing economic behavior presumably have not changed, economic thinking in many subfields of the discipline now differs markedly from what it was in 1970 or 1950 or 1930. (And by 2010 it will almost surely be different than it is today.) No student of economics is well advised to study only developments of the most recent few years, be they conceptual or practical. But especially for those who are learning economics with the hope of advancing the discipline by their own research, it is essential to know where the frontier of the subject lies and what lies on it. Because of the continual and often rapid evolution of thinking that results from the ongoing interaction between axiomatic reasoning and empirical observation, that frontier is, in important ways, a moving target. By the time new advances are fully integrated into textbooks and treatises, their day on the frontier is past. For this reason the student preparing to do economic research must rely to a great extent on new thinking and new findings not yet digested into secondary sources. The MIT Press Readings in Economics series is designed to help students and other potential researchers come rapidly to the frontier by providing carefully selected collections of readings in areas in which rapid progress has recently been made.

These two volumes, edited by N. Gregory Mankiw and David Romer, bring together the major contributions to what the editors describe as "new Keynesian economics." The principal thrust of the "new classical" revolution in macroeconomic thinking was that little or no theoretical grounding existed to explain in an axiomatic way such phenomena as sticky wages and prices, failure of market clearing, and "nonrational" expectations; that the role of such phenomena in macroeconomic models was at best no more than that of ad hoc assumptions; and that macroeconomics should henceforth proceed without them. Scholars working in the new classical tradition demonstrated that these features were central to the character of the description of the economic environment provided by the resulting model, so that analysis without these features delivered sharply different implications for macroeconomic behavior. But as highly visible economic events of the 1980s appeared to many to be more easily understandable in terms of models that did incorporate wage and price stickiness or nonclearing markets or expectations based on less than full and symmetric information, researchers increasingly returned to incorporating these features in macroeconomic analysis while at the same time seeking an enriched understanding of their microeconomic origins. At one level, the outcome of this effort has been to reestablish, albeit with sounder theoretical underpinnings, some traditional ways of thinking about how economies respond to various influences. At a different level, the outcome has been to refocus macroeconomic analysis on the behavior of individuals and institutions and thus to create a new frontier for research. The papers collected by Mankiw and Romer in these two volumes have contributed importantly to that effort.

Benjamin M. Friedman
Lawrence H. Summers

# Acknowledgments

We have benefitted from the comments and suggestions of a large number of colleagues in organizing this collection. We are especially indebted to George Akerlof, Laurence Ball, Olivier Blanchard, and Janet Yellen for their help in our efforts to reduce a vast literature to a coherent collection. In addition, Ben Bernanke, Alan Blinder, Peter Diamond, Richard Froyen, Mark Gertler, Robert Gordon, Stephen O'Connell, Michael Parkin, Robert Shiller, Lawrence Summers, Michael Woodford, and several anonymous reviewers provided thoughtful and useful suggestions about the choice of topics and papers and the structure of the collection. Finally, we are indebted to Jeanette DeHaan, Andrew Metrick, Stefan Oppers, and especially Karen Dynan for their assistance in preparing these volumes.

# New Keynesian Economics

# Introduction

## N. Gregory Mankiw and David Romer

Keynesian economics arose in response to the economic crisis of the 1930s. The Great Depression vividly and painfully convinced most economists that their traditional emphasis on the efficiency of unfettered markets was misplaced. Perhaps the invisible hand guides the economy in normal times, but the invisible hand is susceptible to paralysis. Events like the Great Depression require a different theory, a theory capable of explaining market failure on a grand scale.

The ascent of Keynesian economics reached its peak with the Keynesian consensus of the 1960s. Many macroeconomists at that time believed that our understanding of the economy was nearly complete, that there were only details left to fill in. The *IS-LM* model provided the theory of aggregate demand. Although the theory of aggregate supply remained murky, the Phillips Curve was widely viewed as providing a useful empirical summary of how wages and prices adjust over time. This consensus rested crucially on the assumption that wages and prices adjust only gradually to changes in aggregate demand.

This Keynesian consensus in macroeconomics faltered in the 1970s with the birth of the new classical macroeconomics. The new classical economists argued persuasively that Keynesian economics was theoretically inadequate, that macroeconomics must be built on a firm microeconomic foundation. They also argued, less persuasively, that Keynesian economics should be replaced with macroeconomic theories based on the assumptions that markets always clear and that economic actors always optimize. This research program evolved in the 1980s into real-business-cycle theory. Because these real-business-cycle models are Walrasian general equilibrium models, they imply that the invisible hand always guides the economy to the efficient allocation of resources.

New Keynesian economics arose in the 1980s in response to this theoretical crisis of the 1970s. Much research during the past decade was devoted to providing rigorous microeconomic foundations for the central elements of Keynesian economics. Because wage and price rigidities are often viewed as central to Keynesian economics, much effort was aimed at showing how these rigidities arise from the microeconomics of wage and price setting,

In these two volumes we collect some of the papers that have been central in this resurgence of Keynesian economics. Our goal in bringing together this work is to help researchers and students see what progress has been made and where the most promising directions for future research lie. We should emphasize that this work is not finished. There remain many open questions for future theoretical and empirical research.

## What Is New Keynesian Economics?

There are many authors in these volumes, and undoubtedly they disagree with each other on many important economic and policy questions. Yet we have chosen to bring these papers together because we see a common theme. Here we should try to define, at least broadly, what we mean by "new Keynesian economics."

There are two questions that one may ask about any theory of economic fluctuations.

• Does the theory violate the classical dichotomy? Does it posit that fluctuations in nominal variables like the money supply influence fluctuations in real variables like output and employment?

• Does the theory assume that real market imperfections in the economy are crucial for understanding economic fluctutations? Are such considerations as imperfect competition, imperfect information, and rigidity in relative prices central to the theory?

New Keynesian economics answers an emphatic yes to both of these questions. The classical dichotomy fails because prices are sticky. Real imperfections are crucial because imperfect competition and rigidity in relative prices are central to understanding why prices are sticky.

Among the prominent approaches to macroeconomics, new Keynesian economics is alone in answering both of these questions in the affirmative. Real-business-cycle theory emphasizes technological disturbances and perfect markets; it therefore answers both questions in the negative. Many older macroeconomic theories rejected the classical dichotomy, but they usually did not emphasize real imperfections as a key part of the story. For example, most of the Keynesian economics of the 1970s imposed wage and price rigidities on otherwise Walrasian economics. Thus the interaction of nominal and real imperfections is a distinguishing feature of new Keynesian economics.

Having said what new Keynesian economics is, perhaps we should also say what it is not. Because the debate over macroeconomic theory and policy has covered so much ground since Keynes wrote *The General Theory*, the term "Keynesian" can mean different things to different people. There are therefore many views called Keynesian that are not necessarily encompassed by new Keynesian economics as exposited by the authors in these volumes. Most important, one should not view new Keynesians as protagonists in what has been called the monetarist-Keynesian debate, for two reasons.

First, new Keynesian economists do not a hold a single view on the relative potency of monetary and fiscal policy. This debate over the control of aggregate demand is largely unrelated to new Keynesian theories of aggregate supply. An economist can be a monetarist by believing that fluctuations in the money supply are the primary source of fluctuations in aggregate demand and a new Keynesian by believing that microeconomic imperfections lead to macroeconomic price rigidities. Indeed, since monetarists believe that fluctuations in the money supply have real effects but often leave price rigidities unexplained, much of new Keynesian economics could also be called new monetarist economics.

Second, new Keynesian economists do not necessarily believe that active government policy is desirable. Because the theories developed in this book emphasize market imperfections, they usually imply that the unfettered market reaches inefficient equilibria. Thus these models show that government intervention can potentially improve the allocation of resources. Yet whether the government should intervene in practice is a more difficult question that entails political as well as economic judgements. Many of the traditional arguments against active stabilization policy, such as the long and variable lags with which policy works, may remain valid even if one is persuaded by new Keynesian economics.

## A Whirlwind Tour of New Keynesian Economics

We have divided the collection into seven parts. Parts 1 and 2 examine how frictions in price setting at the microeconomic level—costs of price adjustment and staggered timing of price changes—lead to nominal rigidity at the macroeconomic level. Parts 3 and 4 are devoted to the macroeconomic consequences of imperfect competition, including aggregate demand externalities, multipliers, and coordination failures. Parts 5, 6, and 7 are devoted to recent papers on non-Walrasian features of the labor, credit, and goods markets that may have important macroeconomic implications.

Imperfections in these markets are important both because they may play central roles in models of nominal rigidity arising from frictions in price setting and because they can give rise to other Keynesian phenomena, such as involuntary unemployment.

## 1 Costly price adjustment

The distinctive features of new Keynesian research on nominal rigidity is the idea that considerable aggregate nominal rigidity can be generated by small barriers to nominal price flexibility.[1] This basic insight is due independently to Mankiw (this collection, chap. 1), Akerlof and Yellen (this collection), and Parkin (1986). The Keynesian view that nominal disturbances are a primary source of aggregate fluctuations appears to encounter immediately a fatal objection: Economic theory (and common sense) tells us that agents should be concerned primarily with real rather than nominal magnitudes; thus it appears that nominal shocks and barriers to nominal adjustment could not be the source of, for example, large recessions and the obvious large costs they entail. Mankiw, Akerlof and Yellen, and Parkin answer this objection by building models in which frictions in price adjustment at the level of individual firms cause shifts in aggregate demand to have large real effects. In Mankiw's and Parkin's models the friction is a fixed cost of changing nominal prices (a "menu cost"); in Akerlof and Yellen's it is a small departure from full optimization ("near rationality"). As Blanchard and Kiyotaki emphasize (part 3 of this collection), the reason that small barriers to price adjustment can result in downturns with large social costs is that under imperfect competition, individual firms' decisions about price adjustment affect other firms through an "aggregate demand externality."

Ball and Romer (this collection) address the question not of whether small frictions can in principle lead to considerable nominal stickiness but of what conditions are needed for this to occur in practice. They establish that simply adding small barriers to price adjustment to an otherwise Walrasian model is likely to generate only modest amounts of nominal rigidity for plausible cases. They then go on to show that the addition of appropriate "real rigidities" to the model can reverse this result. The paper thus links the final three parts of the collection to the first two.

Caplin and Spulber (this collection) also address, but in a very different way, the question of whether microeconomic frictions will in practice have important macroeconomic effects. Specifically, they show that if the barrier to price adjustment takes the form of a fixed cost of changing prices, there are simple conditions—the most important of which are that there are no firm-specific shocks and that aggregate demand never falls—under which there is *no* price stickiness at the aggregate level. Caplin and Spulber's results have been challenged along two dimensions. The first concerns the conditions under which their results hold, *given* their assumption about the form of the barrier to price adjustment. Caplin and Leahy (1989) analyze a simple case in which the possibility that aggregate demand may either rise or fall causes demand disturbances to have real effects over a wide range. In addition, Tsiddon (1987a, 1987b), Blanchard (1987), and Caballero and Engel (1989) analyze more complex cases, also finding that shifts in demand generally move real output. The second and perhaps more important challenge to Caplin and Spulber's result focuses on the form of the friction in price adjustment. Specifically, if the friction takes some form other than a pure fixed cost, the implications for aggregate behavior may be very different; this occurs, for example, under the fixed-timing rules considered in part 2 of this collection.

One obvious implication of this discussion is that the microeconomics of price adjustment are extremely important to the macroeconomics of nominal rigidity. Barro (1972), Sheshinski and Weiss (1977), and Caplin and Sheshinski (1987) present theoretical analyses of firm behavior in the presence of costs of price adjustment.[2] Empirical studies of price adjustment by individual firms, which are essential to determining the nature and the magnitude of barriers to nominal adjustment, include Carlton (this collection), Godley and Gillian (1965), Cecchetti (1986), and Kashyap (1987). These studies suggest that the extent of nominal stickiness at the microeconomic level is large and that price-adjustment policies are quite complex. To date the reasons for those policies have defied explanation (but see Carlton 1987 for an attempt).

Finally, Ball, Mankiw, and Romer (this collection) derive and test a straightforward empirical prediction of models of aggregate nominal rigidity arising from microeconomic frictions that differs from the predictions both of the Lucas imperfect-information model and of traditional Keynesian models that take the degree of nominal rigidity as exogenous.[3]

## 2  The staggering of wages and prices

The papers in the second part of this collection explore the consequences of an additional friction in nominal adjustment: not all prices and wages are changed simultaneously. In two classic papers Fischer (this collection) and Phelps and Taylor (1977) showed that the presence of long-term nominal contracts can cause demand shifts to have real effects even if expectations are rational and the shifts are anticipated. Taylor (this collection, 1980) then showed that with two additional assumptions those real effects will continue even after all contracts have expired and hence all prices and wages have been adjusted. The needed additional features are, first, that contract negotiations are staggered and, second, that the prices and wages specified in the contracts are not continuously adjusted along a predetermined path but instead are fixed for considerable periods (such as a year at a time). Under these assumptions, if firms do not wish their prices or wages to get far out of line with others', then those firms that can adjust their prices or wages at any point will make only small changes. The result is slow adjustment of the aggregate price level to a nominal disturbance.[4] Blanchard (this collection) extends Taylor's results, which focus on wages, to prices, and demonstrates that the extent of inertia increases with the length of the chain of producton.[5] Note that a third assumption is in fact necessary for this result: firms must be reluctant to have their prices and wages deviate greatly from the prevailing level. This in turn requires the same types of conditions that Ball and Romer show are necessary for small frictions in price adjustment to generate substantial nominal rigidity. Thus again there is a link between nominal stickiness and the real imperfections considered in the final three parts of this collection.[6]

The Taylor and Blanchard papers take the timing of price and wage adjustments as exogenous. There are at least three distinct questions one can ask about this assumption. The first is why adjustment is not continuous; the answer is presumably that there are barriers of some type to costless adjustment. The second question is why adjustment policies might take a form that resembles a fixed-timing rule. This must depend on the precise nature of the barriers. As described above, empirical studies of price adjustment have not resolved the issue of what form the barriers take; they do suggest, however, that there is an important element of time dependence in actual adjustment rules. Danzinger (1983) presents a model in which fixed timing is optimal.

The third and most thoroughly explored question is why the pattern of adjustments should be staggered rather than synchronized. Fethke and Policano (1984) were the first to tackle the question of when staggered rather than synchronized price setting would arise. Fethke and Policano (this collection), Ball and Cecchetti (this collection), and Ball and Romer (1989) show that if timing is endogenous, then there are simple cases— among them the ones considered by Taylor and Blanchard—in which adjustment would in fact be synchronized. The leading proposed sources of endogenous staggering are firms' desires to learn the information contained in others' price changes before setting their own prices (Ball and Cecchetti) and the simple fact that firm-specific shocks affect different firms at different times (Ball and Romer). These two papers, along with the Fethke and Policano paper, also examine the welfare economics of equilibrium timing and show that the equilibrium pattern can be staggered even if synchronization is superior. Other possible sources of staggering have been explored by Parkin (1986), Matsukawa (1986), Fethke and Policano (1987), and Maskin and Tirole (1988).

## 3  Imperfect competition

A recurrent theme in new Keynesian economics is that deviations from perfect competition may be crucial for understanding economic fluctuations. In most goods markets, firms are price setters rather than price takers. The literature on costly price adjustment discussed above maintains the assumption of monopolistically competitive firms; indeed, it is almost impossible to comprehend the question of how firms adjust prices in a world in which firms are price takers. Yet imperfect competition has implications for macroeconomics beyond the issue of price adjustment. In a provocative paper Weitzman (1982) went so far as to argue that one could make sense of unemployment only in a world of increasing returns and imperfect competition.

Economists are only beginning to explore the macroeconomic implications of general-equilibrium models with imperfect competition. Imperfect competition has been a central feature of many models trying to provide a theoretical underpinning for the Keynesian multiplier. The first such model is that of Hart (this collection), who emphasizes the noncompetitive feature of labor markets. Mankiw (this collection, chap. 14) and Startz (1989) emphasize imperfectly competitive firms. The existence of imperfect competition creates a wedge between private and social costs, which in turn leads to an "aggregate demand externality" and a demand multiplier. Blanchard and Kiyotaki (this collection) discuss the relationship between this externality and models of costly price adjustment.

Empirical work on the macroeconomics of imperfect competition is also only beginning. In two influential papers Hall (this collection, 1988) argues that imperfect competition is the most natural way to explain the procyclical behavior of total-factor productivity. His estimates, together with those of Shapiro (1987), suggest that price is many times marginal cost in most industries. These empirical findings suggest that the aggregate-demand externalities identified in the theoretical models are potentially important in the world.

## 4  Coordination failures

If the Keynesian multipliers described above are sufficiently strong, the result can be multiple equilibria: if each firm's optimal output is increasing more than one for one with others' output, it is possible for there to be multiple equilibrium levels of output. And if there are positive externalities to higher output, the high-output equilibria can be Pareto-superior to the low-output equilibria. Thus there can be fluctuations in aggregate output and in welfare driven not by any extrinsic shocks but by changes in "confidence" and "animal spirits." Cooper and John (this collection) provide a unifying framework for examining models of coordination failure and analyze the welfare economics of coordination failure.

Perhaps the best-known candidate source of coordination failure is "thick-market externalites": markets may function better—and it may therefore be more attractive for any given firm or individual to be economically active—when many individuals are economically active. The classic model capturing this idea is due to Diamond (this collection). A second possible source of coordination failure is that production under increasing returns is more attractive when demand is high; thus actions that affect others' demands have externalities and can lead to multiple equilibria. This idea is investigated by Shleifer (this collection), Kiyotaki (1988), Shleifer and Vishny (1988), and Murphy, Shleifer, and Vishny (1989a, 1989b). Other models of coordination failure have been developed by Bryant (this collection) and Heller (1986).

The simplest models of coordination failure are static. Yet the models are often intended to provide insights into the nature of fluctuations. For example, the models are often interpreted as providing support for the views that there can be larger fluctuations in real activity without any changes in fundamentals and that there may be a role for government intervention to "coordinate" a movement to a superior equilibrium. Haltiwanger and

Waldman (1985, 1989) show how the same kinds of phenomena that give rise to coordination failure can have important implications for the response of the economy to shocks. Howitt and McAfee (1988) and Durlauf (1989) show how the final resting place of the economy can be affected by initial conditions. And Diamond and Fudenberg (1989), Murphy, Shleifer, and Vishny (1988, 1989c), and Cooper and Haltiwanger (1989) show how thick-market externalities and increasing returns can lead to recurrent cyclical fluctuations.

Ball and Romer (1989) link the literature on coordination failure with the research on nominal rigidity arising from small nominal frictions. They show that there can be multiple equilibria in the degree of nominal rigidity and that equilibria with greater price flexibility are often Pareto-superior; thus nominal price rigidity itself can represent a coordination failure.

Finally, Cooper, DeJong, Forsythe, and Ross (1990) and Van Huyck, Battalio, and Beil (1990) report experimental evidence about behavior in coordination-failure games. Both sets of authors find that individuals often fail to reach the Pareto-superior equilibrium.

Recent work on "sunspots" and "self-fulfilling prophecies" is closely related to the work on coordination failures. The central idea is that if the economy does not possess a unique equilibrium, variables of no extrinsic importance, "sunspots," can have real effects. Much of the research in this literature takes overlapping-generation models, which often have vast numbers of equilibrium paths, as the underlying economic model of multiple equilibria (Woodford 1984, Kehoe and Levine 1985, Azariadis 1981, Cass and Shell 1983). In addition, if one of the equilibrium responses to an aggregate demand disturbance involves unchanged nominal prices, the models then provide a candidate explanation of nominal stickiness without any barriers to nominal adjustment (Azariadis and Cooper 1985, Farmer and Woodford 1984, Geanakoplos and Polemarchakis 1982). But the models must then confront the questions of why, in the absence of *any* barriers to nominal adjustment, nominal rigidity is somehow selected as the equilibrium and of whether there is an important connection between nominal rigidity in overlapping-generation models, where nominal rigidity corresponds to rigidity in real rates of return, and nominal rigidity in settings where money is the medium of exchange. Finally, Grandmont (1985) shows how similar considerations can give rise to "chaotic" aggregate dynamics. Woodford (this collection) surveys this work and discusses some of the central issues.

## 5   The labor market

New Keynesian research on the labor market focuses on two issues. The first is unemployment. Is it possible for the labor market to be in equilibrium when some individuals wish to work at the prevailing wage but cannot do so? The second question concerns the cyclical behavior of real wages and unemployment. A fundamental difficulty confronting virtually all theories of short-run fluctuations, whether real or nominal, is how large movements in labor input in the short run can be reconciled with an apparently low elasticity of labor supply. If there are imperfections in the labor market, then workers are not necessarily on their labor-supply curves throughout the business cycle; thus there is no longer a necessary link between the elasticity of labor supply and the cyclical behavior of the real wage. It follows that imperfections that may lead to unemployment also have at least the potential to lead to large short-run changes in labor input accompanied by small short-run changes in real wages.

The real imperfection in the labor market that has received the most attention recently is the possibility that productivity may be affected by wages and thus create a reason that firms might choose not to cut wages in the face of an excess supply of labor. These models have been surveyed by Yellen (this collection) and Katz (1986).[7] A variety of reasons that productivity might depend on wages have been suggested. One prominent possibility is captured in "shirking" models. In these models, firms' ability to monitor workers is imperfect; firms therefore pay wages above the market-clearing level to confer rents and thereby provide workers with incentives not to engage in behavior that might cause them to lose their jobs (for example, Shapiro and Stiglitz, this collection). Bulow and Summers (1986) argue that shirking models can account for a variety of other important features of the labor market in addition to unemployment. A second candidate source of efficiency wages involves workers' notions of "fairness": workers' efforts may depend on whether they believe they are bring treating fairly by the firm, and their perceptions of fairness may depend on the wages they are paid (Akerlof 1980, 1982, 1984; Akerlof and Yellen 1989; Romer 1984). A variety of other reasons that firms might pay efficiency wages have been suggested; see for example Weiss (1980) and Salop (1979).

Little work has been done on the implications of efficiency wages for the cyclical behavior of real wages. Akerlof and Yellen (part 1 of this collection), Sparks (1986), Solow (1979), Blanchard (1987), and Ball and Romer (part

1 of this collection) all observe in various forms that it is possible for efficiency-wage considerations to make the real wage much less procyclical than in a market-clearing model. Kimball (1989) explicitly examines the dynamic implications of the Shapiro and Stiglitz shirking model, and he finds that the implications are quite complex.

Efforts to test efficiency-wage models have focused on interindustry wage differentials. Papers that have documented these differentials and discussed their implications for efficiency-wage theory include Krueger and Summers (this collection, 1987), Dickens and Katz (1987, 1988), and Katz and Summers (1989). Both efficiency-wage theory and the interpretation of the interindustry wage differentials are controversial; see for example Carmichael (1985), Murphy and Topel (1987), Topel (1989), and Hall (1989).

A second imperfection that has been extensively explored is the existence of long-term relationships between workers and firms. Work investigating the consequences of this feature of labor markets falls into two broad categories. The first category investigates the consequences of the fact that firms and workers may have different tolerances toward risk, and thus that labor contracts may have not only an allocative role but also an insurance function. These "implicit contract" models, due originally to Azariadis (1975), Baily (1974), and Gordon (1974), have been surveyed by Azariadis and Stiglitz (this collection), Azariadis (1979), Hart (1983), Rosen (1985), Stiglitz (1986), and Hart and Holmstrom (1987). The early versions of these models assumed symmetric information, with the result that contracts in effect served only an insurance role. In later models there is asymmetric information, so that both the incentive and insurance funtions are relevant.

The second line of research investigating long-term relationships between workers and firms focuses on bargaining issues. McDonald and Solow (this collection, 1985) demonstrate that the cyclical behavior of employment and real wages may be very different when it is determined by bargaining than when it is determined competitively. Gregory (1986), Blanchard and Summers (this collection, 1986), and Lindbeck and Snower (1986, 1987) argue that the presence of labor-management bargaining can cause temporary shocks to have permanent effects—so-called "hysteresis" models. And Katz and Summers (1989) argue that there may be important interactions between worker-firm bargaining and efficiency-wage considerations.

A final imperfection is the simple presence of heterogeneity among jobs and workers—"matching" or "search" models. Heterogeneity has received relatively little attention from macroeconomists, and thus its potential macroeconomic importance is unknown. Mortenson (1986) surveys the microeconomic work on matching models. Howitt (1988) notes that heterogeneity and search are potentially important for the cyclical behavior of the labor market. And Blanchard and Diamond (1989) have recently investigated the macroeconomics of job matching empirically.

## 6  The credit market

Work on credit market imperfections has focused on the consequences of asymmetric information between lenders and borrowers.[8] Borrowers may be better informed than lenders about the quality of their investment projects, about their expenditures of effort, and about the final payoffs to the projects. Research on the microeconomics of credit markets has demonstrated that these types of information asymmetries can have a variety of important microeconomic consequences: they can give rise to equilibrium credit rationing (Jaffee and Russell 1976; Stiglitz and Weiss, this collection), they can explain why contracts in the credit market often take the form of debt contracts (Townsend 1979, Gale and Hellwig 1985), they can provide an explanation of financial intermediation (Diamond 1984, Boyd and Prescott 1986), and they can create inefficiencies that potentially justify government intervention (Stiglitz and Weiss, this collection; Mankiw, this collection, chap. 28). Recent work by Hoshi, Kashyap, and Scharfstein (1988) and Fazzari, Hubbard, and Petersen (1988) has found evidence of the microeconomic importance of credit-market imperfections.

Research on the macroeconomic importance of credit-market imperfections has pursued two general directions. The first concerns the role of credit markets in the determination of aggregate demand and in the monetary-transmission mechanism. In the traditional textbook model, restrictive monetary policy is transmitted to aggregate demand by reducing the money stock and thus raising interest rates to clear the market for money. The higher interest rates then cause consumers and firms to reduce their purchases. Research on credit-market imperfections has challenged two separate features of this account. The first concerns the special role of money. By reducing the quantity of bank reserves, monetary policy may have a direct impact on banks' ability to lend. If imperfect information is important in credit markets, other potential lenders may not be able to make the loans instead. Thus, the transmission mechanism may operate in part through a direct impact on bank loans; in the extreme, the impact on money may be irrelevant. Fama (1985) discusses the competing views about whether the liability (that is, money) or asset (loan) side of banks' balance sheets is what makes banks distinctive, and he discusses the implications for the burden of reserve requirements. Bernanke and Blinder (this collection) extend the *IS-LM* model to incorporate a distinct role for bank loans and discuss the implications of the extended model.

The second challenge to the traditional view of the transmission mechanism focuses on whether the reduction in lending takes place through increases in interest rates or through rationing. Stiglitz and Weiss (this collection), Mankiw (this collection, chap. 28), and Blinder (1987) demonstrate that rationing may be central to the transmission mechanism.

Finally, if bank loans are important to the determination of aggregate demand, shocks to the intermediation process will affect demand. This point is made at a general level by Bernanke and Blinder (this collection) and concretely in the context of the Great Depression by Bernanke (this collection). And if debt contracts are written in nominal terms, unanticipated inflation will itself be a shock to intermediation by redistributing wealth between lenders and borrowers. Thus with nominal debt contracts, nominal shocks may have important real consequences even if prices and wages are flexible (Farmer 1984, Bernanke and Gertler 1989).

The second general direction of research on the macroeconomic consequences of credit-market imperfections concerns how these imperfections can propagate and exacerbate real disturbances. A variety of authors, including Bernanke (this collection), Bernanke and Gertler (1989), Greenwald and Stiglitz (1988a), and Williamson (1987), have shown how finanical-market imperfections can magnify the effects of disturbances and introduce new propagation mechanisms into the economy. The basic idea is simple. The smaller the extent of self-finance or the higher the probability of bankruptcy, the more important are credit market imperfections. Shocks that act initially to reduce output (or to redistribute wealth from borrowers to lenders) thus cause credit markets to function less well, which leads to further declines in output.[9] Even more strikingly, Mankiw (this collection, chap. 28) and Bernanke and Gertler (1990) show how disturbances that would have only mild effects with Walrasian credit markets can cause discontinuous change ("financial collapse") in the presence of credit-market imperfections.

Empirical research on the macroeconomic consequences of credit-market imperfections is still in its early stages. Friedman (1982, 1983, 1986) shows that the correlation between aggregate measures of credit and real activity is as high and as stable over time as the money-output correlation. Similarly, Bernanke (this collection) shows that measures of financial-market disturbances were significant predictors of real economic activity during the Great Depression, and Greenwald and Stiglitz (1986b) argue that the "stylized facts" about the business cycle are more consistent with theories focusing on capital-market imperfections than with traditional theories. Wojnilower (1980) and Eckstein and Sinai (1986) provide descriptive accounts emphasizing the importance of credit-market disturbances in postwar fluctuations. Finally, King (1986), Bernanke and Blinder (1989), and Romer and Romer (1990) examine the role of bank lending in particular in cyclical fluctuations and in the monetary transmission mechanism; none find strong evidence of a role for bank loans.

## 7 The goods market

The central focus of new Keynesian research on the goods market—beyond the general research on imperfect competition that is the topic of part 3—is the cyclical behavior of the markup. Firms' incentives to raise prices in response to changes in aggregate output are central to the question of whether small frictions in nominal adjustment can generate substantial nominal rigidity. One critical determinant of those incentives is the behavior of marginal cost, which in turn depends on the degree of returns to scale (parts 3 and 4), the behavior of the real wage (part 5), and the behavior of capital costs (part 6). The other critical determinant is the behavior of price for a given marginal cost—the markup.

The classic early theoretical discussions of possible sources of counter-cyclical markups include Phelps and Winter (1970) and Okun (this collection). Phelps and Winter emphasize that a change in the price of a firm's product affects sales along two margins—sales to a given set of customers and the actual number of customers—and that this may have important implications for the cyclical behavior of prices.[10] Okun focuses on the importance of long-term relationships for firms' pricing policies, an idea that is investigated further by Woglom (1982). Okun's paper also discusses a wide range of other issues related to the subject of this collection, including the link between real imperfections and nominal rigidity and the welfare costs of inflation.

Stiglitz (this collection) surveys a wide variety of candidate reasons for a countercyclical markup. One natural possibility is that a higher level of economic activity reduces the importance of costs of acquiring and disseminating information and thus makes markets more competitive; that is, "thick-market" effects may be important to the cyclical behavior of the markup (see for example Barsky, Kimball, and Warner 1988). Another possibility, due to Rotemberg and Saloner (this collection), is that the increased profits created by greater economic activity make it more difficult for oligopolists to sustain collusion and thereby place downward pressure on markups. A variety of other possible sources of countercyclical markups have been proposed; see for example Blinder (1982) and Rotemberg and Summers (1988).

Since the markup is the ratio of price to marginal cost, the key step in empirically determining the cyclical behavior of the markup is determining the cyclical behavior of marginal cost. Empirical work in this area is at an early stage and has yielded decidedly mixed results. Bils (this collection), noting that overtime is expensive to firms and that overtime is highly procyclical, argues that marginal cost must be strongly procyclical and thus that the markup is countercyclical. Ramey (1989) and Miron and Zeldes (1988), on the other hand, observe that firms show no desire to use inventories to smooth production and conclude that marginal cost is largely unaffected by the level of output and thus that the markup is approximately acyclical.

## Conclusion

After two decades of ferment, macroeconomics may be in the process of returning to a state similar to that of the 1960s. The new classical argument that the Keynesian assumption of nominal rigidities was incapable of being given theoretical foundations has been refuted. More importantly, the broad outlines of an account of macroeconomic fluctuations based on nominal rigidity are becoming clear. The key ingredients are small barriers to full and immediate nominal adjustment and the real rigidities in the markets for labor, goods, and credit that cause those small barriers to generate large amounts of nominal stickiness.

But the recent progress in Keynesian economics has not merely provided justifications for the models of the 1960s. Real imperfections are now a central part of the Keynesian world view, and those imperfections have important implications for many subjects—unemployment, rationing, the possibility of beneficial government intervention, and so on—beyond the

failure of the classical dichotomy. Indeed, much of the progress in understanding real imperfections—including work on such subjects as efficiency
wages, credit rationing, and thick-market externalities—has been a spill-
over from efforts to provide microeconomic foundations for Keynesian
macroeconomics. Thus the reconstruction of Keynesian economics has not
only provided a basis for the assumption of nominal stickiness and improved our understanding of the macroeconomy; it has also been part of
a revolution in microeconomics as well.

There is much that remains to be done. Only the most general outline of
a complete account of economic fluctuations is visible. The precise source
and nature of the frictions in price adjustment and the real imperfections that magnify their effects are unknown. Thus, after a frustrating two
decades when the most fundamental questions in macroeconomics were
unanswered and at times appeared unanswerable, we might be entering a
period in which rapid progress on important issues will lead to large strides
in macroeconomic knowledge.

## Notes

1. The research covered in this section is surveyed by Blanchard (1987); Rotemberg (1987);
Ball, Mankiw, and Romer (this collection); and Romer (1990).

2. In addition, Sheshinski and Weiss (1979), Rotemberg and Saloner (1987), and Benabou
(1988, 1989) investigate the implications of costs of price adjustment for a variety of microeconomic questions.

3. In addition, the work on the macroeconomic consequences of small nominal frictions has
been extended in a variety of directions. Ball (1987) and Ball and Romer (1989) consider the
welfare economics of output fluctuations caused by demand movements and barriers to price
adjustment. Akerlof and Yellen (1985b), Jinushi and Romer (1988), and Rotemberg (1982a,
1982b) consider dynamic cases. And Akerlof and Yellen (1985c) discuss other ways in which
small frictions of various kinds can have large aggregate consequences.

4. Early hints of this result are contained in the classic papers of Akerlof (1969) and Phelps
(1978).

5. A recent paper by Ball (1990) establishes that Taylor's and Blanchard's result of slow
adjustment of *prices* does not imply slow adjustment of *inflation*: in standard models of
staggered adjustment the central bank can rapidly reduce the rate of inflation without causing
a recession. Thus the presence of inertia not just in prices but in inflation as well remains a
puzzle.

6. In addition, Blanchard (1986) considers the case of a mix of wage and price adjustment,
Taylor (1983) and Blanchard (1987) investigate staggering models empirically, and Calvo
(1983) and Romer (1989) propose a potentially more tractable model of staggered adjustment.

7. Some of the most important papers in this literature are collected in Akerlof and Yellen
(1986).

8. Gertler (1988) surveys the work covered in this section.

9. Thus credit-market imperfections serve to raise the cost of capital in downturns and thereby reduce firms' incentives to cut their prices and expand output. This strengthens the ability of small frictions in price setting to lead to price rigidity and real effects of nominal shocks. Thus again, there is a link between real rigidities and the nominal rigidities that are the subject of the first part of this collection.

10. Bils (1989, 1988) develops this idea further.

## References

### 1 Costly price adjustment

Akerlof, George A., and Yellen, Janet L., 1985a. "A Near-Rational Model of the Business Cycle, with Wage and Price Inertia." *Quarterly Journal of Economics* 100 supplement: 823–838. Reprinted in volume 1 of this collection.

Akerlof, George A., and Yellen, Janet L., 1985b. "The Theory of Near Rationality and Small Menu Costs with Continued Shocks." Mimeo. University of California, Berkeley.

Akerlof, George A., and Yellen, Janet L. 1985c. "Can Small Deviations from Rationality Make Significant Differences to Economic Equilibria?" *American Economic Review* 75 (September): 708–721.

Ball, Laurence. 1987. "Externalities from Contract Length." *American Economic Review* 77 (September): 615–629.

Ball, Laurence, Mankiw, N. Gregory, and Romer, David. 1988. "The New Keynesian Economics and the Output-Inflation Trade-off." *Brookings Papers on Economic Activity*, no. 1: 1–65. Reprinted in volume 1 of this collection.

Ball, Laurence, and Romer, David. 1989. "Are Prices Too Sticky?" *Quarterly Journal of Economics* 104 (August): 507–524.

Ball, Laurence, and Romer, David. 1990. "Real Rigidities and the Non-neutrality of Money." *Review of Economic Studies* 57 (April): 183–302. Reprinted in volume 1 of this collection.

Barro, Robert. 1972. "A Theory of Monopolistic Price Adjustment." *Review of Economic Studies* 34 (January): 17–26.

Benabou, Roland. 1988. "Search, Price Setting, and Inflation." *Review of Economic Studies* 55 (July): 353–376.

Benabou, Roland. 1989. "Optimal Price Dynamics and Speculation with a Storable Good." *Econometrica* 57 (January): 41–80.

Blanchard, Olivier J. 1990. "Why Does Money Affect Output? A Survey." In B. M. Friedman and F. H. Hahn, eds., *Handbook of Monetary Economics*, Vol. 2 (Elsevier Science Publishers); 779–835.

Blanchard, Olivier J., and Kiyotaki, Nobuhiro. 1987. "Monopolistic Competition and the Effects of Aggregate Demand." *American Economic Review* 77 (September): 647–666. Reprinted in volume 1 of this collection.

Caballero, Ricardo J., and Engel, M. R. A. 1989. "The $S-s$ Economy: Aggregation, Speed of Convergence, and Monetary Policy Effectiveness." Mimeo. Columbia University.

Caplin, Andrew, and Leahy, John. 1989. "State Dependent Pricing and the Dynamics of Money and Output." Mimeo. Columbia University. *Quarterly Journal of Economics*, forthcoming.

Caplin, Andrew, and Sheshinski, Eytan. 1987. "Optimality of $(S, s)$ Pricing Policies." Mimeo. Hebrew University of Jerusalem.

Caplin, Andrew S., and Spulber, Daniel F. 1987. "Menu Costs and the Neutrality of Money." *Quarterly Journal of Economics* 102 (November): 703–725. Reprinted in volume 1 of this collection.

Carlton, Dennis. 1986. "The Rigidity of Prices." *American Economic Review* 76 (September): 637–658. Reprinted in volume 1 of this collection.

Carlton, Dennis. 1987. "The Theory and Facts of How Markets Clear: Is Industrial Organization Valuable for Understanding Macroeconomics?" National Bureau of Economic Research, working paper no. 2178, March. *Handbook of Industrial Organization*, forthcoming.

Cecchetti, Steven G. 1986. "The Frequency of Price Adjustment: A Study of Newsstand Prices of Magazines, 1953 to 1979." *Journal of Econometrics* 31 (April): 255–274.

Godley, W. A. H., and Gillon, C. 1965. "Pricing Behavior in Manufacturing Industry." *National Institute Economic Review* 33 (August): 43–47.

Jinushi, Toshiki, and Romer, David. 1988. "Real Rigidities and the Non-neutrality of Money." Mimeo.

Kashyap, Anil K. 1987. "Sticky Prices: New Evidence from Retail Catalogues." Mimeo. Massachusetts Institute of Technology.

Mankiw, N. Gregory. 1985. "Small Menu Costs and Large Business Cycles: A Macroeconomic Model of Monopoly." *Quarterly Journal of Economics* 100 (May): 529–539. Reprinted in volume 1 of this collection.

Parkin, Michael. 1986. "The Output-Inflation Trade-off When Prices Are Costly to Change." *Journal of Political Economy* 94 (February): 200–224.

Romer, David, 1990. "Aggregate Demand and Economic Fluctuations." Mimeo. University of California. *Journal of Economic Perspectives*, forthcoming.

Rotemberg, Julio. 1982a. "Monopolistic Price Adjustment and Aggregate Output." *Review of Economic Studies* 44 (October): 517–531.

Rotemberg, Julio. 1982b. "Sticky Prices in the United States." *Journal of Political Economy* 90 (December): 1187–1211.

Rotemberg, Julio. 1987. "The New Keynesian Microeconomic Foundations." *NBER Macroeconomic Annual*, 69–114.

Rotemberg, Julio, and Saloner, Garth. 1987. "The Relative Rigidity of Monopoly Pricing." *American Economic Review* 77 (December): 917–926.

Sheshinski, Eytan, and Weiss, Yoram. 1977. "Inflation and Costs of Price Adjustment." *Review of Economic Studies* 44 (June): 287–303.

Sheshinski, Eytan, and Weiss, Yoram. 1979. "Demand for Fixed Factors, Inflation, and Adjustment Costs." *Review of Economic Studies* 46 (January): 31–45.

Tsiddon, Daniel. 1987a. "The (Mis)behavior of the Aggregate Price Level." Mimeo. Columbia University.

Tsiddon, Daniel. 1987b. "On the Stubbornness of Sticky Prices." Mimeo. Columbia University.

## 2   The staggering of wages and prices

Akerlof, George A. 1969. "Relative Wages and the Rate of Inflation." *Quarterly Journal of Economics* 83 (August): 353–374.

Ball, Laurence. 1990. "Disinflation with Staggered Price Setting: The Case of Full Credibility." Mimeo. Princeton University.

Ball, Laurence, and Cecchetti, Stephen G. 1988. "Imperfect Information and Staggered Price Setting." *American Economic Review* 78 (December): 999–1018. Reprinted in volume 1 of this collection.

Ball, Laurence, and Romer, David. 1989. "The Equilibrium and Optimal Timing of Price Changes." *Review of Economic Studies* 56 (April): 179–198.

Blanchard, Olivier J. 1983. "Price Asychronization and Price Level Inertia." In Rudiger Dornbusch and Mario Henrique Simonsen, eds., *Inflation, Debt, and Indexation* (MIT Press, 1983), 3–24. Reprinted in volume 1 of this collection.

Blanchard, Olivier J. 1986. "The Wage-Price Spiral." *Quarterly Journal of Economics* 101 (August): 543–565.

Blanchard, Olivier J. 1987. "Individual and Aggregate Price Adjustment." *Brookings Papers on Economic Activity* 1: 57–122.

Calvo, Guillermo A. 1983. "Staggered Prices in a Utility-Maximizing Framework." *Journal of Monetary Economics* 12 (November): 383–398.

Danziger, Leif. 1983. "Price Adjustments with Stochastic Inflation. *International Economic Review* 24 (October): 699–707.

Fethke, Gary, and Policano, Andrew. 1984. "Wage Contingencies, the Pattern of Negotiation, and Aggregate Implications of Alternative Contract Structures." *Journal of Monetary Economics* 14 (September): 151–170.

Fethke, Gary, and Policano, Andrew. 1986. "Will Wage Setters Ever Stagger Decisions?" *Quarterly Journal of Economics* 101 (November): 867–877. Reprinted in volume 1 of this collection.

Fethke, Gary, and Policano, Andrew. 1987. "Monetary Policy and the Timing of Wage Negotiations." *Journal of Monetary Economics* 19 (January): 89–105.

Fischer, Stanley. 1977. "Long-term Contracts, Rational Expectations, and the Optimal Money Supply Rule." *Journal of Political Economy* 85 (February): 191–205. Reprinted in volume 1 of this collection.

Maskin, Eric, and Tirole, Jean. 1988. "A Theory of Dynamic Oligopoly. I: Overview and Quantity Competition with Large Fixed Costs." *Econometrica* 56 (May): 549–570.

Matsukawa, S. 1986. "The Equilibrium Distribution of Wage Settlements and Economic Stability." *International Economic Review* 27 (June): 415–437.

Parkin, Michael. 1986. "The Output-Inflation Trade-off When Prices Are Costly to Change." *Journal of Political Economy* 94 (February): 200–224.

Phelps, Edmund S. 1978. "Disinflation without Recession: Adaptive Guideposts and Monetary Policy." *Weltwirtschaftliches Archiv* 114: 783–809.

Phelps, Edmund S., and Taylor, John B. 1977. "Stabilizing Powers of Monetary Policy with Rational Expectations." *Journal of Political Economy* 85 (February): 163–190.

Romer, David. 1989. "Staggered Price Setting with Endogenous Frequency of Adjustment." National Bureau of Economic Research, working paper no. 3134, October. *Economics Letters*, forthcoming.

Taylor, John B. 1979. "Staggered Wage Setting in a Macro Model." *American Economic Review* 69 (May): 108–113. Reprinted in volume 1 of this collection.

Taylor, John B. 1980. "Aggregate Dynamics and Staggered Contracts" *Journal of Political Economy* 88 (February): 1–23.

Taylor, John B. 1983. "Union Wage Settlements During a Disinflation." *American Economic Review* 73 (December): 981–993.

## 3  Imperfect competition

Blanchard, Olivier J., and Kiyotaki, Nobuhiro. 1987. "Monopolistic Competition and the Effects of Aggregate Demand." *American Economic Review* 77 (September): 647–666. Reprinted in volume 1 of this collection.

Hall, Robert E. 1986. "Market Structure and Macroeconomic Fluctuations." *Brookings Papers on Economic Activity*, no. 2: 285–322. Reprinted in volume 1 of this collection.

Hall, Robert. 1988. "The Relationship between Price and Marginal Cost in U.S. Industry." *Journal of Political Economy* 96 (October): 921–947.

Hart, Oliver. 1982. "A Model of Imperfect Competition with Keynesian Features." *Quarterly Journal of Economics* 97 (February): 109–138. Reprinted in volume 1 of this collection.

Mankiw, N. Gregory. 1988. "Imperfect Competition and the Keynesian Cross." *Economics Letters* 26: 7–14. Reprinted in volume 1 of this collection.

Shapiro, Matthew D. 1987. "Measuring Market Power in U.S. Industry." National Bureau of Economic Research, working paper no. 2212, April.

Startz, Richard. 1989. "Monopolistic Competition as a Foundation for Keynesian Macroeconomic Models." *Quarterly Journal of Economics* 104 (November): 737–752.

Weitzman, Martin. 1982. "Increasing Returns and the Foundations of Unemployment Theory." *Economic Journal* 92 (December): 787–804.

## 4  Coordination failures

Azariadis, Costas. 1981. "Self-fulfilling Prophecies." *Journal of Economic Theory* 25 (December): 380–396.

Azariadis, Costas, and Cooper, Russell. 1985. "Nominal Wage-Price Rigidity as a Rational Expectations Equilibrium." *American Economic Review* 75 (May): 31–35.

Ball, Laurence, and Romer, David. 1989. "Sticky Prices as Coordination Failure." Mimeo. Princeton University.

Bryant, John. 1983. "A Simple Rational Expectations Keynes-Type Model." *Quarterly Journal of Economics* 98 (August): 525–528. Reprinted in volume 2 of this collection.

Cass, David, and Shell, Karl. 1983. "Do Sunspots Matter?" *Journal of Political Economy* 91 (April): 193–227.

Cooper, Russell, DeJong, Douglas V., Forsythe, Robert, and Ross, Thomas W. 1990. "Selection Criteria in Coordination Games: Some Experimental Results." *American Economic Review* 80 (March): 218–233.

Cooper, Russell, and Haltiwanger, John. 1989. "Macroeconomic Implications of Production Bunching: Factor Demand Linkages." National Bureau of Economic Research, working paper no. 2976, May.

Cooper, Russell, and John, Andrew. 1988. "Coordinating Coordination Failures in Keynesian Models." *Quarterly Journal of Economics* 103 (August): 441–463. Reprinted in volume 2 of this collection.

Diamond, Peter. 1982. "Aggregate Demand Management in Search Equilibrium." *Journal of Political Economy* 90 (October): 881–894. Reprinted in volume 2 of this collection.

Diamond, Peter, and Fudenberg, Drew. 1989. "An Example of Rational Expectations Business Cycles in Search Equilibrium." *Journal of Political Economy* 97 (June): 606–619.

Durlauf, Steven N. 1989. "Locally Interacting Systems, Coordination Failure, and the Behavior of Aggregate Activity." Mimeo. Stanford University.

Farmer, Roger E. A., and Woodford, Michael. 1984. "Self-Fulfilling Prophecies and the Business Cycle." Center for Analytic Research in Economics and Social Science, working paper no. 84–12, University of Pennsylvania.

Geanakoplos, J. D., and Polemarchakis, H. M. 1982. "We Can't Disagree Forever." *Journal of Economic Theory* 28 (October): 192–200.

Grandmont, Jean-Michel. 1985. "On Endogenous Competitive Business Cycles." *Econometrica* 53 (September): 995–1045.

Haltiwanger, John, and Waldman, Michael. 1985. "Rational Expectations and the Limits of Rationality: An Analysis of Heterogeneity." *American Economic Review* 75 (June): 326–340.

Haltiwanger, John, and Waldman, Michael. 1989. "Limited Rationality and Strategic Complements: The Implications for Macroeconomics." *Quarterly Journal of Economics* 104 (August): 463–484.

Heller, Walter. 1986. "Coordination Failure with Complete Markets, with Applications to Effective Demand." In Walter Heller, Ross M. Starr, and David Starrett, eds., *Equilibrium Analysis: Essays in Honor of Kenneth J. Arrow* (Cambridge: Cambridge University Press).

Howitt, Peter, and McAffee, R. Preston. 1988. "Stability of Equilibria with Externalities." *Quarterly Journal of Economics* 103 (May): 261–278.

Kehoe, Timothy J., and Levine, David K. 1985. "Comparative Statics and Perfect Foresight in Infinite Horizon Economics." *Econometrica* 53 (March): 433–453.

Kiyotaki, Nobuhiro. 1988. "Multiple Expectational Equilibria under Monopolistic Competition." *Quarterly Journal of Economics* 102 (November): 695–714.

Murphy, Kevin M., Shleifer, Andrei, and Vishny, Robert W. 1988. "Increasing Returns, Durables, and Economic Fluctuations." Mimeo. University of Chicago.

Murphy, Kevin M., Shleifer, Andrei, and Vishny, Robert W. 1989a. "Income Distribution, Market Size, and Industrialization." *Quarterly Journal of Economics* 104 (August): 537–564.

Murphy, Kevin M., Shleifer, Andrei, and Vishny, Robert W. 1989b. "Industrialization and the Big Push." *Journal of Political Economy* 96 (December): 1221–1231.

Murphy, Kevin M., Shleifer, Andrei, and Vishny, Robert W. 1989c. "Building Blocks of Market-Clearing Business Cycle Models." *NBER Macroeconomics Annual*, 247–286.

Shleifer, Andrei. 1986. "Implementation Cycles." *Journal of Political Economy* 94 (December): 1163–1190. Reprinted in volume 2 of this collection.

Shleifer, Andrei, and Vishny, Robert W. 1988. "The Efficiency of Investment in the Presence of Aggregate Demand Spillovers." *Journal of Political Economy* 96 (December): 1221–1231.

Van Huyck, John B., Battalio, Raymond C., and Beil, Richard O. 1990. "Tacit Coordination Games, Strategic Uncertainty and Coordination Failure." *American Economic Review* 80 (March): 234–248.

Woodford, Michael. 1984. "Indeterminacy in the Overlapping Generations Model: A Survey." Mimeo. Columbia University.

Woodford, Michael. 1990. "Self-Fulfilling Expectations and Fluctuations in Aggregate Demand." National Bureau of Economic Research, working paper no. 3361, May. Reprinted in volume 2 of ths collection.

## 5  The labor market

Akerlof, George A. 1980. "A Theory of Social Custom, of Which Unemployment May Be One Consequence." *Quarterly Journal of Economics* 94 (June): 749–775.

Akerlof, George A. 1982. "Labor Contracts as Partial Gift Echange." *Quarterly Journal of Economics* 97 (November): 543–589.

Akerlof, George A. 1984. "Gift Exchange and Efficiency Wage Theory: Four Views." *American Economic Review* 74 (May): 79–83.

Akerlof, George A., and Yellen, Janet L. 1985a. "A Near-Rational Model of the Business Cycle, with Wage and Price Inertia." *Quarterly Journal of Economics* 100 supplement: 823–838. Reprinted in volume 1 of this collection,

Akerlof, George A., and Yellen, Janet L. eds. 1986. *Efficiency Wage Models of the Labor Market.* Cambridge: Cambridge University Press.

Akerlof, George A., and Yellen, Janet L. 1989. "The Fair Wage/Effort Hypothesis and Unemployment." Mimeo. University of California, Berkeley. *Quarterly Journal of Economics,* forthcoming.

Azariadis, Costas. 1975. "Implicit Contracts and Underemployment Equilibria." *Journal of Political Economy* 83 (December): 1183–1202.

Azariadis, Costas. 1979. "Implicit Contracts and Related Topics: A Survey." In Z. Hornstein et al., eds., *The Economics of the Labor Market* (London: Her Majesty's Stationery Office).

Azariadis, Costas, and Stiglitz, Joseph E. 1983. "Implicit Contracts and Fixed Price Equilibria." *Quarterly Journal of Economics* 98 supplement: 1–22. Reprinted in volume 2 of this collection.

Baily, Martin. 1974. "Wages and Employment under Uncertain Demand." *Review of Economic Studies* 41 (January): 37–50.

Blanchard, Olivier J. 1987. "Why Does Money Affect Output? A Survey." National Bureau of Economic Research, working paper no. 2285, June. *Handbook of Monetary Economics,* forthcoming.

Blanchard, Olivier J., and Diamond, Peter. 1989. "The Beveridge Curve." *Brookings Papers on Economic Activity* no. 1: 1–60.

Blanchard, Olivier J., and Summers, Lawrence. 1986. "Hysteresis and the European Unemployment Problem." *NBER Macroeconomics Annual,* 15–77.

Blanchard, Olivier J., and Summers, Lawrence. 1987. "Hysteresis in Unemployment." *European Economic Review* 31: 288–295. Reprinted in volume 2 of this collection.

Bulow, Jeremy, and Summers, Lawrence. 1986. "A Theory of Dual Labor Markets with Applications to Industrial Policy, Discrimination, and Keynesian Unemployment." *Journal of Labor Economics* 4 (July): 376–414.

Carmichael, Lorne. 1985. "Can Unemployment Be Involuntary? Comment." *American Economic Review* 75 (December): 1213–1214.

Dickens, William T., and Katz, Lawrence F. 1987. "Inter-industry Wage Differences and Industry Characteristics." In Kevin Lang and Jonathan S. Leonard, eds., *Unemployment and the Structure of Labor Markets* (Basil Blackwell, 1987).

Dickens, William T., and Katz, Lawrence F. 1988. "Further Note on the Inter-industry Wage Structure." Mimeo. Harvard University.

Gordon, David. 1974. "A Neoclassical Theory of Underemployment." *Economic Inquiry* 12 (December): 432–459.

Gregory, R. C. 1986. "Wages Policy and Unemployment in Australia." *Economica* 53 supplement: S53–74.

Hall, Robert E. 1989. "Industry Rents: Evidence and Implications. Comment." *Brookings Papers on Economic Activity: Microeconomics,* 276–280.

Hart, Oliver. 1983. "Optimal Labour Contracts under Asymmetric Information: An Introduction." *Review of Economic Studies* 50 (January): 3–35.

Hart, Oliver, and Holmstrom, Bengt. 1987. "The Theory of Contracts." In T. Bewley, ed., *Advances in Economic Theory: Fifth World Congress* (Cambridge: Cambridge University Press).

Howitt, Peter. 1988. "Business Cycles with Costly Search and Recruiting." *Quarterly Journal of Economics* 103 (February): 147–167.

Katz, Lawrence. 1986. "Efficiency Wage Theories: A Partial Evaluation." *NBER Macroeconomics Annual*: 235–276.

Katz, Lawrence, and Summers, Lawrence. 1989. "Industry Rents: Evidence and Implications." *Brookings Papers on Economic Activity: Microeconomics*, 209–275.

Kimball, Miles S. 1989. "Labor Market Dynamics When Unemployment Is a Worker Discipline Device." National Bureau of Economic Research, working paper no. 2967, May.

Krueger, Alan B., and Summers, Lawrence. 1987. "Reflections on the Inter-industry Wage Structure." In Kevin Lang and Jonathan S. Leonard, eds., *Unemployment and the Structure of Labor Markets*. (Basil Blackwell).

Krueger, Alan B., and Summers, Lawrence. 1988. "Efficiency Wages and the Inter-industry Wage Structure." *Econometrica* 56 (March): 259–293. Reprinted in volume 2 of this collection.

Lindbeck, Assar, and Snower, Dennis. 1986. "Wage Setting, Unemployment, and Insider-Outsider Relations," *American Economic Review* 76 (May): 235–239.

Lindbeck, Assar, and Snower, Dennis. 1987. "Union Activity, Unemployment Persistence, and Wage Employment Ratchets." *European Economic Review* 31 (February–March): 157–167.

McDonald, Ian M., and Solow, Robert M. 1981. "Wage Bargaining and Employment." *American Economic Review* 71 (December): 896–908. Reprinted in volume 2 of this collection.

McDonald, Ian M., and Solow, Robert M. 1985. "Wages and Unemployment in a Segmented Labor Market." *Quarterly Journal of Economics* 100 (November): 1115–1141.

Mortenson, Dale T. 1986. "Job Search and Labor Market Analysis." In Orley Ashenfelter and Richard Layard, eds., *Handbook of Labor Economics*, volume 2 (Amsterdam: North-Holland).

Murphy, Kevin M., and Topel, Robert H. 1987. "Efficiency Wages Reconsidered: Theory and Evidence." Mimeo. University of Chicago.

Romer, David. 1984. "The Theory of Social Custom: A Modification and Some Extensions." *Quarterly Journal of Economics* 99 (November): 717–727.

Rosen, Sherwin. 1985. "Implicit Contracts." *Journal of Economic Literature* 23 (September): 1144–1175.

Salop, Steven. 1979. "A Model of the Natural Rate of Unemployment." *American Economic Review* 69 (March): 117–125.

Shapiro, Carl, and Stiglitz, Joseph E. 1984. "Equilibrium Unemployment as a Worker Discipline Device." *American Economic Review* 74 (June): 433–444. Reprinted in volume 2 of this collection.

Solow, Robert. 1979. "Another Possible Source of Wage Stickiness." *Journal of Macroeconomics* 1 (Winter): 79–82.

Sparks, Roger. 1986. "A Model of Involuntary Unemployment and Wage Rigidity: Worker Incentives and the Threat of Dismissal." *Journal of Labor Economics* 4 (October): 560–581.

Stiglitz, Joseph. 1986. "Theories of Wage Rigidities." In J. L. Butkiewicz et al., eds., *Keynes' Economic Legacy: Contemporary Classic Theories* (New York: Praeger).

Topel, Robert H. 1989. "Industry Rents: Evidence and Implications: Comment." *Brookings Papers on Economic Activity: Microeconomics*, 283–288.

Weiss, Andrew. 1980. "Job Queues and Layoffs in Labor Markets with Flexible Wages." *Journal of Political Economy* 88 (June): 526–538.

Yellen, Janet L. 1984. "Efficiency Wage Models of Unemployment." *American Economic Review* 74 (May): 200–205. Reprinted in volume 2 of this collection.

## 6  The credit market

Bernanke, Ben S. 1983. "Nonmonetary Effects of the Financial Crisis in the Propagation of the Great Depression." *American Economic Review* 73 (June): 257–276. Reprinted in volume 2 of this collection.

Bernanke, Ben S., and Blinder, Alan S. 1988. "Credit, Money, and Aggregate Demand." *American Economic Review* 78 (May): 435–439. Reprinted in volume 2 of this collection.

Bernanke, Ben S., and Blinder, Alan S. 1989. "The Federal Funds Rate and the Channels of Monetary Transmission." Mimeo. Princeton University.

Bernanke, Ben S., and Gertler, Mark. 1989. "Agency Costs, Net Worth, and Business Fluctuations." *American Economic Review* 79 (March): 14–31.

Bernanke, Ben S., and Gertler, Mark. 1990. "Financial Fragility and Economic Performance." *Quarterly Journal of Economics* 105 (February): 87–114.

Blinder, Alan S. 1985. "The Stylized Facts about Credit Aggregates." Mimeo. Princeton University.

Blinder, Alan S. 1987. "Credit Rationing and Effective Supply Failures." *Economic Journal* 97 (June): 327–352.

Boyd, John H., and Prescott, Edward C. 1986. "Financial Intermediary Coalitions," *Journal of Economic Theory* 38 (April): 211–232.

Diamond, D. W. 1984. "Financial Intermediation and Delegated Monitoring." *Review of Economic Studies* 51: 393–414.

Eckstein, Otto, and Sinai, Allen. 1986. "The Mechanisms of the Business Cycle in the Postwar Period." In Robert J. Gordon, ed., *The American Business Cycle: Continuity and Change* (Chicago: University of Chicago Press), 39–105.

Fama, Eugene F. 1985. "What's Different about Banks?" *Journal of Monetary Economics* 15 (January): 29–39.

Farmer, Roger E. A. 1984. "A New Theory of Aggregate Supply." *American Economic Review* 74 (December): 920–930.

Fazzari, Steven M., Hubbard, R. Glenn, and Petersen, Bruce C. 1988. "Financing Constraints and Corporate Investment." *Brookings Papers on Economic Activity*, no. 1: 141–195.

Friedman, Benjamin M. 1982. "Debt and Economic Activity in the United States." In Benjamin M. Friedman, ed., *The Changing Roles of Debt and Equity Financing in U.S. Capital Formation* (Chicago: University of Chicago Press), 91–110.

Friedman, Benjamin M. 1983. "The Roles of Money and Credit in Macroeconomic Analysis." In James Tobin, ed., *Macroeconomics, Prices, and Quantities: Essays in Memory of Arthur M. Okun* (Washington, D.C.: Brookings Instiution), 161–189.

Friedman, Benjamin M. 1986. "Money, Credit, and Interest Rates in the Business Cycle." In Robert J. Gordon, ed., *The American Business Cycle: Continuity and Change* (Chicago, University of Chicago Pres), 395–438.

Gale, Douglas, and Hellwig, Martin. 1985. "Incentive-Compatible Debt Contracts. I: The One-Period Problem." *Review of Economic Studies*, October, 647–664.

Gertler, Mark. 1988. "Financial Structure and Aggregate Economic Activity: An Overview." *Journal of Money, Credit, and Banking* 20 part 2 (August): 559–588.

Greenwald, Bruce C., and Stiglitz, Joseph E. 1988a. "Financial Market Imperfections and Business Cycles." National Bureau of Economic Research, working paper no. 2494, January.

Greenwald, Bruce C., and Stiglitz, Joseph E. 1988b. "Examining Alternative Macroeconomic Theories." *Brookings Papers on Economic Activity*, no. 1: 207–260.

Hoshi, Takeo, Kashyap, Anil K., and Scharfstein, David. 1988. "Corporate Structure, Liquidity, and Investment: Evidence from Japanese Panel Data." Mimeo. Massachusetts Institute of Technology.

Jaffee, Dwight, and Russell, Thomas. 1976. "Imperfect Information and Credit Rationing." *Quarterly Journal of Economics* 90 (November): 651–666.

King, Stephen R. 1986. "Monetary Transmission: Through Bank Loans or Bank Liabilities?" *Journal of Money, Credit, and Banking* 18 (August): 290–303.

Mankiw, N. Gregory. 1986. "The Allocation of Credit and Finanical Collapse." *Quarterly Journal of Economics* 101 (August): 455–470. Reprinted in volume 2 of this collection.

Romer, Christina D., and Romer, David H. 1990. "New Evidence on the Monetary Transmission Mechanism." Mimeo. University of California, Berkeley. *Brookings Papers on Economic Activity*, forthcoming.

Stiglitz, Joseph E., and Weiss, Andrew. 1981. "Credit Rationing in Markets with Imperfect Information." *American Economic Review* 71 (June): 393–410. Reprinted in volume 2 of this collection.

Townsend, Robert M. 1979. "Optimal Contracts and Competitive Markets with Costly State Verification." *Journal of Economic Theory* 21 (October): 265–293.

Williamson, Stephen D. 1987. "Financial Intermediation, Business Failures and Real Business Cycles." *Journal of Political Economy* 95 (December): 1196–1216.

Wojnilower, Albert M. 1980. "The Central Role of Credit Crunches in Recent Financial History." *Brookings Papers on Economic Activity*, no. 2, 277–326.

## 7  The goods market

Barsky, Robert B., Kimball, Miles, and Warner, Elizabeth. 1988. "A Model of Weekend and Holiday Sales." Mimeo. University of Michigan.

Bils, Mark. 1987. "The Cyclical Behavior of Marginal Cost and Price." *American Economic Review* 77 (December): 838–855. Reprinted in volume 2 of this collection.

Bils, Mark. 1988. "Cyclical Pricing of Durable Goods." Manuscript. University of Rochester.

Bils, Mark. 1989. "Pricing in a Customer Market." *Quarterly Journal of Economic* 104 (November): 699–718.

Blinder, Alan S. 1982. "Inventories and Sticky Prices: More on the Microfoundations of Macroeconomics." *American Economic Review* 72 (June): 334–348.

Miron, Jeffrey A., and Zeldes, Stephen P. 1988. "Seasonality, Cost Shocks, and the Production-Smoothing Model of Inventories." *Econometrica* 56 (July): 877–908.

Okun, Arthur M. 1975. "Inflation: Its Mechanics and Welfare Costs." *Brookings Papers on Economic Activity*, no. 2. Reprinted in volume 2 of this collection.

Phelps, Edmund S., snd Winter, Sidney G., Jr. 1970. "Optimal Price Policy under Atomistic Competition." In E. S. Phelps, ed., *Microeconomic Foundations of Inflation and Employment Theory* (New York: Norton).

Ramey, Valerie. 1989. "Inventories as Factors of Production and Economic Fluctuations." *American Economic Review* 79 (June): 338–354.

Rotemberg, Julio J., and Saloner, Garth. 1986. "A Supergame-Theoretic Model of Price Wars during Booms." *American Economic Review* 76 (June): 390–407. Reprinted in volum 2 of this collection.

Rotemberg, Julio J., and Summers, Lawrence. 1988. "Labor Hoarding, Inflexible Prices, and Procyclical Productivity." National Bureau of Economic Research, working paper no. 2591, May.

Stiglitz, Joseph E. 1984. "Price Rigidities and Market Structure." *American Economic Review* 74 (May): 350–355. Reprinted in volume 2 of this collection.

Woglom, Geoffrey. 1982. "Underemployment with Rational Expectations." *Quarterly Journal of Economics* 97 (February): 89–108.

# I COSTLY PRICE ADJUSTMENT

# 1 Small Menu Costs and Large Business Cycles: A Macroeconomic Model of Monopoly

N. Gregory Mankiw

## 1 Introduction

The conflict between modern neoclassical and traditional Keynesian theories of the business cycle centers upon the pricing mechanism.[1] In neoclassical models, prices are fully flexible. They represent the continuous optimization of economic agents and the continuous intersection of supply and demand. In Keynesian models, prices are often assumed to be sticky. They do not necessarily equilibrate all markets at all times. One of the reasons for the resurgence of the equilibrium approach to macroeconomics has been the absence of a theoretical underpinning for this Keynesian price stickiness.

This note shows that sticky prices can be both privately efficient and socially inefficient. The business cycle results from the suboptimal adjustment of prices in response to a demand shock. To the extent that policy can stabilize aggregate demand, it can mitigate the social loss due to this suboptimal adjustment.

In some Keynesian models, prices are simply exogenously fixed.[2] In others, agents must set their prices in advance of the transaction date.[3] The act of altering a posted price is certainly costly. These costs include such items as printing new catalogs and informing salesmen of the new price. Yet these "menu" costs are small and, therefore, generally perceived as providing only a weak foundation for these fixed-price models. However, this inference is flawed. Small menu costs can cause large welfare losses. The claim that price adjustment costs are small does not rebut the claim that they are central to understanding economic fluctuations.

I present a simple static model of a monopoly firm's pricing decision. The firm sets its price in advance, and changes that price ex post only by incurring a small menu cost. I show the firm's price adjustment decisions are in no sense socially optimal.[4]

## 2 A Partial-Equilibrium Analysis

Consider a monopoly firm facing a constant cost function (1) and the inverse demand function (2):[5]

*Quarterly Journal of Economics* 100 (May 1985): 529–539. Copyright © 1985 by the President and Fellows of Harvard College. Reprinted by permission of John Wiley & Sons.

$$C = kqN \tag{1}$$

$$P = f(q)N, \tag{2}$$

where $C$ is the total nominal cost of producing quantity $q$, $k$ is simply a constant, $P$ is the nominal price the firm obtains if it places $q$ on the market, and $N$ is a nominal scale variable. The variable $N$ denotes the exogenous level of aggregate demand. It can be regarded as the overall price level, the money stock, or the level of nominal GNP. Both the nominal cost to the firm $C$ and the nominal price it receives $P$ increase proportionally to the level of nominal demand $N$.

Figure 1 shows the standard profit-maximizing solution to the monopoly firm's problem.[6] An increase in the nominal scale variable shifts the cost and demand functions proportionally, thereby increasing $P_m$ without affecting the firm's output $q_m$.

Let $c = C/N$ and $p = P/N$. The firm's problem is then viewed as independent of aggregate demand. That is, if faces (1') and (2'), which do not shift when $N$ changes:

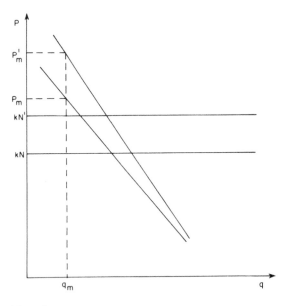

**Figure 1**

$$c = kq \tag{1'}$$

$$p = f(q) \tag{2'}$$

(see figure 2). The firm chooses $p$ and $q$ to maximize profits. The nominal price it sets is $p_m N$. (I hereafter refer to $p$ as the "price," even though it is the nominal price normalized by the nominal scale variable.) The firm earns profits (producer surplus) equal to the rectangular area between $k$ and $p_m$. Consumer surplus—the excess of value over price—equals the triangle above profits. Total surplus, which is the measure of welfare used in this paper, is the sum of profits and consumer surplus.

Now suppose that the firm needs to set its nominal price one period ahead based upon its expection of aggregate demand $N^e$. It sets the nominal price equal to $p_m N^e$. If its expectation turns out correct ex post, then the observed price $p_0$ is $p_m$. If it turns out incorrect, then the observed price is $p_0 = p_m(N^e/N)$.[7]

If $N$ is lower than expected, $p_0$ is higher than $p_m$ (see figure 3). In this case, the firm's profits are lower by the area $B - A$, which is positive, since $p_m$ is

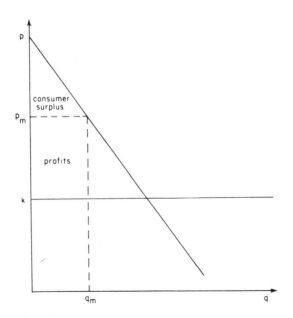

**Figure 2**

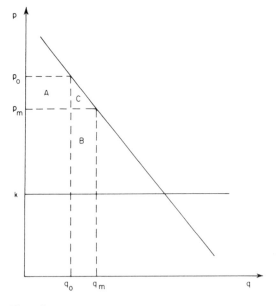

**Figure 3**

by definition the profit-maximizing price. Total surplus is reduced by
$B + C$. Hence, the reduction in welfare due to a contraction in aggregate
demand is greater than the reduction in the firm's profits.

Suppose that the firm is able to change its nominal price ex post, but
only at a menu cost of $z$. If it chooses to do so, it reduces the price from $p_0$
to $p_m$ and obtains the additional profits $B - A$. Hence, it lowers its price if
and only if $B - A > z$. Yet, from the standpoint of a social planner, the
firm should lower its price to $p_m$ if and only if $B + C > z$. Thus, we obtain
these results:

PROPOSITION 1    Following a contraction in demand, if the firm cuts its
price, then doing so is socially optimal.

*Proof of proposition 1*    If the firm cuts its price, then $B - A > z$. Hence,
$B + C > z + A + C > z$. Thus, doing so is socially optimal.

PROPOSITION 2    Following a contraction in demand, if $B + C > z >
B - A$, then the firm does not cut its price to $p_m$, even though doing so
would be socially optimal.

Proposition 2 suggests the downward price rigidity often mentioned in macroeonomic debate. The inefficiency results because there is an external benefit of $C + A$ in printing new menus. How large is this externality? A natural measure is the ratio of the social benefit from a price adjustment $B + C$ to the private benefit $B - A$. This ratio, of course, depends upon the size of the demand shock. Since the firm would adjust to the profit-maximizing price $p_m$, rather than the first-best price $k$, the increment to profits $B - A$ is of second order, while the increment to welfare $B + C$ is of first order. Therefore, this ratio approaches infinity as the size of the shock approaches zero. The ratio is more meaningful if evaluated for a shock of typical size. Hence, I compute it for a 1 percent contraction.[8] If the demand function has a constant price elasticity of ten, the ratio is twenty-three. If the elasticity is two, the ratio is over two hundred. For any plausible demand function, the social gains from price adjustment far exceed the private gains.

PROPOSITION 3    A contraction in aggregate demand unambiguously reduces welfare as measured by the sum of producer and consumer surplus. If the firm cuts its price in response, then the contraction only has the menu cost $z$. If not, then the contraction has the possibly much larger cost $B + C$.

Now let us examine an expansion in aggregate demand. Since $N > N^e$, we know that $p_0 < p_m$. At first, let $p_0 > k$ ($N/N^e < p_m/k$,) as in figure 4. The firm's profits are reduced by $D - F$, which is positive, since $p_m$ is profit-maximizing. Total surplus is increased by $E + F$. The firm resets its price if the cost of doing so is justified by increased profit. That is, the firm raises its price back to $p_m$ if and only if $D - F > z$.

PROPOSITION 4    Following an expansion in demand in which $N/N^e < p_m/k$, if the firm resets its price, total surplus is decreased by the menu cost. If the firm does not reset its price, surplus is increased by $E + F$.

If $N/N^e > p_m/k$, then after the demand expansion, $p_0$ is below $k$ (see figure 5). Total surplus decreases by $I - J$, which could be negative or positive, making the welfare effect ambiguous. Firm profits (now negative) have been reduced by $G + H + I$. The firm resets its price to $p_m$ if $G + H + I > z$. It is socially optimal to do so if $I - J > z$.

PROPOSITION 5    Following an expansion in which $N/N^e > p_m/k$, if the firm resets its price, total surplus is decreased by the menu cost. If the firm does

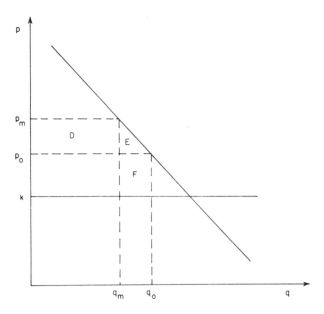

**Figure 4**

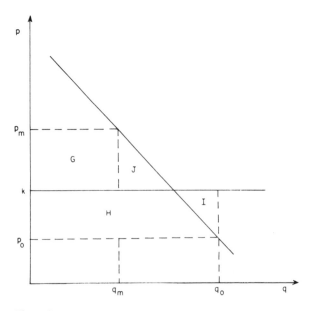

**Figure 5**

not reset its price, total surplus change is ambiguous, but total surplus does not decrease by more than the menu cost.

*Proof of proposition 5* If the firm does not reset its price, then $G + H + I < z$. This implies that $I - J < z - J - G - H < z$. Hence, total surplus reduction, $I - J$, is less than the menu cost.

As a partial summary of the above results:

PROPOSITION 6 An expansion in aggregate demand reduces welfare by no more than the menu cost, and may even increase welfare. A contraction in aggregate demand unambiguously reduces welfare, possibly by much more than the menu cost.

## 3 Conclusion

The economy I describe is Keynesian, even though all agents are optimizing and all prices result from that optimization. The central postulate is that monopoly firm must incur a small menu cost if it alters its posted price after an aggregate demand shock. I show that the firm's price adjustment decisions are suboptimal. In addition, the welfare loss can far exceed the menu cost that is its cause.

The model also displays an asymmetry between contractions and expansions, since the natural rate of output is below the social optimum. Private incentives produce too much price adjustment following an expansion in aggregate demand and too little price adjustment following a contraction in aggregate demand. From the viewpoint of a social planner, the nominal price level may be stuck too high, but it is never stuck too low. In this sense, prices are downwardly rigid but not upwardly rigid.[9] Furthermore, the model's asymmetry parallels another observed phenomenon; namely, that while aggregate demand contractions are associated with grotesquely inefficient underproduction, aggregate demand expansions are not associated with similarly inefficient overproduction. There is no obverse to the Great Depression. Instead, periods of expansion, such as the late 1960s in the United States, are often considered periods of economic prosperity.[10]

The analysis presented here is all in the context of partial equilibrium. It is, however, possible to construct simple general equilibrium examples that encompass exactly these partial-equilibrium results.[11] I suspect that a more complete general equilibrium model would exhibit more pronounced price stickiness. In particular, the introduction of interfirm purchases would exacerbate price rigidity. In such a model the failure of one firm to reduce its price following a contraction in demand would prevent the costs of other firms from falling, thereby reducing those firms' incentive to cut prices. The primary qualitative conclusion—that trivial menu costs can have important efficiency effects—would certainly remain true in the context of general equilibrium.[12]

The theme of this paper appears robust: In almost all economic models, agents who have the power to affect prices, exert that power by restricting output. The economy's equilibrium, or natural rate, is thus below the social optimum.[13] Because of this, deviations below the natural rate impose greater costs on society than on the price-setting agents. These agents, therefore, have inadequate incentive to return the economy to its equilibrium.

An economy of this sort does not recommend passive monetary policy. As long as new information about exogenous demand factors (e.g., velocity) is made available to the monetary authority after private agents set their prices, systematic feedback rules can stabilize output.[14] These exogenous demand shocks cause substantial and inefficient fluctuations in output and employment if the monetary authority does not react. Although firms optimize, their prices are not socially optimal, and in particular, respond too little to adverse demand shocks. This inefficiency appears to be the target of policies that aim directly at the pricing mechanism, such as wage-price controls and tax-based incomes policy.

## Appendix: A General-Equilibrium Example[15]

The real world is replete with intricate interrelations between product markets and labor markets. For the most part, individuals sell their labor at a determined wage and buy goods at a determined price. Firms buy labor at a determined wage and sell their goods in markets were they exercise at least some control over their prices. To illustrate how menu costs fit into a general equilibrium, I present a simple example that encompasses the partial equilibrium results in the paper.

This economy is composed of individuals and firms, both of which are distributed along the unit interval. All individuals are identical. Thus, their behavior is represented by a single individual, and I need not be concerned hereafter with the fact that there is more than one. The firms produce differentiated products. They also differ in their menu costs. Thus, after a monetary shock, some firms decide to alter their posted price, and some firms do not.

The economy comprises a labor market, a money market, and a continuum of product markets. It differs from a standard market-clearing competitive economy in only one respect. On the supply side of each product market is a monopolist. The Walrasian auctioneer, who costlessly adjusts prices, is replaced with price-setting firms, each with its own menu cost.[16]

Our representative individual has the following utility function:

$$U = (1 - \phi)^{-1} \int_0^1 q_i^{1-\phi} \, di + \theta \log(M^d/P) - L, \tag{A1}$$

where $U$ is utility, $q_i$ is the quantity of product i he consumes, $\phi$ is the reciprocal of the elasticity of substitution between the different products $(0 < \phi < 1)$, $M^d$ is his money demand, $P$ is the general price level, $L$ is his labor supply, and $\theta$ is a money demand parameter $(\theta > 0)$. The general price level $P$ is the geometric average of all $P_i$, where $P_i$ is the nominal price of the good produced by firm $i$. That is,

$$P = \exp\left(\int_0^1 \log P_i \, di\right). \tag{A2}$$

Given $P_i$ for all $i$ and the nominal wage $W$, our individual maximizes $U$ subject to his budget constraint (A3).

$$\int_0^1 P_i q_i \, di + M^d = WL + M + \text{Profits} \tag{A3}$$

$M$ is the money supply, which begins with the individual. Profits of the firms go to the individual to assure that Walras's Law is satisfied. Of course, the individual takes profits as fixed in his maximization problem.

With this particular utility function, the first-order conditions give product demand and money demand.

$$q_i = (P_i/W)^{-1/\phi} \quad \text{for all } i \tag{A4}$$

$$M^d = \theta W \tag{A5}$$

Labor supply comes from (A3), (A4), and (A5). I do not explicitly solve for equilibrium in the labor market, as this is guaranteed by Walras's Law coupled with equilibrium both in the product markets and in the money market.

Equilibrium in the money market is simply money supply equaling money demand.

$$M = M^d \tag{A6}$$

From (A4) and (A5), with simple algebraic rearrangement, we obtain

$$P_i = \theta^{-1} M q_i^{-\phi}, \tag{A7}$$

$$W = \theta^{-1} M. \tag{A8}$$

Equation (A7) is the inverse demand function (1) faced by the firm. The price elasticity of demand is $1/\phi$.

Each firm takes (A7) as its demand function and (A9) as its production function:

$$q_i = L_i, \tag{A9}$$

where $L_i$ is labor input of firm $i$. From (A8) and (A9) we obtain the nominal cost function (A10).

$$C_i = W L_i = \theta^{-1} M q_i \tag{A10}$$

The implied profit function is

$$\Pi_i = (q_i^{1-\phi} - q_i)\theta^{-1} M. \tag{A11}$$

The profit maximizing output $q_m$ for each firm is

$$q_m = (1 - \phi)^{1/\phi}. \tag{A12}$$

At this quantity, each price is

$$P_m = \theta^{-1} M (1 - \phi)^{-1}. \tag{A13}$$

Since $\theta^{-1} M$ is all that enters into the above expressions, increases in money supply $M$ are exactly the same as reductions in money demand $\theta$. For simplicity I hold $\theta$ constant hereafter and examine changes in $M$ only.

Suppose each firm in the economy is at its "natural rate" of $q_m$. The money supply is $M_0$, and thus each price is $P_0 = \theta^{-1} M_0 (1 - \phi)^{-1}$. Suddenly the money supply is changed to $M_1$. Suppose all the posted prices at first remain unchanged at $P_0$ even though the profit-maximizing price is now $P_m = \theta^{-1} M_1 (1 - \phi)^{-1}$. Through the money market equilibrium (A6), the nominal wage changes from $\theta^{-1}M_0$ to $\theta^{-1}M_1$. Through product demand (A7), output changes from $q_m$ to $q_0 = (M_1/M_0)^{1/\phi} q_m$ for all firms.

Now suppose each firm can change its menu ex post, but to do so would require a small labor input $g$. In particular, let the menu cost of firm $i$ be

$$z_i = g(i)W = g(i)\theta^{-1}M \quad g' > 0 \tag{A14}$$

Each firm, when deciding whether to post a new price, compares the increment in profit $\Delta\Pi$, as calculated from (A11), to its menu cost $z_i$. Thus, the marginal firm $I$ is

$$I = g^{-1}(\Delta\Pi/W) = g^{-1}[(q_m^{1-\phi} - q_0^{1-\phi}) - (q_m - q_0)] \tag{A15}$$

If $i < I$, then the firm finds it profitable to incur the menu cost, post the price $P_m$, and produce output $q_m$. If $i > I$, then the firm leaves its price at $P_0$, and produces $q_0$. Total output is therefore

$$Q = \int_0^1 q_i \, di = Iq_m + (1 - I)q_0. \tag{A16}$$

The general price level is

$$P = \exp\left(\int_0^1 \log P_i \, di\right) = \exp\left[I \log P_m + (1 - I)\log P_0\right]. \tag{A17}$$

Employment equals output through the production functions (A9) plus the labor input necessary for changing prices.

$$L = Q + \int_0^I g(i) \, di \tag{A18}$$

Utility is

$$U = (1 - \phi)^{-1}[Iq_m^{1-\phi} + (1 - I)q_0^{1-\phi}] + \theta \log M$$
$$- \theta[I \log P_m + (1 - I)\log P_0]$$
$$- \left[Iq_m + (1 - I)q_0 + \int_0^I g(i) \, di\right]. \tag{A19}$$

In addition, straightforward algebra demonstrates that the real wage is procyclical.

The partial equilibrium analysis of the paper shows that the ex post price-adjustment decisions by profit-maximizing firms are not socially efficient. The same result can be shown in this general equilibrium example. Suppose a social planner could dictate which firms adjust prices ex post. In other words, instead of $I$ being determined endogenously as in (A15), the planner chooses the optimal $I^*$ to maximize $U$ in (A19). The first-order condition[17] is

$$\frac{dU}{dI} = 0. \tag{A20}$$

This implies

$$I^* = g^{-1}[(1 - \phi)^{-1}(q_m^{1-\phi} - q_0^{1-\phi}) - \theta \log(P_m/P_0) - (q_m - q_0)]. \tag{A21}$$

For a monetary expansion, $P_m > P_0$ and $q_m < q_0$. Comparing (A15) and (A21) shows that $I^* < I$. The social planner would have fewer firms adjust prices. Similarly, for a monetary contraction, $P_m < P_0$, $q_m > q_0$, and thus $I^* > I$. The social planner would have more firms adjust prices.[18] Private incentives produce too much price adjustment following a monetary expansion and too little price adjustment following a monetary contraction.[19]

## Acknowledgements

I am grateful to Olivier Blanchard, Alan Blinder, Avery Katz, Eric Rasmusen, James Rauch, Deborah Roloff, David Romer, Julio Rotemberg, Robert Solow, Lawrence Summers, and two anonymous referees for helpful comments and to the National Science Foundation for financial support.

## Notes

1. See Gordon (1981) for a general discussion of the role of price adjustment in macroeconomic debate.

2. See, for example, Malinvaud (1977). Gordon (1981) references other fixed-price models.

3. See, for example, Fischer (1977) and Blinder and Mankiw (1984). The economy I describe in this paper is a relative of the Type 3 (nominal price contracts) economy in Blinder and Mankiw.

4. Rotemberg (1982) examines a model of monopoly firms with quadratic price adjustment costs. He emphasizes the dynamic behavior of prices and aggregate output, rather than the welfare properties of the firm's decisions.

5. Allowing a more general cost function does not alter the results.

6. Although the demand functions in the figures are linear, the results do not depend upon this functional form.

7. I assume that the firm cannot ex ante announce a nominal price $P$ indexed to $N$. The reasons why indexation might or might not arise are beyond the scope of this note. See Gray (1976) for one discussion.

8. Barro and Rush (1980) find that the standard deviation of the postwar U.S. monetary shocks is 1.4 percent with annual data and 0.5 percent with quarterly data.

9. The price adjustment rule followed by the firm is not itself asymmetric. Instead, the welfare properties of the adjustment process exhibit asymmetry. Studies that concentrate upon the positive aspects of the adjustment process (e.g., Barro 1972), rather than its normative aspects, thus report no asymmetry.

10. These periods are often considered times of excessive inflationary pressure. Yet there is little concern about the level of output per se.

11. An earlier version of this paper contained such an example. The simplest general equilibrium example contains $n$ yeoman farmers, each choosing between leisure and production of his uniquely differentiated output. In equilibrium, each produces too little. The price adjustment rule each follows is suboptimal, as in the partial-equilibrium analysis presented in this note.

12. The dynamic nature of the price-setting process, which is undoubtedly important, is ignored in this paper. Whether a contraction is viewed as temporary or permanent probably affects the reaction of firms. Rotemberg (1982), in the context of a somewhat different model, considers the dynamics of price adjustment in more detail. Another important aspect of the problem ignored here is the effects of price desynchronization. Blanchard (1982) explicitly examines this issue.

13. Okun (1981, p. 267), in his already well-known *Prices and Quantities*, writes that "there are strong grounds for the presumption that in macro equilibrium the output of the price-tag economy is below a social optimum, and that the extra output generated by a strengthening of aggregate demand augments social welfare."

14. See Blinder and Mankiw (1984) for a more complete exposition of this issue.

15. This appendix was circulated as part of the 1982 working paper version of this article, but was not included in the version published in the *Quarterly Journal of Economics*.

16. An analogous model of monopoly unions in the labor market would imply similarly inefficient employment fluctuations and wage rigidity. Real economies are characterized by a variety of different types of wage-price stickiness, as is discussed in Blinder and Mankiw (1984).

17. This first-order condition holds with equality only if the optimum $I^*$ is strictly inside the unit interval. Examination of the more general Kuhn-Tucker conditions does not alter the conclusions.

18. A larger monetary contraction would induce more firms to adjust their prices, but those that do not are even farther from the optimal output. The marginal effect upon aggregate output and welfare depends upon $g(\cdot)$ and is in general ambiguous.

19. Some numbers may be helpful. Let $\phi = .1, \theta = 1$, and $g(i) = .03i^8$. Simple calculation shows total menu costs for this economy are less than 1% of its natural rate output. A 2% monetary expansion causes a 6.9% reduction in output, since only 62% of the firms adjust their prices. The social planner would have every firm adjust its price, in which case there is no drop in output.

# References

Barro, Robert J., "A Theory of Monopolistic Price Adjustment," *Review of Economic Studies*, 39 (1972), 17–26.

Barro, Robert J., and Mark Rush, "Unanticipated Money and Economic Activity," *Rational Expectations and Economic Policy*, Stanley Fischer, ed. (Chicago: University of Chicago Press, 1980).

Blanchard, Olivier J., "Price Desynchronization and Price Level Inertia," National Bureau of Economic Research Working Paper No. 900, 1982.

Blinder, Alan S., and N. Gregory Mankiw, "Aggregation and Stabilization Policy in a Multi-Contract Economy." *Journal of Monetary Economics*, 13 (1984), 67–86.

Fischer, Stanley, "Long-Term Contracts, Rational Expectations, and the Optimal Money Supply Rule," *Journal of Political Economy*, 85 (1977), 191–206.

Gordon, Robert J., "Output Fluctuations and Gradual Price Adjustment," *Journal of Economic Literature*, 19 (1981), 493–530.

Gray, Jo Anna, "Wage Indexation: A Macroeconomic Approach," *Journal of Monetary Economics*, 2 (1976), 221–235.

Malinvaud, Edmond, *The Theory of Unemployment Reconsidered* (Oxford: Blackwell, 1977).

Okun, Arthur M., *Prices and Quantities: A Macroeconomic Analysis* (Washington, D.C.: Brookings Institution, 1981).

Rotemberg, Julio, "Monopolistic Price Adjustment and Aggregate Output," *Review of Economic Studies*, 44 (1982), 517–531.

# 2 A Near-Rational Model of the Business Cycle, with Wage and Price Inertia

George A. Akerlof and Janet L. Yellen

## 1 Introduction

This paper offers an explanation of why changes in the nominal supply of money are not neutral in the short run. It shows that aggregate demand shocks can cause significant changes in output and employment if agents adjust wages and prices in ways that are "insignificantly" suboptimal from their individual standpoints. Alternatively, very small transaction costs of decision making or changing prices could account for large fluctuations in real economic activity.

The argument proceeds in six steps.

1. The property of nonneutrality is shown to be important for business cycle theory.

2. The concept of near-rationality is introduced. Near-rational behavior is nonmaximizing behavior in which the gains from maximizing rather than nonmaximizing are small in a well-defined sense.

3. It is argued that in a wide class of models—those models in which objective functions are differentiable with respect to agents' own wages or prices—the cost of inertial money wage and price behavior as opposed to maximizing behavior, is small when a long-run equilibrium with full maximization has been perturbed by a shock. If wages and prices were initially at an optimum, the loss from failure to adjust them will be smaller, by an order of magnitude, than the shock.

4. The economic meaning of objective functions differentiable in agents' own prices and wages will be explained. Profit functions do *not* have this property when there is perfect competition in the labor and product markets. But in a wide class of models, including those with imperfect competition, objective functions *do* have this property.

5. Some intuition will be provided to explain why nonmaximizing behavior that results in only second-order losses to the individual nonmaximizers will nevertheless have first-order effects on real variables.

6. An example will be presented of a model in which inertial price and wage behavior causes first-order changes in real activity but imposes only in-

*Quarterly Journal of Economics* 100 supplement (1985): 823–838. Copyright © 1985 by the President and Fellows of Harvard College. Reprinted by permission of John Wiley & Sons.

significant losses on nonmaximizing agents. In this model the typical firm's profits are a continuous, differentiable function of the price it charges and the wage it offers. The model assumes imperfect competition in the product market and a relationship between wages and labor productivity leading to "efficiency wage" payments in the labor market. It will be argued that the assumption of efficiency wages is appealing because it rationalizes one important stylized view of the economy—the dual labor market— and because it provides a coherent explanation of persistent involuntary unemployment.

**The need for a model without money neutrality**

As is well-known, *anticipated* changes in aggregate demand cause no fluctuations in employment or output in neoclassical models with market clearing (see Sargent 1973). The insensitivity of employment and output to aggregate-demand shifts generalizes, however, beyond such neoclassical models. As long as a model postulates behavior that is rational—i.e., derived from maximization of objective functions that depend only on real variables—there is no reason why anticipated demand shocks should have any effect on real output. Thus, recent models in which involuntary unemployment can be rationalized as a result of staggered or implicit contracts, imperfect information, labor turnover, or efficiency wages still leave unanswered the question of how changes in the money supply, unless unanticipated, can affect real output.

In the Keynesian model, changes in aggregate demand cause fluctuations in real output because of agents' inertia in changing money wages and prices. There is abundant empirical evidence for the phenomenon of wage and price sluggishness (see, for example, the discussion in Okun 1981). Nevertheless, the reasons why prices and wages do not adjust quickly to changes in aggregate demand remain mysterious. In the standard Keynesian model with competitive markets, there are substantial gains to be made by agents who do adjust wages and prices quickly; so inertial behavior, in that model, is both irrational and costly. In partial answer to this problem the new classical macroeconomics has proposed models in which money is neutral with full information but is nonneutral insofar as unanticipated money shocks fool agents who are imperfectly informed about wage and price distributions. The applicability of this model has been the subject of considerable debate. This paper suggests an alternative.

### Near-rational behavior

The alternative explanation of nonneutrality offered in this paper is based on the idea that inertial wage-price behavior by firms may not, in fact, be very costly; it may be near-rational. Firms that behave suboptimally, adjusting prices and wages slowly, may suffer losses from failure to optimize, but those losses may be very small. Near-rational behavior is behavior that is perhaps suboptimal but that nevertheless imposes very small individual losses on its practitioners relative to the consequences of their first-best policy. Technically, *very small* is defined as being second-order in terms of the policy shocks that create a disturbance from a long-run, fully maximizing equilibrium. This paper argues that inertial wage and price behavior that is near-rational, in the sense that it causes only second-order losses to its practitioners, can nevertheless cause first-order changes in real activity. As a result, changes in the money supply can cause first-order changes in employment and output if agents are near-rational. In sum, this paper argues that a small amount of nonmaximizing behavior can cause a significant business cycle in response to money supply shocks that would be neutral in the absence of such inertial behavior.

### The crucial requirement for the near-rationality of inertial behavior: Differentiability of objective functions in agents' own wages and prices

Consider a shock that perturbs an equilibrium in which all agents are maximizing. Sticky wage and price behavior will be near-rational for any agent whose objective function is differentiable as a function of *his own wages and prices*. The error in wages or prices caused by inertial behavior will result in losses to the agent that are second-order in terms of the policy shock, since at the equilibrium prior to the shock, the agent chose prices (wages) so that the marginal benefits of higher prices (wages) was just offset by the marginal costs. An error in wages and prices therefore has a second-order effect on the value of the objective function. This is just an application of the envelope theorem (see Varian 1978).

### The assumption of differentiability

The condition that the objective function is differentiable in an *agent's own wages and prices* requires explanation. This assumption does not hold in a competitive model. Consider firms' profits in a competitive model. In this model a firm that individually pays a wage lower than the market wage can hire no labor. At the market wage, labor availability jumps discontinuously and consequently so do profits. With the firm's own wage higher than the market-clearing, profits decline proportionately with the excess of the wage over the market-clearing level. Accordingly, profit as a function of the firm's wage is not differentiable at the optimum wage, which is the market-clearing wage. A similar story is true with regard to prices. If the firm charges a price above the market-clearing level, a competitive firm has no sales. Profits jump discontinuously when a firm's own price falls to the market-clearing level because the firm can then have all the sales it wants. And at prices lower than the market-clearing level, profits decline proportionately to the gap between the market-clearing price and the firm's own price. In the competitive model, prices lower or wages higher than the market-clearing levels confer no benefits on the firm.

In contrast, there are many models of price and wage setting in which profits are a differentiable function of the firm's own price or wage. In models with imperfect information by buyers, monopoly or oligopoly in the product market, or monopolistic competition with differentiated products, a firm's profits vary *differentiably* with its own price because its sales do not fall to zero as its price departs marginally from the prices charged by other firms. In these models, price reductions by firms result in marginal benefits due to increased sales as well as the marginal cost of less revenue per unit of output sold.

Similarly, there are models of the labor market in which profits are a differentiable function of the firm's own wage offer. This occurs in models where workers have imperfect information, which confers at least temporary monopsony power on firms, and in monopsonistic and oligopsonistic labor markets.[1] In most models of staggered contracts, the profit function is differentiable with respect to the *timing* of wage changes. Finally, in the efficiency wage model of unemployment, as will be presently described, profits are a differentiable function of wages because the higher labor costs per employee that result from higher wage offers are at least partially offset by a reduction in labor cost due to increased productivity.

Thus, there is a wide class of models in which firms' profits are a differentiable function of wage and price variables. In any such model, inertial wage or price-setting behavior in response to a shock, starting from a long-run equilibrium with full maximization, will impose only small losses on nonmaximizing agents.

**First-order consequences of sticky wages and prices for real variables**

It has now been seen that in a wide class of models the effect of wage and price stickiness on agents' objective functions is second-order in terms of the magnitude of a shock starting from a long-run equilibrium in which all agents maximize. Nevertheless, such wage and price stickiness commonly has a first-order effect on equilibrium values of real variables following the shock. Although this property must be checked in any particular variant of the model proposed, there is a general intuition why it usually occurs.

If *all* agents maintain sticky prices following a change in the money supply by a fraction $\epsilon$, there would be a change in real balances by the same fraction. The change in real balances would clearly be of the same order of magnitude as the shock, and in most models all other real variables would change by the same order of magnitude. The property that most real variables change by the same order of magnitude as the shock continues to hold, although the argument is more subtle, in models of short-run equilibrium when only a fraction of agents have sticky prices or wages while the remainder of agents maximize.

**The example chosen**

The next section presents a specific model that illustrates the proposition that near-rational wage and price stickiness can account for business cycle fluctuations. The model presented has three basic features. The first of these is sticky wage and price behavior. By that we mean that following a shock to a long-run equilibrium in which all agents exactly maximize, a fraction $\beta$ of agents maintain the same nominal prices and wages, while the remaining agents are full maximizers.

The second feature of the model guarantees that *price* stickiness is a near-rational policy in response to a shock of a long-run equilibrium with full maximization. We assume that firms are monopolistic competitors with their sales dependent on the level of real aggregate demand and the firm's own price relative to the averge prices charged by other firms. For simplicity, we assume that real aggregate demand is proportional to real balances. As the logic of the previous discussion should indicate, price stickiness in such a model is near-rational. Even with a market-clearing labor market, such price inertia suffices to explain how money-supply changes could cause proportional changes in real variables.

It is the intent of this paper to present an example that shows not only how monetary nonneutrality can result from near-rational behavior but also how equilibria can be characterized by involuntary unemployment. Involuntary unemployment occurs in our model because the productivity of workers is assumed to depend on the real wage they receive, inducing firms to set wages above the market-clearing level. Because such efficiency wage models may be unfamiliar, they will be briefly described, with some comments on why we consider them to be a realistic basis for a model of nonclearing labor markets.

**Efficiency wage models of unemployment**

There is now a burgeoning literature that explains involuntary unemployment in developed countries as the result of *efficiency wages*.[2] According to the efficiency wage hypothesis, real wage cuts may harm productivity. If this is the case, each firm sets its wage to minimize labor cost per efficiency unit, rather than labor cost per worker. The wage that minimizes labor cost per efficiency unit is known as the efficiency wage. The firm hires labor up to the point where its marginal revenue product is equal to the real wage it has set. And it easily happens that the aggregate demand for labor, when each firm offers its efficiency wage, falls short of labor supply, so that there is involuntary unemployment.

There are three basic variants of this model (see Yellen 1984 for a survey). In one case, firms pay higher wages than the worker's reservation wages so that employees have an incentive not to shirk. In a second version, wages greater than market-clearing are offered so that workers have an incentive not to quit and turnover is reduced. In the third version, wages greater than market-clearing are paid to induce loyalty to the firm.

Although there are potential problems with these models (e.g., complicated contracts in some cases will be Pareto-superior and eliminate equilibrium unemployment; these models may exhibit countercyclical, rather than procyclical productivity), nevertheless, with modification, they have real promise as an explanation of involuntary unemployment. Furthermore, any model of the *dual labor market* must explain why primary-sector firms pay more than the market-clearing wage, and such an explanation can only come from an efficiency wage theory.

## 2   A Model of Cyclical Unemployment

As motivated in the introduction, this section constructs a model in which changes in the money supply will cause changes of the same order in the level of employment in near-rational short-run equilibrium. As indicated earlier, the model is based on monopolistic competition and efficiency wage theory.

**The model**

Assume a monopolistically competitive economy with a fixed number of identical firms. In the initial equilibrium, each firm sets its price and wage to maximize profits under the assumption that changes in its own price will have no effect on the prices charged by rivals or on the average price level. In this sense, each firm is a Bertrand maximizer. There are two different types of firms. One type, which is a fraction $\beta$ of all firms, sets its price and wage according to a rule of thumb in the short run. The variables pertaining to such firms are denoted $n$, since these are *non*maximizing firms. The remaining fraction $(1 - \beta)$ are short-run maximizers, as well as long-run maximizers. They set their price and wage at the levels that maximize profits on the Bertrand assumption that the prices charged by competitors (and the average price level) will be unaffected by their decision. Variables relating to these firms are denoted $m$, since they are *maximizing* firms.

Accordingly, let the demand curve facing each firm be

$$X = (p/\bar{p})^{-\eta}(M/\bar{p}) \qquad \eta > 1, \tag{1}$$

where $X$ = output of the firm, $p$ = the price of the firm's output, $\bar{p}$ = the average price level, and $M$ = the money supply per firm. The parameter $\eta$ is chosen to be greater than 1, so that each firm has increasing revenues as its own price falls. The average price level, $\bar{p}$, is given as the geometric mean of the prices charged by all firms. In long-run equilibrium all firms charge the same price, $p = \bar{p}$, and so the system of demand equations (1) is consistent with a quantity theory:

$$\bar{p}X = M \tag{2}$$

Firms produce output according to the production function:

$$X = (eN)^{\alpha} \qquad 0 < \alpha < 1, \tag{3}$$

where $e$ = average effort of laborers hired and $N$ = number of laborers hired.

Effort $e$ is assumed to depend on the real wage paid $\omega$ according to the function $e = e(\omega)$. The function $e(\omega)$ is assumed to have elasticity with respect to $\omega$ of less than 1 at high $\omega$ and greater than 1 at low $\omega$. An example of such a function is

$$e(\omega) = -a + b\omega^\gamma \qquad 0 < \gamma < 1, \quad a > 0, \quad b > 0. \tag{4}$$

In most efficiency-wage theories, $e$ realistically depends not only on $\omega$ but also on the unemployment rate and the wages paid by other firms. The dependence of $e$ on unemployment plays an important role in these models: through this dependence, increases in the supply of labor cause more workers to be hired in equilibrium. An increase in labor supply, in the absence of any other repercussions, causes unemployment to rise. This rise in unemployment causes a rise in $e$, which in turn, causes firms to increase their demand for labor. (Other repercussions will also follow, as the equilibrium real wage and other things also change.) Our example omits the dependence of $e$ on unemployment and other wages with the result that equilibrium employment is independent of labor supply. The peculiarity of this outcome should not be disturbing, since this is not an essential property of efficiency wage models. Our goal is to illustrate, in the simplest fashion, how first-order changes in welfare can occur because of inertial wage and price behavior whose individual cost is second-order. Since that property does not turn on the dependence of $e$ on unemployment or other wages and since such dependence considerably complicates the model, we have adopted the simpler assumption: $e = e(\omega)$.

**Long-run equilibrium**

The production function and demand function can be used to compute the profit function for each firm, which is revenue (price times output sold) net of factor costs (money wages times labor hired). The profits of each firm are accordingly

$$\Pi = p(p/\bar{p})^{-\eta}(M/\bar{p}) - (p/\bar{p})^{-\eta/\alpha}(M/\bar{p})^{1/\alpha}\omega(e(\omega))^{-1}\bar{p}. \tag{5}$$

In long-run equilibrium each firm chooses the price of its own output and the wage paid its own workers, so as to maximize profits (provided that the demand for labor is less than the supply), on the assumption that the average price level $\bar{p}$ is unaffected by that decision.

For notational convenience, let us denote the price level in the initial period as $p_0$; this is the average price level, the price of maximizing firms, and the price of nonmaximizing firms. With an initial money supply $\overline{M}_0$, the first-order condition for profit maximization and the condition $p = \bar{p}$ yields an equilibrium price of

$$p_0 = k\overline{M}_0, \quad \text{where } k = \left(\frac{\eta\omega^*}{\alpha(\eta - 1)e(\omega^*)}\right)^{\alpha/(1-\alpha)}. \tag{6}$$

The real wage $\omega$ is chosen at the optimizing level $\omega^*$, where the elasticity of effort with respect to the real wage is unity. (This is a standard result in such models [Solow 1979] and represents the condition that the firm chooses the real wage that minimizes the unit cost of a labor efficiency unit.) With this choice of real wage $\omega^*$, the demand for labor is

$$N_0 = k^{-1/\alpha}/e(\omega^*). \tag{7}$$

The total supply of labor per firm $\overline{L}$ is assumed to exceed total labor demanded (which is the right-hand side of (7)). In this case, there will be unemployment, and the firm will be able to obtain all the labor it wants at its preferred real wage $\omega^*$.

### Assumption concerning short-run equilibrium

This characterization of the initial (long-run) equilibrium lays the foundation for determing how much employment will change if there is a change in the money supply when some of the firms are nonmaximizers in the short run. Also to be calculated is the difference between the actual profits of a nonmaximizing firm and its expected profits if it were to continue setting its prices and wages in the Bertrand-maximizing fashion.

The description of short-run behavior follows. Suppose that the money supply changes by a fraction $\epsilon$ so that $M = M_0(1 + \epsilon)$. Suppose also that there are two groups of firms that behave differently in the short run. The $m$ firms, which are the short-run maximizers, set both the price of their output and the wage paid their workers at those levels that exactly maximize profits on the assumption that the average price level is unaffected by their individual decisions. The $n$ firms, which follow a rule of thumb, continue to charge the same price for output and to pay the same money wage. This assumption corresponds to the common finding that money wages are sticky over the business cycle, and also that prices are a constant markup over normal average unit cost. (See Nordhaus and Godley 1972 and Nordhaus 1974 for such a model of pricing and further references. This behavior of wages corresponds to any standard Phillips curve.) An increase in the money supply induces the nonmaximizing firms to hire more labor to an extent dependent on the reduction in the relative price of output, the increase in aggregate real balances, and the number of laborers needed to produce output according to the production function.

**The nature of short-run equilibrium**

The first key task with respect to this short-run model is to compute the difference between the profit of a typical nonmaximizing firm and its profits if it were to abandon its rule-of-thumb behavior and adopt instead the Bertrand behavior of the maximizing firms. It will be shown that for $\epsilon$ equal to zero, the derivative of this difference with respect to $\epsilon$ is zero. In this sense, the prospective loss in profits to the nonmaximizing firms due to their *individual* nonmaximizing behavior is a second-order effect. The second key task is to calculate the derivative, with respect to $\epsilon$, of the ratio between total employment and initial employment. This derivative is positive for $\epsilon$ equal to zero.

In short-run equilibrium the key endogenous variables are determined by (8) to (12):

$$p^n = p_0 \tag{8}$$

It is obvious from our assumptions that $p^n = p_0$.

$$\omega^m = \omega^* \tag{9}$$

Setting the derivative of the profit function (5) with respect to $\omega$ equal to zero yields the optimizing condition that the elasticity of effort with respect to the real wage $\omega^m$ be unity. It follows that in equilibrium $\omega^m$ is unchanged from its long-run value of $\omega^*$.

$$p^m = p_0(1 + \epsilon)^\theta, \tag{10}$$

where $\theta = \dfrac{(1 - \alpha)/\alpha}{\beta(\eta/\alpha - \eta + 1) + (1 - \beta)((1 - \alpha)/\alpha)} \leq 1$

Setting the derivative of the profit function with respect to $p^m$ equal to zero, with $\omega = \omega^*$, yields the optimizing $p^m$ as a function of $\bar{p}$ and $M$. Remembering that $\bar{p}$ is a geometric mean of prices, so that $\bar{p} = (p^n)^\beta (p^m)^{1-\beta}$, and setting $p^n = p_0$ and $M = \bar{M}_0(1 + \epsilon)$ yields $p^m = p_0(1 + \epsilon)^\theta$.

$$\bar{p} = p_0(1 + \epsilon)^{(1-\beta)\theta} \tag{11}$$

This follows directly from the definition of $\bar{p} = (p^n)^\beta (p^m)^{1-\beta}$ and the values of $p^n = p_0$, $p^m = p_0(1 + \epsilon)^\theta$.

$$\omega^n = \omega^*(1 + \epsilon)^{-(1-\beta)\theta}. \tag{12}$$

The money wage paid by the nonmaximizing firm is unchanged at its initial value $w_0$. The real wage is accordingly $w_0/\bar{p}$, which can be rewritten as the product $(w_0/p_0)(p_0/\bar{p})$. The first term of this product is $\omega^*$, and the second is $(1 + \epsilon)^{-(1-\beta)\theta}$.

**Calculation of $p^n$, $\omega^m$, $p^m$, $\bar{p}$ and $\omega^n$**

Each of these variables will be explained in turn. Consider the position of nonmaximizing firms. Their actual profits $\Pi^n$ in the short-run equilibrium are given by the profit function (5) evaluated with $p^n = p_0$, $\bar{p} = p_0(1 + \epsilon)^{(1-\beta)\theta}$, $\omega^n = \omega^*(1 + \epsilon)^{-(1-\beta)\theta}$, and $M = \overline{M}_0(1 + \epsilon)$. Whether or not it is reasonable for these firms to follow rule-of-thumb behavior, we assume, depends upon the difference between their maximum expected profits and their actual profits. The optimum price for any nonmaximizing firm to charge, on the assumption of constant $\bar{p}$, is just the price being charged by the maximizing firms, which is $p^m = p_0(1 + \epsilon)^{\theta}$. The maximum expected profits of any nonmaximizing firm are thus identical with the actual profits $\Pi^m$ being earned by the typical maximizing firm. $\Pi^m$ is found by substituting $p^m = p^m(\epsilon) = p_0(1 + \epsilon)^{\theta}$, $\bar{p} = p_0(1 + \epsilon)^{(1-\beta)\theta}$, $\omega^m = \omega^*$, and $M = \overline{M}_0(1 + \epsilon)$ into the profit function (5). Accordingly, $\Pi^n$ and $\Pi^m$ can be written, respectively, as functions of $\epsilon$:

$$\Pi^n = (p_0)^{1-\eta}f(\epsilon) - (p_0)^{-\eta/\alpha}g(\epsilon)h(\epsilon)\omega^*[e(h(\epsilon)\omega^*)]^{-1} \qquad (13)$$

$$\Pi^m = (p^m(\epsilon))^{1-\eta}f(\epsilon) - (p^m(\epsilon))^{-\eta/\alpha}g(\epsilon)\omega^*(e(\omega^*))^{-1} \qquad (14)$$

The precise functional forms of $f(\epsilon)$ and $g(\epsilon)$ are unimportant. What is crucial is their similar role in the $\Pi^n$ and $\Pi^m$ functions. They can be calculated explicitly by substituting $p_0(1 + \epsilon)^{(1-\beta)\theta}$ and $M_0(1 + \epsilon)$ for $\bar{p}$ and $M$, respectively, into the profit function (5). Similary, $h(\epsilon)$ can be found as $(1 + \epsilon)^{-(1-\beta)\theta}$, since $\omega^n = \omega^*(1 + \epsilon)^{-(1-\beta)\theta}$; $h(\epsilon)$ has the property that $h(0) = 1$.

$\Pi^n$ and $\Pi^m$ are not very different. Their first and second terms have the common factors $f(\epsilon)$ and $g(\epsilon)$, respectively. The derivative of $\Pi^m$ with respect to $p^m$ is zero, since that variable is chosen to maximize that function. And the derivative of $\Pi^m$ with respect to $\omega$ is equal to zero for $\omega = \omega^*$. These properties are useful in showing that the derivative of the difference between $\Pi^m$ and $\Pi^n$ with respect to $\epsilon$ vanishes for $\epsilon = 0$.

The derivative of $\Pi^m - \Pi^n$ with respect to $\epsilon$ can be grouped into four separate terms, each one corresponding to one set of curly brackets in (15):

$$\frac{d(\Pi^m - \Pi^n)}{d\epsilon} = \{(1 - \eta)(p^m(\epsilon))^{-\eta}f(\epsilon)$$

$$+ (\eta/\alpha)(p^m(\epsilon))^{-\eta/\alpha-1}g(\epsilon)\omega^*(e(\omega^*))^{-1}\}\frac{dp^m}{d\epsilon}$$

$$+ \{\omega^*[e(h(\epsilon)\omega^*)]^{-1} - h(\epsilon)\omega^{*2}e'(h(\epsilon)\omega^*)$$

$$\times [e(h(\epsilon)\omega^*)]^{-2}\}\cdot\frac{dh}{d\epsilon}(p_0)^{-\eta/\alpha}g(\epsilon)$$

$$+ \{(p^m(\epsilon))^{1-\eta}f'(\epsilon) - (p^m(\epsilon))^{-\eta/\alpha}\omega^*[e(\omega^*)]^{-1}g'(\epsilon)\}$$

$$- \{(p_0)^{1-\eta}f'(\epsilon) - (p_0)^{-\eta/\alpha}h(\epsilon)\omega^*[e(h(\epsilon)\omega^*)]^{-1}g'(\epsilon)\}. \quad (15)$$

The first term in curly brackets in (15) is zero because of the first-order condition for $p^m$ as the maximand of the profit function $\Pi^m$. The second term in curly brackets vanishes for $\epsilon$ equal to zero, since $h(0) = 1$ and since $\omega^*$ has been chosen to maximize profits. (This causes $\omega^*e'(\omega^*)[e(\omega^*)]^{-1}$ to equal unity.) Thus, the first two terms in curly brackets in (15) are zero for $\epsilon$ equal zero because of the optimizing choice of the respective variables $p$ and $\omega$. The third and fourth terms in curly brackets cancel for $\epsilon$ equal to zero, becasue $p^m(0) = p_0$ and $h(0) = 1$. These terms reflect the common effect of $\epsilon$ on $\Pi^m$ and $\Pi^n$. Since all four terms in curly brackets either vanish or cancel for $\epsilon$ equal zero, it follows that

$$\frac{d(\Pi^m - \Pi^n)}{d\epsilon}\bigg|_{\epsilon=0} = 0. \quad (16)$$

This is a key result of this paper. It says that the loss to the nonmaximizers over their maximum possible profits in this model is second order with respect to $\epsilon$. It also follows trivially that this loss in percentage terms is equal to zero for $\epsilon$ equal zero and has a derivative of zero.

### Employment

The elasticity of total employment with respect to changes in the money supply is not zero. For $\epsilon$ equal zero, this elasticity can be calculated as

$$\frac{d(N/N_0)}{d\epsilon} = (1/\alpha)(1 - (1 - \beta)\theta) + \beta(1 - \beta)\theta. \quad (17)$$

Two comments are in order about (17). First, since $\theta$ is less than one, an increase in the money supply causes an increase in employment. Also, since $\theta = 1$ for $\beta = 0$, the elasticity of employment with respect to changes in the money supply vanishes as the fraction of nonmaximizers approaches zero. Such a result should be expected, since as $\beta$ approaches zero, the model approaches one of monetary neutrality.

## Simulations

We did some simulations of the preceding model of unemployment for various values of the elasticity of output with respect to labor input ($\alpha$), the elasticity of demand for each firm ($\eta$), and the fraction of nonmaximizers ($\beta$). The parameters of the wage-effort function, $a$, $b$, and $\gamma$, were chosen equal to 1.0, 2.0 and 0.5, respectively, so that $\omega^*[e(\omega^*)]^{-1}$ would conveniently equal one.[3]

For each set of parameter values, table 1 reports the percentage difference between the profits of maximizers and nonmaximizers for changes in the

**Table 1**
Percentage loss in profits due to nonmaximizing behavior for different percentage changes in employment, elasticity of output with respect to labor input ($\alpha$), elasticity of demand ($\eta$), and proportion of nonmaximizers ($\beta$) ($a = 1.0, b = 2.0, \gamma = 0.5$)

| | 5% change in employment | | | 10% change in employment | | |
|---|---|---|---|---|---|---|
| | $\beta = 0.25$ | $\beta = 0.5$ | $\beta = 0.75$ | $\beta = 0.25$ | $\beta = 0.5$ | $\beta = 0.75$ |
| $\alpha = 0.25$ | | | | | | |
| $\eta = 1.5$ | 0.084 | 0.023 | 0.011 | 0.309 | 0.088 | 0.043 |
| $\eta = 3.0$ | 0.220 | 0.059 | 0.028 | 0.808 | 0.226 | 0.107 |
| $\eta = 5.0$ | 0.298 | 0.079 | 0.036 | 1.090 | 0.303 | 0.142 |
| $\eta = 20.0$ | 0.408 | 0.107 | 0.049 | 1.496 | 0.410 | 0.189 |
| $\eta = 100.0$ | 0.443 | 0.116 | 0.052 | 1.623 | 0.442 | 0.203 |
| $\alpha = 0.5$ | | | | | | |
| $\eta = 1.5$ | 0.088 | 0.024 | 0.012 | 0.330 | 0.092 | 0.045 |
| $\eta = 3.0$ | 0.295 | 0.080 | 0.038 | 1.109 | 0.306 | 0.146 |
| $\eta = 5.0$ | 0.459 | 0.122 | 0.057 | 1.726 | 0.471 | 0.222 |
| $\eta = 20.0$ | 0.768 | 0.201 | 0.091 | 2.892 | 0.774 | 0.356 |
| $\eta = 100.0$ | 0.888 | 0.231 | 0.104 | 3.343 | 0.889 | 0.405 |
| $\alpha = 0.75$ | | | | | | |
| $\eta = 1.5$ | 0.046 | 0.012 | 0.006 | 0.175 | 0.045 | 0.021 |
| $\eta = 3.0$ | 0.207 | 0.054 | 0.025 | 0.796 | 0.209 | 0.097 |
| $\eta = 5.0$ | 0.397 | 0.103 | 0.048 | 1.533 | 0.402 | 0.186 |
| $\eta = 20.0$ | 0.974 | 0.251 | 0.114 | 3.769 | 0.979 | 0.447 |
| $\eta = 100.0$ | 1.304 | 0.334 | 0.151 | 5.046 | 1.304 | 0.591 |

money supply, which respectively produce 5 percent and 10 percent increases in employment. For 5 percent changes in employment, all values but one, even for values of $\eta$ (the elasticity of demand) as large as 100, are less than 1 percent. For changes in employment of 10 percent, these differences are mainly below 1 percent for low values of $\eta$ and at the maximum value in the table, for $\alpha = 0.75$, $\eta = 100$, and $\beta = 0.25$, only reaches 5.05 percent. Although this loss in profits is extreme in the table, it is not beyond the bounds of possibility. Quite conceivably, over the course of the business cycle, a quarter of all firms could fail to correct a policy that caused a 5 percent loss in profits.

## 3  Conclusion

In conclusion, a model has been presented in which changes in aggregate demand cause significant changes in equilibrium output. This model meets Lucas's criterion that there are "no $500 bills lying on the sidewalk." There is a class of maximizers in this model who are ready to take advantage of *any* profitable opportunity, and those agents who are not maximizing can make at most only small gains from altering their behavior.

The model presented also satisfies the condition that there is involuntary unemployment. This occurs because of the assumption that wages in excess of market-clearing are determined according to the efficiency-wage criterion of minimization of cost-per-labor efficiency unit.

As the introduction made clear, the basic method applied in this paper to show the short-run nonneutrality of money should be applicable in a wide range of models, of which the monopolistic-competition, efficiency-wage model of the last section was only one example.

## Acknowledgements

This is a revised version of Akerlof and Yellen (1983). The authors would like to thank Andrew Abel, Alan Blinder, Richard Gilbert, Hajime Miyazaki, John Quigley, James Tobin, and James Wilcox for helpful conversations. The research for this paper was supported by National Science Foundation Grant No. SES 81-19150 administered by the Institute for Business and Economic Research of the University of California, Berkeley.

## Notes

1. In an implicit contract model without severance pay and with money, it is possible to show the existence of near-rational contracts in which money is nonneutral. If firms alter their

short-run hiring when the money supply changes on the false assumption that unemployment benefits are fixed in money terms rather than in real terms, their policies are near-rational. But the effect of these policies on equilibrium employment and output are first-order in states of the world where there was some unemployment in the long-run equilibrium prior to the money supply shock. Thus, changes in aggregate demand can have a first-order effect on equilibrium in implicit contract models if contracts are near-rational.

2. See, for example, Akerlof (1982); Bowles (1981, 1983); Calvo (1979); Foster and Wan (1984); Malcomson (1981); Miyazaki (1984); Salop (1979); Schlicht (1978); Shapiro and Stiglitz (1984); Stoft (1982a, 1982b); Weiss (1980); and Weisskopf, Bowles, and Gordon (1983).

3. Another choice of the $a$, $b$, $\gamma$ parameters showed negligible differences from the results reported in table 1.

# References

Akerlof, George A., "Labor Contracts as Partial Gift Exchange," *Quarterly Journal of Economics*, 97 (Nov. 1982), 543–569.

Akerlof, George A., and Janet Yellen L., "The Macroeconomic Consequences of Near-Rational Rule-of-Thumb Behavior," mimeo, September 1983.

Bowles, Samuel, "Competitive Wage Determination and Involuntary Unemployment: A Conflict Model," mimeo, University of Massachusetts, May 1981.

Bowles, Samuel, "The Production Process in a Competitive Economy: Walrasian, Neo-Hobbesian and Marxian Models," mimeo, University of Massachusetts, May 1983.

Calvo, Guillermo, "Quasi-Walrasian Theories of Unemployment," *American Economic Review Proceedings*, 69 (May 1979), 102–107.

Foster, James E., and Henry Y. Wan, Jr., "Involuntary Unemployment as a Principal-Agent Equilibrium," *American Economic Review*, 74 (June 1984).

Malcomson, James, "Unemployment and the Efficiency Wage Hypothesis," *Economic Journal*, 91 (Dec. 1981) 848–866.

Miyazaki, Hajime, "Work Norms and Involuntary Unemployment," *Quarterly Journal of Economics*, 94 (May 1984), 297–312.

Nordhaus, William D., "The Falling Share of Profits," *Brookings Papers on Economic Activity*, 1 (1974), 169–208.

Nordhaus, William D., and Wynne A. H. Godley, "Pricing in the Trade Cycle," *Economic Journal*, 82 (Sept. 1972), 853–882.

Okun, Arthur M., *Prices and Quantities: A Macroeconomic Analysis* (Washington, D.C.: Brookings Institution, 1981).

Salop, Steven, "A Model of the Natural Rate of Unemployment," *American Economic Review*, 69 (March 1979), 117–125.

Sargent, Thomas J., "Rational Expectations, the Real Rate of Interest, and the Natural Rate of Unemployment," *Brookings Papers on Economic Activity*, 2 (1973), 429–480.

Schlicht, Ekkehart, "Labor Turnover, Wage Structure, and Natural Unemployment," *Zeitschrift für die Gesamte Staatswissenschaft*, 134 (June 1978), 337–346.

Shapiro, Carl, and Joseph E. Stiglitz, "Equilibrium Unemployment as a Worker Discipline Device," *American Economic Review*, 74 (June 1984).

Solow, Robert M., "Another Possible Source of Wage Stickiness," *Journal of Macroeconomics*, 1 (Winter 1979), 79–82.

Stoft, Steven, "Cheat-Threat Theory," unpublished Ph.D. thesis, University of California, Berkeley, 1982a.

Stoft, Steven, "Cheat-Threat Theory: An Explanation of Involuntary Unemployment," mimeo, Boston University, May 1982b.

Varian, Hal, *Microeconomic Analysis* (New York: Norton, 1978).

Weiss, Andrew, "Job Queues and Layoffs in Labor Markets with Flexible Wages," *Journal of Political Economy*, 88 (June 1980), 526–538.

Weisskopf, Thomas, Samuel Bowles, and David Gordon, "Hearts and Minds: A Social Model of Aggregate Productivity Growth in the U.S., 1948–1979," *Brookings Papers on Economic Activity*, 2 (1983), 381–441.

Yellen, Janet L., "Efficiency Wage Models of Unemployment," *American Economic Review Proceedings*, 74 (May 1984), 200–205.

# 3 Real Rigidities and the Nonneutrality of Money

Laurence Ball and David Romer

## 1  Introduction

According to Keynesian economics, nominal wages and prices are rigid, and so nominal disturbances have real effects. Researchers have presented a wide range of explanations for wage and price rigidities; examples include implicit contracts, customer markets, social customs, efficiency wages, inventory models, and theories of countercyclical markups.[1] These explanations have a common weakness, however: they are theories of *real* rather than *nominal* rigidities. That is, they attempt to explain why real wages or prices are unresponsive to changes in economic activity. Real rigidity does not imply nominal rigidity: without an independent source of nominal stickiness, prices adjust fully to nominal shocks regardless of the extent of real rigidities.

The purpose of this paper is to show that real rigidities nonetheless have a crucial role in explaining nominal rigidities and the nonneutrality of nominal shocks. While real rigidities alone are not sufficient, nominal rigidities can be explained by a *combination* of real rigidities and small frictions in nominal adjustment.

Real rigidities are important because nominal frictions alone—like real rigidities alone—are not enough to cause a large amount of nominal rigidity. In practice, the costs of making nominal prices and wages more flexible—for example, by adjusting prices more frequently or adopting greater indexation—appear small. Mankiw (1985) and Akerlof and Yellen (1985) show that small costs of changing prices ("menu costs")—or equivalently small departures from full optimization ("near rationality")—can *in principle* produce large nominal rigidities. We show, however, that without real rigidities, this result holds only for implausible parameter values; for example, labor supply must be highly elastic. For plausible parameter values, small nominal frictions produce only small rigidities. Thus Mankiw's and Akerlof and Yellen's argument, by itself, is not successful in providing foundations for the Keynesian assumption of nominal rigidity.

This paper shows that the argument can be rescued by introducing real rigidities. The degree of nominal rigidity arising from a given menu cost

*Review of Economic Studies* 57 (April 1990): 183–203. Copyright © 1990 by the Society for Economic Analysis Limited. Reprinted with permission.

(or a given departure from full rationally) is increasing in the degree of real rigidity. Substantial real rigidity implies a large amount of nominal rigidity even if the menu cost is small.

The intuition behind these results is the following. Rigidity of prices after a nominal shock is a Nash equilibrium if the gain to a firm from changing its nominal price, given that other nominal prices are unchanged, is less than the cost of changing prices. But a change in one firm's nominal price when other nominal prices are fixed is a change in the firm's real price. Further, if other prices do not change, then the nominal shock affects real aggregate demand. Thus nominal rigidity is a equilibirum if a firm's gain from adjusting its real price in response to the change in real aggregate demand is less than the cost of changing price. If the firm desires only a small change in its real price—that is, if there is a large degree of real rigidity—then the gain from making the change is small. Since real rigidity reduces the gain from adjustment, it increases the range of nominal shocks for which nonadjustment is an equilibrium.[2]

The remainder of the paper consists of five sections. Since our point is not tied to any specific source of real rigidity, section 2 studies a quite general model. In this model imperfectly competitive price setters face a small menu cost. We show that the degree of nominal rigidity is increasing in the degree of real rigidity under broad conditions.

Section 3 shows that nominal frictions alone are not sufficient for large nonneutralities. We present a specific example of the general model of section 2 in which imperfect competition and the menu cost are the only departures from Walrasian assumptions. We show that for plausible parameter values the model implies only small nominal rigidities.

The following two sections illustrate the general relation between real and nominal rigidity. Each section adds a specific source of real rigidity to the model of section 3 and shows that large nonneutralities can result. In section 4 the real rigidity arises in the goods market. Specifically, we combine our basic model with a model of imperfect information and customer markets based on Stiglitz (1979, 1984) and Woglom (1982). Real price rigidity arises from an asymmetry in the demand curves facing firms. In section 5 the real rigidity arises in the labor market. Real wages are rigid because firms pay efficiency wages to deter shirking.

Section 6 offers concluding remarks.

## 2   General Results

### A.   Assumptions and overview

Consider an economy consisting of a large number of price-setting agents. We assume that agent $i$'s utility depends on aggregate real spending in the economy, $Y$, and on the agent's relative price, $P_i/P$.[3] In addition, there is a small cost, $z$, of changing nominal prices—the menu cost. Thus agent $i$'s utility is given by

$$U_i = W\left(Y, \frac{P_i}{P}\right) - zD_i, \tag{1}$$

where $D_i$ is a dummy variable that indicates whether the agent changes his nominal price. In the specific models of later sections an agent is usually a "yeoman farmer" who sells a differentiated good that he produces with his own labor. We also, however, consider the case in which farmers hire each other in a labor market. Finally, it is straightforward to extend our analysis to the case in which (1) is the profit function of an imperfectly competitive firm; the model is then closed by assuming that firms are owned by households. Under all these interpretations, $Y$ affects an agent's utility (or profits) by shifting out the demand curve that he faces—greater aggregate demand implies that the agent's sales are higher at a given relative price. $P_i/P$ affects utility by determining the point on the demand curve at which the agent produces.

To make nominal disturbances possible, we introduce money. Assume that a transactions technology determines the relation between aggregate spending and real money balances:

$$Y = \frac{M}{P}, \tag{2}$$

where $M$ is the nominal money stock.[4] Substituting (2) into (1) yields

$$U_i = W\left(\frac{M}{P}, \frac{P_i}{P}\right) - zD_i. \tag{3}$$

We assume that in the absence of menu costs, there is a symmetric equilibrium in prices ($P_i/P = 1$, $\forall i$) for a unique level of $M/P$. We normalize this level to be one; in other words, we assume that $W_2(1, 1) = 0$ (subscripts denote partial derivatives). We also assume that $W_{22}(1, 1) < 0$ (the price setters' second-order condition) and that $W_{12} > 0$ (which guarantees stability of the equilibrium).

Part B of this section derives the degree of real price rigidity. We measure real rigidity by the responsiveness of agents' desired real prices, neglecting the menu cost, to shifts in real economic activity. Part C derives the degree of nominal rigidity, defined by the largest monetary shock to which prices do not adjust. Under broad conditions, changes in $W(\cdot)$ that raise the degree of real rigidity lead to greater nominal rigidity as well. Finally, part D computes the welfare loss from equilibrium nominal rigidity and shows that it also usually increases with real rigidity. Thus real rigidities bolster the Keynesian view that economic fluctuations resulting from nominal shocks are highly inefficient.

## B. Real rigidity

Let $P_i^*/P$ be agent $i$'s utility-maximizing real price in the absence of menu costs. This price is defined by the first-order condition $W_2(M/P, P_i^*/P) = 0$. Differentiating this condition with respect to $M/P$ yields

$$\frac{d(P_i^*/P)}{d(M/P)} = \frac{-W_{12}}{W_{22}} \equiv \pi, \tag{4}$$

where henceforth we evaluate all derivatives at $(1, 1)$, the equilibrium in the absence of menu costs. We define a high degree of real rigidity as a small value of $\pi$, a small responsiveness of an agent's desired real price to changes in aggregate real spending.

Equation (4) shows that a high degree of real rigidity can result from a large value of $-W_{22}$ or a small value of $W_{12}$. Intuitively, when $-W_{22}$ is large—that is, when utility is very concave in an agent's relative price—changes in the price are very costly. When $W_{12}$ is small, shifts in real money have little effect on $W_2$, which determines the desired price.

## C. The equilibrium degree of nominal rigidity

We measure nominal rigidity through an experiment similar to ones in previous work on menu costs (Mankiw 1985, Blanchard and Kiyotaki 1987, Ball and Romer 1989). Suppose that agents set prices believing that $M$ will equal one (a normalization). Each agent sets his price to one, the frictionless equilibrium in this case. After prices are set, however, there is an unanticipated shock to $M$. At this point each agent has the option of paying the menu cost $z$ and adjusting his price. We solve for the range of realizations of $M$ for which nonadjusting of all prices is a Nash equilibrium. This range is symmetric around one; we therefore denote it by $(1 - x^*, 1 + x^*)$ and use $x^*$ as our measure of nominal rigidity. We show that a broad class of changes in $W(\cdot)$ that raise real rigidity raise $x^*$ as well.

To determine when nonadjustment is an equilibrium, we compare an agent's utility if he adjusts his price and if he does not, given that other agents do not adjust. If agent $i$ maintains a rigid price of one along with the others, then $D_i = 0$, $M/P = M$, and $P_i/P = 1$. Thus the agents' utility is $W(M, 1)$. If the agent adjusts despite others' nonadjustment, then $D_i = 1$ and the agent sets $P_i/P$ to $P_i^*/P$, the utility-maximizing level given $M/P$. Since one agent's behavior does not affect the aggregate price level, $M/P$ is still simply $M$. Thus the agent's utility is $W(M, P_i^*/P) - z$.

These results imply that agent $i$ does not adjust—and so rigidity is an equilibrium—if

$$PC < z, \qquad PC = W\left(M, \frac{P_i^*}{P}\right) - W(M, 1). \tag{5}$$

$PC$ is the "private cost" of nominal rigidity: an agent's loss from not setting his relative price at the utility-maximizing level. Rigidity is an equilibrium if this loss is less than the menu cost. A second-order Taylor approximation around $M = 1$ yields

$$PC \simeq \frac{-(W_{12})^2}{2W_{22}} x^2, \tag{6}$$

where $x \equiv M - 1$.[5] Equations (5) and (6) imply that rigidity is an equilibrium when $M$ lies with $(1 - x^*, 1 + x^*)$, where

$$x^* = \sqrt{\frac{-2W_{22}z}{(W_{12})^2}}. \tag{7}$$

We can now show the connection between real and nominal rigidity. Using $\pi = -W_{12}/W_{22}$, we can rewrite (7) as

$$x^* = \sqrt{\frac{2z}{\pi W_{12}}}. \tag{8}$$

If there is no nominal friction, then nominal prices are completely flexible: $x^* \equiv 0$ if $z = 0$. But for a positive menu cost, increasing real rigidity—that is, decreasing $\pi$—by either decreasing $W_{12}$ or increasing $-W_{22}$ leads to greater nominal rigidity. (A lower $W_{12}$ raises $x^*$ directly as well as through $\pi$.) As $\pi$ approaches zero, the degree of nominal rigidity becomes arbitrarily large.[6]

To understand the connection between $x^*$ and $\pi$, recall that nominal rigidity is an equilibrium if an agent does not adjust his nominal price to a nominal shock given that others do not adjust. As explained in the introduction, nonadjustment along with the others implies a constant real price, and the others' behavior implies that the nominal shock affects real aggregate demand; thus nominal rigidity is an equilibrium if an agent does not adjust his real price when demand shifts. An increase in real rigidity means that an agent desires a smaller change in his real price after a given change in demand. When the desired change is smaller, the cost of foregoing it is smaller; thus a menu cost is sufficient to prevent adjustment for a wider range of shocks.

So far we have focused on the conditions under which nominal rigidity is an equilibrium. It is also natural to ask when *flexibility* is an equilibrium. Analysis parallel to the derivation of (7) shows that adjustment of all prices is an equilibrium if $|x| > x^{**}$, where

$$x^{**} = \sqrt{\frac{2z}{-W_{22}}}. \tag{9}$$

As discussed in Ball and Romer (1988), $x^{**}$ can be less than $x^*$. In this case there is a range of shocks, $x^{**} < |x| < x^*$, for which both rigidity and flexibility are equilibria. Intuitively, multiple equilibria arise from "strategic complementarity" in price setting: an agents' desired price depends positively on others' prices, so adjustment by others raises his incentive to adjust.

Equations (9) and (7) imply that $x^*/x^{**} = 1/\pi$. Thus multiple equilibria require sufficient real rigidity ($\pi < 1$), and greater real rigidity increases the range of multiple equilibria. Real rigidity strengthens strategic complementarity in price setting—when agents want stable real prices, their desired nominal prices are closely tied to others' prices.

These results suggest a caveat to our main argument. According to (9), increasing real rigidity by raising $-W_{22}$ widens not only the range of shocks for which rigidity is an equilibrium but also the range for which flexibility is an equilibrium. If we measure rigidity by $x^{**}$ rather than $x^*$, real rigidity can lead to *less* nominal rigidity. This result does not, however, affect our conclusion that real rigidity is necessary for substantial nominal rigidity.

As we show below, without real rigidities the degree of nominal rigidity is small even using the generous measure $x^*$. That is, without real rigidities, *all* equilibria have little nominal rigidity. Introducing real rigidities means that $x^*$ can be large, so considerable nominal rigidity can be an equilibrium. The result that $x^{**}$ can fall means only that the amount of rigidity in other equilibria can go from small to smaller.[7]

## D. The welfare loss from nominal rigidity

Since real rigidity increases nominal rigidity, it increases the economic fluctuations resulting from shocks to aggregate demand. Conventional Keynesian doctrine holds not only that such fluctuations are large but also that they are highly undesirable. In an earlier paper (Ball and Romer 1989) we analyze the welfare costs of fluctuations arising from nominal rigidity in a model with few departures from Walrasian assumptions. We find that the costs are small for plausible parameter values. Here we show that real rigidities can alter this conclusion: greater real rigidity implies greater welfare costs of equilibrium nominal rigidity.

For our welfare analysis we modify the experiment of the last section in two ways. First, as in our previous paper, we assume for simplicity that agents must decide whether to pay the menu cost *before* observing the money supply. If an agent pays, he can always adjust his price ex post; if he does not pay, his price is always rigid. This nominal rigidity is a zero/one variable. This simplification does not affect the qualitative results.

Second, to study the effects of fluctuations, we posit a distribution for $M$ rather than simply considering an unanticipated shock. Let the mean of $M$ be one and let $\sigma^2$ denote its variance. In this case, the price $P_0$, that agents set before observing $M$ is not equal to the expected value of $M$: certainly equivalence fails because utility is not quadratic. Following our earlier paper, one can show the following:[8]

$$\frac{1}{P_0} \simeq 1 - \frac{W_{211}}{2W_{12}} \sigma^2 \tag{10}$$

Thus the mean level of output under rigidity, $E[M]/P_0$, differs from one, its level under flexibility.

In this version of the model, reasoning parallel to the derivation of (5) and (6) shows that (complete) rigidity is an equilibrium if

$$PC < z, \qquad PC \simeq \frac{-(W_{12})^2}{2W_{22}} \sigma^2. \tag{11}$$

Comparing (11) with (6) shows that $\sigma^2 = E[(M - 1)^2]$ replaces $x^2 = (M - 1)^2$. In choosing between rigidity and flexibility ex ante, agents compare the menu cost to the *expected* private loss from rigidity.

The welfare loss from equilibrium rigidity depends on the relation between $PC$ and the "social cost" or rigidity: the difference between $E[W(\cdot)]$ when all agents pay the menu cost and when none pays. If all agents pay, then $M/P = 1$ and $P_i/P = 1$ (the equilibrium under flexible prices); thus $E[W(\cdot)] = W(1, 1)$. If no agent pays, then all nominal prices equal $P_0$ and $E[W(\cdot)] = E[W(M/P_0, 1)]$. Thus the social cost is

$$SC = W(1, 1) - E[W(M/P_0, 1)] \simeq \frac{W_1 W_{211} - W_{11} W_{12}}{2 W_{12}} \sigma^2, \tag{12}$$

where we again approximate around $M = 1$.

Combining (11) and (12) yields the ratio of the social to the private cost of rigidity:

$$R = \frac{SC}{PC} = \frac{W_{22}(W_{11} W_{12} - W_1 W_{211})}{(W_{12})^3}. \tag{13}$$

Recall that nominal rigidity is an equilibrium as long as the private cost does not exceed $z$. The largest possible social cost of equilibrium rigidity is thus $R$ times $z$. Since the losses from rigidity disappear when $\sigma^2 = 0$, $Rz$ is also the maximum gain from stabilizing aggregate demand. Thus, for a given menu cost $z$, the welfare cost of rigidity and the gains from demand stabilization are increasing in $R$. As discussed in Ball and Romer (1989), $R$ can be greater than one—the social cost of nominal rigidity can exceed the private cost—because rigidity has a negative externality. Rigidity in one agent's price contributes to rigidity in the aggregate price level. Greater price-level rigidity causes larger fluctuations in real spending, which harms all agents.

The size of $R$, like the degree of nominal rigidity, is linked to the degree of real rigidity. Consider first an increase in real rigidity caused by an increase in $-W_{22}$. As described above, this reduces the private cost of nominal rigidity—the gain from adjusting to a shock if others do not adjust. In contrast, the social cost of nominal rigidity is unaffected. Intuitively, real rigidity is irrelevant to the difference in welfare when all prices adjust and when none adjusts because all real prices are one in both cases. Thus real rigidity increases the ratio of social to private costs of nominal rigidity by reducing the denominator while leaving the numerator unchanged.

The effect of an increase in real rigidity caused by a decrease in $W_{12}$ is more complicated. A lower $W_{12}$, like a higher $-W_{22}$, reduces the private cost of rigidity. But in principle $W_{12}$ affects the social cost as well, because it affects $P_0$ and hence the mean level of output under rigidity. As a result, reducing $W_{12}$ has in general an ambiguous effect on $R$. In the specific models of sections 4 and 5, however, the effect of rigidity on mean output proves to be unimportant. If we ignore this effect, a smaller $W_{12}$ has the same implications as a larger $-W_{22}$: $R$ rises because its denominator falls and its numerator is unchanged.

## 3   A Baseline Model

This section considers a simple example of the class of models studied above. Aside from imperfect competition and the menu cost, the model's assumptions are Walrasian. We use the model to show that menu costs are not enough to produce large real effects of money; specifically, we show that the degree of nominal rigidity and the welfare loss from rigidity are small for plausible parameter values. The model is also the basis for sections 4 and 5. In those sections we add specific sources of real rigidity and show that large nonneutralities can result.

### A.   The model

We consider a simple "yeoman farmer" economy similar to those in Ball and Romer (1988, 1989). There is a continuum of agents ("farmers") indexed by $i$ and distributed uniformly on $[0, 1]$. Each farmer uses his own labor to produce a differentiated good, then sells this product and purchases the products of all other farmers. Farmer $i$'s utility function is

$$U_i = C_i - \frac{\epsilon - 1}{\gamma \epsilon} L_i^\gamma - z D_i, \qquad C_i = \left[ \int_{j=0}^1 C_{ij}^{(\epsilon-1)/\epsilon} \, dj \right]^{\epsilon/(\epsilon-1)}, \qquad (14)$$

where $L_i$ is farmer $i$'s labor supply, $C_i$ is an index of farmer $i$'s consumption, $C_{ij}$ is farmer $i$'s consumption of the product of farmer $j$, $\epsilon$ is the elasticity of substitution between any two goods ($\epsilon > 1$), and $\gamma$ measures the extent of increasing marginal disutility of labor ($\gamma > 1$). The coefficient on $L_i$ is chosen so that equilibrium output neglecting menu costs is one.

Farmer $i$ has a linear production function:

$$Y_i = L_i, \tag{15}$$

where $Y_i$ is the farmer's output. As in section 2, a transaction technology implies

$$Y = \frac{M}{P}, \tag{16}$$

where in this model

$$Y = \int_{i=0}^{1} Y_i \, di \qquad P = \left[ \int_{i=0}^{1} P_i^{1-\epsilon} \, di \right]^{1/(1-\epsilon)}. \tag{17}$$

$P$ is the price index for consumption $C_i$.

Equations (14) to (17) determine the demand for farmer $i$'s product:

$$Y_i^D = \left( \frac{M}{P} \right) \left( \frac{P_i}{P} \right)^{-\epsilon}. \tag{18}$$

Substituting (18) and the farmer's budget constraint ($PC_i = P_i Y_i$) into (14) yields the specific form of $W(\cdot)$ in this model:

$$U_i = \left( \frac{M}{P} \right) \left( \frac{P_i}{P} \right)^{(1-\epsilon)} - \frac{\epsilon-1}{\gamma\epsilon} \left( \frac{M}{P} \right)^{\gamma} \left( \frac{P_i}{P} \right)^{-\gamma\epsilon} - zD_i \equiv W \left( \frac{M}{P}, \frac{P_i}{P} \right). \tag{19}$$

**B.  Are the nonneutralities large?**

We can now determine the degree of nominal rigidity and the welfare loss from rigidity in this model. Taking the appropriate derivatives of (19), evaluating at $(1, 1)$, and substituting into (7) and (13) yields

$$x^* = \sqrt{\frac{2(1 + \gamma\epsilon - \epsilon)z}{(\epsilon-1)(\gamma-1)^2}}, \qquad R = \frac{(1 + \epsilon\gamma - \epsilon)^2}{\epsilon(\epsilon-1)(\gamma-1)^2}. \tag{20}$$

As in previous papers, a second-order menu cost leads to first-order nominal rigidity ($x^*$ is proportional to $\sqrt{z}$). But this does not imply that menu costs prevent adjustment to sizable shocks. Similarly, $R$ is greater than one, but this does not imply that menu costs cause large welfare losses; since the loss from equilibrium rigidity is $Rz$ and $z$ is small, $R$ must be much greater than one. We now show that in this model $x^*$ and $R$ are small for

**Table 1**
Baseline model

| Labor supply elasticity $(1/(\gamma - 1))$ | Markup $(1/(\varepsilon - 1))$ | | | |
|---|---|---|---|---|
| | 5% | 15% | 50% | 100% |
| | Private cost/$R$ | | | |
| 0.05 | 2.38/1.05 | 2.16/1.16 | 1.64/1.55 | 1.22/2.10 |
| 0.15 | 0.79/1.06 | 0.71/1.19 | 0.53/1.65 | 0.39/2.31 |
| 0.50 | 0.23/1.10 | 0.20/1.30 | 0.14/2.04 | 0.10/3.13 |
| 1.00 | 0.11/1.15 | 0.10/1.47 | 0.06/2.67 | 0.04/4.50 |

Note: Private cost is for a 5% change in money and is measured as a percentage of revenue when prices are flexible.

plausible parameter values. The results for $R$ are more clear-cut than the results for $x^*$.

Table 1 shows the private cost of nonadjustment to a 5% change in the money supply, measured as a percentage of a farmer's revenue when all prices are flexible, for various values of $\epsilon$ and $\gamma$.[9] The private cost equals the menu cost needed to prevent adjustment to the shock—that is, to make $x^*$ greater than 0.05. The table also shows the values of $R$ corresponding to the values of $\epsilon$ and $\gamma$. To interpret the results, note that nonadjustment to a 5% change in money implies a 5% change in real output. Recall that $\epsilon$ is the elasticity of demand for a farmer's product and $\gamma$ measures the degree of increasing marginal disutility of labor. The table presents the private cost and $R$ as functions of $1/(\epsilon - 1)$, the markup of price over marginal cost, and $1/(\gamma - 1)$, farmer's labor supply elasticity.

We focus on a base case in which, using evidence from empirical studies, we take 0.15 as the value of the markup and 0.15 again as the labor supply elasticity; these numbers imply $\epsilon = \gamma = 7.7$.[10] For these values, the private cost of rigidity is 0.7% of revenue, which appears nonnegligible. Thus while it is difficult to determine "realistic" values for costs of adjusting nominal prices, trivial costs would not be sufficient to prevent adjustment in this example. In any case, the welfare result is very clear. When both the markup and the labor supply elasticity are 0.15, $R$ is 1.2—the social cost of rigidity is only slightly greater than the private cost. Since the welfare loss from rigidity is bounded by $Rz$, $R = 1.2$, and small menu costs imply that this loss is small.

Table 1 shows that it is difficult to reverse these results. The private cost of rigidity is decreasing in both the markup and the labor supply elasticity and approaches zero as either approaches infinity. But implausibly large values of these parameters are required for large nonneutralities. To see this, consider a labor supply elasticity of one (well above most estimates) and a markup of one (generous even compared with the high estimates in Hall 1988). In this case the private cost of nonadjustment to a 5% change in money is 0.04% of revenue, which is perhaps trivial. But $R = 4.5$; the welfare cost of the business cycle is only 4.5 times the menu cost. Only outlandish parameter values yield a large $R$—for example, a markup of one and labor supply elasticity of 10 imply $R = 72$.

Intuitively, the crucial problem for the model is that labor supply appears to be unelastic (that is, realistic values of $\gamma$ are large). Since workers are reluctant to vary their hours of work, they have a strong incentive to adjust their wages (equal to their product prices in our yeoman farmer model) when demand changes. Large private gains from flexibility imply that farmers pay the menu cost after a nominal shock unless the shock is very small and thus that only small shocks affect output and welfare.

These results are strengthened by a natural modification of the model. In studying a yeoman farmer economy, we implicitly introduce an additional imperfection besides the menu cost and imperfect competition: immobile labor. If farmers sell labor to each other in a competitive market (a case considered in section 5), the private cost of price rigidity is greatly increased. If, for example, the money stock falls and prices do not adjust, then output falls and the lower labor demand reduces the real wage. Since a producer can hire as much labor as he wants at the low wage, he can greatly increase profits by cutting his price and raising output. With self-employment, the gains from increasing output are smaller because the producer faces his own upward-sloping labor-supply curve. If labor supply is inelastic, this difference in incentives to adjust is very large. For a markup and labor-supply elasticity of 0.15, introducing labor mobility raises the private cost in table 1 from 0.7% of revenue to 38%. With such strong incentives to adjust, nominal frictions produce *extremely* small nonneutralities.

## 4  Imperfect Information and Customer Markets

### A.  Overview

This section and the next present examples in which we add sources of real rigidity to the model of section 3 and show that large nonneutralities can result. Here the source of rigidity is an asymmetry in the effects on demand of price increases and decreases, which has been explored by Stiglitz (1979, 1984) and Woglom (1982). The central assumption is that changes in a firm's price are observed by the firm's current customers but not by other consumers. If the firm raises its price, it loses sales both because some of its customers leave for other sellers and because its remaining customers buy less. If the firm lowers its price, it sells more to current customers, but it does *not* attract other firms' customers, because they do not observe the lower price.[11]

To introduce this asymmetry in demand, we modify our basic model by assuming that each good is produced by many farmers rather than by one and that each farmer sells to a group of customers rather than to everyone. In addition, we introduce heterogeneity in tastes, which causes the proportion of a farmer's customers who leave to be a smooth function of the farmer's price. Thus, while Stiglitz and Woglom study demand curves with kinks, we focus on the more appealing case of demand curves that bend sharply but are nonetheless differentiable at all points. (Kinked demand curves are a limiting case of our model; we discuss the special features of this case below.)

Part B of this section presents the revised model. Part C derives the demand curve facing a farmer and shows that it is asymmetric. Part D shows that the asymmetry in demand leads to real price rigidity. Part E demonstrates the link between real and nominal rigidity in this example. Finally, part F asks how much real rigidity is needed to generate nominal rigidity that is quantitively important.

## B. Assumptions

There is a continuum of differentiated goods each produced by a continuum of farmers. Goods are indexed by $j$ and distributed uniformly on the unit interval; farmers are indexed by $j$ and $k$ and distributed uniformly on the unit square. We let $i = (j, k)$ denote a point in the unit square.

Each farmer consumes all products but purchases a given product from only one farmer, his "home seller" of that good. A farmer observes the prices of his home sellers. He does not observe other individual prices, but he knows the distribution of prices for each good. In his role as a seller, each farmer is the home seller to a continuum of farmers, his customers. Each producer of good $j$ begins as the home seller of an equal proportion of all farmers.

As in our other models, each seller sets a nominal price before observing the money stock and adjusts after $M$ is revealed if he pays the menu cost. After prices are determined, each farmer chooses whether to leave each of his home sellers for another seller of the same product. For simplicity, we assume that this search is costless but that a farmer can search for a seller of a given product only once; if the farmer leaves his home seller, he is assigned to another and can neither search again nor return to his original home seller. (Our results would not change if we introduced a search cost and allowed farmers to choose how many times to search). If a farmer leaves his home seller of a given product, he has an equal chance of being assigned to each other seller of the product.

We introduce heterogeneity in tastes by modifying the utility function, (14), to be

$$U_i = AC_i - BL_i^\gamma - zD_i, \tag{21}$$

where

$$C_i = \left\{ \int_{j=0}^1 [(\theta_{ij})^{D(ij)} C_{ij}]^{(\epsilon-1)/\epsilon} \, dj \right\}^{\epsilon/(\epsilon-1)}. \tag{22}$$

$D(ij)$ is a dummy variable equal to one if farmer $i$ remains with his home seller of product $j$, $\theta_{ij}$ measures farmer $i$'s taste for remaining with his home seller of product $j$, and $A$ and $B$ are constants chosen for convenience.[12] The important change in the utility function is the addition of the $\theta_{ij}$s to the consumption index. In words, farmer $i$'s utility gain from one unit of product $j$ provided by his home seller equals his gain from $\theta_{ij}$ units from a different seller. We can interpret farmer's tastes for their home sellers as arising from location, service, and the like. For simplicity, a farmer is indifferent among all sellers of a given product who are not his home seller.

We assume that $\theta_{ij}$ is distributed across $i$ with a cumulative distribution function, $F(\cdot)$, which is the same for all $j$. We also assume that the mean of $\theta_{ij}$, $\bar{\theta}$, is greater than one and that the density function of $\theta_{ij}$, $f(\cdot)$, is symmetric around $\bar{\theta}$ and single-peaked. The assumption that $\bar{\theta}$ is greater than one means that, all else being equal, most buyers prefer to remain with their home sellers. This plausible assumption is necessary for imperfect information to lead to asymmetric demand. If $\theta$ had mean one, then half of a farmer's customers would leave if he charged a real price of one, and this would imply that price decreases save as many customers as price increases drive away.

Aside from the modifications described here, the model is the same as in section 3.

## C.  Product demand

The first step in studying this model is to derive the demand curve facing a seller. We consider the case in which all other sellers charge a real price of one; the analysis below requires only the results for this case. Farmer $i$ sells to two groups of customers: original customers who remain with him after they observe his price and customers of other sellers who leave and are assigned to him. An original customer stays if this maximizes his utility gain per unit of expenditure; when others' real prices are one, this occurs for $P_i/P < \theta$.[13] One can show that if a customer stays, his demand for the farmer's product is

$$(A\theta)^{(\epsilon-1)}\left(\frac{P_i}{P}\right)^{-\epsilon}\left(\frac{M}{P}\right). \tag{23}$$

The fraction of other farmers' customers who leave is $F(1)$, the fraction with $\theta$ less than the others' real price of one. By our symmetry assumptions, the new customers assigned to farmer $i$ are a proportion $F(1)$ of his original customers. Finally, the demand from each new customer is given by (23) with $\theta$ replaced by one, since $\theta^{D(ij)} \equiv 1$ for buyers who switch sellers. Combining these results leads to total demand for farmer $i$'s product:

$$Y_i^D = A^{\epsilon-1}\left\{F(1) + \int_{\theta=P_i/P}^{\infty} \theta^{\epsilon-1}f(\theta)\,d\theta\right\}\left(\frac{P_i}{P}\right)^{-\epsilon}\left(\frac{M}{P}\right)$$

$$\equiv A^{\epsilon-1}h\left(\frac{P_i}{P}\right)\left(\frac{P_i}{P}\right)^{-\epsilon}\left(\frac{M}{P}\right). \tag{24}$$

Intuitively, $h(P_i/P)$ gives the effect of farmer $i$'s price on his number of customers, and as usual, $(P_i/P)^{-\epsilon}$ determines how much each customer buys.

Equation (24) implies asymmetric responses to increases and decreases in a farmer's price. Straightforward computations lead to

$$\eta \equiv -\left.\frac{\partial \ln Y_i^D}{\partial \ln (P_i/P)}\right|_{(P_i/P)=1} = \epsilon + \frac{f(1)}{h(1)};$$

$$\rho \equiv -\left.\frac{\partial^2 \ln Y_i^D}{\partial \ln (P_i/P)^2}\right|_{(P_i/P)=1} = \eta\frac{f(1)}{h(1)} + \frac{f'(1)}{h(1)}. \tag{25}$$

Here $\eta$ is the elasticity of demand evaluated at one, the farmer's ex ante real price, and $\rho$ measures the change in the elasticity as the farmer's price rises around one. If $\rho > 0$, it implies that price increases have larger effects on demand than price decreases. A sufficient condition for $\rho > 0$ is $f'(1) > 0$, which is guaranteed by our assumptions that $E[\theta] > 1$ and that $f(\cdot)$ is increasing below its mean. If $f'(1)$ is large, then the asymmetry in demand is strong—the demand curve bends sharply around one.

As in Stiglitz and Woglom, imperfect information is the source of asymmetric demand. A price increase drives away customers, but a decrease does not attract new customers, because customers of other sellers do not observe it. The details of the results are more complicated than in previous papers, however. Stiglitz and Woglom assume that a firm retains all its customers if it charges a real price of one, but we assume that the firm loses some customers (those with $\theta < 1$). Thus in our model a price decrease *does* raise the number of customers: it saves some old customers who otherwise would leave. Demand is still asymmetric, because our assumptions about $F(\cdot)$ imply that the number saved is less than the number lost by an increase.

Figure 1 illustrates the asymmetry in our model. Since farmer $i$ retains original customers for whom $\theta > P_i/P$, the proportion of customers who stay is given by the area under $f(\cdot)$ to the right of $P_i/P$. The change in this

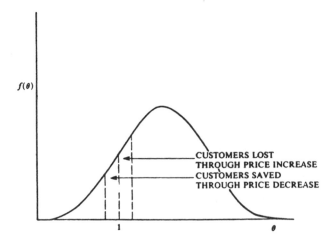

**Figure 1**
Asymmetric effects of price changes in a model of imperfect information

proportion resulting from a price change is the area under $f(\cdot)$ between the old and new prices. Figure 1 shows that a price increase starting from $P_i/P = 1$ has a larger effect on the proportion who stay than a price decrease, because $f'(1) > 1$.

There are two limiting cases of our model. The first is $f(1) = f'(1) = 0$, which implies that all customers remain with a farmer if his price is in the neighborhood of one. In this case, $\eta = \epsilon$, $\rho = 0$, and the demand function reduces to (18), the symmetric function in the basic model. The second case is $f(\theta) = 0$ for $\theta < 1$ and $f'(1) \to \infty$. This implies that $\rho \to \infty$: the demand curve is kinked, as in Stiglitz and Woglom. In this case all customers remain as long as $P_i/P \le 1$, but a nonnegligible proportion leaves as soon as the price rises above one.

## D.  Real rigidity

Substituting the demand equation, (24), into the utility function, (21), yields $W(\cdot)$ for this model:

$$U_i = A^{(\epsilon-1)}\left(\frac{M}{P}\right)h\left(\frac{P_i}{P}\right)\left(\frac{P_i}{P}\right)^{(1-\epsilon)} - A^{\gamma(\epsilon-1)}B\left[h\left(\frac{P_i}{P}\right)\right]^{\gamma}\left(\frac{M}{P}\right)^{\gamma}\left(\frac{P_i}{P}\right)^{-\gamma\epsilon} - zD_i$$

$$\equiv W\left(\frac{M}{P},\frac{P_i}{P}\right) - zD_i. \tag{26}$$

Substituting the appropriate derivatives of $W(\cdot)$ into the definition of $\pi$ yields

$$\pi = \frac{\eta(\gamma - 1)(\eta - 1)}{\eta(\eta - 1)(1 + \gamma\eta - \eta) + \rho}, \qquad \frac{\partial\pi}{\partial\rho} < 0, \qquad \lim_{\rho\to\infty}\pi = 0. \tag{27}$$

According to (27), real prices become more rigid as demand becomes more asymmetric. As the bend in the demand curve approaches a kink ($\rho \to \infty$), real prices become completely rigid. Intuitively, a sharply bent demand curve means that price increases greatly reduce demand but decreases raise demand only a little. In this case, both increases and decreases are unattractive and farmers maintain rigid prices.

## E.  Nominal rigidity

We can now show the connection between real and nominal rigidity in this model. Substituting the derivates of (26) into (7) and (13) yields

$$x^* = \sqrt{\frac{2[(\eta - 1)(1 + \gamma\eta - \eta) + (\rho/\eta)]z}{(\gamma - 1)^2(\eta - 1)^2}}; \tag{28}$$

$$R = \frac{(1 + \gamma\eta - \eta)^2}{\eta(\eta - 1)(\gamma - 1)^2} + \frac{\rho}{\eta^2(\eta - 1)(\gamma - 1)}. \tag{29}$$

Both $x^*$ and $R$ are increasing in $\rho$, and both approach infinity as $\rho$ approaches infinity. Thus increasing real rigidity by bending the demand curve leads to greater nominal rigidity, and complete real rigidity arising from kinked demand implies complete nominal rigidity. In terms of our general model, increases in $\rho$ raise $x^*$ and $R$ because they increase $-W_{22}$ while leaving $W_{12}$ unchanged—the bend in the demand curve makes a seller's utility more concave in his price.[14]

**F.  How much real rigidity is necessary?**

In the baseline model of section 3, plausible parameter values imply that there is little nominal rigidity. We now ask how much real rigidity is needed to reverse this result. Table 2 presents the private cost of nominal rigidity (again on the assumption of a 5% change in money) and $R$ for various values of the markup, the labor-supply elasticity, and the degree of real rigidity $\pi$. The markup is now $1/(\eta - 1)$. With the markup and labor supply elasticity, there is a one-to-one relation between $\pi$ and $\rho$; we present results in terms of $\pi$ because $\rho$ is difficult to interpret. Since the results about $R$ are the most disappointing in section 3, we focus the present discussion on $R$.

    Table 2 shows that a large degree of real rigidity is necessary for a large $R$. As a benchmark, note first that if $\rho = 0$—there is no asymmetry in demand, so the model reduces to the one in section 3—a markup of 0.15 and a labor supply elasticity of 0.15 imply that $\pi = 0.127$ and (as shown above) $R = 1.2$. Increasing $\rho$ so that $\pi$ falls to 0.05—that is, reducing the response of real prices to demand shifts by more than half—raises $R$ to 3.0, but this is still small ($\pi = 0.05$ combined with a markup and labor-supply elasticity of one implies $R = 30$). Larger reductions in $\pi$ produce better results: $\pi = 0.01$ implies $R = 15$ for a markup and labor supply elasticity of 0.15 (and $R = 150$ for a markup and elasticity of one), and $\pi = 0.001$ implies $R = 152$ (and 1,500).

    While these results show that the necessary amount of real rigidity is large, they do not determine whether this much rigidity is realistic. It is plausible that customer-market considerations are quantitatively important—certainly there is no presumption that they are trivial, as with the costs of

**Table 2**
A model of customer markets. Private cost/$R$ for various degrees of real rigidity

| $1/(\eta - 1) = 0.15, 1/(\gamma - 1) = 0.15$ | | $1/(\eta - 1) = 0.15, 1/(\gamma - 1) = 1.00$ | |
|---|---|---|---|
| $\pi$ | $PC/R$ | $\pi$ | $PC/R$ |
| 0.127* | 0.71/1.19 | 0.115* | 0.10/1.47 |
| 0.050 | 0.28/3.04 | 0.050 | 0.04/3.37 |
| 0.025 | 0.14/6.09 | 0.025 | 0.02/6.75 |
| 0.010 | 0.06/15.2 | 0.010 | 0.01/16.9 |
| 0.005 | 0.03/30.4 | 0.005 | 0.00/33.7 |
| 0.002 | 0.01/76.1 | 0.002 | 0.00/84.3 |
| 0.001 | 0.01/152.1 | 0.001 | 0.00/168.6 |
| $1/(\eta - 1) = 1.00, 1/(\gamma - 1) = 0.15$ | | $1/(\eta - 1) = 1.00, 1/(\gamma - 1) = 1.00$ | |
| $\pi$ | $PC/R$ | $\pi$ | $PC/R$ |
| 0.474* | 0.39/2.31 | 0.333* | 0.04/4.50 |
| 0.200 | 0.17/5.37 | 0.200 | 0.03/7.50 |
| 0.050 | 0.04/21.5 | 0.050 | 0.01/30.0 |
| 0.025 | 0.02/43.0 | 0.025 | 0.00/60.0 |
| 0.010 | 0.01/107.5 | 0.010 | 0.00/150.0 |
| 0.005 | 0.00/214.9 | 0.005 | 0.00/300.0 |
| 0.002 | 0.00/537.3 | 0.002 | 0.00/750.0 |

Note: Private cost is for a 5% change in revenue and is measured as a percentage of revenue when prices are flexible.
* Real rigidity when $\rho = 0$

adjusting nominal prices. Research has not progressed far enough, however, to produce estimates of $\rho$, the sharpness of the bend in demand, or of the resulting real rigidity. Thus the question of whether customer markets are an important source of nominal rigidity remains open.

## 5   The Labor Market and Real Wage Rigidity

### A.   Discussion

Section 4 suppresses the labor market and studies the implications of real price rigidity arising from product-market imperfections. Traditionally, however, macroeconomists have viewed labor-market imperfections as central to aggregate fluctuations. Motivated by this view, we now present a model with a labor market in which rigidity in firms' real prices is caused

Laurence Ball and David Romer

by rigidity in their real wages. Real wage rigidity arises because firms pay efficiency wages to elicit effort.[15]

The results of previous sections provide two more specific motivations for this section. First, the small degree of nominal rigidity in our basic yeoman-farmer model arises largely from inelastic labor supply, which gives farmers strong incentives to stabilize their employment by adjusting prices. The analogue when firms hire workers in a Walrasian labor market is that inelastic labor supply implies highly procyclical real wages—large wage increases are needed to bring forth more labor supply. Highly procyclical real wages imply highly procyclical marginal costs, which in turn imply strong incentives for price adjustment when demand changes. A potential advantage of efficiency wage models is that firms set wages above the market clearing level. Since real wages are not tied directly to labor supply, inelastic labor supply need not imply procyclical real wages.

A second motivation for this section is the difficulty in section 4 of determining how much real price rigidity is realistic. This difficulty reflects uncertainty about the key parameter, the sharpness of the demand asymmetry. In this section the degree of real price rigidity is determined by the degree of real wage rigidity—the responsiveness of real wages to demand shifts. We know something about this parameter; in particular, the acyclicality of real wages in actual economies suggests that a high degree of rigidity is realistic.

The analysis in this section is tentative because economists are not yet certain of the cyclic behavior of efficiency wages. If firms pay efficiency wages to deter "shirking," real wages are procyclical (Shapiro and Stiglitz 1984): when unemployment is high, workers fear the consequences of losing their jobs, and so firms can reduce wages without inducing shirking. It appears, however, that wages are less procyclical than in a competitive labor market. The degree of procyclicality depends on how steeply the cost of job loss rises with unemployment. If unemployed workers enter a secondary labor market (Bulow and Summers 1986), this steepness depends on the extent of decreasing returns in the secondary sector, which may not be large. If unemployed workers simply search for new jobs, as in Shapiro and Stiglitz, the effect of unemployment on the cost of job loss depends on several parameters, including the rate at which exogenous separations create job openings. In this setting, unemployment has a smaller effect on efficiency wages than on competitive wages (Blanchard 1990).

While efficiency-wage considerations appear to reduce the cyclicality of real wages, current models are too stylized to produce meaningful quantitative estimates of this effect. In the analysis below we therefore calibrate the model using aggregate evidence that real wages are quite acyclical. It is not yet clear whether this aggregate behavior can be generated by efficiency wage models with realistic microeconomic parameters. We simply show that *if* efficiency wages are highly acyclical, they help to explain nominal rigidities.

## B. A model

Since efficiency wages are a labor market phenomenon, a preliminary step is to modify our basic model by assuming that farmers work for each other rather than for themselves. Farmers have two sources of income, profits from their own farms and wages from working for others. Using the production function, (15), and the product-demand equation, (18), one can derive the following expression for a farmer's utility:

$$U_i = wL_i + \left(\frac{M}{P}\right)\left(\frac{P_i}{P}\right)^{(1-\epsilon)} - w\left(\frac{M}{P}\right)\left(\frac{P_i}{P}\right)^{-\epsilon} - \frac{\epsilon - 1}{\gamma\epsilon}L_i^\gamma - zD_i, \tag{30}$$

where $w$ is the real wage. The first term in (30) is the farmer's labor income, the second (as in the basic model) the revenue from his farm, the third the wage bill he pays, and the fourth the disutility from the labor he supplies.

To see the importance of efficiency wages, first suppose that the labor market is Walrasian. Deriving a labor supply function from (30) and combining it with the production function and our assumption that $Y = M/P$, we obtain

$$w = \frac{\epsilon - 1}{\epsilon}\left(\frac{M}{P}\right)^{\gamma-1}. \tag{31}$$

Equation (31) describes the cyclical behavior of real wages with a Walrasian labor market. Note that inelastic labor supply (a large $\gamma$) implies highly procyclical wages. Equations (30) and (31) lead to the form of $W(\cdot)$ for this case:

$$W_{\text{Wal}}\left(\frac{M}{P}, \frac{P_i}{P}\right) = \frac{\epsilon - 1}{\epsilon}\left(\frac{M}{P}\right)^\gamma\left[1 - \left(\frac{P_i}{P}\right)^{-\epsilon}\right] + \frac{M}{P}\left(\frac{P_i}{P}\right)^{1-\epsilon} - \frac{\epsilon - 1}{\gamma\epsilon}\left(\frac{M}{P}\right)^\gamma. \tag{32}$$

Now suppose that, as in Shapiro and Stiglitz, firms pay efficiency wages to deter shirking. That is, with imperfect monitoring of workers, firms pay wages above the market-clearing level to make it costly for workers to lose

their jobs, thereby inducing effort. Effort is a zero/one variable, so firms
pay the lowest wage that induces effort. As described above, a fall in
aggregate employment raises the cost of job loss and thus reduces the
necessary wage. Choosing a convenient functional form, we assume that
the "no shirking" wage is

$$
w = b\left(\frac{\epsilon - 1}{\epsilon}\right)L^{\phi-1} = b\left(\frac{\epsilon - 1}{\epsilon}\right)\left(\frac{M}{P}\right)^{\phi-1} \qquad b > 1, \phi > 1. \tag{33}
$$

Here $b > 1$ implies that in the vicinity of the no-shock equilibrum, wages
are set above the market-clearing level, and so suppliers of labor are
rationed. (Below we assume that $b$ is close to one, so that the equilibrium
unemployment rate is low.) Since workers are off their labor-supply curves,
the behavior of the wage no longer depends on $\gamma$. As long as $\phi < \gamma$, real
wages are less procyclical—that is, more rigid in the face of fluctuations in
demand—than in a Walrasian market.

Following other efficiency-wage models, we assume that part of the
rationing of hours of work occurs through unemployment. Specifically, the
division of labor input into workers and hours is given by

$$
E_i = (L_i^D)^a \qquad 0 < a < 1 \tag{34}
$$

$$
H_i = (L_i^D)^{1-a} \qquad 0 < a < 1, \tag{35}
$$

where $E_i$ is the number of workers hired by farmer $i$, $H_i$ is hours per worker,
and $L_i^D = E_i H_i$ is the amount of labor the farmer hires. We assume that
workers are divided between employment and unemployment randomly.
(The division of $L_i^D$ into $E_i$ and $H_i$ proves irrelevant to the degree of nominal
rigidity, $x^*$ but relevant to the welfare loss from rigidity.)

In this model $W(\cdot)$ is a farmer's expected utility given his probability of
employment. Since the size of the labor force is one, this probability is equal
to $E_i$ (equation (34)). The farmer's utility is determined by (30) with the
wage given by (33) and the farmer's labor supply equal to $H_i$ (equation (35))
when employed and zero when unemployed. Combining these results and
using the fact that $L_i^D = Y_i = M/P$ yields

$$
W_{\text{EW}}\left(\frac{M}{P}, \frac{P_i}{P}\right) = b\frac{\epsilon - 1}{\epsilon}\left(\frac{M}{P}\right)^{\phi}\left[1 - \left(\frac{P_i}{P}\right)^{-\epsilon}\right] + \frac{M}{P}\left(\frac{P_i}{P}\right)^{1-\epsilon}
$$

$$
- \frac{\epsilon - 1}{\gamma\epsilon}\left(\frac{M}{P}\right)^{(1-a)\gamma+a}. \tag{36}
$$

## C. Real and nominal rigidity

The solutions for $W(\cdot)$ in the two models lead to simple expressions for the degree of real price rigidity:

$$\pi_{\text{Wal}} = \gamma - 1 \qquad \pi_{\text{EW}} = \phi - 1 \tag{37}$$

If real wages are more rigid under efficiency wages ($\phi < \gamma$), real prices are also more rigid. In terms of our general model, efficiency wages increase real price rigidity by lowering $W_{12}$ while leaving $W_{22}$ unchanged. In this respect the current model differs from the one in section 4, where real rigidity arises from a higher $-W_{22}$.

To see the implications of efficiency wages for nominal rigidity, we calculate $x^*$ and $R$ for the two models. We assume for simplicity that $b \simeq 1$. The results are

$$x_{\text{Wal}}^* = \sqrt{\frac{2z}{(\gamma - 1)^2(\epsilon - 1)}}; \tag{38}$$

$$x_{\text{EW}}^* = \sqrt{\frac{2z}{(\phi - 1)^2(\epsilon - 1)}}; \tag{39}$$

$$R_{\text{Wal}} = \frac{1 + \epsilon\gamma - \epsilon}{\epsilon(\epsilon - 1)(\gamma - 1)^2}; \tag{40}$$

$$R_{\text{EW}} = \frac{\phi + [(\epsilon - 1)/\gamma\epsilon][(1 - a)\gamma + a][(1 - a)(\gamma - 1) - \phi]}{(\phi - 1)^2(\epsilon - 1)}. \tag{41}$$

The expression for $x_{\text{EW}}^*$ is identical to the one for $x_{\text{Wal}}^*$ except that $\phi$ replaces $\gamma$. Efficiency wages increase nominal rigidity if $\phi < \gamma$, and the degree of nominal rigidity becomes large as the real wage becomes acyclical ($\phi$ approaches one). The effect of efficiency wages on $R$ is more complex, but $R_{\text{EW}}$ also becomes large as the real wage becomes acyclical.

As in section 4 we can ask how much real rigidity is needed for large nonneutralities. For various parameter values table 3 shows the degree of real price rigidity, the private cost of nonadjustment to a 5% change in money, and the value of $R$ in both the Walrasian and the efficiency-wage models. In contrast to the customer-market example, the degree of real price rigidity is determined by parameters for which we know plausible values, and so we can ask whether the amount of real rigidity needed for substantial nominal rigidity is realistic.

**Table 3**
Efficiency wage model

| $1/(\gamma - 1) = 1/(\varepsilon - 1) = 0.15$ <br> $a = 0.50$ | | | | $1/(\gamma - 1) = 1/(\varepsilon - 1) = 1.00$ <br> $a = 0.50$ | | | |
|---|---|---|---|---|---|---|---|
| | $\phi$ | $\pi$ | $PC$ | $R$ | $\phi$ | $\pi$ | $PC$ | $R$ |

| | $\phi$ | $\pi$ | $PC$ | $R$ | | $\phi$ | $\pi$ | $PC$ | $R$ |
|---|---|---|---|---|---|---|---|---|---|
| Wal | — | 6.70 | 37.60 | 0.02 | Wal | — | 1.00 | 0.13 | 1.50 |
| EW | 2.00 | 1.00 | 0.84 | 0.40 | EW | 2.00 | 1.00 | 0.13 | 1.44 |
| | 1.50 | 0.50 | 0.21 | 1.44 | | 1.50 | 0.50 | 0.03 | 4.50 |
| | 1.10 | 0.10 | 0.01 | 32.93 | | 1.10 | 0.10 | 0.00 | 87.50 |
| | 1.05 | 0.05 | 0.00 | 130.19 | | 1.05 | 0.05 | 0.00 | 337.50 |

| $1/(\gamma - 1) = 1/(\varepsilon - 1) = 0.15$ <br> $a = 0$ | | | | | $1/(\gamma - 1) = 1/(\varepsilon - 1) = 0.15$ <br> $a = 1.00$ | | | | |
|---|---|---|---|---|---|---|---|---|---|

| | $\phi$ | $\pi$ | $PC$ | $R$ | | $\phi$ | $\pi$ | $PC$ | $R$ |
|---|---|---|---|---|---|---|---|---|---|
| Wal | — | 6.70 | 37.60 | 0.02 | Wal | — | 6.70 | 37.60 | 0.02 |
| EW | 2.00 | 1.00 | 0.84 | 0.91 | EW | 2.00 | 1.00 | 0.84 | 0.26 |
| | 1.50 | 0.50 | 0.21 | 3.60 | | 1.50 | 0.50 | 0.21 | 0.79 |
| | 1.10 | 0.10 | 0.01 | 89.15 | | 1.10 | 0.10 | 0.01 | 14.56 |
| | 1.05 | 0.05 | 0.00 | 356.19 | | 1.05 | 0.05 | 0.00 | 55.60 |

Note: Private cost is for a 5% change in money and is measured as a percentage of revenue when prices are flexible.

As an empirically plausible base case, we assume that $\phi = 1.1$ (real wages are only slightly procyclical under efficiency wages) and $a = 0.5$ (variations in labor are divided equally between hours and employment).[16] We assume as above that the markup and labor supply elasticity are both 0.15. For these parameter values the introduction of efficiency wages has dramatic effects. In a Walrasian labor market, the private cost of rigidity is a huge 38% of revenue, and $R$ is a tiny 0.02.[17] But with efficiency wages, the private cost is less than 0.01% and $R$ is 33. Intuitively, the private cost is small because, with nearly acyclical real wages, shifts in aggregate output have little effect on marginal cost and so firms' desired price adjustments are small. As in section 4, substantial nominal rigidity requires substantial real price rigidity: in our base case, introducing efficiency wages reduces $\pi$ from 6.7 to 0.1. In this model, however, it is clear that this much real rigidity can arise from plausible underlying assumptions, in particular, the assumption that real wages are nearly acyclical.

# 6 Conclusion

Rigidities in real wages and prices are not sufficient to explain real effects of nominal disturbances. In the absence of nominal frictions, prices adjust fully to nominal shocks regardless of the degree of real rigidity. Small costs of adjusting nominal prices are also not enough to explain important nonneutralities. With no real rigidities, these frictions cannot prevent adjustment to sizable nominal shocks or cause nominal fluctuations to have large welfare effects. This paper shows, however, that the *combination* of substantial real rigidity and small costs of nominal flexibility can lead to large real effects of money. We derive this result both in general and for two specific examples of real rigidities.

We do not fully resolve whether the degrees of real rigidity needed for large nominal rigidities are realistic. In our customer-market model, the degree of real rigidity depends on the sharpness of the asymmetry in demand, a parameter for which we do not know realistic values. In our efficiency-wage model, real rigidity is tied to the cyclical behavior of the real wage, for which there is evidence, but the microeconomic foundations of this behavior are not settled. Further research on real rigidities is therefore crucial for strengthening the foundations of Keynesian economics. This paper shows that better explanations for real rigidities will yield better explanations for nominal rigidities as well.

## Acknowledgements

We are grateful for excellent research assistance from Charles Larson; for helpful suggestions from Charles Bean, Herschel Grossman, N. Gregory Mankiw, Christina Romer, Geoffrey Woglom, and seminar participants at Harvard, Johns Hopkins, Michigan, Penn, Wisconsin, Yale, and the National Bureau of Economic Research; and for financial support from the National Science Foundation.

## Notes

1. For implicit contracts, see for example Azariadis (1975) and Baily (1974); for customer markets, Okun (1981); for social customs, Akerlof (1980) and Romer (1984); for efficiency wages, Solow (1979), Shapiro and Stiglitz (1984), and Bulow and Summers (1986); for inventories, Blinder (1982); and for countercyclical markups, Stiglitz (1984), Rotemberg and Saloner (1986), and Bils (1986, 1987).

2. Blanchard (1987, 1990) also argues that real rigidities increase the real effects of nominal disturbances.

3. Our general results do not depend on particular definitions of $Y$ and the price level $P$ (that is, they do not depend on how we aggregate over agents). Our only assumption is that if all agents (or since the economy is large, all but one) choose the same price, then $P$ equals this price.

4. The purpose of (2) is not to advance a particular theory of money but simply to introduce a downward-sloping aggregate-demand curve, a negative relation between $Y$ and $P$. Our results would not change, if following Blanchard and Kiyotaki (1987), we introduced money by adding real balances to utility. In addition, while we assume below that fluctuations in aggregate demand arise from fluctuations in money, it would be straightforward to introduce velocity shocks instead.

5. A second-order approximation of $W(M, P_i^*/P) - W(M, 1)$ yields

$$\left\{ W(1, 1) + \left[ W_1 + W_2 \frac{\partial P_i^*/P}{\partial M} \right] x + \frac{1}{2} \left[ W_{11} + 2W_{12} \frac{\partial P_i^*/P}{\partial M} + W_{22} \left( \frac{\partial P_i^*/P}{\partial M} \right)^2 + W_2 \frac{\partial^2 P_i^*/P}{\partial M^2} \right] x^2 \right\}$$

$$- \{ W(1, 1) + W_1 x + \frac{1}{2} W_{11} x^2 \}.$$

Using $W_2 = 0$ (agents initially set prices optimally given expected $M$) and $\partial(P_i^*/P)/\partial M = -W_{12}/W_{22}$ (from (4)), this expression simplifies to (6).

6. Because the degree of nominal rigidity depends on more than the degree of real rigidity, one can construct examples in which changing a parameter increases real rigidity but lowers $x^*$. Specifically, this can occur if the change raises $W_{12}$ and also raises $-W_{22}$ by a greater amount. But this is not a natural case. As we show in the specific models of later sections, plausible sources of real rigidity simply raise $-W_{22}$ or lower $W_{12}$.

7. When both rigidity and flexibility are equilibria, perhaps the more "natural" equilibrium is rigidity—doing nothing. This idea can be formalized by allowing agents to delay adjustment until they see what others do.

8. The first-order condition for agents $i$'s price under rigidity, $P_{0i}$, is $E[W_2(M/P_0, P_{0i}/P_0)] = 0$. Equilibrium requires $P_{0i} = P_0$. Thus the equilibrium $P_0$ is defined by $E[W_2(M/P_0, 1)] = 0$. Expanding this condition around $M = 1$ gives (10).

9. Blanchard and Kiyotaki (1987) present similar calculations. While the private cost is measured in units of utility and revenue is measured in dollars, it is legitimate to compare them because the marginal utility of income is one.

10. For evidence on markups, see Scherer (1980); for labor-supply elasticities, see Killingsworth (1983).

11. We choose this source of real rigidity because we are able to formalize it rigorously. If one is willing to introduce an ad hoc rigidity, our results can be illustrated more simply. Ball and Romer (1987) present an example in which we simply add a quadratic cost of adjusting real prices to agents' objective functions. The resulting increase in real rigidity implies greater nominal rigidity as well.

12. The definitions of $A$ and $B$ are

$$A = \left[ F(1) + \int_{\theta=1}^{\infty} \theta^{\epsilon-1} f(\theta) \, d\theta \right]^{1/(1-\epsilon)}, \qquad B = \frac{(\epsilon-1)A^{1-\epsilon} + f(1)}{[\epsilon A^{1-\epsilon} + f(1)]\gamma}$$

where $F(\cdot)$ and $f(\cdot)$ are as defined below.

13. More precisely, if farmer $i$ sells product $j$ to farmer $i'$, then farmer $i'$ remains if $P_i/P < \theta_{i'j}$. In the text we suppress subscripts for simplicity.

14. Stiglitz and Woglom argue that kinked demand can lead to nominal rigidity without referring explicity to nominal frictions, which suggests that real rigidities alone can cause

nominal rigidity. Nominal frictions are implicit in the Stiglitz and Woglom argument, however. Neglecting menu costs, kinked demand curves imply multiple real equilibria—for example, each firm will raise its price a small amount if all others do (this leaves relative prices unchanged but reduces real money). Crucially, nominal disturbances do not affect the set of real equilibria. Stiglitz and Woglom argue informally that nominal disturbances may move the economy from one real equilibrium to another—for example, if nominal money falls and prices do not adjust, which is one equilibrium response, then real money falls. This argument depends, however, on the idea that when there are several equilibrium responses to a shock, the one with fixed nominal prices, rather than the one with fixed real prices, is "natural." In turn this depends on a notion of the convenience of fixing prices in nominal terms, which amounts to a small cost of nominal flexibility.

15. Nominal rigidity still arises in prices but not wages because we do not introduce nominal frictions in wage setting. If we added such frictions, real wage rigidity would increase nominal wage rigidity just as real price rigidity increases nominal price rigidity.

Akerlof and Yellen (1985) also add efficiency wages to a model with a small nominal friction ("near rationality"). They do not, however, investigate the link between real and nominal rigidity or the importance of efficiency wages for their quantitive results; they imply that imperfect competition and near rationality alone are sufficient for large nominal rigidities. Akerlof and Yellen introduce efficiency wages so that nominal shocks affect involuntary unemployment as well as employment and output and so that the costs to firms of control *wage* rigidity are not first-order in the size of shocks.

16. Estimates of the cyclical behavior of real wages vary, but many studies find that real wages are approximately acyclical (for example, Geary and Kennan 1982). The choice of $a = 0.5$ is based on the common finding (for example, Barksy and Miron 1989) that at business-cycle frequencies the elasticity of output with respect to employment is roughly two and the elasticity with respect to total man hours is roughly one.

17. $R = 0.02$ implies that with a Walrasian labor market the private gains from adjustment are much greater than the social gains. An individual producer can greatly increase profits by cutting his price when the real wage is low, but society cannot realize similar gains: if all sellers cut their prices, then output rises and the real wages rises, which greatly reduces each seller's gain from adjustment.

# References

Akerlof, G. A. 1980. "A Theory of Social Customs, of Which Unemployment May Be One Consequence." *Quarterly Journal of Economics* 94:749–775.

Akerlof, G. A., and Yellen, J. L. 1985. "A Near-Rational Model of the Business Cycle, with Wage and Price Inertia." *Quarterly Journal of Economics* 100:823–838.

Azariadis, C. 1975. "Implicit Contracts and Underemployment Equilibria." *Journal of Political Economy* 83:1183–1202.

Baily, M. N. 1974. "Wages and Unemployment under Uncertain Demand." *Review of Economic Studies* 41:37–50.

Ball, L., and Romer, D. 1987. "Real Rigidities and the Non-Neutrality of Money." National Bureau of Economic Research, working paper no. 2476.

Ball, L., and Romer, D. 1988. "Sticky Prices as Coordination Failure." Mimeo.

Ball, L., and Romer, D. 1989. "Are Prices Too Sticky?" *Quarterly Journal of Economics* 104:507–524.

Barsky, R., and Miron, J. 1989. "The Seasonal Cycle and the Business Cycle." *Journal of Political Economy* 97:503–534.

Bils, M. 1986. "Pricing in a Customer Market." Rochester Center for Economic Research, working paper no. 30.

Bils, M. 1987. "Cyclical Pricing of Durable Luxuries." Rochester Center for Economic Research, working paper no. 83.

Blanchard, O. J. 1987. "Aggregate and Individual Price Adjustment." *Brookings Papers on Economic Activity* 1987, no. 1:57–109.

Blanchard, O. J. 1990. "Why Does Money Affect Output?" In B. Friedman and F. Hahn, (eds.), *Handbook of Monetary Economics* (Amsterdam: North-Holland).

Blanchard, O. J., and Kiyotaki, N. 1987. "Monopolistic Competition and the Effects of Aggregate Demand." *American Economic Review* 77:647–666.

Blinder, A. 1982. "Inventories and Sticky Prices." *American Economic Review* 72:334–348.

Bulow, J. I., and Summers, L. H. 1986. "A Theory of Dual Labour Markets with Applications to Industrial Policy, Discrimination, and Keynesian Unemployment." *Journal of Labor Economics* 4:376–414.

Geary, P., and Kennan, J. 1982. "The Employment-Real Wage Relationship: An International Study." *Journal of Political Economy* 90:854–871.

Hall, R. E. 1988. "The Relation between Price and Marginal Cost in U.S. Industry." *Journal of Political Economy* 96:921–947.

Killingsworth, M. 1983. *Labor Supply.* Cambridge: Cambridge University Press.

Mankiw, N. G. 1985. "Small Menu Costs and Large Business Cycles." *Quarterly Journal of Economics* 100:529–537.

Okun, A. M. 1982. *Prices and Quantities: A Macroeconomic Analysis.* Washington, D.C.: Brookings Institution.

Romer, D. 1984. "The Theory of Social Custom: A Modification and Some Extensions." *Quarterly Journal of Economics* 99:717–727.

Rotemberg, J. J., and Saloner, G. 1984. "A Supergame-Theoretic Model of Price Wars during Booms." *American Economic Review* 76:390–407.

Scherer, F. M. 1980. *Industrial Market Structure and Economic Performance.* 2nd ed. Chicago: Rand-McNally.

Shapiro, C., and Stiglitz, J. E. 1984. "Equilibrium Unemployment as a Worker Discipline Device." *American Economic Review* 74:433–444.

Solow, R. M. 1979. "Another Possible Source of Wage Stickiness." *Journal of Macroeconomics* 1:79–82.

Stiglitz, J. E. 1979. "Equilibrium in Product Markets with Imperfect Information." *American Economic Review* 69:339–345.

Stiglitz, J. E. 1984, "Price Rigidities and Market Structure." *American Economic Review* 69:350–355.

Woglom, G. 1982. "Underemployment Equilibrium with Rational Expectations." *Quarterly Journal of Economics* 97:89–107.

# 4 Menu Costs and the Neutrality of Money

Andrew S. Caplin and Daniel F. Spulber

## 1 Introduction

Historically determined nominal prices can lead to inertia in the aggregate level of prices, leaving room for monetary shocks to influence real variables. Formal models connecting the microeconomic behavior of nominal prices with aggregate price stickiness include models with staggered price and wage decisions (Fischer 1977, Taylor 1980, Blanchard 1983, Parkin 1986), models with partial adjustment of prices (e.g., Rotemberg 1982), and the more recent "menu cost" models of Akerlof and Yellen (1985), Blanchard and Kiyotaki (1985), and Mankiw (1985). We present an alternative aggregate model with microeconomic price stickiness that emphasizes the importance of endogenous timing of price adjustments. The model provides conditions under which money shocks have no real effects.

A number of macroeconomic models of price stickiness have a common microeconomic base: infrequent but large changes in nominal variables are assumed to be more economical than frequent small changes.[1] The models also share the assumption that the time between successive price revisions is preset and hence unresponsive to shocks to the economy. This assumption is questionable both at the microeconomic level and in the aggregate. Formal microeconomic models (e.g., Sheshinski and Weiss 1983) strongly suggest that more rapid inflation will shorten the time between price revisions. Empirical evidence against the fixed-timing assumption is presented by Cecchetti (1986) and Liebermann and Zilbefarb (1985). At the aggregate level, large monetary shocks may increase the number of agents revising their nominal prices in a given period. This in turn reduces the extent of price-level inertia. An important open question remains: what are the real effects of monetary shocks with endogenous timing of price revisions?

The present paper assumes that individual firms adjust their prices using the $(s, S)$ pricing policies of Sheshinski and Weiss (1977, 1983). To model asychronization, we make a cross-sectional assumption on initial prices. The price level is derived endogenously by aggregating across firms. Ag-

*Quarterly Journal of Economics* 102 (November 1987): 703–725. Copyright © 1987 by the President and Fellows of Harvard College and the Massachusetts Institute of Technology. Reprinted with permission.

gregate price stickiness then vanishes despite the presence of nominal price
rigidity and imperfectly synchronized price revisions.

The presence of *relative price variability* as a consequence of inflation is
also observed endogenously through aggregation of cross-sectional price
data. A simple formula is derived linking nominal price adjustment by firms
with cross-sectional variability of inflation rates.

The basic model is outlined in section 2. The neutrality proposition is
presented in section 3. In section 4 the model is applied to study relative
price variability. Section 5 provides further discussion of the model and its
assumptions. Conclusions are given in section 6.

## 2   The Model

### The aggregate setting

We provide an aggregate model of price dynamics with individual firms
pursuing asynchronous $(s, S)$ pricing policies. The structure of the aggregate
model is kept as simple as possible to highlight the distinction between our
model and others with asynchronous price and wage decisions. These
alternative models frequently assume a staggered pattern of timing (e.g.,
Akerlof 1969, Fischer 1977, Taylor 1980, and Blanchard 1983).

Money growth is subject to continuous shocks. The stochastic process
governing monetary growth is taken as exogenous by all firms in the
economy.[2] Let $M(t)$ denote the logarithm of the money supply at time $t$,
where time is measured continuously. We assume that the money-supply
process is increasing over time and does not make discrete jumps.

ASSUMPTION 1: MONOTONICITY AND CONTINUITY    The money supply does
not decrease over time, $M(t_2) \geq M(t_1)$ for $t_2 \geq t_1$. Also, the money-supply
process is continuous in the time parameter $t$. Normalize so that $M(0) = 0$.

The monetary assumption will rule out periods of deflation. The continuity
assumption allows a simple characterization of firm pricing policies. The
assumption also plays a role in analyzing the cross-sectional behavior of
prices. This issue is taken up below. The monetary process is sufficiently
general as to accommodate feedback rules. We shall consider particular
examples of monetary processes below.

There is a continuum of firms in the economy indexed by $i \in [0, 1]$. All
firms face identical demand and cost conditions. The assumed microeconomic structure is based on the menu-cost model of Sheshinski and

Weiss (1977, 1983). Let $q_i(t)$ and $Q(t)$ represent firm $i$'s *nominal price* and the *aggregate price index*, respectively, with $p_i(t)$ and $P(t)$ their respective logarithms. The aggregate price index, $P(t)$, is endogenously derived below from individual firm prices. It is convenient to express firm $i$'s *real price*, $q(t)/Q(t)$, in log form, $r_i(t)$,

$$r_i(t) \equiv p_i(t) - P(t) = \ln\left[q_i(t)/Q(t)\right], \tag{1}$$

for all $i \in [0, 1]$. We take $r_i(0)$ as given.

The *aggregate price index* $Q(t)$ is determined endogenously by aggregating individual firms' nominal prices $q_i(t)$. The index is assumed to depend only on the frequency distribution over nominal prices. Because firms have menu costs of price adjustment, prices may remain dispersed in the long run. Thus the set of observed prices at any date may be described by a time-dependent frequency-distribution function, say $G_t(q)$. The index is assumed also to satisfy homogeneity; when nominal prices double, so does the index.[3]

ASSUMPTION 2: SYMMETRIC PRICE INDEX   The aggregate price index $Q(t)$ depends only on the frequency distribution of nominal prices and satisfies homogeneity:

$$Q(t) = Q(G_t(q)), \tag{2}$$

where $G_t(q)$ is the proportion of firms $i \in [0, 1]$ such that $q_i(t) \leq q$.

If $G_{t_1}(q) = G_{t_2}(\lambda q)$ for all $q$,

then $\lambda Q(t_1) = Q(t_2)$, for any $t_1, t_2 \geq 0$. $\tag{3}$

This condition is satisfied by a wide variety of common price indices.[4] An example of a price index that satisfies assumption 2 is a simple *average* of nominal prices based on their frequency distribution, $Q(t) = \int q \, dG_t(q)$. More generally, let $Q(t) = \int w(q, G_t(\cdot))q \, dG_t(q)$, where $w(q, G)$ represents weights as a function of prices $q$ and the distribution of nominal prices $G$. The assumption requires the weights to satisfy $w(q, G_{t_1}) = w(\lambda q, G_{t_2})$ when $G_{t_1}(q) = G_{t_2}(\lambda q)$ for all $q$. An example of such a set of weights is $w(q, G) = q/\int q \, dG(q)$.

### The market setting

Consumer demand is assumed to depend only on the firm's real price and on real money balances. Writing the arguments in log form, *consumer demand* faced by firm $i$, $\Gamma_i$, is defined by

$$\Gamma_i(t) \equiv \Gamma(r_i(t), M(t) - P(t)), \tag{4}$$

where $r_i(t)$ and $M(t) - P(t)$ are the log of firm $i$'s price and the log of real balances, respectively.[5] One rationale for this is to assume that real balances enter consumer utility functions, as in Rotemberg (1982, 1983), for example. Note also that all firms can have some positive demand even though prices are dispersed. This may arise if the commodities are imperfect substitutes. It may also be that consumer search across firms is costly and that consumers do not recall prices posted by firms in earlier periods (see Benabou 1985b).

Costs are assumed to be fixed in real terms. Production at rate $X_i(t)$ gives rise to real flow costs, $C(X_i(t))$. This assumption rules out stickiness in nominal input prices, including contractual wages. This prevents us from addressing the relationship between price stickiness and wage stickiness, a topic of independent interest (see Blanchard 1983).[6] Additional study of the present model with input price stickiness is clearly desirable. All profits are distributed to consumers, and firm costs accrue to consumers as income.[7]

The good is assumed to be nonstorable, so that the firm's output is supplied at the same date it is produced. This removes intertemporal linkages embodied in inventories. As a result, the only variables that influence the firm's *flow rate of real profits* $B_i(t)$ are the instantaneous real price and the level of real money balances.[8]

$$B_i(t) \equiv B[r_i(t), M(t) - P(t)]$$

$$= \max_{X_i(t) \leq \Gamma_i(t)} [e^{r_i(t)} X_i(t) - C(X_i(t))] \tag{5}$$

Thus the *output* of firm $i$, $X_i(t)$, is a function of its real price and the level of real money balances that solves the problem in equation (5):

$$X_i(t) = X(r_i(t), M(t) - P(t)) \tag{6}$$

Let $X(t)$ represent the constant dollar value of *aggregate output*:

$$X(t) \equiv \int_0^1 (q_i(t)/Q(t)) X_i(t) \, di = \int_0^1 e^{r_i(t)} X_i(t) \, di$$

In the absence of menu costs the firm picks its instantaneous price $r_i(t)$ to maximize flow profits $B(r_i(t), M(t) - P(t))$.[9] Nominal price stickiness is introduced into the model in the form of a real *menu cost*, $\beta$, which is incurred each time the firm changes its nominal price.[10] This fixed transaction cost results in price stickiness at the level of the individual firm. Rather than responding smoothly and continuously to changes in the overall price level, the firm responds only occasionally and with discrete price jumps.

We consider a firm that continuously monitors the price level, and pursues an $(s, S)$ *pricing policy*, as introduced by Sheshinski and Weiss. The impact of this policy on the dynamics of the firm's real price is illustrated in figure 1. The instant the log of the real price $r(t)$ hits the fixed lower limit $s$, the firm adjusts its nominal price, returning the log of the real price to its upper limit $S$. Let $D \equiv S - s$ represent the size of the firm's price increase. Then the changes in the firm's nominal price within any time period $[0, t]$ are always an integer multiple of the price range, $p(t) - p(0) = k(t)D$, where $k(t) \geq 0$ is an integer. Noting that $r_i(0) = p_i(0)$ and using the definition of the firm's real price in equation (1), we may formally characterize the $(s, S)$ pricing policy as follows: $r_i(t) \in (s, S)$ and

$$r_i(t) - r_i(0) = (p_i(t) - p_i(0)) - (P(t) - P(0))$$

$$= k_i(t)D - (P(t) - P(0)). \tag{7}$$

Hence, changes in the log of the firm's real price are an integer multiple of $D$ minus the log of the price level.

Two important requirements are necessary for $(s, S)$-type policies to be optimal. One requirement is stationarity of real balances over time—$M(t) - P(t) = -P(0)$—so that demand $\Gamma_i$ is stationary. We shall demonstrate that

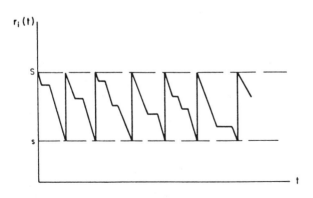

Figure 1

in equilibrium this requirement is satisfied. The other requirement concerns restrictions on the form of the anticipated inflation process. Conditions for optimality of $(s, S)$ pricing policies in a stochastic setting have been considered by Sheshinski and Weiss (1983), Danziger (1984), and more recently by Caplin and Sheshinski (1987).[11] Danziger considers a world with discrete inflationary shocks. He demonstrates that when inflationary shocks arrive one at a time with exponentially distributed interarrival times, then the optimal pricing policy is of the $(s, S)$ variety.[12] With general inflationary processes, the optimal pricing policy may take a more complex form.

The central qualitative feature of $(s, S)$ pricing policies is that they make the time between successive price versions endogenous: prices change more frequently when inflation is rapid than when it is slow. Alternative models of asynchronous price setting involve fixed decision times regardless of ensuing shocks to the economy. Seen in this light, one may be less concerned with the precise optimality of $(s, S)$ pricing policies.[13] Rather, they may be seen as a simple and tractable alternative to the assumption of a predetermined pattern of price revisions.

Analysis of the time path of aggregate prices in our framework requires specification of the initial distribution of prices across firms in the economy. It is assumed that firms' initial real prices $r_i(0)$ are uniformly distributed over the range $(s, S]$. For ease of exposition we restate the uniformity assumption with a frequency distribution $F_0(p)$ that defines the proportion of firms with the logs of their initial prices $p_i(0)$ no higher than $p$.

ASSUMPTION 3: UNIFORMITY   The frequency distribution over initial real prices satisfies

$$F_0(p) = \begin{cases} 0 & \text{for } p \leq s, \\ b/D & \text{for } p = s + b, \text{with } 0 \leq b \leq D, \\ 1 & \text{for } p \geq S. \end{cases} \tag{8}$$

The uniform initial distribution of prices across the price range $(s, S]$ is the analogue in prices of the standard assumption of uniformly staggered price changes over time. Indeed, assumption 3 is equivalent to an assumption of uniform staggered timing in the special case where inflation is constant at some rate $\lambda > 0$. However, it will be apparent that in a stochastic setting a uniform distribution of initial prices has significantly different implications.

In a fundamental sense, assumption 3 may be viewed as a statement about the endogenous tendency of prices to become uniformly distributed after a long history of inflationary shocks and pursuit of fixed $(s, S)$ policies. This lies outside the current framework, since firms pursuing identical $(s, S)$ policies in the face of inflation retain forever the initial differences in their real prices. However, if firms pursue slightly distinct $(s, S)$ policies or randomize on their trigger price $s$ (as in Benabou 1985a), their real prices become statistically independent of one another with the passage of time. A related result for inventories states that without degeneracies, firms that pursue $(s, S)$ inventory policies have inventory levels that are independent in the long run (Caplin 1985).

## 3  Neutrality

We address the connection between asynchronous price decisions and aggregate price stickiness. To what extent is the individual-firm stickiness in nominal prices reflected in aggregate price inertia? The central result of the paper is that *real balances and aggregate output are invariant to monetary shocks.* Price stickiness disappears in the aggregate. Given $(s, S)$ pricing rules, the initial distribution of real prices is invariant and remains uniform. The aggregate nominal price index exactly reflects nominal money shocks. Consumer demand as a function of real prices and real balances remains stationary. This results in constant aggregate output.

In the absence of real shocks to the economy, money neutrality is appropriately defined as follows.

DEFINITION 1    Money is *neutral* if aggregate real output is invariant to monetary shocks, $X(t) = X(0)$, for all $t \geq 0$.

Monetary policy may influence the *distribution* of real prices across firms in our model, as will be seen in section 4. However, these distributional effects cancel out in the aggregate.

Suppose that firms follow $(s, S)$ policies in anticipation of constant real balances. That is, firms expect that $P(t) = M(t)$. Then by the description of $(s, S)$ pricing policies in equation (7), we may calculate each firm's nominal price as a function of cumulative money growth and the firm's initial price:

$$p_i(t) = k_i(t)D + p_i(0), \tag{9}$$

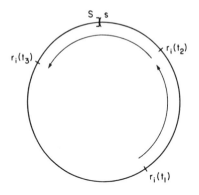

**Figure 2**

where $k_i(t)$ is an integer determined by the requirement that $r_i(t) \in (s, S]$. Proposition 1 verifies that aggregation of these nominal prices yields a price level equal to cumulative money growth at each time $t$, so that money is neutral.

The neutrality result may be understood by observing that the $(s, S)$ policy moves real prices around a circle. The method of proof is easily illustrated using figure 2. Points on the circle represent the range of the log of the firm's real prices. At the apex of the circle the outer limits of the range are adjacent. At time $t_1$, $r_i(t_1)$ is firm $i$'s real price. Inflation occurring between time $t_1$ and $t_2$ reduces the real price to $r_i(t_2)$ as indicated by the counterclockwise motion. Between time $t_2$ and $t_3$ inflation drives the real price down to $s$; the price is then readjusted up to $S$, and further inflation drives that real price to $r_i(t_3)$. It is critical to note that the rotation engendered by monetary growth is invariant to the location of the initial real price on the circle. Thus the initial uniformity of real prices is preserved.

PROPOSITION 1    Given assumptions 1 to 3, money is neutral if firms follow $(s, S)$ pricing policies in anticipation of constant real balances.

*Proof of proposition 1*    Let money growth be written as an integer multiple of $D$ and a remainder $b(t)$:

$$M(t) = k(t)D + b(t), \tag{10}$$

where $k(t) \geq 0$ and $b(t) \geq 0$ are chosen such that $b(t) < D$. If firms follow $(s, S)$ pricing policies and anticipate constant real balances, then by equation (9), the log of each firm $i$'s nominal price can be expressed in terms of the components of money-supply growth in equation (10):

$$p_i(t) = \begin{cases} p_i(0) + k(t)D & \text{for } p_i(0) > s + b(t) \\ p_i(0) + [k(t) + 1]D & \text{for } p_i(0) \leq s + b(t) \end{cases} \tag{11}$$

Equation (11) shows that if $s + b(t) < p_i(0) \leq S$, then $s + M(t) < p_i(t) \leq s + M(t) + D - b$. Also, if $s < p_i(0) \leq s + b(t)$, then $s + M(t) + D - b < p_i(t) \leq S + M(t)$. By uniformity of initial real prices (assumption 3), it follows that $p_i(t) - M(t)$ is uniform over the interval $(s, S]$, or equivalently,

$$F_t(p) = \begin{cases} 0 & \text{for } p \leq s + M(t), \\ b/D & \text{for } p = s + M(t) + b, \text{ with } 0 \leq b \leq D, \\ 1 & \text{for } p \geq S + M(t). \end{cases} \tag{12}$$

The frequency distribution over nominal prices is then given by $G_t(q) \equiv F_t(\ln q)$. Note that $G_t(q)$ is defined over $(e^{s+M(t)}, e^{S+M(t)}]$. Thus we may define $G_t(e^{M(t)}x)$ over $(e^s, e^S)$ so that $G_t(e^{M(t)}x) = G_0(x)$ for $x \in (e^s, e^S)$. Therefore, by the assumption of a symmetric price index, $Q(t) = e^{M(t)}Q(0)$. Thus we have verified that endogenously derived inflation matches monetary growth and real balances are constant: $Q(t)/e^{M(t)} = Q(0)$. Furthermore, since $r_i(t) = p_i(t) - P(t) = p_i(t) - M(t)$ is uniform over $(s, S]$ for $t \geq 0$, we have

$$X(t) = \int_0^1 e^{r_i(t)} X(r_i(t), P(0)) \, di = \int_0^1 e^{r_i(0)} X(r_i(0), P(0)) \, di, \tag{13}$$

so $X(t) = X(0)$. Q.E.D.

Consider an illustrative example. Note first that since $p_i(t)$ is uniformly distributed on $(s + M(t), S + M(t))$, $q_i(t)$ is distributed on $(e^{sM(t)}, e^{sM(t)})$ with distribution $G_t(q) = (\ln q)/D$. If we use the simple arithmetic mean as our symmetric price index, the price level is then

$$Q(t) \equiv \left(\frac{1}{D}\right) \int_{e^{sM(t)}}^{e^{SM(t)}} dq = e^{M(t)} \frac{e^S - e^s}{D} = e^{M(t)}Q(0).$$

The central feature of proposition 1 is that it provides a simple framework in which there are monetary shocks and asynchronous nominal price revisions but no stickiness in the aggregate price level. In fact, $P(t) - M(t) = P(0)$. Thus it contrasts strongly with monetary models with a fixed staggered pattern of price and wage revisions, which can generate significant aggregate price stickiness (e.g., Akerlof 1969, Blanchard 1983, and Fischer 1977.) In qualitative terms the difference between the results can be simply explained. In the staggered-timing framework, large monetary shocks draw a response from a fixed fraction of the population, with the remainder pursuing an unchanged policy. The size of the predetermined pool of decision makers will influence the extent of price revision by those currently free to decide: on average, agents' prices adjust only partially to large monetary shocks. In contrast, the $(s, S)$ model makes the fraction of firms that revise prices in any given period endogenous. Hence, rapid growth of the monetary supply causes an increase in the number of price increases in a given period. Surprisingly, our simple form of endogenous timing completely removes aggregate inertia.

The result also provides a new perspective on the emerging study of menu costs and monetary policy in a *static* setting (e.g., Akerlof and Yellen 1985, Blanchard and Kiyotaki 1985, Mankiw 1985). Here Akerlof and Yellen (1985) argue that the presence of a small menu cost may make it optimal for an individual firm to maintain a fixed nominal price in the face of a monetary shock. This may lead to a welfare loss larger than the menu cost itself. The extension from the case of a single firm to the economy as a whole is based on a representative-agent framework. Since one firm fails to adjust its price, so do all firms, and as a result the open market operation can have a significant real impact.

Taken literally, such reasoning can only be applied for the first monetary shock to an economy that had never before been out of static equilibrium. Even the second monetary shock may have a different effect, since after the first shock the hypothesis that the initial real price is at its equilibrium level fails. Proposition 1 presents a simple setting where the presence of menu costs indeed prevents many firms from revising prices. However, those who do adjust their prices do so discontinuously. Although only a few firms may adjust their prices, they adjust their prices by a large amount. The net result is that monetary shocks are absorbed with no real impact.

Proposition 1 also provides a positive answer to a question posed by Sheshinski and Weiss (1983) for their model of $(s, S)$ pricing policies. They are concerned with providing a consistent aggregate version of their model. They consider identical firms facing exogenous inflationary shocks, uniformly distributed with respect to the time of their last price increase. Sheshinski and Weiss note, "Large and/or closely spaced shocks may lead to synchronization and hence change the distribution. There is thus no simple correspondence between the process of exogenous shocks and the process followed by the aggregate price level" (1983, p. 523). Proposition 1 demonstrates that with identical firms, consistent aggregation requires that firms be uniformly distributed in terms of the log of their *initial real price* levels rather than the time of their last price change. The distinction is that in a stochastic setting, uniformity in timing is unstable, while uniformity in real prices is continuously sustained.[14]

## 4   Menu Costs and Relative-Price Variability

In this section we develop formulas linking inflation and firm pricing policies to relative price variability. These formulas can be seen as stochastic generalizations of the deterministic price dispersion models of Rotemberg (1981), and Cecchetti (1985), which are based on staggered price setting. Our results also clarify the relationship between price variability and the time period between successive observations of the economy.[15]

The association between inflation and relative price variability has been widely investigated (see Fischer 1981 for a survey). The empirical research suggests a positive association between relative price variability and both the mean and the variance of the overall rate of inflation.[16] One important line of research into inflation and relative prices originates with Barro (1976). Here it is inflationary variability rather than the rate of inflation per se that drives relative price variability. As the variability of inflation increases, individual-firm estimates of inflation become more widely dispersed, which drives firms' preset prices apart.[17] Barro's approach is further developed by Cukierman (1979), Cukierman and Wachtel (1982), Hercowitz (1981), and Parks (1978).

An alternative theory holds that inflationary variations in relative prices can be caused by nominal price inflexibility (Cecchetti 1985, Mussa 1981, Rotemberg 1983).[18] Our formulas lie in this alternative tradition, stressing the costs of changing nominal prices.

The basic characterization of relative price variability to be given here is based on repeated observations of the economy, with successive observations separated by a fixed time period of arbitrary length $\tau > 0$. With this discrete pattern of observations, cumulative inflation during the $t$th time period is denoted $\Pi^\tau(t)$. Proposition 1 allows us to identify the inflation rate with the (stochastic) growth of the money supply:

$$\Pi^\tau(t) \equiv P[\tau(t + 1)] - P[\tau t] = M[\tau(t + 1)] - M[\tau t]. \tag{14}$$

Our results of this section require only that $\Pi^\tau(t)$ is a stationary stochastic process. It is also convenient to restrict attention to inflation or money-supply processes that are regularly behaved.

ASSUMPTION 1: STATIONARITY    For any $\tau > 0$, the process $\Pi^\tau(t)$ of equation (14) is a stationary stochastic process, with long-run probabilities specified by the density function $\phi^\tau(\Pi)$. The density of $\phi^\tau(\Pi)$ is assumed to be nonatomic, with compact support.

As in the proof of proposition 1, it is useful to separate inflation into an integer multiple of $D$ and a residual.[19] Definition 2 provides the appropriate formalization.

DEFINITION 2    With cumulative inflation measured over periods of length $\tau > 0$, the *residual inflation process* $b^\tau(t)$ is defined as $\Pi^\tau(t)$ taken modulo $D$.

In light of assumption 1, the residual process $b^\tau(t)$ is itself stationary and has compact support, with long-run probabilities specified by the density function $\eta^\tau(b)$ satisfying

$$\eta^\tau(b) = \sum_{k=0}^{\infty} \phi^\tau(kD + b). \tag{15}$$

Individual firm price increases are also measured at intervals of length $\tau$:

$$\Pi_i^\tau(t) \equiv p_i[\tau(t + 1)] - p_i(\tau t) \tag{16}$$

To measure *inflation*, we use a specific price index. This is the standard *Divisia* index of inflation, with equal expenditure shares for distinct firms $i \in [0, 1]$:

$$\Pi^\tau(t) \equiv \int_0^1 \Pi_i^\tau(t)\,di \tag{17}$$

The Divisia index is a standard employed in empirical studies of relative price variability (e.g., Fischer 1981, Hercowitz 1981, Parks 1978, and Vining and Elwertowski 1976). The Divisia index is symmetric. By proposition 1 it follows that the endogenous inflation measure in equation (17) is consistent with monetary growth in equation (14).

*Relative price variability* $V^\tau(t)$ is measured as the dispersion of individual firm inflation rates around the aggregate rate of inflation:

$$V^\tau(t) \equiv \int_0^1 [\Pi_i^\tau(t) - \Pi^\tau(t)]^2\,di \tag{18}$$

We are interested in the statistical properties of $V^\tau(t)$ and in particular the influence of $D$, the size of individual price increases. Intuition suggests that increases in $D$ may raise the general level of relative price variability. A precise characterization of the expected level of relative price variability is contained in proposition 2.

PROPOSITION 2 Expected relative price variability is related to price changes $D$ and the residual inflation process $b^\tau(t)$ as follows:

$$E[V^\tau(t)] = E\{b^\tau(t)[D - b^\tau(t)]\}, \tag{19}$$

with $b^\tau(t)$ as in defintion 2.

*Proof of proposition 2* To simplify notation, the superscript $\tau$ is supposed throughout the proof. We first separate period $t$ inflation in the standard manner,

$$\Pi(t) = k(t)D + b(t), \tag{20}$$

with $k(t)$ a nonnegative integer and $0 \leq b(t) < D$. The $(s, S)$ pricing policies imply that individual firm price increases obey

$$\Pi_i(t) = \begin{cases} k(t)D & \text{for } r_i(t) > s + b(t) \\ [k(t) + 1]D & \text{for } r_i(t) \leq s + b(t). \end{cases} \tag{21}$$

Hence, $(\Pi_i(t) - \Pi(t))^2$ takes value $b^2$ for $r_i(t)$ above $s + b(t)$ and $(D - b)^2$ otherwise. But from proposition 1 we know that real prices $r_i(t)$ are distributed uniformly over $(s, S]$ for $t \geq 0$. Hence, using the definition of $V(t)$, we have

$$V(t) = \left(\frac{D - b(t)}{D}\right)b^2(t) + \left(\frac{b(t)}{D}\right)[D - b(t)]^2$$

$$= b(t)(D - b(t)). \tag{22}$$

Finally, assumption 1 implies that $b(t)$ is a stationary process, which allows us to take expectations in (22). Q.E.D.

Proposition 2 shows that the range of individual price variation $D$ is a central determinant of the variability of individual price increases. However, interpretation of the result is complicated by the presence of the residual process, $b^\tau(t)$. While the formula does suggest a positive association between $D$ and relative price variability, examples with a negative association are readily constructed.[20]

By changing the time interval between observations, it is possible to greatly simplify the formulas of proposition 2. The results are stated for a restricted class of inflation imposed to simplify proofs: the analysis may incorporate more general conditions.

ASSUMPTION 1: TWO-RATE INFLATION PROCESS   Monetary growth (and hence inflation) can take place at one of two distinct rates, $g_H$ ang $g_L$ with $g_H > g_L \geq 0$. The time spent with inflation of $g_H$ (respectively, $g_L$) is distributed exponentially with parameter $\lambda_H$ (respectively, $\lambda_L$).

A desirable feature of the two-rate inflation processes of assumption 1 is that their simple Markovian structure is inherited by the discretely observed process $\Pi^\tau(t)$. The state of the system at time $t$ comprises a specification of all firms' instantaneous real prices $r_i(t)$ and the current inflation rate, $H$ or $L$. State transitions in the ensuing interval depend only on cumulative inflation over the interval and the level of inflation at the end of the interval. Such state transitions are then Markovian, since information available prior to $t$ is irrelevant to the probabilistic progress of the system.[22]

With this background we can provide the simple formulas of propositon 3 that apply respectively to "widely spaced" and "closely spaced" observations of the economy. This proposition is proved in the appendix.

PROPOSITION 3   Given assumptions 1, 2, and 3, if firms follow $(s, S)$ pricing policies and $\tau$ is the period of observation, then expected relative-price variability satisfies

$$\lim_{\tau \to \infty} EV^\tau(t) = D^2/6, \tag{a}$$

$$\lim_{\tau \to 0} \left[ \frac{EV^\tau(t)}{E\Pi^\tau(t)} \right] = D. \tag{b}$$

The surprising feature of (a) of proposition 3 is that with widely separated observations, relative price variability depends only on $D$. It may be that the formula is roughly appropriate for semiannual data where firms change prices at intervals ranging from one to three months. The applicability of (b) of proposition 3 is harder to gauge: the observation period must be considerably shorter than the time between successive price revisions.

Sheshinski and Weiss (1983) provide useful formulas for assessing the impact of parameter changes on $D = S - s$, the range of the log of real prices.[23] For $g_L = 0$ they establish that the range $D$ is increasing in the price adjustment cost $\beta$ and increasing in the certainty-equivalent rate of inflation $\bar{g}$, where $\bar{g} = (\lambda_L + \rho)g_H/(\lambda_L + \lambda_H + \rho)$ and where $\rho$ is the rate of interest. Changes in parameter values $\lambda_L$, $\lambda_H$, $\rho$, and $g_H$ will affect the price range and thus relative price variability as defined in proposition 3. However, it is difficult to establish a direct relation between the mean and variance of inflation and relative price variability.

It is possible to determine the effects of menu costs on relative price variability. Because $(s, S)$ policies may not be optimal, we assume that firms choose the *best* $(s, S)$ bounds. Then we use a time period $\tau \leq D/g_H$. Since $\Pi(t) = k(t)D + b(t)$ from equation (20), the number of nominal price changes within the time period under observation is always zero, so that $\Pi(t) = b(t)$. We may thus write expected relative price variability, using proposition 2, as follows:

$$E[V^\tau(t)] = E\{\Pi(t)[D - \Pi(t)]\} \tag{23}$$

The inflation process $\Pi(t)$ is independent of adjustment costs, and the range of prices is increasing in $\beta$. Thus if firms follow the best $(s, S)$ pricing policy, expected relative price variability is increasing in the menu costs of price adjustment $\beta$.

## 5   The Interpretation of Assumptions

The neutrality of money in our model is particularly dependent on the $(s, S)$ form of firm pricing policies. For firms to follow $(s, S)$ policies, the monetary process must at least exhibit monotonicity and continuity. These requirements may be quite restrictive.

When the monetary process is nonmonotone, it will sometimes be necessary for the firm to *lower* its nominal price. The one-sided $(s, S)$ pricing policies must be replaced by two-sided pricing policies, as anaylzed by Barro (1972).[24] With the two-sided pricing policies, the neutrality proposition no longer holds: it may even be that unusually rapid monetary expansion is associated with increased real balances and vice versa.[25] A theoretical difficulty in modeling two-sided policies is that their properties under aggregation appear highly complex. Specifically, it is not possible to specify an initial cross-sectional distribution of prices that survives shocks.[26] In economic terms, this implies that a second positive shock to the money supply may have very different effects than the first positive shock. Such effects may well have nonintuitive implications: for example, after two successive positive shocks, output may be higher in response to a negative shock to the money supply than in response to a third positive shock. In the absence of a fully developed model, such comments remain speculative.

The assumed continuity of the money-supply process has two roles. First, it gives rise to the simple form of the individual firm equations for price transitions. In particular, (7) no longer holds in the absence of continuity, since if the real price falls by a discrete amount at any given instant, it may at some point fall strictly below $s$. The immediate response of increasing the real price to $S$ then involves a discrete jump in the real price in excess of $D \equiv S - s$, which contradicts (7). Sample-path continuity plays an additional role in relation to the uniformity assumption 3. Jumps in the price level act as a coordinating device pulling many firms in the economy to adjust at the same instant and eliminating uniformity. The uniform distribution over initial prices, however, is the only distribution that is invariant to shocks.

Finally, there are conditions under which alternative pricing policies may be optimal. Significant alterations in the monetary process may lead agents to revise trigger points.[27] One possibility is that a sudden increase in the rate and variability of money growth causes all agents to broaden their trigger range, which raises $S$ and lowers $s$. In this case, real balances may rise in the short run as firms find insufficient benefit from a price change. This increase in real balances corresponds to the effect noted in the literature on the impact of menu costs in a static setting (as in Akerlof and Yellen 1985). Once again, note that the short-run expansionary impact of monetary policy is not stable. When real balances have risen enough, a sudden burst of price increases may be triggered as all firms go to the very top of their real price range. This process will result in a reduction of real balances to below their initial level and a corresponding slowdown in activity.

The neutrality result depends on firms anticipating constant real money balances. What would happen if firms anticipated systematic changes in real money balances? For example, if firms expect real money balances, and therefore demand, to increase, this may trigger an earlier price increase and thus counteract the rise in real balances. A formal analysis of this possibilty is of interest.

It is worthwhile noting a concern about the exogenous demand functions $\Gamma_i$, particularly in evaluating comparative dynamics. It would, of course, be desirable to construct the demand functions endogenously from consumer utility functions with either differentiated products or consumer search. Ball and Romer (1986) derive such demand functions in a general equilibrium model with differentiated products. With endogenous search activity, demand at a real price of $r_i(t) > 0$ may be zero if all other firms have identical prices $r_j(t) = 0$ but positive if other firms have widely dispersed prices. Hence, the functions $\Gamma[r_i(t), M(t) - P(t)]$ must be treated as conditional on the levels of $S$ and $s$ in the rest of the economy. Benabou (1985b) provides a thorough treatment of the interaction between search and menu costs.

## 6  Conclusion

This paper presents a model in which inflation is derived endogenously through price adjustment by firms. If firms pursue $(s, S)$ price adjustment policies and the logs of real prices are initially uniformly dispersed, then money shocks are shown to be neutral. Thus nominal changes, such as monetary growth, do not have aggregate real effects, despite the presence of menu costs of price adjustment. Although money is neutral, we observe the presence of relative price variability.

The model illustrates that individual firm price stickiness and staggered timing need not lead to aggregate price stickiness. This suggests that real effects of money shocks may depend more on fixed-length contracts than simply on asynchronous nominal price adjustment. Overall, the analysis highlights the importance of cross-sectional timing assumptions in macroeconomic models.

## Appendix

### Proof of proposition 3

To prove (a) in light of proposition 2 requires only that

$$\lim_{\tau \to \infty} \{E[b^\tau(t)(D - b^\tau(t))]\} = D^2/6, \tag{A1}$$

with $b^\tau(t)$ as in definition 2. Let $H^\tau(x)$ denote the long-run cumulative distribution of $b^\tau(t)$:

$$H^\tau(x) = \int_0^x \eta^\tau(b) \, db \tag{A2}$$

The heart of the proof of (a) is contained in lemma 1.

LEMMA 1   For $0 \le b \le D$, $\lim_{\tau \to \infty} H^\tau(x) = b/D$.

*Proof*   With the simple two-level inflation process of assumption 6, the individual firm's discretely observed real-price behavior is ergodic, with a unique stationary density $\psi(r_i(t))$, which is uniform over $(s, S]$. Ergodicity can be proved by applying the procedure of Caplin and Spulber (1985, proposition 1). The trivial amendment concerns the fact that $g_H$ and $g_L$ may both be positive in the current case; in the earlier version $g_L = 0$. The existence of this simple ergodic distribution implies that

$$\lim_{\tau \to \infty} P\{r_i(t + \tau) \in (S - b, X) | r_i(t) = S\} = b/D. \tag{A3}$$

But $r_i(t) \in (s, S]$ and equation (7) show that the events $\{r_i(t + \tau) \in (S - b, S) | r_i(t) = S\}$ and $\{b^\tau(t) \le b | r_i(t) = S\}$ are equivalent. An identical argument applies conditions on other initial prices. This allows the conditioning to be removed so that

$$\lim_{\tau \to \infty} P\{b^\tau(t) \le b\} = b/D, \tag{A4}$$

as claimed. Q.E.D.

Lemma 1 demonstrates that for $0 \le b \le D$, $F^m(b) \to b/D$ in distribution. Application of proposition 8.12 of Breiman (1968) allows us to take limiting expectations using the uniform density:

$$\lim_{\tau \to \infty} \{E[b^\tau(t)(D - b^\tau(t))]\} = \frac{1}{D} \int_0^D b(D - b) \, db$$

$$= \frac{1}{D} \left[ \frac{Db^2}{2} - \frac{b^3}{3} \right]_0^D = \frac{D^2}{6}, \tag{A5}$$

as claimed.

To establish (b), it must be shown that for $\tau$ sufficiently small,

$$1 \ge \frac{E[b^\tau(t)(D - b^\tau(t))]}{DE(\Pi^\tau(t))} \ge 1 - \epsilon \tag{A6}$$

for any given $\epsilon \in (0, 1)$. To confirm this, pick a time interval $\tau$ below $\epsilon(D/g_H)$, so that the maximal inflation rate in any given period is below $\epsilon D$. Then

$$E[b^\tau(t)(D - b^\tau(t))] = E[\Pi^\tau(t)(D - b^\tau(t))] < DE(\Pi^\tau(t)). \tag{A7}$$

In addition,

$$E[b^\tau(t)(D - b^\tau(t))] \geq E[\Pi^\tau(t)(D - \epsilon D)] = (1 - \epsilon)DE[\Pi^\tau(t)]. \qquad (A8)$$

Together, (A7) and (A8) establish (b). Q.E.D.

## Acknowledgments

We thank Andrew Abel, Roland Benabou, Olivier Blanchard, Dennis Carlton. Stanley Fischer, Benjamin Friedman, Barry Nalebuff, William Nordhaus, David Romer, Julio Rotemberg, Eytan Sheshinski, John Veitch, and an anonymous referee for valuable comments. Spulber's research was supported by the National Science Foundation under grant no. SES-82-19121. The paper was presented at the Fifth World Congress of the Econometric Society, Cambridge, Mass., 1985, and at the Program in Economic Fluctuations Conference of the National Bureau of Economic Research, October, 1985.

## Notes

1. An exception is Rotemberg (1983), who considers increasing marginal costs of nominal price revisions instead.

2. In general, the money growth process may be set as a feedback rule based on the history of output.

3. Individual firms set $s$ and $S$ taking the price level as exogenously given. However, for given levels $s$ and $S$, the index endogenously determines $P(0)$. Will the exogenous and endogenous indices be consistent? The answer is generally no. However, if we associate higher real balances with higher levels of $s$ and $S$, there will be some initial specification of real balances guaranteeing this static consistency, since higher real balances raise the desired average real price, raising the endogenous level of $P(0)$ relative to the exogenous level.

4. Blanchard and Kiyotaki (1985) and Ball and Romer (1986) derive symmetric price indices based on an underlying symmetric utility framework.

5. The assumption that demand is independent of future prices rules out consumer speculation. Benabou (1985a) presents an analysis of optimal pricing policies in the face of consumer storage and speculation. In principle, the future path of real money balances may also influence real demand. For present purposes, proposition 1 will allows us to ignore this potentially complex dependence.

6. Gordon (1981) finds evidence for price stickiness for periods with widely different forms of labor contracts. This suggests that there are important sources of price stickiness other than the behavior of input prices.

7. By Walras's law, market clearing in the commodity market implies market clearing in the money market (see, for example, Rotemberg 1982).

8. The present formulation allows the firm to ration its customers. The case without rationing can also be handled by the model (see Sheshinski and Weiss 1983).

9. With standard assumptions, increases in real money balances that increase demand for the commodity will also raise the firm's optimal real price.

10. There is an issue here concerning the proper treatment of menu costs. If these are indeed real costs, they should be explicit included as part of output. Hence, a closed model of the economy should properly include a sector of variable size dedicated to the production of menus. This is ignored in our formulation.

11. Sheskinski and Weiss (1983) employ a special form of the stochastic inflation process. Caplin and Sheshinski (1987) present a discrete time formulation with i.i.d. inflationary shocks.

12. While the discrete nature of Danziger's inflation process contradicts assumption 1 of our analysis, including the neutrality proposition, nevertheless applies.

13. Even in the inventory literature, Arrow, Harris, and Marschak (1951) study $(s, S)$ policies because of their relative simplicity. The first general proof of optimality is due to Scarf (1959). Further, stationary $(s, S)$ policies are frequently analyzed and applied in situations where they are undoubtedly suboptimal, such as in multiechelon inventory systems (Schwarz 1981) and in more general nonstationary environments (Karlin and Fabens 1959).

14. In a deterministic world with constant inflation, the two forms of uniformity are equivalent.

15. As Cecchetti (1985) notes in a nonstochastic setting, there is no cross-sectional variance of inflation rates when the observation period is an integer multiple of the period between price revisions.

16. Early studies include Graham (1930) and Mills (1927). More recent work includes Vining and Elwertowski (1976); Pagan, Hall, and Trivedi (1983); Balk (1985); and Marquez and Vining (1984).

17. According to this approach, the apparent association between the level of inflation and relative price variability is a statistical artifact resulting from an actual association between the mean level of inflation and the variability of inflation. This relationship is explicitly investigated by Taylor (1981).

18. See also Carlton (1978) and Hubbard and Weiner (1985), who consider markets with both spot transactions and nominal contracting.

19. The formal identification between $(s, S)$ policies and modulo arithmetic also plays a role in the inventory literature (see Caplin 1985).

20. For example with $\Pi^\tau(t)$ uniform over $[9, 10]$ an increase in $D$ from 8 to 9 reduces $EV^\tau(t)$ from $9\frac{2}{3}$ to $4\frac{1}{6}$.

21. Assumption 1 represents a slightly more general form of the inflation process studied by Sheshinski and Weiss (1983).

22. Note that transitions in the rate of inflation between observations are not independent of cumulative inflation. High cumulative inflation is associated with an ensuing inflation rate of $g_H$. Hence, transition probabilities for the Markov process are nonseparable between real price transitions and transitions in the inflation rate.

23. The related $(s, S)$ inventory literature suggests that increases in the mean and variance of sales will raise order size. The well-known Wilson lot-size formula (more familiar as the square-root formula for money demand) expresses the relationship in simple form. The more recent approximation formula of Ehrhardt (1979) has similar properties.

24. An analogous model of money holding with both inflows and outflows is due to Miller and Orr (1966).

25. A suggestive example is presented in Blanchard and Fischer (1985).

26. This will, of course, invalidate the neutrality proposition.

27. Blinder (1981) examines the related issue of changing trigger points and their impact on aggregate inventory behavior.

## References

Akerlof, George A., "Relative Wages and the Rate of Inflation," *Quarterly Journal of Economics*, 83 (1969), 353–374.

Akerlof, George, A., and Janet Yellen L., "A Near-Rational Model of the Business Cycle, with Wage and Price Inertia," *Quarterly Journal of Economics*, 100 (1985), 823–838.

Arrow, Kenneth J., Thomas Harris, and Jacob Marschak, "Optimal Inventory Policy," *Econometrica*, 19 (1951), 250–272.

Balk, B. M., "Inflation Variability and Relative Price Change Variability in the Netherlands, 1951–1981," *Economics Letters*, 19 (1985), 27–30.

Ball, Laurence, and David Romer, "Are Prices Too Sticky," Princeton University, Department of Economics, mimeo, August 1986.

Barro, Robert J., "A Theory of Monopolistic Price Adjustment," *Review of Economic Studies*, 39 (January 1972), 17–26.

Barro, Robert J., "Rational Expectations and the Role of Monetary Policy," *Journal of Monetary Economics*, 2 (1976), 1–32.

Benabou, Roland, "Optimal Price Dynamics and Speculation with a Storable Good," mimeo, 1985a, MIT.

Benabou, Roland, "Searchers, Price Setters and Inflation," mimeo, 1985b, MIT.

Blanchard, Olivier, "Price Asynchronization and Price Level Inertia," in R. Dornbusch and M. Simonsen, eds., *Indexation, Contracting, and Debt in an Inflationary World* (Cambridge: MIT Press, 1983).

Blanchard, Olivier, and Stanley Fischer, "Notes on Advanced Macroeconomic Theory," chapters 9 and 10, mimeo, 1985.

Blanchard, Olivier, and N. Kiyotaki, "Monopolistic Competition, Aggregate Demand Externalities, and Real Effects of Nominal Money," National Bureau of Economic Research, working paper no. 1770, 1985.

Blinder, Alan S., "Retail Inventory Investment and Business Fluctuations," *Brookings Papers on Economic Activity*, 2 (1981), 443–505.

Breiman, Leo, *Probability* (Reading, Mass.: Addison-Wesley, 1968).

Caplin, Andrew S., "The Variability of Aggregate Demand with $(S, s)$ Inventory Policies," *Econometrica*, 53 (November 1985), 1395–1410.

Caplin, Andrew S., and Eytan Sheshinski, "Optimality of $(s, S)$ Pricing Policies," mimeo, 1987.

Caplin, Andrew S., and Daniel F. Spulber, "Inflation, Menu Costs, and Relative Price Variability," Harvard Institute of Economic Research, discussion paper no. 1181, 1985.

Carlton, Dennis W., "Market Behavior with Demand Uncertainty and Price Inflexibility," *American Economic Review*, 58 (1978), 571–587.

Cecchetti, Steven, "The Frequency of Price Adjustment: A Study of the Newsstand Prices of Magazines," *Journal of Econometrics*, 31 (1986), 255–274.

Cecchetti, Steven, "Staggered Contracts and the Frequency of Price Adjustment," *Quarterly Journal of Economics*, 100 (1985) 935–960.

Cukierman, Alex, "The Relationship between Relative Prices and the General Price Level, A Suggested Interpretation," *American Economic Review*, 69 (September 1979), 595–609.

Cukierman, Alex, and Paul Wachtel, "Relative Price Variability and Nonuniform Inflationary Expectations," *Journal of Political Economy*, 90 (1982), 146–157.

Danziger, Leif, "Stochastic Inflation and the Optimal Policy of Price Adjustment," *Economic Inquiry*, 22 (1984), 98–108.

Ehrhardt, R. A., "The Power Approximation for Computing $(s, S)$ Inventory Policies," *Management Science*, 25 (1979), 777–786.

Fischer, Stanley, "Long Term Contracts, Rational Expectations, and the Optimal Money Supply Rule," *Journal of Political Economy*, 85 (1977), 191–205.

Fischer, Stanley, "Relative Shocks, Relative Price Variability, and Inflation," *Brookings Papers on Economic Activity* (1981), 381–431.

Graham, Frank D., *Exchange, Prices, and Production in Hyper-inflation: Germany 1920–1923* (Princeton, N.J.: Princeton University Press, 1930).

Gordon, Robert J., "Output Fluctuations and Gradual Price Adjustment," *Journal of Economic Literature*, 19 (1981), 493–530.

Hercowitz, Zvi, "Money and the Dispersion of Relative Prices," *Journal of Political Economy*, 89 (April 1981), 328–356.

Hubbard, Robert G., and Robert J. Weiner, "Nominal Contracting and Price Flexibility in Product Markets," National Bureau of Economic Research, working paper no. 1738, 1985.

Karlin, Samuel, and A. Fabens, "A Stationary Inventory Model with Markovian Demand," in K. Arrow, S. Karlin, and P. Suppes, eds., *Mathematical Methods in the Social Sciences* (Stanford: Stanford University Press, 1959).

Liebermann, Y., and B. Z. Zilbefarb, "Price Adjustment Strategy under Conditions of High Inflation: An Empirical Examination," *Journal of Economics and Business*, 37 (1985), 253–265.

Mankiw, N. Gregory, "Small Menu Costs and Large Business Cycles: A Macoreconomic Model of Monopoly," *Quarterly Journal of Economics*, 100 (1985), 529–539.

Marquez, John, and Daniel R. Vining, "Inflation and Relative Price Behavior: A Survey of the Literature," in M. Ballabou, ed., *Economic Perspectives*, vol. 3, (New York: Harwood Academic Publishers, 1984).

Miller, M., and D. Orr, "A Model of the Demand for Money by Firms," *Quarterly Journal of Economics*, 80 (1966), 413–435.

Mills, Frederick C., *The Behavior of Prices* (New York: Arno Press, 1927; National Bureau of Economic Research, reprint, 1975).

Mussa, Michael, "Sticky Prices and Disequilibrium Adjustment in a Rational Model of the Inflationary Process," *American Economic Review*, 71 (December 1981), 1020–1027.

Pagan, A. R., A. D. Hall, and P. K. Trivedi, "Assessing the Variability of Inflation," *Review of Economic Studies*, 50 (October 1983), 585–596.

Parkin, Michael, "The Output-Inflation Tradeoff When Prices Are Costly to Change," *Journal of Political Economy*, 94 (1986), 200–224.

Parks, Richard W., "Inflation and Relative Price Variability," *Journal of Political Economy*, 86 (February 1978), 79–95.

Rotemberg, Julio, "Monopolistic Price Adjustment and Aggregate Output," *Review of Economic Studies*, 49 (October 1982), 517–531.

Rotemberg, Julio, "Aggregate Consequences of Fixed Costs of Price Adjustment," *American Economic Review*, 73 (June 1983), 433–436.

Rotemberg, Julio, "Fixed Costs of Price Adjustment and the Costs of Inflation," Sloan School of Management, mimeo, December 1981.

Scarf, Herbert E., "The Optimality of (s, S) Policies in the Dynamic Inventory Problem," chapter 13 in K. J. Arrow, S. Karlin, and P. Suppes, eds., *Mathematical Methods in the Social Sciences* (Stanford: Stanford University Press, 1959).

Schwarz, L. B., ed., *Multi-level Production/Inventory Control Systems: Theory and Practice* (Amsterdam: North-Holland, 1981).

Sheshinski, Eytan, and Yoram Weiss, "Inflation and Costs of Price Adjustment," *Review of Economic Studies*, 54 (1977), 287–303.

Sheshinski, Eytan, and Yoram Weiss, "Optimum Pricing Policy under Stochastic Inflation," *Review of Economic Studies*, 50 (July 1983), 513–529.

Taylor, John B., "Aggregate Dynamics and Staggered Contracts," *Journal of Political Economy*, 88 (1980), 1–23.

Taylor, John B., "On the Relation between the Variability of Inflation and the Average Inflation Rate," in Karl Brunner and Allan H. Meltzer, eds., *The Costs and Consequences of Inflation*, Carnegie-Rochester Conference Series on Public Policy, vol, 15 (Amsterdam: North-Holland, 1981), pp. 57–85.

Vining, Daniel R., Jr., and Thomas C. Elwertowski, "The Relationship between Relative Prices and the General Price Level," *American Economic Review*, 66 (September 1976), 699–708.

# 5 The Rigidity of Prices

Dennis W. Carlton

Economists focus on price as a mechanism to allocate resources efficiently. It is well recognized that inefficient resource allocation could occur if prices are not free to adjust. Much of macroeconomics relies on some, usually unexplained, source of price rigidity to generate inefficient unemployment. And in industrial organization there is a large literature on "administered" prices that fail to respond to the forces of supply and demand. Recently, there have been several attempts to explain price rigidity (see, for example, Okun 1981 and Williamson 1975) and to develop a theory to explain why efficient resource allocation requires prices to be unchanging or "rigid" (see, for example, my forthcoming paper and Hall 1984). Whether or not price rigidity is efficient, one common conclusion emerging from models with price rigidity is that markets with rigid prices behave very differently than markets with flexible prices. Therefore, an important unanswered question is, just how rigid are prices? Despite the great interest in this question, there have been virtually no attempts to answer it with data on individual transaction prices.

The purpose of this paper is to present evidence on the amount of price rigidity that exists in individual transaction prices. Previous studies of price rigidity have relied almost exclusively on an examination of aggregate price indices collected by the Bureau of Labor Statistics (BLS).[1] The use of BLS data has been strongly criticized on the grounds that the BLS data are inaccurate measures of transaction prices. George Stigler and James Kindahl sought to remedy this deficiency by collecting price data on actual transactions. Stigler and Kindahl then showed that price indices of average transaction prices were more flexible than the BLS price indices.

The difficulty with using indices is that they can mask the behavior of individual transaction prices. For example, suppose that two people buy varying amounts of commodity $A$ monthly for many years. Suppose that each buyer pays a constant price on each transaction for a period of several years, that when the price to one buyer changes, the price to the other buyer is unaffected, and that the price rigidity that exists is more pronounced for a downward price movement. All of these facts could be perfectly consistent with a flexible aggregate price index as long as the amount purchased by

*American Economic Review* 76 (September 1986): 637–658. Copyright © 1986 by the American Economic Association. Reprinted with permission.

each buyer varies from month to month. Yet the implication that many draw from a flexible price index, namely that price is allocating resources efficiently, could be completely inappropriate. Moreover, there are several interesting questions that cannot be answered by examining aggregate price indices. For example, how long do prices to a buyer remain unchanged, what is the relationship between contract length and price rigidity, and how closely together do the prices to different buyers move?

Using the Stigler-Kindahl data, I have examined the behavior of individual buyers' prices for certain products used in manufacturing. My main conclusions are as follows:

• The degree of price rigidity in many industries is significant. It is not unusual in some industries for prices to individual buyers to remain unchanged for several years.

• Even for what appear to be homogeneous commodities, the correlation of price changes across buyers is very low.

• There is a (weak) negative correlation between price rigidity and length of buyer-seller association. The more rigid are prices, the shorter the length of association.

• There is a positive correlation between price rigidity and average absolute price change. The more rigid are prices, the greater is the price change when prices do change.

• There is a negative correlation between length of buyer-seller association and average absolute price change. The longer a buyer and seller deal with each other, the smaller is the average price change when prices do change.

• There is no evidence that there is an asymmetry in price rigidity. In particular, prices are not rigid downward.

• The fixed costs of changing a price at least to some buyers may be small. There are plenty of instances where small price changes occur. It appears that for any particular product, the fixed cost of changing the price varies across firms and buyers.

• There is at best very weak evidence that buyers have systematic preferences across products for unchanging prices.

• The level of industry concentration is strongly correlated with rigid prices. The more concentrated the industry, the longer is the average spell of price rigidity.

The most startling finding to me is that for many products, the correlation of price changes across buyers is low. Some of the theories referred to earlier explain why this is likely to occur, especially for specialized goods. The fact that it occurs for what most economists (though not necessarily businessmen) would regard as a homogeneous product emphasizes how erroneous it is to focus attention on price as the exclusive mechanism to allocate resources. Nonprice rationing is not a fiction. It is a reality of business and may be the efficient response to economic uncertainty and the cost of using the price system. (See my forthcoming paper.)

Two general caveats deserve mention. First, a rigid price by itself does not necessarily imply an inefficiency. If supply and demand are unchanging, prices will be rigid. Moreover, even in a changing market, a fixed-price contract for a fixed quantity creates no economic inefficiency in the standard competitive model. If prices change subsequent to the signing of the contract, the buyer incurs a capital gain or loss, but his marginal price remains the same as every other buyer as long as the product can be readily bought and sold. However, if either the buyer cannot readily resell his product or the buyer does not have a fixed quantity contract, then a fixed price may well lead to buyers facing different marginal prices. My understanding of the data I use is that the contracts typically leave the quantity unspecified, so that different buyers paying different prices do indeed face different marginal prices. Although this is inefficient in the standard competitive model, it need not be under more realistic assumptions that recognize the cost of making a market. (See my forthcoming paper. See also my 1978, 1979, 1982, and 1983 papers for analyses reconciling observed price behavior with market equilibrium.) But the finding of different prices and price movements to different buyers does emphasize the inadequacy of the simple market-clearing model.

Second, the time period I examine is one with relatively low levels of inflation, and therefore, I have made no adjustment for it. However, even if inflation were rampant and all prices indexed so that no (nominal) price rigidity existed, the main conclusion of the paper would stand as long as some of the other empirical findings (such as the low correlation of price movements across buyers) continue to hold. The conclusion is that price alone is not allocating goods and new theories are required to justify what looks like non-market-clearing behavior.

This paper is organized as follows. Section 1 describes the Stigler and Kindahl data and discusses measures of price rigidity. Section 2 analyzes the characteristics of price rigidity found in several general product group-ings. Section 3 investigates the relationship between price rigidity, price change, and length of buyer-seller associations. Section 4 examines whether buyers have systematic preferences for price stability across different prod-ucts. One criticism of using broadly defined product groups as the unit of analysis is that there is so much heterogeneity of products within a single product grouping that results can be biased. Therefore, in section 5 I redo the analysis for a select group of narrowly defined products. Section 6 shows how to measure whether the prices to different buyers move in concert and classifies the various products according to how similar price changes are to different buyers. Section 7 examines some specific implications the results have for the prediction of price behavior. Section 8 examines whether there is any relationship of the various characteristics of price movements to the structural characteristics of the industry.

## 1   The Stigler and Kindahl Data

Stigler and Kindahl collected data mainly from buyers on actual transac-tion prices paid for a variety of products. They tried to correct for any explicit or implicit discounting and for any changes in the specifications of the product. Although there are undoubtedly some misreporting of prices and some unrecorded product changes (for example, physical characteris-tics, point of delivery, time of delivery), it is the most accurate and compre-hensive data I know of on individual transaction prices.

The buyers who report prices are typically firms in the *Fortune* 500. The identity of the seller is not known.[2] Typically, there is only scant informa-tion on quantity purchased, though it is believed that during the course of the reporting, buyers were using the product regularly. Ideally, actual transaction prices are reported monthly. However, in several instances prices are reported less frequently. A decision on how (or whether) to interpolate prices had to be made.

If the price is unchanged between reportings, I assume that the inter-vening price is also unchanged. If the price is not the same, I create two different series. One method assumes a change in each unobserved month. The other assumes only one change over the entire period. For example, suppose that for January the price is $10 and for April it is $20, with missing reports for February and March. The first interpolation approach assumes that the price was $13.33 in February and $16.67 in March (i.e., linear interpolation), while the second interpolation approach assumes that the price changed to $20 in either February, March, or April. (It turns out that the results on length of rigidity are unaffected by which particular month is assumed for the price change in this second approach.)

The period of observation is January 1, 1957 through December 31, 1966. Few associations between buyers and sellers last for the entire ten-year period, a point that I analyze later on. Transactions often take place under contract and the length of the contract (for example, semiannual, annual) is indicated. The appendix provides additional information on each type of transaction. Many contracts specify neither a price nor quantity. They seem not to be binding legal documents but rather more like agreements to agree.

The commodities chosen for study were preselected by Stigler and Kindahl to contain many that others had claimed were characterized by inflexible prices. The commodities are intermediate products used in manufacturing. Within broad commodity classes, finer product distinctions are made. So, for example, one can examine the general category of steel or a specific product category like carbon-steel pipe less than 3 inches in diameter. Even within fine product specifications the individual transactions will probably not involve perfectly homogeneous goods. Therefore, I never compare absolute price levels across products but instead look only at percentage changes in price and compare movements in percentage changes in price across buyers.

There are a few instances where price series are believed to be list prices, and those prices have been excluded from the analysis. Also excluded are price series that contain inconsistent information. For example, a series is excluded if the reporter claims to produce prices through 1965 but instead prices only through 1960 appear. For several transactions the product undergoes a specification change. When this occurs, I treat the prices under the new specification change as a new transaction.

## 2 An Analysis of Product Groups

Table 1 describes the price rigidity present in the individual transaction prices by product group. The first column in table 1 lists the type of product purchased. Column 2 lists the number of buyer-seller pairings that are observed for goods of unchanged specification. (One pairing could last anywhere from 1 month to 10 years.) Column 3 lists the average duration of

**Table 1**
Price rigidity by product group

| Product group (1) | Number of buyer-seller pairings[a] (2) | Average duration of price rigidity (spells) (months) (3) | Standard Deviation of duration (spells) (months) (4) | Average duration of price rigidity, monthly contracts (spells) (months) (5) | Average duration of price rigidity (transactions) (months) (6) |
|---|---|---|---|---|---|
| Steel | 348 | 13.0 | 18.3 | 9.4 | 17.9 |
| Nonferrous metals | 209 | 4.3 | 6.1 | 2.8 | 7.5 |
| Petroleum | 245 | 5.9 | 5.3 | 2.5 | 8.3 |
| Rubber tires | 123 | 8.1 | 12.0 | 7.8 | 11.5 |
| Paper | 128 | 8.7 | 14.0 | 8.8 | 11.8 |
| Chemicals | 658 | 12.8 | 10.7 | 9.6 | 19.2 |
| Cement | 40 | 13.2 | 14.7 | 5.6 | 17.2 |
| Glass | 22 | 10.2 | 12.1 | 8.5 | 13.3 |
| Truck motors | 59 | 5.4 | 6.3 | 3.7 | 8.3 |
| Plywood | 46 | 4.7 | 7.7 | 1.2 | 7.5 |
| Household appliances | 14 | 3.6 | 3.6 | 2.5 | 5.9 |

a. A pairing means a transaction over time for a good of constant specification.

price rigidity. This last figure is computed as the average length of spell for which price remains unchanged. For example, if the observations on monthly price were $5, $5, $5, $6, $6, $7, $7, $7, $7, the average rigidity would be three months. The procedure for calculating an average rigidity actually involves an underestimate, since the price before the period of observation may have been $5 and the price after the period of observation may have been $7. Calculations including and excluding the beginning and ending spells were done with no material change in the substantive interpretation of the results. The calculations in table 1 are based on the second method of interpolation of prices (only one price change between missing observations—see section 1) and include the beginning and the end of each price series. Column 4 reports the standard deviation in the rigidity of prices. Column 5 reports the same estimate of price rigidity as in column 3, except that only monthly-contract series are used. These series have fewer missing observations than the other types of transactions, hence much less interpolation is needed. (In fact, the results on rigidity for monthly contracts are similar for the two methods of interpolation.) If the implication of the numbers in column 3 across commodities differ greatly from those in column 5, one might be suspicious of the interpolation used in column 3. I expect price flexibility of monthly contracts to exceed that of all other contract types, so column 5 really puts a lower bound on column 3.

To avoid misinterpretation of the results, it may be helpful to review a standard issue in duration analysis. Imagine that there are two observed transactions, each lasting for a one-year period and each involving the same size of monthly purchase. The first transaction involves a different price each month, while the second involves the same price each month. There are 13 spells of rigidity, 12 of which last one month and one of which lasts twelve months. Based on spells, the average rigidity is 24 ÷ 13 or 1.8 months with 92 percent of the spells lasting one month and 8 percent lasting twelve months. Conditional on a price change just having occurred, the average time to the next price change is 1.8 months. Yet one-half of all goods sold involve a rigid price over the entire period. In other words, if we hold monthly purchases constant, the analysis based on spells underestimates the fraction of goods sold with rigid prices. The results in columns 3 and 5 utilize spells data. Therefore, even though I have no quantity information, I expect that these results underestimate the fraction of goods sold at rigid prices.

In column 6 I calculate price rigidity using a transaction as the unit of analysis, not a "spell." For each transaction I calculate the average price rigidity and then take an average (with each transaction weighted according to its length) over all transactions. Return to the earlier example of two transactions each lasting one year but one involving 12 price changes and the other no price changes. An analysis based on *transactions* (not spells) would calculate average rigidity to be $(1 + 12)/2$ or 6.5 months. It is that type of calculation that is reported on column 6.

Several interesting facts emerge from table 1. In several industries, prices are on average unchanged over periods exceeding one year. The degree of price inflexibility varies enormously across products groups. Steel, chemicals, and cement have average rigidities exceeding one year, while household appliances, plywood, and nonferrous metals have average price rigidities of less than five months. For any one product group the standard deviation of rigidity is quite high. In fact, the standard deviation tends to rise as the average duration of rigidity rises. The simple correlation and the Spearman rank correlation between the standard deviation and the average duration (cols. 3 and 4) are both above .80. This suggests (though it does not prove) either that each product group presented in table 1 contains heterogeneous products that differ widely in their price flexibility or that for even a homogeneous product a great heterogeneity in price flexibility is present.[3]

Column 5 shows that using monthly contracts rather than all contracts does not change the basic implications of column 3 regarding price rigidity across groups. Column 6 shows that, as expected, the average of price rigidity rises when the unit of analysis is a transaction. Indeed, the results of column 6 are striking in that they show that every product group has an average rigidity in excess of roughly six months and that 6 of the 11 product groups have average rigidities of roughly one year or more.

In table 2 more detailed evidence is provided on the time pattern of price rigidity by product group for three types of transactions. The three transaction types are monthly, in which case the transaction occurred monthly (with no necessary future commitment); quarterly-monthly, in which case the transaction was monthly but was observed quarterly; and annual, in which case the transaction was pursuant to an annual contract. For most product groups these three types of transactions account for well over 60 percent of all transactions. (See the appendix for a description of the various types of transactions that comprise the sample.) One important point to note about these transactions is that an annual "contract" rarely means a price change every twelve months, nor does a monthly contract mean a price change every month. Although annual contracts do involve more rigidity than monthly ones, it is incorrect to think of contracts as inflexible price rules set at specified intervals. A more appropriate view is that they are flexible agreements that can be renegotiated when and if the need arises.

The results in table 2 show, as one would expect from table 1, that the pattern of rigidity across product groups is highly varied. As a general rule, all product groups for each of the three transaction types in table 2 are characterized by spells of price rigidity that, in the majority of cases, last less than one year. Some commodities, like nonferrous metals and plywood, are characterized by very flexible prices, with over 60 percent of all spells in the monthly and quarterly-monthly categories lasting less than three months. On the other hand, there are definitely a substantial number of transactions involving very inflexible prices. For example, in steel, over 39 percent of the spells of rigid prices in the annual and quarterly-monthly categories (which comprise over half of all the transactions in steel) last more than one year. Other commodities with important transaction types showing fairly inflexible prices include paper, chemicals, cement, and glass.

**Table 2**
Frequency of duration of price rigidity for various types of transactions based on spells of price rigidity

| Product | Type of transaction | Percent of all transactions | Number of pairings[a] | 0–3 months | 4 mo.–1 year | 1–2 years | 2–4 years | Over 4 years |
|---|---|---|---|---|---|---|---|---|
| Steel | Annual | 3 | 11 | .11 | .41 | .24 | .22 | .03 |
| | Quarterly | 53 | 185 | .34 | .26 | .18 | .12 | .09 |
| | Monthly | 32 | 111 | .48 | .27 | .15 | .07 | .04 |
| Nonferrous metals | Annual | 4 | 8 | .16 | .69 | .12 | .03 | .00 |
| | Quarterly | 19 | 40 | .61 | .29 | .08 | .02 | .02 |
| | Monthly | 42 | 87 | .78 | .20 | .02 | .01 | .00 |
| Petroleum | Annual | 27 | 66 | .20 | .69 | .07 | .04 | .00 |
| | Quarterly | 15 | 37 | .74 | .23 | .02 | .00 | — |
| | Monthly | 7 | 16 | .83 | .15 | .02 | .00 | — |
| Rubber tires | Annual | 26 | 32 | .19 | .72 | .07 | .01 | .01 |
| | Quarterly | 37 | 45 | .34 | .48 | .11 | .04 | .04 |
| | Monthly | 20 | 24 | .44 | .44 | .07 | .01 | .06 |
| Paper | Annual | 17 | 22 | .04 | .69 | .18 | .08 | .01 |
| | Quarterly | 2 | 3 | .17 | .42 | .29 | .08 | .04 |
| | Monthly | 28 | 36 | .46 | .36 | .12 | .04 | .02 |
| Chemicals | Annual | 43 | 286 | .11 | .58 | .17 | .09 | .06 |
| | Quarterly | 11 | 72 | .37 | .30 | .12 | .16 | .04 |
| | Monthly | 20 | 134 | .53 | .27 | .09 | .06 | .04 |
| Cement | Annual | 20 | 8 | .04 | .78 | .13 | .04 | .00 |
| | Quarterly | 50 | 20 | .19 | .27 | .23 | .14 | .05 |
| | Monthly | 10 | 4 | .64 | .29 | .02 | .04 | .02 |
| Glass | Annual | 36 | 8 | .00 | .87 | .10 | .03 | .00 |
| | Quarterly | 9 | 2 | .25 | .50 | .19 | .00 | .06 |
| | Monthly | 41 | 9 | .51 | .22 | .18 | .09 | .00 |

**Table 2** (continued)

| Product | Type of transaction | Percent of all transactions | Number of pairings[a] | 0–3 months | 4 mo.– 1 year | 1–2 years | 2–4 years | Over 4 years |
|---|---|---|---|---|---|---|---|---|
| Truck motors | Annual | 14 | 8 | .05 | .86 | .09 | .00 | .00 |
| | Quarterly | 2 | 1 | .21 | .57 | .21 | .00 | .00 |
| | Monthly | 58 | 34 | .69 | .26 | .04 | .01 | .00 |
| Plywood | Annual | 0 | 0 | .00 | .00 | .00 | .00 | .00 |
| | Quarterly | 96 | 44 | .64 | .29 | .04 | .02 | .01 |
| | Monthly | 4 | 2 | .99 | .02 | .00 | .00 | .00 |
| Household appliances | Annual | 21 | 3 | .00 | .82 | .18 | .00 | .00 |
| | Quarterly | 0 | 0 | .00 | .00 | .00 | .00 | .00 |
| | Monthly | 57 | 8 | .78 | .22 | .00 | .00 | .00 |

Note: The numbers in the rows of the table may not add to one because of rounding.
a. The number of pairings is not the number of spells of price rigidity in all contracts. See the discussion preceding table 1 and the note to table 1.

In fact, a histogram analysis based on transactions (not spells) shows that 50 percent or more of all transactions involving steel, cement, chemicals, or glass have average rigidities of one year or more for frequently used contract types.

As one would expect, the annual category involves less price flexibility than the quarterly category, which itself exhibits less flexibility than the monthly category. It is also interesting to note that even within a particular product group and transaction type there is a high degree of heterogeneity in price flexibility. For example, for chemicals in the monthly category, over 50 percent of spells of rigidity are less than three months, but still a significant fraction (10 percent) involve spells of rigidity in excess of two years. This suggests that within any one product grouping, either the products sold are different, or the buyer-seller pairings have different properties, or the method (i.e., price versus nonprice) chosen to allocate across different pairings of buyers and sellers is simply different.

One issue frequently raised in discussions of price flexiblity is the cost of making a price change (see, for example, Barro 1972). There are many types of costs associated with a price change. New price sheets have to be constructed, price information must be conveyed to buyers, buyers may find planning more difficult, buyers may distrust sellers if prices change often, search costs are higher if prices change often, and so on. The real question is how important are these costs. One way to address this question is to see how important small price changes are. Table 3 reports the percent of all price changes that are less than $1/4$, $1/2$, 1, and 2 percent in absolute value for the same product groups and transaction types reported in table 2.

Table 3 makes two points. First, very small price changes occur more often in monthly than in quarterly-monthly or in annual transaction types. Second and more important, there are a significant number of price changes that one would consider small (i.e., less than 1 percent) for most commodities and transaction types. This finding presents a bit of a puzzle if buyers are homogeneous. Either the cost of changing a price is small or the costs of being at the "wrong" price—even one off by 1 percent—are very high.[5] Yet these explanations have difficulty explaining how it can be that some transactions seem to involve prices that do not change over long periods. Another explanation is that perhaps price does not need to change in those transactions for which prices are unchanging (i.e., neither supply nor demand curves are shifting). This explanation runs into the problem that, as is suggested by table 2 (and as will be confirmed later on), within the

**Table 3**
Frequency of small price changes by product group and contract type

| Product | Percent of price changes less than | | | | Average absolute price change (percent) |
|---|---|---|---|---|---|
| | $\frac{1}{4}\%$ | $\frac{1}{2}\%$ | $1\%$ | $2\%$ | |
| Steel | | | | | |
| Annual | 4 | 8 | 11 | 27 | 3.3 |
| Quarterly | 5 | 11 | 17 | 24 | 4.2 |
| Monthly | 9 | 20 | 36 | 52 | 2.5 |
| Nonferrous metals | | | | | |
| Annual | 2 | 5 | 9 | 27 | 7.0 |
| Quarterly | 2 | 5 | 12 | 25 | 5.0 |
| Monthly | 8 | 15 | 28 | 49 | 2.9 |
| Petroleum | | | | | |
| Annual | 0 | 0 | 8 | 24 | 5.3 |
| Quarterly | 0 | 0 | 2 | 17 | 5.4 |
| Monthly | 1 | 5 | 19 | 47 | 2.9 |
| Rubber tires | | | | | |
| Annual | 12 | 21 | 30 | 44 | 3.0 |
| Quarterly | 7 | 11 | 18 | 34 | 4.5 |
| Monthly | 13 | 23 | 38 | 63 | 2.3 |
| Paper | | | | | |
| Annual | 4 | 9 | 8 | 27 | 6.3 |
| Quarterly | 0 | 19 | 24 | 33 | 3.6 |
| Monthly | 13 | 23 | 43 | 62 | 2.0 |
| Chemicals | | | | | |
| Annual | 4 | 8 | 13 | 24 | 7.7 |
| Quarterly | 0 | 5 | 11 | 24 | 7.3 |
| Monthly | 5 | 14 | 30 | 42 | 5.0 |
| Cement | | | | | |
| Annual | 14 | 22 | 32 | 46 | 3.3 |
| Quarterly | 0 | 0 | 1 | 19 | 4.1 |
| Monthly | 71 | 75 | 85 | 94 | 5.0 |
| Glass | | | | | |
| Annual | 0 | 0 | 7 | 19 | 6.5 |
| Quarterly | 0 | 0 | 20 | 40 | 6.2 |
| Monthly | 3 | 20 | 45 | 67 | 2.1 |
| Truck motors | | | | | |
| Annual | 3 | 3 | 12 | 20 | 3.9 |
| Quarterly | 0 | 0 | 0 | 8 | 7.2 |
| Monthly | 12 | 27 | 50 | 75 | 1.7 |
| Plywood | | | | | |
| Annual | — | — | — | — | — |
| Quarterly | 1 | 2 | 6 | 19 | 6.1 |
| Monthly | 19 | 38 | 54 | 72 | 1.9 |
| Household appliances | | | | | |
| Annual | 0 | 0 | 0 | 25 | 4.3 |
| Quarterly | — | — | — | — | — |
| Monthly | 22 | 44 | 70 | 95 | .8 |

same product grouping there are likely to be changing prices for one transaction at the same time that there are constant prices for another. The only possible explanations consistent with efficiency seem to be either that firms differ in their allocation ability, with some firms relying on price more than others, or alternatively that every firm must rely more on price when dealing with certain buyers than with others.[6]

The foregoing analysis can also shed light on the question of whether there is an asymmetry in price movements. For example, are prices rigid downward? If prices are rigid downward, then one can think of the fixed cost of changing prices as being higher for price declines than price increases. If so, the minimum positive price change should be less than the minimum negative price change. In fact, an analysis of minimum positive and negative price changes reveals no such pattern.

## 3  Relationships among Price Rigidity, Price Change, and Length of Buyer-Seller Association

If within a particular product group there is a wide degree of heterogeneity in price rigidity across buyers, are there any predictable correlations that emerge among price rigidity, price change, and length of buyer-seller association?[7] There are several different theories of price rigidity, and the theories often have different implications for these correlations. I now investigate three questions.

First, is there a positive correlation between length of association and price rigidity across transactions for the same product?[8] That is, if buyer A has been dealing with his seller for ten years while buyer B is beginning a new relationship, are buyer A's prices more rigid? One rationale for this relationship would be that if buyers and sellers deal with each other over long time periods, they set one average price and thereby save on the transaction cost of changing price constantly. However, it is quite possible to justify the reverse relationship. The impediment to changing price may be that the buyer or seller may feel the other side is taking advantage of him (see, for example, Williamson 1975). If buyers and sellers have been dealing with each other for long periods of time, it will be in their interest not to take advantage of the other in the short run for fear of damaging the ongoing relationship (see, for example, Telser 1980). If buyers and sellers know each other well because of their long-standing relationship, this fear of being taken advantage of in the short run will be reduced. In such a case flexible prices may emerge.

Second, is there an inverse correlation between the size of price changes and duration of price rigidity across transactions within the same product group? That is, if buyer *A* purchases steel on a contract in which price changes frequently while buyer *B* has a contract in which price changes infrequently, are the price changes of buyer *A* (when they occur) larger in absolute value than those of buyer *B*? This relationship would make sense if prices are rigid on some transactions because there is a cost to changing prices. If so, one would expect that those transactions with the most rigid prices (those to buyer *B*) have the highest costs of changing prices and therefore only large price changes will be observed on those contracts. An alternative prediction would be that some prices are rigid because buyers (or sellers) want price stability for insurance-type reasons. In such a case price changes on the more rigid contract could well be smaller than on the flexible price contract, since the function of insurance is to smooth out price fluctuations.

The third question is whether there is a negative association between length of association and the size of price changes. If buyers' and sellers' distrust of or lack of knowledge about each other explains rigid prices, then the longer the association, the lower the cost of changing price and hence the more flexible the price and the smaller the observed price changes should be. The opposite prediction could emerge from a theory in which buyers and sellers who deal with each other over long periods care about getting only the average price right. In such a case, one would expect to see rigid prices that infrequently change. When they do change, they will change by larger amounts than prices in less rigid contracts.[9]

Table 4 reports the correlations between length of association, price changes (absolute values), and rigidity for each product group, and it indicates when the correlations are statistically significant at the 10 percent level, the 5 percent level, and the 1 percent level.[10] A strong positive association between length of association and rigidity exists only for chemicals, while a strong negative association exists for petroleum, household appliances, and truck motors. To the extent any general relationship exists between length of association and rigidity, it is a *negative* one. The second column of table 4 indicates that there is a *positive* association between price change and rigidity. All but one correlation is positive, and all seven statistically significant correlations are positive. The third column suggests

**Table 4**
Correlations of contract characteristics

| | Correlation between | | |
|---|---|---|---|
| Product | length of association and rigidity | rigidity and average absolute percent price change | length of association and average absolute percent price change |
| Cement | .28 | .17 | .24 |
| Chemicals | .16ᶜ | .10ᵃ | −.12ᵇ |
| Glass | −.11 | .69ᶜ | −.24 |
| Household appliancesᵈ | −.87ᶜ | .71ᵇ | −.66ᵇ |
| Nonferrous metals | .12 | .12 | −.15ᵇ |
| Paper | .03 | .20 | −.25ᵃ |
| Petroleum | −.25ᶜ | −.06 | −.09 |
| Plywood | .10 | .54ᶜ | −.11 |
| Rubber tires | −.08 | .43ᶜ | −.27ᵇ |
| Steel | .03 | .14ᵇ | .01 |
| Truck motors | −.56ᶜ | .60ᵃ | −.23 |

a. Statistically significant at the 10 percent level.
b. Statistically significant at the 5 percent level.
c. Statistically significant at the 1 percent level.
d. Based on only 11 observations.

that there is a *negative* correlation between length of association and price changes. All but two correlations are negative, and all five statistically significant correlations are negative.

In short, the evidence in table 4 is *consistent* with the following explanation. Buyers and sellers who do not have long associations are more likely to use fixed price contracts because they don't trust or know each other. The "cost" of changing price on such a contract is to risk creation of mutual distrust. Prices change on these contracts only for substantial price movements. Buyers and sellers who have long associations aren't as worried about mutual distrust. Hence, price changes are more frequent (i.e., less rigid prices) and on average smaller.[11]

One common explanation for price (or wage) rigidity has to do with insurance. I have not incorporated that explanation into the one just given for several reasons. First, Sherwin Rosen (1985) casts doubt on the theoretical underpinnings of an insurance explanation. Second, large firms should be able to diversify such risks and hence not need insurance.[12] Third, as we will see in the next section, the insurance explanation does not seem supported by the data.

## 4  Relationships Among Types of Transactions

Do some buyers seek out stable pricing arrangements in which the price changes infrequently? If so, one would expect to see a correlation in the rigidity of pricing across transactions of different commodities. For example, if the transactions of a particular buyer who purchased steel involved price changing much less frequently than the industry average, will it also be the case that the buyer's transactions involving paper have prices that change less frequently than the industry average?

For the product categories of table 1, I have calculated for each buyer a vector of the average price rigidity for each of the commodities he purchases. I then examine pairs of products to see if there is a correlation across firms in these rigidities. (That is, does a firm buying steel with overly rigid prices buy paper with overly rigid prices?) There are 227 buyer firms in my sample. There are many fewer (around 60) who purchase any two commodities. The pairwise correlations were primarily positive, but in most cases the correlations were not statistically significant and were often sensitive to the interpolation method used to calculate price rigidity. The most stable and statistically significant results were the (positive) correlations between price rigidity for contracts in steel and rubber, metals and plywood, and rubber and cement.[13] Because of the instability of the results, they should be regarded as at best weak support that buyers may have certain preferences across transaction types for different products.

## 5  Analysis of Specific Products

One drawback to the analysis of the previous sections is that the product groups may be so broad that in the results a heterogeneity appears that is caused only by the heterogeneous nature of the products in any one commodity group. To remedy this problem, I analyzed 32 specific products. These 32 products were chosen primarily because there were numerous data on them. The products analyzed are listed in table 5 along with information similar to that presented in table 1.

The results are similar to those of table 1 in several respects. As in table 1, there is wide variation across products in the rigidity of price. Even within a single detailed product specification there still exists a great deal of heterogeneity in durations of spells of rigidity. The standard deviation of duration rises with the average duration.[14] One is struck by the rigidity of

**Table 5**
Price rigidity for detailed product specifications

| Product (1) | Number of buyer-seller pairings (2) | Average duration of price rigidity (spells) (months) (3) | Standard deviation of duration (spells) (months) (4) | Average duration of price rigidity, monthly contracts (spells) (months) (5) | Average duration of price rigidity (transactions) (months) (6) |
|---|---|---|---|---|---|
| Steel plates | 28 | 18.5 | 19.4 | 21.6 | 20.3 |
| Hot rolled bars and rods | 33 | 15.1 | 17.6 | 10.6 | 17.5 |
| Steel pipe and tubing (3″ or less in diameter) | 33 | 12.1 | 16.4 | 12.7 | 15.9 |
| Copper wire and cable (bare) | 26 | 3.8 | 5.4 | 2.6 | 4.1 |
| Gasoline (regular) | 66 | 6.2 | 5.7 | 2.7 | 8.9 |
| Diesel oil #2 | 75 | 4.7 | 4.3 | 1.4 | 6.9 |
| Fuel oil #2 | 41 | 7.3 | 4.9 | 4.6 | 8.3 |
| Residual fuel oil #6 | 59 | 6.5 | 6.4 | 2.9 | 9.2 |
| Container board, fiberboard | 28 | 11.6 | 8.0 | 11.5 | 12.6 |
| Caustic soda (liquid) | 33 | 16.2 | 22.9 | 27.6 | 21.3 |
| Chlorine liquid | 28 | 19.9 | 18.7 | 60.0 | 27.1 |
| Oxygen, cylinders | 30 | 16.8 | 14.6 | 36.3 | 21.5 |
| Acetylene | 22 | 16.0 | 16.2 | 26.4 | 21.9 |
| Portland cement (sack) | 28 | 16.4 | 16.8 | — | 19.0 |
| Steel sheet and strip, hot rolled | 25 | 18.6 | 18.5 | — | 19.1 |
| New rail (RR) | 20 | 22.1 | 31.4 | 17.1 | 23.2 |
| Tie plates (RR) | 18 | 21.9 | 33.0 | 20.0 | 23.0 |
| Steel wheels, "one wear" (RR) | 25 | 21.4 | 22.6 | 24.0 | 24.9 |
| Track bolts (RR) | 18 | 14.5 | 17.4 | 4.4 | 17.2 |
| Zinc slab ingots | 9 | 5.1 | 5.4 | 4.4 | 5.6 |
| Coal (RR) | 20 | 6.8 | 12.2 | 1.4 | 15.9 |
| Kraft wrapping paper | 12 | 7.5 | 6.0 | 5.7 | 9.2 |
| Paper bags | 16 | 9.4 | 5.3 | 20.0 | 10.3 |
| Sulfuric acid, bulk | 15 | 14.1 | 18.7 | 22.3 | 20.9 |
| Sulfuric acid | 19 | 11.0 | 17.1 | 5.1 | 19.5 |

**Table 5** (continued)

| Product (1) | Number of buyer-seller pairings (2) | Average duration of price rigidity (spells) (months) (3) | Standard deviation of duration (spells) (months) (4) | Average duration of price rigidity, monthly contracts (spells) (months) (5) | Average duration of price rigidity (transactions) (months) (6) |
|---|---|---|---|---|---|
| Methyl alcohol | 18 | 12.3 | 12.9 | 17.4 | 17.8 |
| Phthalic anhydride | 10 | 7.2 | 6.1 | 6.8 | 8.3 |
| Succinate antibiotic | 16 | 34.4 | 52.1 | 57.0 | 25.4 |
| Kapseals antibiotic | 16 | 56.1 | 66.7 | 40.0 | 44.0 |
| Meprobanate tablets | 16 | 13.8 | 12.0 | 18.7 | 15.5 |
| Librium | 13 | 19.1 | 23.1 | 56.0 | 20.9 |
| Plywood | 25 | 3.7 | 4.8 | 1.1 | 6.2 |

Notes: See table 1. The dashes in col. 5 indicate that no data is available.

some prices. Even for monthly contracts there are many products (for example, chlorine liquid, steel plate) where the average length of a spell of price rigidity is well over one year. And column 6 indicates that with transactions as the unit of analysis, most commodities have average durations of price in excess of eight months.

In table 6 I present spells of price rigidity by commodity for a frequently used contract specification. The pattern that emerges is similar to that in table 2. Even within detailed product specification for a particular contract type there is considerable heterogeneity in length of spells of price rigidity. This suggests that the price of a good is changing for some transactions but not for others.[15] Table 6 reveals that although most prices do not remain in effect for over one year, for many products (for example, steel plate, hot-rolled bars and rods, oxygen) a significant number of spells of rigid prices (over 20 percent) remain in effect for over two years.

In table 7 I present the fraction of price changes that are less than $1/4$, $1/2$, 1, and 2 percent in absolute value in order to assess the importance of the fixed costs of changing prices. Table 7 corroborates the message of table 3. For most products there are numerous instances (over 10 percent) of small price changes (below 1 percent). This fact reinforces my earlier

**Table 6**
Durations of rigidity by detailed product specification, based on spells of rigidity

| Product | 0–3 mo. | 3 mo.– 1 yr. | 1–2 yrs. | 2–4 yrs. | Over 4 yrs. |
|---|---|---|---|---|---|
| Steel plate | .24 | .24 | .23 | .18 | .11 |
| Hot rolled bars and rods | .36 | .21 | .21 | .16 | .07 |
| Steel pipe and tubing (less than 3″ diameter) | .39 | .31 | .16 | .10 | .05 |
| Copper wire and cable (bare) | .67 | .30 | .02 | .00 | .01 |
| Gasoline (regular) (a) | .33 | .59 | .05 | .03 | .00 |
| Diesel oil #2 | .79 | .22 | .00 | .00 | .00 |
| Fuel oil #2 (a) | .03 | .88 | .08 | .02 | .00 |
| Residual fuel oil #6 (a) | .22 | .64 | .07 | .06 | .00 |
| Container board, fiberboard (a) | .00 | .73 | .19 | .06 | .00 |
| Caustic soda (liquid) (a) | .10 | .64 | .14 | .06 | .06 |
| Chlorine liquid (a) | .00 | .69 | .14 | .10 | .06 |
| Oxygen, cylinders | .32 | .27 | .14 | .26 | .01 |
| Acetylene | .37 | .24 | .15 | .21 | .01 |
| Portland cement (bag or sack) | .19 | .32 | .24 | .14 | .05 |
| Steel sheet and strip, hot-rolled | .25 | .27 | .19 | .21 | .08 |
| New rail | .53 | .07 | .16 | .06 | .18 |
| Tie plates | .53 | .08 | .17 | .06 | .16 |
| Steel wheels "one wear" | .13 | .35 | .22 | .22 | .09 |
| Track bolts | .27 | .34 | .23 | .06 | .11 |
| Zinc slab ingots | .44 | .44 | .09 | .03 | .00 |
| Coal for RR | .60 | .23 | .11 | .03 | .03 |
| Kraft wrapping paper | .00 | .40 | .40 | .20 | .00 |
| Paper bags | .17 | .00 | .67 | .17 | .00 |
| Sulfuric acid, bulk | .68 | .18 | .08 | .00 | .05 |
| Sulfuric acid (a) | .13 | .56 | .20 | .05 | .05 |
| Methyl alcohol (a) | .38 | .38 | .15 | .07 | .01 |
| Phthalic anhydride | .47 | .41 | .09 | .03 | .00 |
| Succinate antibiotic | .00 | .30 | .00 | .50 | .20 |
| Kapseals antibiotic | .00 | .08 | .08 | .31 | .54 |
| Meprobanate tablets (a) | .14 | .67 | .11 | .06 | .03 |
| Librium (a) | .13 | .39 | .22 | .17 | .09 |
| Plywood | .73 | .23 | .03 | .01 | .01 |

Notes: All contracts are monthly or quarterly-monthly unless followed by (a), which indicates annual. The numbers in rows may not add to one because of rounding.

**Table 7**
Frequency of small price changes by detailed product specification

| Product | Percent of price changes less than | | | |
|---|---|---|---|---|
| | $\frac{1}{4}\%$ | $\frac{1}{2}\%$ | 1% | 2% |
| Steel plate | 0 | 1 | 11 | 16 |
| Hot-rolled bars and rods | 1 | 8 | 13 | 28 |
| Steel pipe and tubing (less than 3″ diameter) | 4 | 6 | 14 | 27 |
| Copper wire and cable (bare) | 3 | 5 | 8 | 19 |
| Gasoline (regular) (a) | 0 | 1 | 13 | 27 |
| Diesel oil #2 | 0 | 0 | 2 | 19 |
| Fuel oil #2 (a) | 0 | 0 | 7 | 22 |
| Residual fuel oil #6 (a) | 0 | 0 | 2 | 25 |
| Container board, fiberboard (a) | 4 | 4 | 4 | 12 |
| Caustic soda (liquid) (a) | 2 | 5 | 11 | 15 |
| Chlorine liquid (a) | 6 | 13 | 17 | 31 |
| Oxygen, cylinders | 0 | 0 | 3 | 14 |
| Acetylene | 0 | 10 | 18 | 23 |
| Portland cement (bag or sack) | 0 | 0 | 1 | 19 |
| Steel sheet and strip, hot-rolled | 0 | 2 | 7 | 13 |
| New rail | 1 | 3 | 6 | 10 |
| Tie plates | 3 | 5 | 5 | 9 |
| Steel wheels "one wear" | 4 | 4 | 10 | 16 |
| Track bolts | 1 | 3 | 14 | 16 |
| Zinc slab ingots | 6 | 6 | 11 | 20 |
| Coal (RR) | 3 | 8 | 18 | 37 |
| Kraft wrapping paper | 3 | 8 | 20 | 53 |
| Paper bags | 0 | 20 | 20 | 60 |
| Sulfuric acid, bulk | 3 | 12 | 34 | 54 |
| Sulfuric acid | 1 | 1 | 57 | 76 |
| Methyl alcohol (a) | 0 | 15 | 24 | 32 |
| Phthalic anhydride | 0 | 0 | 0 | 0 |
| Succinate antibiotic | 0 | 0 | 0 | 0 |
| Kapseals antibiotic (a) | 0 | 0 | 0 | 50 |
| Meprobanate tablets (a) | 0 | 0 | 0 | 27 |
| Librium (a) | 0 | 0 | 0 | 14 |
| Plywood | 1 | 3 | 7 | 18 |

Notes: see table 6.

**Table 8**
Correlations of contract characteristics

| Product | Correlation between | | |
| --- | --- | --- | --- |
| | length of association and rigidity | rigidity and average absolute percent price change | length of association and average absolute percent price change |
| Steel sheet and strip, hot-rolled | — | −.40[a] | — |
| Steel plate | .07 | −.11 | .27 |
| Hot-rolled bars and rods | −.00 | .32[a] | .26 |
| Steel pipe and tubing (3″ or less in diameter) | −.21 | .19 | −.32[a] |
| Plywood | .10 | .04 | −.34[a] |
| New rail | .14 | .41[a] | −.64[b] |
| Tie plates | — | .47[b] | — |
| Steel wheels, "one wear" | .07 | −.33 | −.14 |
| Track bolts | — | .54[b] | — |
| Copper wire and cable, bare | −.06 | .76[c] | −.20 |
| Coal for RR | — | −.14 | — |
| Gasoline | .02 | .08 | .02 |
| Diesel oil #2 | −.74[c] | −.22 | .27 |
| Fuel oil #6 | −.12 | −.02 | −.14 |
| Sulfuric acid, bulk | .51[b] | −0.6 | −.45[b] |
| Sulfuric acid | −.52[c] | .15 | .10 |
| Caustic soda, liquid | .35 | .58[c] | .22 |
| Chlorine, liquid | .40[a] | −.00 | −.56[b] |
| Oxygen cylinders | .10 | −.17 | .07 |
| Acetylene | .04 | .50[b] | .12 |
| Methyl alcohol | .21 | .53[c] | .02 |
| Portland cement, in bag or sack | .34 | .19 | .33 |

a. Significant at the 10 percent level.
b. Significant at the 5 percent level.
c. Significant at the 1 percent level.

conclusion that theories that postulate rigid prices solely because of a common high fixed cost of changing price to each buyer are not supported by the evidence. (See the discussion of the results of table 3.) The most reasonable explanation is that firms and buyers must differ in their need to rely on the price system to achieve allocative efficiency and that the fixed costs of changing price varies across buyers and across firms.

An analysis of the minimum positive and negative price changes reveals no tendency for one to exceed the other. Just as in the earlier analysis, there appears to be no evidence to support asymmetric price changes.

In table 8 I present information, comparable to table 4, on the relationship between price rigidity, length of association, and average price change for transactions in the same product.[16] (Table A2 in the appendix presents information by product on average absolute price change and average length of association.) The results mirror those of table 4. There may be a weak negative correlation between rigidity and length of association. Of the 18 correlations, only 4 were statistically significant. Two negative correlations were significant at the 1 percent level, while the positive correlations were significant at the 5 and 10 percent levels. (However, the number of positive correlations exceeded the number of negative ones.) The evidence on the correlation between price change and rigidity is clearer. Of the 9 significant correlations, 8 were positive. The number of positive correlations exceeded the number of negative ones. The evidence on the correlation between price change and length of association suggests a negative correlation. Of the 5 significant coefficients, all were negative. (However, the number of negative correlations equaled the number of positives.)

## 6   The Heterogeneity of Price Movements Across Buyers

The previous evidence reveals that price movements across different transaction types for the same commodity may be very different. In this section I investigate in more detail the heterogeneity of price movements for the same commodity. By limiting the analysis to transactions of the same type, I have automatically screened out considerable heterogeneity. Despite this, I still find a startling amount of heterogeneity. I limit the analysis to annual contracts or quarterly-monthly and monthly contracts, depending on the available data. I group quarterly-monthly and monthly price movements together on the grounds that they both represent price series whose prices are not necessarily expected to remain in force for more than one month.

I use two methods to describe how heterogeneous price movements are. The first method measures the difference in the stochastic structure of each price change series, while the second attempts to measure correlation in price movements across different transactions.

The first method computes for each individual price series the variance in the percent changes in price (actually the first difference of the log of the price series). A variance $\sigma$ is computed for each transaction-price series. If all the price series have the same stochastic structure, this variance should be the same across different price series for the same commodity. For each of 30 commodities, I present the mean variance (i.e., the mean of $\sigma^2$), the variance of $\sigma^2$ (i.e., a measure of how $\sigma^2$ varies across transactions), and the coefficient of variation (the square root of variance of $\sigma^2$ divided by the mean).[17]

Table 9 shows that in general the individual price series within any one commodity and transaction type seems to be quite different from the others. The commodities that seem to have the least homogeneous transactions are steel pipe, oxygen, sheet steel, steel railway wheels, and coal.

Another method of characterizing the degree of heterogeneity among price series is to look at the correlation of contemporaneous price changes. A slight extension of this method is to examine the correlation of filtered price series. An example will illustrate.

Suppose two monthly price series are

10  10  10  10  5  5  5  5    7.5  7.5  7.5  7.5,

10  10  10    5  5  5  5  7.5  7.5  7.5  7.5  7.5.

One might be especially interested in seeing how closely the percent changes in the price series are correlated. The two derived series of percent price changes are

—  0  0    0   −50%  0  0   0    50%  0  0  0,

—  0  0  −50%    0    0  0  50%    0  0  0  0.

It appears that the two series have no correlation in percent changes. But that conclusion is misleading. Both series change within one month of each other. Suppose that one constructs a new series that takes the arithmetic average of the last two monthly percent changes in prices. Then one obtains two series that look like

**Table 9**
Measures of heterogeneity among price series

| Product | Mean variance of individual price change | Variances of individual price change | Coefficient of variation |
|---|---|---|---|
| Steel plate | 1.33 (10-6) | 1.56 (10-9) | 29.7 |
| Hot-rolled bars and rods | 1.73 (10-6) | 3.64 (10-9) | 34.9 |
| Steel pipe and tubing (3″ or less in diameter) | 3.31 (10-6) | 2.27 (10-8) | 45.5 |
| Copper wire and cable, bare | 1.45 (10-5) | 4.36 (10-8) | 14.4 |
| Gasoline | 6.22 (10-5) | 1.03 (10-6) | 16.3 |
| Diesel fuel #2 | 1.59 (10-5) | 6.50 (10-8) | 16.0 |
| Fuel oil #2 (a) | 2.93 (10-5) | 1.02 (10-7) | 10.9 |
| Fuel oil #6 | 2.57 (10-5) | 4.54 (10-7) | 26.2 |
| Container board, fiberboard | 2.94 (10-5) | 5.62 (10-9) | 2.5 |
| Caustic soda, liquid | 5.26 (10-5) | 4.89 (10-8) | 4.2 |
| Liquid chlorine (a) | 8.48 (10-6) | 6.57 (10-8) | 30.2 |
| Oxygen, cylinders | 3.07 (10-5) | 2.49 (10-6) | 51.4 |
| Acetylene | 6.66 (10-6) | 4.63 (10-8) | 32.3 |
| Portland cement | 1.97 (10-6) | 4.79 (10-9) | 35.1 |
| Sheet steel and strip (hot rolled) | 4.64 (10-6) | 1.63 (10-7) | 87.0 |
| New rails | 9.95 (10-7) | 1.44 (10-10) | 12.1 |
| Tie plates | 1.55 (10-6) | 1.43 (10-10) | 7.7 |
| Steel railway wheels | 9.51 (10-7) | 8.08 (10-9) | 94.5 |
| Railroad track bolts | 2.87 (10-6) | 4.93 (10-9) | 24.5 |
| Zinc slab, ingot | 6.21 (10-5) | 7.09 (10-8) | 4.3 |
| Coal (RR) | 9.15 (10-6) | 1.60 (10-7) | 43.7 |
| Sulfuric acid, bulk (a) | 5.92 (10-5) | 1.91 (10-6) | 23.3 |
| Sulfuric acid (a) | 5.54 (10-5) | 9.05 (10-7) | 17.2 |
| Methyl alcohol (a) | 7.24 (10-5) | 1.55 (10-7) | 5.4 |
| Phthalic anhydride | 2.78 (10-4) | 1.52 (10-6) | 4.4 |
| Succinate (a) | 5.42 (10-6) | 3.13 (10-8) | 32.6 |
| Kapseals (a) | 2.52 (10-6) | 2.77 (10-9) | 20.9 |
| Meprobanate tablets (a) | 2.59 (10-4) | 3.83 (10-6) | 7.6 |
| Librium (a) | 6.39 (10-5) | 5.40 (10-7) | 11.5 |
| Plywood | 2.08 (10-5) | 1.43 (10-7) | 18.2 |

Notes: See table 6.

$$— \quad — \quad 0 \quad \quad 0 \quad -25\% \quad -25\% \quad 0 \quad 0 \quad 25\% \quad 25\% \quad 0 \quad 0,$$

$$— \quad — \quad 0 \quad -25\% \quad -25\% \quad \quad 0 \quad \quad 0 \quad 25\% \quad 25\% \quad 0 \quad \quad 0 \quad 0.$$

The correlation between the two new series will be positive and will equal .5. If one uses a three-month filter (i.e., averages over the last three monthly percent changes in price), the correlation rises to .67. In general, one initially expects correlation to rise as the period of averaging increases.

Before presenting tabulations of correlations by product for different filter sizes, it will be helpful first to decide what is a "high" or "low" correlation. In other words, we must develop some underlying standard as to how closely two very related series should move. Suppose we adopt the position that two price series that change by identical amounts within, say, three months of each other are "highly" correlated. Let $\rho(F)$ be the contemporaneous correlation of the two price series when averaging over $F$ periods is performed. Suppose that the two series representing percent price changes are identical, are displaced from each other by three months, and that price changes are independent of the preceding price change. Then it is easy to show that

$$\rho(1) = \rho(2) = 0$$

$$\rho(F) = 1 - 3/F \qquad F > 3.$$

This means that the correlation between our two series is .5 for a filter of size 6, and it rises to .75 for filters of one year (12). In general, one should expect that very high correlations (above .7) will probably be unusual for filters below twelve months, even for "well-behaved" price series.

Each of 30 products was analyzed separately. For each product and for each contract type an average correlation for a particular filter size was computed. For example, suppose that there are 10 individual contract transactions for steel plates, each lasting 10 years. The monthly percent change in price (differences in the logs of prices) was calculated for each series for each month. The simple correlation was computed for every combination of contracts (45 pairs), and an average correlation over the 45 pairs was then computed. If the average correlation is high, it says that on average the price series move together. If the average correlation is low, it suggests that price movements for the same good are only very loosely related to each other. If the low correlation persists as the filter increases to say two years, it says that knowing how person $A$'s price has changed

**Table 10**
Heterogeneity measures: correlations among price series

| Product[a] | $\rho(1)$[b] | $\rho(12)$[b] |
|---|---|---|
| Steel plate (m) | .42 | .61 |
| Hot-rolled bars and rods (m) | .42 | .60 |
| Steel pipe and tubing (m) (3″ or less in diameter) | .16 | .25 |
| Copper wire and cable (m) | .53 | .78 |
| Gasoline (a) | .02 | .07 |
| (m) | .04 | .30 |
| Diesel fuel #2 (a) | .00 | .06 |
| (m) | .53 | .69 |
| Fuel oil #2 (a) | .01 | −.03 |
| Fuel oil #6 (a) | .02 | .11 |
| (m) | .26 | .49 |
| Container board, fiberboard (a) | .14 | −.03 |
| (m) | .06 | .16 |
| Caustic soda, liquid (a) | .07 | .07 |
| (m) | .04 | .36 |
| Liquid chlorine (a) | .05 | .08 |
| Oxygen, cylinders (a) | .03 | .17 |
| (m) | .28 | .40 |
| Acetylene (m) | .30 | .54 |
| Portland cement (m) | .15 | .21 |
| Sheet steel and strip, (m) (hot-rolled) | .40 | .44 |
| Rails (m) | .81 | .94 |
| Tie plates (m) | .78 | .88 |
| Steel railway wheels | .37 | .54 |
| Railroad track bolts | .47 | .62 |
| Zinc slab ingots (m) | .52 | .90 |
| Coal (RR) (m) | .14 | .17 |
| Phthalic anhydride (m) | .27 | .68 |
| Sulfuric acid, bulk (a) | .13 | .32 |
| Sulfuric acid (a) | .10 | .07 |
| Methyl alcohol (a) | .22 | .46 |
| Succinate (a) | .00[c] | .00[c] |
| Kapseals (a) | .00[c] | .00[c] |
| Meprobanate tablets (a) | .03 | −.07 |
| Librium (a) | −.02 | −.06 |
| Plywood (m) | .16 | .21 |

a. Contracts are quarterly monthly or monthly (indicated by *m*) or annual (indicated by *a*).
b. $\rho(i)$: correlations of price changes averaged over *i* months.
c. No price movement in most contracts.

over a two-year period doesn't help much in predicting how person $B$'s price will change (averaged over the two-year period).

In table 10, I present measures of average correlations for filters of one month and twelve months for each of the 30 commodities for selected contract types.[18] As expected, $\rho(12)$ usually exceeds $\rho(1)$. If we use the criterion that correlations on the order of .5 and above represent price series that move pretty closely together, we see that for several products there are homogeneities of price movements. On the other hand, there are several products, like cement, container board, plywood, and several chemical products, that have very low (sometimes even negative) correlations even for twelve-month averaging. In fact, it is startling to find so many products where it is clear that some mechanism other than price alone is allocating resources.[19] It is noteworthy that container board exhibits low correlations of price, since I understand that quantity rationing is sometimes used in the paper industry in place of price rationing.[20]

It is interesting to see whether there is any agreement between the two methods of characterizing heterogeneity in tables 9 and 10. In fact, there is a low degree of agreement. The simple correlation between the measures of heterogeneity in tables 9 and 10 is below .1 and is not statistically significant. On the other hand, there is a high negative, statistically significant correlation between $\rho(1)$ (or $\rho(12)$) and such other measures of heterogeneity as the coefficients of variation for rigidity, price change, and length of association. [21] This may imply that the measure in table 9 is capturing an aspect of price different from the other measures or that the measure in table 9 is not a useful one.

## 7 Implications for Price Behavior

Tables 1 through 10 can form the foundation for several predictions. For example, one can predict the following:

• The products with high correlations for $\rho(12)$ in table 10 should tend to have more serial correlation in their WPI (wholesale price index) components than products with low correlations.

• Industrywide price adjustment for products with high values for $\rho(1)$ in table 10 should tend to be swift.

• Price controls on products with long spells of rigid prices (table 1) are less likely to have harmful efficiency effects than controls on products with short spells of rigidity because nonprice methods are probably already used to allocate resources for products with very rigid prices.

I have not systematically investigated these three claims for each of the products listed in table 10. However, I have done some work to corroborate at least some of the claims for some products. For example, from table 10, copper wire and cable has a $\rho(12)$ of .78, while gasoline (monthly) has $\rho(12)$ of only .30. The correlation between the monthly WPI and the monthly WPI lagged once (1957–1966) for copper wire and cable is .99, which, as expected, exceeds that same measure (.88) for gasoline.[22]

Michael Bordo (1980) has estimated adjustment lags in prices for some of the commodity groups well represented in table 10, such as metals and metal products, chemicals, and fuel. Based on the size of $\rho(1)$ in table 10, I would predict the speed of adjustment to be fastest in metals and metal products, and the speed of adjustment in fuels and chemicals to be much slower and roughly equal to each other. In fact, Bordo (p. 1105) finds the mean lag of price adjustments for metals and metal products to be 3.66 months, while the lag for fuels and chemicals are 6.64 and 6.20 months, respectively.

Finally, the only evidence I could find on the difficulty of price controls is John Kenneth Galbraith's *A Theory of Price Control* (1952), which is an account of his experience in controlling prices during World War II when he headed the Office of Price Administration (OPA). Although he does not deal explicitly with all the products in tables 1 through 10, he does talk about steel products, which from table 1 have a high degree of price rigidity. Galbraith states, "The Office of Price Administration controlled the price of all steel mill products with far less manpower and trouble than was required for a far smaller volume of steel scrap. ... It is relatively easy to fix prices that are already fixed" (p. 17).

Although bits of evidence corroborate the predictions for some types of commodities, they are obviously far from conclusive. They do, however, show the value of evidence like that in tables 1 through 10.

## 8  Structural Determinants of Price Behavior

Is there any correlation between industry characteristics and any of the measures of heterogeneity such as those in tables 9 and 10? Using 30 products, I correlated the measures of heterogeneity in price movements of tables 9 and 10 with the following variables:

• Mean absolute growth and variability of price (the higher this number is, the higher the expected correlation of price movements).

• Measures of competitiveness: (a) four-firm concentration ratio and (b) fraction of shipments beyond 500 miles.

• Growth and variability of total industry shipments.

• Length of buyer-seller association.

Simple correlations never emerged as statistically significant (with the exception of the variance of the growth rate in price), though the correlations were generally in the positive direction. However, since no more than 30 observations were available, it would be premature to conclude that these structural characteristics do not influence price heterogeneity in the industry.

Is there any correlation between concentration and duration of price rigidity or length of association or average price change? The only significant correlation was between concentration (four firms) and duration of price rigidity. That correlation was statistically significant at the 5 percent level. The correlation implies that for every 10-point increase in the four-firm concentration ratio, prices remain rigid for an extra 1.6 months.[23] This finding is particularly interesting because it suggests that allocations are performed differently in concentrated and unconcentrated markets. I believe it is premature to draw the conclusions, implicit in the work of Means (1935), Burns (1936), Galbraith (1952), and others, that the markets have stopped working when they become concentrated. Instead, an alternative interpretation is that as firms become large, they supplant the market's exclusive reliance on price as an allocation device and resort to other methods. In a world filled with transaction costs, exclusive reliance on a market-generated price to allocate goods could well be inferior to other nonprice allocation methods. However, markets that use nonprice allocation will respond to market shocks much differently than markets that exclusively use price to allocate. See my forthcoming paper for a fuller development of this theory.

## 9  Conclusions

Since this paper began with a summary of the empirical results, I will not repeat them here. The main conclusion is that several of the empirical results are sufficiently startling that we should reexamine the central, often exclusive, role assigned to the price mechanism in theories of efficient resource allocation. The price mechanism has not necessarily failed; rather, alternative allocation mechanisms are used in addition to the price mechanism to achieve efficiency.

## Appendix

Transactions were classified into one of Stigler and Kindahl's ten categories. The most important classifications include the following:

* Annual contract: contract in force for one year
* Annual average: average of transaction prices during the year
* Annual-monthly: annual observations of a transaction that occurs monthly
* Semiannual contract: contract in force for six months
* Semiannual average: average of transaction prices during six months
* Quarterly contract: contract in force for three months
* Quarterly average: average of transaction prices during the quarter
* Quarterly-monthly: quarterly observation of a transaction that occurs monthly
* Irregular: irregular
* Monthly: monthly observations of a transaction that occurs monthly

Tables A1 and A2 present characteristics of contracts by product, and table A3 presents correlations among measures of heterogeneity.

Tables 1A and 2A of my 1986 working paper report the importance of each classification by product group and for individual products.

## Acknowledgments

I thank the NSF and the Law and Economics Program at the University of Chicago for support. I thank Frederic Miller, Virginia France, Larry Harris, Deborah Lucas, and Steven Oi for research assistance. I also thank Claire Friedland and George Stigler for making these data available to me and for assisting me in their use. I thank Edward Lazear, Sam Peltzman, George Stigler, two anonymous referees, and participants at seminars at the National Bureau of Economic Research (Stanford) and the Universities of Chicago, Montreal, Pennsylvania, and Virginia for helpful comments.

**Table A1**
Characteristics of contracts by product

| Product | Average length of association between buyer and seller (months) | Average size of absolute value of percent price change | Product | Average length of association between buyer and seller (months) | Average size of absolute value of percent price change |
|---|---|---|---|---|---|
| Steel | 105 | 3.5 | Cement | 103 | 3.0 |
| Nonferrous metals | 86 | 4.0 | Glass | 91 | 4.2 |
| Petroleum | 87 | 4.4 | Truck motors | 82 | 2.7 |
| Rubber tires | 98 | 3.9 | | | |
| Paper | 91 | 3.4 | Plywood | 114 | 5.0 |
| Chemicals | 81 | 7.0 | Household appliances | 75 | 1.0 |

**Table A2**
Characteristics of contracts by product

| Product | Average length of association between buyer, seller (months) | Average size of absolute value of percent price change |
|---|---|---|
| Steel plates | 108 | 3.8 |
| Hot-rolled bars and rods | 109 | 3.7 |
| Steel pipe and tubing (3″ or less in diameter) | 114 | 4.6 |
| Copper wire and cable (bare) | 68 | 4.4 |
| Gasoline (regular) | 91 | 3.3 |
| Diesel oil #2 | 94 | 4.3 |
| Fuel oil #2 | 89 | 4.6 |
| Residual fuel oil #6 | 73 | 5.8 |
| Container board, fiberboard | 78 | 5.2 |
| Caustic soda (liquid) | 84 | 7.8 |
| Chlorine liquid | 89 | 5.0 |
| Oxygen, cylinders | 109 | 11.5 |
| Acetylene | 116 | 6.9 |
| Portland cement (by sack) | 104 | 3.7 |
| Steel sheet and strip, hot-rolled | 120 | 5.9 |
| New rail (RR) | 116 | 3.9 |
| Tie plates (RR) | 119 | 4.5 |
| Steel wheels, "one wear" (RR) | 119 | 3.8 |
| Track bolts (RR) | 119 | 4.2 |
| Zinc slab ingots | 104 | 4.8 |
| Coal (RR) | 119 | 3.7 |
| Kraft wrapping paper | 94 | 4.3 |
| Paper bags | 88 | 4.8 |
| Sulfuric acid, bulk | 96 | 4.8 |
| Sulfuric acid | 103 | 3.5 |
| Methyl alcohol | 91 | 7.1 |
| Phthalic anhydride | 93 | 11.7 |
| Succinate antibiotic | 58 | 8.3 |
| Kapseals antibiotic | 70 | 14.9 |
| Meprobanate tablets | 64 | 12.1 |
| Librium | 48 | 8.6 |
| Plywood | 110 | 5.2 |

**Table A3**
Correlations among measures of heterogeneity

|            | CV DP | CV assoc. | CV var. | $\rho(1)$ | $\rho(12)$ |
|------------|-------|-----------|---------|-----------|------------|
| CV dur.    | .88[a] | .41[a]   | −.03    | −.63[a]   | −.60[a]    |
| CV DP      |       | .35[a]    | .39[a]  | −.57[a]   | −.66[a]    |
| CV assoc.  |       |           | −.58[a] | −.47[a]   | −.30       |
| CV var.    |       |           |         | .08       | −0.1       |
| $\rho(1)$  |       |           |         |           | .91[a]     |
| $\rho(12)$ |       |           |         |           |            |

Notes: CV dur. = coefficient of variation of durations; CV DP = coefficient of variation of the absolute values of price changes (log difference); CV assoc. = coefficient of variation of the lengths of association; CV var. = coefficient of variation of the actual price changes; $\rho(1)$, $\rho(12)$ = correlations of price changes averaged over $i$ months.
a. Significant at 5 percent level.

# Notes

1. Research on prices includes the early and important work of Frederick Mills (1926), Gardiner Means (1935), and more recently George Stigler and James Kindahl (1970).

2. The form in which the data exist do not allow conclusive determination that the buyer is dealing with only one seller. However, it is believed that only one seller is involved when the buyer is reporting prices pursuant to a contract. Furthermore, when prices remain unchanged or when the specification of the good remains unchanged from observation to observation, the buyer is also likely to be dealing with only one seller. I thank Claire Friedland, who helped collect the original data, for helpful discussions on this matter. For expositional ease I will regard each price series as arising from a transaction between one buyer and one seller. I will point out when this assumption would substantially alter the interpretation of the results.

3. An alternative explanation is that price movements for the same product are similar across different transactions at any one instant but not across time. As we will see in section 6, this explanation will turn out to be incorrect.

4. Alternatively, the heterogeneity in spells could arise because supply and demand are changing over time. This last explanation turns out not to provide the full answer, as we will see in section 6. Moreover, a table analogous to table 2 but based on transactions, not spells, confirms the heterogeneity across transactions.

5. Even if the fixed cost of changing price is small, one cannot necessarily rule out large welfare effects caused by this fixed cost. In a model with distortions, even small fixed costs can lead to large welfare losses. See, for example, Mankiw (1985) and Akerlof and Yellen (1985). Furthermore, the presence of even small fixed costs might affect the time-series properties of economic variables. See, for example, Rotemberg (1982) and Blanchard (1982).

6. I recognize the possibility that nonefficiency explanations may help explain some pricing behavior (Akerlof and Yellen 1985; Kahneman, Knetsch, and Thaler 1986), but feel that the efficiency explanations have not yet been fully explored (see my forthcoming paper).

7. Length of association is measured as the total time the buyer and seller have engaged in a transaction for a product whose specifications may change over the time of the association. This measure is a noisy one, because the buyer and seller may be engaged in other transactions that affect their knowledge of each other and may have been dealing with each other prior to the beginning of the data set. Moreover, to the extent that a buyer reported prices from several suppliers, rather than one, for each reported price series, the measure of length of association is flawed. (See note 2.)

8. See table A1 for data by product group on average length of association and average price change. Table 1 reports average duration of price rigidity. Correlation of these three variables across product groups is not as good a way of uncovering systematic relationships among these three variables as is correlation of the three variables across transactions for the same product, because many factors differ between product groups.

9. This assumes that price changes are motivated by changes in the permanent price component, whose changes are assumed larger than the transitory component. The reverse relation between permanent and transitory would flip the prediction.

10. My 1986 working paper reports data on average rigidity, average price change, and average length of association by product and type of contract.

11. A model that would generate such results would be one where costs are undergoing a random walk, production is constant returns to scale, and the cost of changing price is negatively related to length of association.

12. This must be qualified by agency theories of monitoring.

13. One curious finding is that price rigidity is negatively correlated at a statistically significant level for truck and steel contracts.

14. The simple and rank correlations of average duration and the standard deviation of duration exceed .9.

15. Data based on transactions (not spells) as the unit of analysis, like table 6, confirm this.

16. Most correlations involve between 20 to 30 observations, with 15 being the minimum number of observations required in order to be reported.

17. Some products from table 5 were dropped because of incompleteness of the data.

18. Filters of 2 years produced results similar to those for filters of 1 year. Correlations were also calculated on the timing of price changes (0 or $\pm 1$ indicating whether or not a price change occurred and its direction), and the same low correlations persisted.

19. My 1979 article presents a theory on buyer heterogeneity, which shows how prices to different buyers can exhibit low (or negative) correlations.

20. Based on personal discussions with industry members.

21. Table A3 in the appendix reports these correlations.

22. The source for WPI data was Stigler and Kindahl (1970, appendix C).

23. The OLS equation is (with standard errors in parentheses)

$$\text{Av. duration} = 4.97 + 16.12\,\text{CR4} \qquad R^2 = .22$$
$$\phantom{\text{Av. duration} = }(3.12) \quad (6.08) \qquad \text{SEE} = 4.9$$

where Av. duration is the average length of a spell of price rigidity and CR4 is the four-firm concentration ratio. This equation is based on 27 observations. The CR4 variable is the 1963 four-firm concentration ratio for the 5-digit SIC code that seems to correspond to the product. This correspondence is not exact and for that reason, together with the small number of observations, the results should be regarded with some caution. Another interesting finding involving concentration is that concentrated industries have a greater frequency of small price changes.

# References

Akerlof, George A., and Yellen, Janet L. "Can Small Deviations from Rationality Make Significant Differences to Economic Equilibrium?" *American Economic Review*, September 1985, 75, 708–720.

Barro, Robert. "A Theory of Monopolistic Price Adjustment." *Review of Economic Studies*, January 1972, 39, 17–26.

Blanchard, Olivier J. "Price Desynchronization and Price Level Inertia." National Bureau of Economic Research, working paper 900, 1982.

Bordo, Michael. "The Effects of Monetary Change on Relative Commodity Prices and the Role of Long-Term Contracts." *Journal of Political Economy*, December 1980, 88, 1088–1109.

Burns, Arthur. *The Decline of Competition*. New York: McGraw-Hill, 1936.

Carlton, Dennis W. "The Rigidity of Prices." National Bureau of Economic Research, working paper 1813, 1986.

Carlton, Dennis W. "Market Behavior with Demand Uncertainty and Price Inflexibility." *American Economic Review*, September 1978, 68, 571–87.

Carlton, Dennis W. "Contracts, Price Rigidity, and Market Equilibrium." *Journal of Political Economy*, October 1979, 87, 1034–1062.

Carlton, Dennis W. "The Disruptive Effect of Inflation on the Organization of Markets." In R. E. Hall, ed., *Inflation*. Chicago: University of Chicago Press, 1982.

Carlton, Dennis W. "Equilibrium Fluctuations When Price and Delivery Lags Clear the Market." *Bell Journal of Economics*, Autumn 1983, 14, 562–572.

Carlton, Dennis W. "The Theory and the Facts of How Markets Clear: Is Industrial Organization Valuable for Understanding Macroeconomics?" In R. Schmalensee and R. Willig, ed., *Handbook of Industrial Organization*. Amsterdam: North-Holland, forthcoming.

Galbraith, J. K. *A Theory of Price Control*. Combridge: Harvard University Press, 1952.

Hall, Robert E. "The Apparent Rigidity of Prices." National Bureau of Economic Research, working paper 1347, 1984.

Kahneman, Daniel, Knetch, Jack L., and Thaler, Richard. "Fairness as a Constraint on Profit Seeking: Entitlements in the Market." *American Economic Review*, September 1986, 76, 728–41.

Mankiw, N. Gregory. "Small Menu Costs and Large Business Cycles: A Macroeconomic Model of Monopoly." *Quarterly Journal of Economics*, May 1985, 100, 529–538.

Means, Gardiner C. "Industrial Prices and Their Relative Inflexibility." U.S. Senate document 13, 74th Congress, 1st session, Washington 1935.

Mills, Frederick C. *The Behavior of Prices*. National Bureau of Economic Research, General Series, no. 11. New York: Arno Press, 1927.

Okun, Arthur. *Prices and Quantities: A Macroeconomic Analysis*. Washington: Brookings Institution, 1981.

Rosen, Sherwin. "Implicit Contracts: A Survey." *Journal of Economic Literature*, September 1985, 23, 1144–1175.

Rotemberg, Julio. "Monopolistic Price Adjustment and Aggregate Output." *Review of Economic Studies*, October 1982, 49, 517–531.

Stigler, George, and Kindahl, James. *The Behavior of Industrial Prices*. National Bureau of Economic Research, General Series, no. 90. New York: Columbia University Press, 1970.

Telser, Lester. "A Theory of Self-Enforcing Agreements." *Journal of Business*, January 1980, 53, 27–44.

Williamson, Oliver. *Markets and Hierarchies—Analysis and Antitrust Implications: A Study in the Economies of Internal Organization*. New York: Free Press, 1975.

# 6 The New Keynesian Economics and the Output-Inflation Trade-off

**Laurence Ball, N. Gregory Mankiw, and David Romer**

In the early 1980s the Keynesian view of business cycles was in trouble. The problem was not new empirical evidence against Keynesian theories but weakness in the theories themselves.[1] According to the Keynesian view, fluctuations in output arise largely from fluctuations in nominal aggregate demand. These changes in demand have real effects because nominal wages and prices are rigid. But in Keynesian models of the 1970s, the crucial nominal rigidities were assumed rather than explained—assumed directly, as in disequilibrium models, or introduced through theoretically arbitrary assumptions about labor contracts.[2] Indeed, it was clearly in the interests of agents to eliminate the rigidities they were assumed to create. If wages, for example, were set above the market-clearing level, firms could increase profits by reducing wages. Microeconomics teaches us to reject models in which, as Robert Lucas puts it, "there are $500 bills on the sidewalk." Thus the 1970s and early 1980s saw many economists turn away from Keynesian theories and toward new classical models with flexible wages and prices.

But Keynesian economics has made much progress in the past few years. Recent research has produced models in which optimizing agents choose to create nominal rigidities. This accomplishment derives largely from a central insight: nominal rigidities, and hence the real effects of nominal demand shocks, can be large even if the frictions preventing full nominal flexibility are slight. Seemingly minor aspects of the economy, such as costs of price adjustment and the asynchronized timing of price changes by different firms, can explain large nonneutralities.

Theoretical demonstrations that Keynesian models can be reconciled with microeconomics do not constitute proof that Keynesian theories are correct. Indeed, a weakness of recent models of nominal rigidities is that they do not appear to have novel empirical implications. As Lawrence Summers argues,

> While words like menu costs and overlapping contracts are often heard, little if any empirical work has demonstrated connection between the extent of these phenomena and the pattern of cyclical fluctuations. It is difficult to think of any anomalies that Keynesian research in the "nominal rigidities" tradition has resolved, or of any new phenomena that it has rendered comprehensible.[3]

*Brookings Papers on Economic Activity*, 1988, no. 1: 1–65. Copyright © 1988 by the Brookings Institution. Reprinted with permission.

The purpose of this paper is to provide evidence supporting new Keynesian theories. We point out a simple prediction of Keynesian models that contradicts other leading macroeconomic theories and show that it holds in actual economies. In doing so, we point out a "new phenomenon" that Keynesian theories "render comprehensible."

The prediction that we test concerns the effects of steady inflation. In Keynesian models, nominal shocks have real effects because nominal prices change infrequently. An increase in the average rate of inflation causes firms to adjust prices more frequently to keep up with the rising price level. In turn, more frequent price changes imply that prices adjust more quickly to nominal shocks and thus that the shocks have smaller real effects. We test this prediction by examining the relation between average inflation and the size of the real effects of nominal shocks both across countries and over time. We measure the effects of nominal shocks by the slope of the short-run Phillips curve.

Other prominent macroeconomic theories do not predict that average inflation affects the slope of the Phillips curve. In particular, our empirical work provides a sharp test between the Keynesian explanation for the Phillips curve and the leading new classical alternative, the Lucas imperfect-information model.[4] Indeed, one goal of this paper is to redo Lucas's famous analysis and dramatically reinterpret his results. Lucas and later authors show that countries with highly variable aggregate demand have steep Phillips curves. That is, nominal shocks in these countries have little effect on output. Lucas interprets this finding as evidence that highly variable demand reduces the perceived relative price changes resulting from nominal shocks. We provide a Keynesian interpretation of Lucas's result: more variable demand, like high average inflation, leads to more frequent price adjustment. We then test the differing implications of the two theories for the effects of average inflation. Our results are consistent with the Keynesian explanation for the Phillips curve and inconsistent with the classical explanation.

In addition to providing evidence about macroeconomic theories, our finding that average inflation affects the short-run output-inflation tradeoff is important for policy. For example, it is likely that the trade-off facing policymakers in the United States has changed as a consequence of disinflation in the 1980s. Our estimates imply that a reduction in average inflation from 10 percent to 5 percent substantially alters the short-run impact of aggregate demand.

The body of the paper consists of three major sections. The first discusses the new research that provides microeconomic foundations for Keynesian theories. The second presents a model of price adjustment. It demonstrates the connection between average inflation and the slope of the Phillips curve and contrasts this result with the predictions of other theories. The third section provides cross-country and time-series evidence that supports the predictions of the model.

## New Keynesian Theories

According to Keynesian economics, fluctuations in employment and output arise largely from fluctuations in nominal aggregate demand. The reason that nominal shocks matter is that nominal wages and prices are not fully flexible. These views are the basis for conventional accounts of macroeconomic events. For example, the consensus explanation for the 1982 recession is slow growth in nominal demand resulting from tight monetary policy. The research program described here is modest in the sense that it seeks to strengthen the foundations of this conventional thinking, not to provide a new theory of fluctuations. In particular, its goal is to answer the theoretical question of how nominal rigidities arise from optimizing behavior, since the absence of an answer in the 1970s was largely responsible for the decline of Keynesian economics.

In the following discussion we first describe the central point of the recent literature: large nominal rigidities are possible even if the frictions preventing full nominal flexibility are small. We next describe some phenomena that greatly strengthen the basic argument, including rigidities in *real* wages and prices and asynchronized timing of price changes. We then discuss two innovations in recent models that are largely responsible for their success: the introduction of imperfect competition and an emphasis on price as well as wage rigidity. Finally, we argue that the ideas in recent work are indispensable for a plausible Keynesian account of fluctuations.[5]

### Small nominal frictions and large nominal rigidities

The recent literature on nominal rigidities enters an argument that Keynesians appeared to be losing. Members of the new classical school that developed in the 1970s challenged Keynesians to explain the rigidities in Keynesian models. In response Keynesians sometimes cited costs of adjusting prices. But as the classicals pointed out, these costs, while surely present, appear small. Indeed, the frequently mentioned "menu costs"—the costs of printing new menus and catalogs, of replacing price tags, and so on—sound trivial. Thus the impediments to nominal flexibility in actual economies appear too small to provide a foundation for Keynesian models.

A common but mistaken response is that there are many obvious sources of large wage and price rigidities: implicit contracts, customer markets, efficiency wages, insider-outsider relationships, and so on. The problem is that these phenomena imply rigidities in *real* wages and prices, while the Keynesian theory depends on rigidities in *nominal* wages and prices. Real rigidities are no impediment to complete flexibility of nominal prices, because full adjustment to a nominal shock does not require any change in real prices. The absence of models of nominal rigidity reflects the microeconomic proposition that agents do not care about nominal magnitudes. The only apparent departures from this proposition in actual economies are the small costs of nominal adjustment.

Thus recent work begins with the premise that it is inexpensive to reduce nominal rigidity and asks how substantial rigidity nonetheless arises. The central answer of the literature is presented by Mankiw, Akerlof and Yellen, Blanchard and Kiyotaki, and Ball and Romer.[6]

**Second-order private costs and first-order business cycles**   Mankiw and Akerlof and Yellen make a simple but important point. They study imperfectly competitive economies and show that the cost of nominal rigidities to price setters can be much smaller than the macroeconomic effects. An example that illustrates the cost to price setters is a firm that initially sets its price at the profit-maximizing level but does not adjust after the money supply falls. We let $\pi(\cdot)$ denote the firm's profits as a function of its price and let $P$ be the firm's predetermined price and $P^*$ its profit-maximizing price, which it would set if it adjusted. Using a Taylor expansion, we can approximate the firm's profit loss from not adjusting as

$$\pi(P^*) - \pi(P) \approx \pi'(P^*)(P^* - P) - \tfrac{1}{2}\pi''(P^*)(P^* - P)^2. \tag{1}$$

But since $P^*$ maximizes profits, $\pi'(P^*)$ is zero. Thus the profit loss from nonadjustment is second order, that is, proportional to the square of $(P^* - P)$. As long as the predetermined price is close to the profit-maximizing price, the cost of price rigidity to the firm is small.

But rigidity can have first-order macroeconomic effects. An increase in nominal money with nominal prices fixed leads to a first-order increase in real aggregate demand and hence in real output. For example, if the aggregate-demand curve is simply $Y = M/P$, rigid prices imply a change in output proportional to the change in money.

The effect on social welfare is also first order, as follows from the assumption of imperfect competition. Under imperfect competition, the profit-maximizing price is socially suboptimal. The price is too high, and output is too low. Thus at $P*$ the first derivative of welfare with respect to the firm's price is negative: welfare would rise if the price fell below $P*$. Nonadjustment to a fall in money implies that $P$ is greater than $P*$. Since the first derivative of welfare is negative, the welfare loss is first order.

Because the cost of rigidity to a price setter is second order while the macroeconomic effects are first order, the latter can be much larger. This finding resolves the puzzle of why price setters refuse to incur the small costs of reducing the business cycle through more flexible prices. Despite the large macroeconomic effects, the private incentives are small.

**Aggregate demand externalities**    Blanchard and Kiyotaki provide an important interpretation of the result in Mankiw and in Akerlof and Yellen: the macroeconomic effects of nominal rigidity differ from the private costs because rigidity has an "aggregate demand externality." A few equations make this clear. Suppose the demand for the product of firm $i$ depends on aggregate spending and on the firm's relative price:

$$Y_i^D = \left(\frac{P_i}{P}\right)^{-\epsilon} Y. \tag{2}$$

For simplicity, aggregate demand is given by a quantity equation:[7]

$$Y = \frac{M}{P}. \tag{3}$$

Combining equations 2 and 3 yields

$$Y_i^D = \left(\frac{M}{P}\right)\left(\frac{P_i}{P}\right)^{-\epsilon}. \tag{4}$$

According to equation 4, firm $i$'s demand depends on its relative price and on real money, which determines aggregate demand. Changes in real money shift the demand curve facing firm $i$, and the firm's price determines its position on the demand curve.

If $M$ falls and firm $i$ does not adjust, the second-order cost to firm $i$ is that $P_i/P$ does not adjust to the new profit-maximizing level. The externality is that rigidity in firm $i$'s price contributes to rigidity in the aggregate price level. Given the fall in nominal money, rigidity in $P$ implies a first-order fall in real money, which reduces demand for all firms' goods. In other words, there is an externality because adjustment of all prices would prevent a fall in real aggregate demand, but each firm is a small part of the economy and thus ignores this macroeconomic benefit.

The importance of the externality is illustrated by a firm in a recession caused by tight money. To the firm, the recession means an inward shift of its demand curve and a resulting first-order loss in profits. The firm would very much like to shift its demand curve back out, but of course it cannot do so by changing its price. Instead, price adjustment would yield only the second-order gain from optimally dividing the losses from the recession between reduced sales and a lower price. The recession would end and everyone would be much better off if all firms adjusted. But each firm believes that it cannot end the recession and therefore may fail to adjust even if the costs of adustment are much smaller than the costs of the recession.

This argument resembles standard microeconomic analyses of externalities. Consider the classic example of pollution. Pollution would be greatly reduced, and social welfare greatly improved, if each person incurred the small cost of walking to the trash can at the end of the block. But each individual ignores this when he throws his wrapper on the street because he is only one of many polluters. Because of externalities, economists do not find highly inefficient levels of pollution puzzling even though the costs of reducing pollution are small. For similar reasons, highly inefficient nominal rigidities are not a mystery even though menu costs are small.

**Externalities from fluctuations in demand**   Keynesians believe not only that shocks to nominal aggregate demand cause large fluctuations in output and welfare, but also that these fluctuations are inefficient, and thus that stabilization of demand is desirable. The models surveyed so far do not provide a foundation for this view. As explained above, nonadjustment of prices to a fall in demand leads to large reductions in output and welfare. But nonadjustment to a *rise* in demand leads to higher output and, because output is initially too low under imperfect competition, to higher welfare. Thus the implications of fluctuations for *average* welfare, and hence the desirability of reducing fluctuations, are unclear. Indeed, Ball and Romer show that the first-order welfare effects of fluctuations average to zero, which means that the first-order/second-order distinction is irrelevant to this issue.[8]

Nonetheless, Ball and Romer show, by comparing the average social and private costs of nominal rigidity, that small nominal frictions are sufficient for large reductions in average welfare. The private cost is fluctuations of a firm's relative price around the profit-maximizing level. The social cost is the private cost plus the cost of fluctuations in real aggregate demand. Greater flexibility would stabilize real demand, but each firm ignores its effect on the variance of demand, just as it ignores its effect on the level of demand after a given shock. Although both the average social and average private costs are second order, Ball and Romer show that the former may be much larger: fluctuations in aggregate demand can be much more costly than fluctuations in relative prices. As a result, small frictions can prevent firms from adopting greater flexibility even if business cycles are highly inefficient.

### Still larger rigidities

The papers discussed so far establish that nominal rigidities can be far larger than the frictions that cause them. But as we now describe, the simple models in these papers cannot fully explain nonneutralities of the size and persistence observed in actual economies. Therefore, we turn to more complicated models that incorporate realistic phenomena that magnify nominal rigidities. These phenomena include rigidities in *real* wages and prices and asynchronized timing of price changes by different firms.

**Real rigidities**     As we argue above, real rigidities alone are no impediment to full nominal flexibility. But Ball and Romer show that a high degree of real rigidity, defined as small responses of real wages and real prices to changes in real demand, greatly increases the nonneutralities arising from small nominal frictions.[9]

This finding is important because, although models with nominal frictions but no real rigidities can in principle produce large nominal rigidities, they do so only for implausible parameter values. Most important, large rigidities arise only if labor supply is highly elastic, while labor supply elasticities in actual economies appear small. The role of labor supply is illustrated by a hypothetical economy with imperfect competition and menu costs in the goods market but a Walrasian labor market. If menu costs led to nominal price rigidity, then nominal shocks would cause large shifts in labor demand. But if labor supply were inelastic, these shifts in labor demand would cause large changes in the real wage and thereby create large incentives for price setters to adjust their prices. As a result, nominal rigidity would not be an equilibrium.

While for plausible parameter values nominal frictions alone produce little nominal rigidity, Ball and Romer show that considerable rigidity can arise if the frictions are combined with real rigidities arising from efficiency wages, customer markets, and the like. For example, substantial nominal rigidity can arise from a combination of real rigidity in the labor market and imperfect competition and menu costs in the goods market. If firms pay efficiency wages, for instance, then real wages may be set above the market-clearing level, so that workers are off their labor supply curves. In this situation a fall in labor demand can greatly reduce employment without a large fall in the real wage even if labor supply is inelastic.

The importance of real rigidities for explaining nominal rigidities is not settled, because there is no consensus about the sources and magnitudes of real rigidities in actual economies. In particular, phenomena like efficiency wages and customer markets increase nominal rigidity to the extent that they reduce desired responses of real wages and real prices to demand shifts, but economists are still unsure of the sizes of these effects. Further research on real rigidities will lead to a better understanding of nominal rigidities.

**Staggered price setting**    Even when real rigidities are added, the models surveyed so far cannot fully explain the size and persistence of the real effects of nominal shocks. In these models, the effects of shocks are eliminated when nominal prices adjust. In actual economies, recessions following severe demand contractions can last for several years, and while individual prices are fixed for substantial periods, these periods are generally shorter than several years. Thus models with sticky prices must explain why the effects of shocks persist after all prices are changed.

An explanation is provided by the literature on staggered price setting, which shows that if firms change prices at different times, the adjustment of the aggregate price level to shocks can take much longer than the time between adjustments of each individual price.[10] The "price level inertia" caused by staggering implies that nominal shocks can have large and long-lasting real effects even if individual prices change frequently.

A simple example makes clear the importance of the timing of price changes. Suppose first that every firm adjusts its price on the first of each month, so that price setting is synchronized. If the money supply falls on June 10, output is reduced from June 10 to July 1, because nominal prices are fixed during this period. But on July 1 all prices adjust in proportion to the fall in money, and the recession ends.

Now suppose that half of all firms set prices on the first of each month and half on the fifteenth. If the money supply falls on June 10, then on June 15 half the firms have have an opportunity to adjust their prices. But in this case they may choose to make little adjustment. Because half of all nominal prices remain fixed, adjustment of the other prices implies changes in *relative* prices, which firms may not want. (In contrast, if all prices change simultaneously, full nominal adjustment does not affect relative prices.) If the June 15 price setters make little adjustment, then the other firms make little adjustment when their turn comes on July 1, because they do not desire relative price changes either. And so on. The price level declines slowly as the result of small decreases every first and fifteenth, and the real effects of the fall in money die out slowly. In short, price adjustment is slow because neither group of firms is willing to be the first to make large cuts.[11]

As Blanchard emphasizes, if staggering occurs among firms at different points in a chain of production, its effects are strengthened.[12] A firm's profit-maximizing price is tied to both the prices of its inputs and the prices of goods for which its product is an input (the latter influence demand for the firm's product). Thus a firm does not want to adjust its price to a shock if these other prices do not adjust at the same time. This reluctance to make asynchronized adjustments causes price level inertia. Blanchard shows that the degree of inertia increases the longer the chain of production: it takes a long time for the gradual adjustment of prices to make its way through a complicated system.

The literature on staggered price setting complements that on nominal rigidities arising from menu costs. The degree of rigidity in the aggregate price level depends on both the frequency and the timing of individual price changes. Menu costs cause prices to adjust infrequently. For a given frequency of individual adjustment, staggering slows the adjustment of the price level. Large aggregate rigidities can thus be explained by a combination of staggering and nominal frictions: the former magnifies the rigidities arising from the latter.

**Asymmetric effects of demand shocks**   We conclude this part of our discussion by mentioning a little-explored possibility for strengthening Keynesian models. The models surveyed imply symmetric responses of the economy to rises and falls in nominal aggregate demand. For example, in menu cost models the range of shocks to which prices do not adjust is symmetric around zero, and so is the range of possible changes in output. But traditional Keynesian models often imply asymmetric effects of demand shifts. In undergraduate texts, for example, the aggregate supply curve is often drawn so that decreases in demand lead to large output losses while the effects of increases are mostly dissipated through higher prices. Such asymmetries are intuitively appealing, and they greatly strengthen the Keynesian view that demand stabilization is desirable: stabilization raises the average levels of output and employment as well as reducing the variances. It is unclear whether plausible modifications of new Keynesian models can produce asymmetries. Asymmetric effects of shocks could arise from asymmetric price rigidity—prices that are sticky downward but not upward—but this is another appealing notion that is difficult to formalize.[13]

### The new assumptions in new Keynesian models

Aside from the specific arguments outlined above, recent research establishes the general point that nominal rigidities can result from optimizing choices of agents in well-specified models. This contrasts with the ad hoc imposition of rigidities in many of the Keynesian models of the 1970s. Recent progress is largely a result of two innovations in modeling: the introduction of imperfect competition and greater emphasis on price rather than wage rigidities.

**Imperfect competition**   Microeconomists have long recognized that sticky prices and perfect competition are incompatible.[14] In a competitive market, a firm does not set its price, but accepts the price quoted by the Walrasian auctioneer. Only under imperfect competition, when firms set prices, does it make sense to ask whether a firm adjusts its price to a shock. Nonetheless, Keynesian models of the 1970s, most clearly disequilibrium models, imposed nominal rigidities on otherwise Walrasian economies. The result was embarrassments in the form of unappealing results or the need for additional arbitrary assumptions. Many recent models simply generalize earlier models by allowing the firms' demand curves to slope down. This single modification sweeps away many of the problems with older models. Specifically, the new models with imperfect competition offer six advantages:

• *Private costs of rigidity are second order.* Under perfect competition, the gains from nominal adjustment are large. For example, if nominal demand rises and prices do not adjust, there is excess demand. In this situation, an individual firm can raise its price significantly and still sell as much output as before, which implies a large increase in profits. In contrast, under imperfect competition a higher price always implies lower sales. Starting from the profit-maximizing price-quantity combination, the gains from trading off price and sales after a shock are second order.

• *Output is demand determined.* When price rigidity is imposed on a Walrasian market, so that the market does not clear, it is natural to assume that quantity equals the smaller of supply and demand, so that output falls below the Walrasian level when price is either above or below the Walrasian level. But Keynesians believe that when prices are rigid, increases in demand, which mean prices below Walrasian levels, raise output, just as decreases in demand reduce output. This result is built into many Keynesian models through the unappealing assumption that output is demand determined even if demand exceeds supply. For example, in the Gray-Fischer contract model, firms hire as much labor as they want, regardless of the preferences of workers.[15] In contrast, under imperfect competition, demand determination arises naturally. Firms set prices and then meet demand. Crucially, if demand rises, firms are happy to sell more even if they do not adjust their prices, because under imperfect competition price initially exceeds marginal cost. Thus changes in demand always cause changes in output in the same direction.

• *Booms raise welfare.* Under perfect competition, the equilibrium level of output in the absence of shocks is efficient. Thus increases in output resulting from positive shocks, as well as decreases resulting from negative shocks, reduce welfare. In the Gray-Fischer model, for example, half the welfare loss from the business cycle occurs when workers are required to work more than they want. In actual economies, unusually high output and employment mean that the economy is doing well.[16] And this is the case in models of imperfect competition. Since imperfect competition pushes the no-shock level of output below the social optimum, welfare rises when output rises above this level.

• *Wage rigidity causes unemployment through low aggregate demand.* In 1970s models with sticky nominal wages, unemployment occurs when prices fall short of the level expected when wages were set, so that real wages rise and firms move up their labor demand curves. In actual economies, however, firms often appear to reduce employment because demand for their output is low, not because real wages are high. This fact is not necessarily a problem for Keynesian theories if the goods market is imperfectly competitive. In this case, a firm's labor demand depends on real aggregate demand as well as the real wage, because changes in aggregate demand shift the firm's product demand (see equation 2).

• *Real wages need not be countercyclical.* Imperfect competition can remedy an embarrassing empirical failure of traditional models based on sticky nominal wages—the cyclical behavior of real wages. We can tautologically write $P = \mu W/MPL$, where $P$ is the price level, $W$ is the wage, $MPL$ is the marginal product of labor, and $\mu$ is the markup of price over marginal cost. If the markup is constant and marginal product of labor is diminishing, as many 1970s models assumed, then the real wage, $W/P = MPL/\mu$, must be countercyclical. In actual economies, however, real wages appear acyclical or a bit procyclical. This fact can be explained if the marginal product of labor is constant, as suggested by Hall, or if the markup is countercyclical, as suggested by Rotemberg and Saloner and by Bils.[17] Thus there need not be a link between changes in employment and changes in real wages.

• *Nominal rigidities have aggregate demand externalities.* As we have explained, since real aggregate demand affects the demand curves facing individual firms, nominal rigidities have externalities. Rigidity in one firm's price contributes to rigidity in the price level, which causes fluctuations in real aggregate demand and thus harms all firms. These externalities are crucial to the finding that small frictions can have large macroeconomic effects. The externalities depend on imperfect competition, for under perfect competition, aggregate demand is irrelevant to individual firms because they can sell all they want at the going price.

**Product market Rigidities**   Keynes and most Keynesians emphasize rigidities in nominal wages. But recent work focuses largely on rigidities in product prices. The change offers two advantages.

• *Goods are sold in spot markets.* Although there is clearly much nominal wage rigidity in actual economies—in U.S. labor contracts, for example, wages are set up to three years in advance—the allocative effects of this rigidity are unclear. The implicit contracts literature shows that it may be efficient for contract signers to make employment independent of wages. That is, given long-term relationships with their workers, firms may choose the efficient amount of employment rather than moving along their labor demand curves when real wages change.[18] In many product markets, on the other hand, buyers clearly operate on their demand curves. For example, the local shoe store has no agreement, explicit or implicit, from its customers to buy the efficient number of shoes regardless of the prices. Instead, rigidity in the store's prices affects its sales of shoes.

• *Real wages need not be countercyclical.* As we argue above, acyclical real wages are possible even if nominal rigidities occur only in wages. But it is easiest to explain acyclical or procyclical real wages if prices as well as wages are sticky. In this case, the effect of a shock on real wages depends on the relative sizes of the adjustments of prices and wages.

Despite the advantages of studying rigidities in goods markets, we are ambivalent about the deemphasis of labor markets because the apparent rigidities in nominal wages may have important allocative effects. Further research on the relative importance of wage and price rigidities is needed.

### Discussion

We conclude this section by discussing several issues concerning the importance of recent theories and their plausibility.

**The importance of nominal rigidities**   Nominal rigidities are essential for explaining important features of business cycles. As we have emphasized, real effects of nominal disturbances, such as changes in the money stock, depend on some nominal imperfection. The only prominent alternative to nominal rigidities is imperfect information about the aggregate price level, an explanation that many economists find implausible. It is possible, of course, to maintain that money is neutral in the short run—that Paul Volcker, for example, had nothing to do with the 1982 recession—but this also appears unrealistic to many economists. Thus it is difficult to explain the relation of output to nominal variables without nominal rigidities.

Nominal rigidities are also important for explaining the effects of *real* shocks to aggregate demand, resulting, for example, from changes in government spending or in the expectations of investors. The point is clear if we interpret $M$ in the aggregate demand equation, $Y = M/P$, as simply a shift term, in which case real disturbances that shift demand affect output through the same channels as changes in money.

Not all explanations for the output effects of real demand shocks depend on nominal imperfections. Robert Barro's model of government purchases, for one, does not.[19] But such explanations invoke implausibly large labor supply elasticities. Thus nominal rigidities, while not the only explanation for the effects of real demand, are perhaps the most appealing.

In the models we have surveyed, slow adjustment of prices implies that shocks cause temporary deviations of output and employment from their "natural rates." Recently, however, models of hysteresis, in which shocks have permanent effects, have become popular. For example, Blanchard and Summers argue that the natural rate of unemployment in European countries changes when actual unemployment changes, so that there is no unique level to which unemployment returns.[20] If these theories are correct, then nominal rigidities cannot fully explain unemployment, because nominal prices eventually adjust to shocks; some additional explanation, such as the insider-outsider model in Blanchard and Summers, is needed for the persistence of unemployment. But nominal rigidities may be crucial for explaining the initial impulses in unemployment. For example, after rising during the late 1970s, unemployment in Britain has remained high, suggesting hysteresis. But the best explanation for the original increase is arguably a conventional one: slow adjustment of wages and prices to shocks like tight monetary policy and increases in import prices.

**The importance of externalities from rigidity**   Externalities from nominal rigidity, the central element of menu cost models, are essential for a plausible theory of rigidities. If rigidities exist, one of the following statements must be true: rigidities do not impose large costs on the economy; rigidities have large costs to the firms and workers who create them, but these are exceeded by the costs of reducing rigidities; or rigidities have small private costs, and so small frictions are sufficient to create them, but externalities from rigidity impose large costs on the economy. The problem with the first statement is the difficulty of explaining apparently costly events, such as rises in unemployment following monetary contractions, without nominal rigidities. The second seems implausible: it would not be costly for magazine publishers to print new prices every year rather than every four years, as they typically do.[21] Thus the third statement is the best hope for explaining rigidities.

**What are menu costs?**   Models of nominal rigidity depend on some cost of full flexibility, albeit a small one. The term menu cost may be misleading because the physical costs of printing menus and catalogs may not be the most important barriers to flexibility. Perhaps more important is the lost convenience of fixing prices in nominal terms—the cost of learning to think in real terms and of computing the nominal price changes corresponding to desired real price changes. More generally, we can view infrequent revision of nominal prices as a rule of thumb that is more convenient than continuous revision. Thus, rather than referring to menus, we can state the central argument of recent papers as follows. Firms take the convenient shortcut of infrequently reviewing and changing prices. The resulting profit loss is small, so firms have little incentive to eliminate the shortcut, but externalities make the macroeconomic effects large.

At a somewhat deeper level, we can interpret the convenience of fixing nominal rather than real prices as that of using the medium of exchange, dollars, as a unit of account.[22] Alternatively, following Akerlof and Yellen, we can view simple rules of thumb as arising from "near-rationality," a small departure from full optimization.[23] In any case, the precise source of frictions is not important. The effects of nominal shocks are the same whether rigidity arises from printing costs, near-rationality, or something else.

## Inflation, the Frequency of Adjustment, and Phillips Curve

Recent research shows that nominal rigidity is possible in principle—that one can construct a model with firm microeconomic foundations in which rational agents choose substantial rigidity. But the validity of Keynesian theories is not thereby established. For these theories to be convincing, they must have empirical implications that contradict other macroeconomic theories, and these predictions must be confirmed by evidence. This section derives implications of recent Keynesian models, and the next section tests them. As explained in the introduction, the main prediction is that the real effects of nominal shocks are smaller when average inflation is higher. Higher average inflation erodes the frictions that cause nonneutralities, for example by causing more frequent wage and price adjustments.

This section studies a specific model of the class described in the previous section. In the model, a cost of price adjustment leads firms to change prices at intervals rather than continuously. In addition to providing a basis for the empirical tests of the next major section, the model is of theoretical interest. Previous models of nominal rigidity are highly stylized; for example, most menu cost models are static. Our model is dynamic and has the appealing feature that the price level adjusts slowly over time to a nominal shock. The speed of adjustment, which is treated as exogenous in older Keynesian models, is endogenous. It depends on the frequency of price adjustment by individual firms, which in turn is derived from profit-maximization.[24]

We first present the model and show that high average inflation reduces the output effects of nominal shocks. We also show that highly variable aggregate demand reduces these effects. We then investigate the model's quantitative implications by calculating the real effects of shocks for a range of plausible parameter values. The results suggest that the effects of average inflation and demand variability are large. Next we argue that the implications of our model are robust: they carry over to broad classes of other Keynesian models.

Finally, we compare the predictions of Keynesian theories with those of models in the new classical or equilibrium tradition, focusing on Lucas's model of imperfect information. Like our model, Lucas's predicts that the size of the real effects of shocks depends negatively on the variance of aggregate demand. Since this prediction is common to Keynesian and new classical theories, testing it empirically, as Lucas and others have done, is not useful for distinguishing between the two theories. Crucially, Lucas's model differs from ours by predicting that the effects of shocks do *not* depend on average inflation. This difference leads to the tests of the models in the next section.

### The model and qualitative results

Our model of price adjustment is similar in spirit to those of John Taylor and Olivier Blanchard.[25] The model is set in continuous time. The economy contains imperfectly competitive firms that change prices at discrete intervals rather than continuously, because adjustments are costly. Price setting is staggered, with an equal proportion of firms changing prices at every instant. The crucial departure from Taylor and Blanchard is that the length of time between price changes, and hence the rate at which the price level adjusts to shocks, is endogenous. Thus we can study the determinants of the speed of adjustment.

Consider the behavior of a representative firm, firm $i$. Rather than derive a profit function from specific cost and demand functions, we simply assume that firm $i$'s profits depend on three variables: aggregate spending in the economy, $y$; firm $i$'s relative price, $p_i - p$; and a firm-specific shock, $\theta_i$ (all variables are in logs). The aggregate price level $p$ is defined simply as the average of prices across firms. Aggregate spending $y$ affects firm $i$'s profits by shifting the demand curve that it faces. When aggregate spending rises, the firm sells more at a given relative price. The term $p_i - p$ affects the firm's profits by determining the position on the demand curve at which it operates. And $\theta_i$ is an idiosyncratic shock to either demand or costs (the presence of $\theta_i$ is not needed for our main qualitative results, but it strongly affects the quantitative results of the next section).

We assume that the elasticity of firm $i$'s profit-maximizing real price, $p_i^* - p$, with respect to $y$ is a positive constant, $v$. Without loss of generality, we assume that the elasticity of $p_i^* - p$ with respect to $\theta_i$ is one, and that $\theta_i$ has zero mean. Thus we can write the profit-maximizing real price as

$$p_i^*(t) - p(t) = v[y(t) - \bar{y}(t)] + \theta_i(t), \qquad v > 0, \tag{5}$$

where $\bar{y}$ is the natural rate of output—the level at which, if $\theta_i$ equals its mean, the firm desires a relative price of one. (Relative prices equal to one is the condition for a symmetric equilibrium of the economy when prices are flexible.)[26]

If price adjustment were costless, firm $i$ would set $p_i = p_i^*$ at every instant. We assume, however, that an adjustment cost leads firms to change prices only at intervals of length $\lambda$, which for simplicity is constant over time (later in this section we discuss the implications of allowing $\lambda$ to vary). Specifically, each price change has a fixed cost $F$, so adjustment costs per period are $F/\lambda$.

As noted above, an equal proportion of firms sets prices at every instant.[27] If firm $i$ sets a price at $t$, it chooses the price and $\lambda$ to maximize its expected profits, averaged over the life of the price (from $t$ to $t + \lambda$). Maximizing profits is equivalent to minimizing profit losses from two sources: adjustment costs and deviations of price from the profit-maximizing level. We approximate the latter by $\frac{1}{2}K(p_i - p_i^*)^2$, where $K$ is the negative of the second derivative of profits with respect to $p_i^* - p_i$. Thus firm $i$'s loss per unit of time is

$$\frac{F}{\lambda} + \frac{1}{\lambda}\frac{1}{2}K \int_{s=0}^{\lambda} E_t[p_i^*(t + s) - p_i]^2 \, ds. \tag{6}$$

Minimization of equation 6 implies a simple rule for choosing $p_i$:

$$p_i = \frac{1}{\lambda} \int_{s=0}^{\lambda} E_t p_i^*(t + s)\, ds. \tag{7}$$

That is, a firm sets its price to the average of its expected profit-maximizing prices for the period when the price is in effect. We describe the more complicated determination of $\lambda$ below.

To study the effects of nominal shocks, we must introduce a stochastic nominal variable. We assume that the log of nominal aggregate demand, $x \equiv y + p$, is exogenous and follows the continuous-time analogue of a random walk with drift:

$$x(t) = gt + \sigma_x W(t), \tag{8}$$

where $W(t)$ is a Wiener process. The first term in the expression for $x(t)$ captures trend growth of $g$ per unit time; the second captures random walk innovations with variance $\sigma_x^2$ per unit time. Our analysis below focuses on the effects of the parameters $g$ and $\sigma_x$ on the economy. A monetarist interpretation of equation 8 is that $x(t) = m(t) + V$—the velocity of money is constant, and aggregate demand is driven by random walk movements in the money stock. A more general interpretation is that a variety of exogenous variables—fiscal policy, the expectations of investors, and so on—drive $x(t)$.

We make two final assumptions. First, the natural rate of output grows smoothly at rate $\mu$:

$$\bar{y}(t) = \mu t. \tag{9}$$

Along with the process for $x(t)$, this implies that average inflation is $g - \mu$. Second, the firm-specific disturbances, the $\theta_i$s, are uncorrelated across firms and follow continuous-time random walks whose innovations have mean zero and variance $\sigma_\theta^2$ per unit time.[28]

**The behavior of the economy for a given frequency of price changes**    Below we show that average inflation, by influencing the interval between price changes, affects the output-inflation trade-off in our model. A preliminary step is to solve for the behavior of the economy for a given interval, $\lambda$. We do this by combining our assumptions about price setting by individual firms and then aggregating. The behavior of individual firms determines the behavior of the price level. As described above, the behavior of price level—which each firm, being small, takes as given—in turn determines the behavior of firms. The condition for equilibrium is that individual and aggregate behavior are consistent; that is, that profit-maximizing price-setting rules for indivdual firms given the behavior of the price level in fact yield that behavior of the price level. The details are complicated, so we leave them for the appendix. Here we simply present our main results.

The solution for the behavior of the price level takes the form

$$p(t) = (g - \mu)t + \int_{s=0}^{x} w(s; \lambda) \, dZ(t - s), \tag{10}$$

where $dZ(t - s) \equiv \sigma_x \, dW(t - s)$ is the innovation in aggregate demand at $t - s$. The first term in equation 10 captures average inflation of $g - \mu$, and the second captures the effects of shocks. The term $w(s; \lambda)$ gives the effect of a demand shock at $t - s$ on the price level at $t$.

The appendix derives the expression that defines $w(\cdot)$. We cannot find an analytic solution to the expression and therefore solve it numerically; the appendix describes how. We find when we solve for $w(\cdot)$ that, assuming $v < 1$, $w(s; \lambda)$ equals zero when $s = 0$, increases with $s$, and approaches one as $s$ approaches infinity. That is, the immediate effect of a shock on the price level is zero (because an infinitesimal proportion of firms changes prices at $t$); the effect of the shock grows over time; and asymptotically the shock is passed one-for-one into prices.

The crucial result about $w(\cdot)$ concerns the frequency of price changes: when $v < 1$, $w(s; \lambda)$ is decreasing in $\lambda$. A longer interval between changes in individual prices leads to slower adjustment of the aggregate price level—for any $s$, a smaller proportion of a shock at $t - s$ is passed into prices by $t$.[29]

The behavior of real output follows directly from the behavior of the price level, the stochastic process for aggregate demand, and the identity $y = x - p$:

$$y(t) - \bar{y}(t) = \int_{s=0}^{x} [1 - w(s; \lambda)] \, dZ(t - s). \tag{11}$$

The sizes of the real effects of nominal shocks are given by $1 - w(\cdot)$; this is the theoretical counterpart of the parameter that we estimate in the following section.

Finally, equation 11 implies an expression for the variance of output:

$$E\{[y(t) - \bar{y}(t)]^2\} = \sigma_x^2 \int_{s=0}^{x} [1 - w(s; \lambda)]^2 \, ds. \tag{12}$$

The variance of output depends on the variance of demand shocks, $\sigma_x^2$, and the size of the effects of shocks, $1 - w(\cdot)$. This result is also used in the empirical work of the next major section.

**The equilibrium frequency of price changes**   We now derive a condition defining the equilibrium interval between price changes. Consider firm $i$'s problem of choosing its interval, $\lambda_i$, given that all other firms in the economy choose an interval $\lambda$. The value of a firm's loss function, $L$ (equation 6), is affected by both $\lambda_i$ and $\lambda$; the latter matters because it determines the behavior of the price level. Minimization of $L(\lambda_i, \lambda)$ with respect to $\lambda_i$ yields the first-order condition $\partial L(\lambda_i, \lambda)/\partial \lambda_i = 0$. A symmetric Nash equilibrium for $\lambda$, $\lambda^E$ is defined implicitly by setting $\lambda_i = \lambda$ in this condition:

$$\left. \frac{\partial L(\lambda_i, \lambda^E)}{\partial \lambda_i} \right|_{\lambda_i = \lambda^E} = 0 \tag{13}$$

In other words, an interval $\lambda$ is an equilibrium if, when $\lambda$ is chosen throughout the economy, it is in firm $i$'s interest to choose $\lambda$ as well.[30]

Because we can find $w(\cdot)$ only numerically, we must also find the equilibrium $\lambda$ numerically, as described in the appendix. We find that $\lambda$ is decreasing in $\bar{\pi}$, $\sigma_x$, and $\sigma_\theta$, where $\bar{\pi} \equiv g - \mu$ is the average inflation rate. Thus the interval between price changes decreases the higher average inflation. High inflation causes a firm's profit-maximizing nominal price to change rapidly, which raises the benefits from frequent adjustment. The interval $\lambda$ also decreases the greater the variances of aggregate and firm-specific shocks. When either variance is large, a firm's future profit-maximizing price is highly uncertain, so the firm does not wish to fix its price for long.

These results, along with the results about the effects of $\lambda$, imply that the Phillips curve is steeper when $\bar{\pi}$, $\sigma_x$, or $\sigma_\theta$ is larger. Higher average inflation reduces the interval between price changes, which in turn raises $w(\cdot)$, the proportion of a shock that is passed into prices. A larger variance of aggregate or firm-specific shocks also reduces $\lambda$ and thus raises $w(\cdot)$. These results imply that increases in $\bar{\pi}$, $\sigma_x$, or $\sigma_\theta$ lead to *decreases* in $1 - w(\cdot)$, the real effects of shocks. These predictions lead to the empirical tests of the next section.

**Quantitative results**

We now ask whether the effects of inflation and demand variability identified above are quantitatively important. We do so by computing the interval between price changes and the real effects of shocks for a range of plausible parameter values.

**The choice of parameters**    Since our focus is the effects of average inflation, $g - \mu$, and the standard deviation of demand, $\sigma_x$, we experiment with wide ranges of values of these parameters ($g$ and $\mu$ affect the results only through their difference). This leaves three other parameters for which we need baseline values: $F/K$, the ratio of the cost of changing prices to the negative of the second derivative of the profit function ($F$ and $K$ enter only through their ratio); $\sigma_\theta$, the standard deviation of firm-specific shocks; and $v$, the elasticity of a firm's profit-maximizing real price with respect to aggregate output.

We choose baseline parameters by experimenting with values of $F/K$, $\sigma_\theta$, and $v$ to find a combination that implies plausible sizes for the real effects of shocks. We then ask whether these parameter values are realistic. Finally, we investigate robustness by calculating the effects of changing each parameter from its baseline value.

It is difficult to measure $F$ and $K$ directly, so we take an indirect approach. In a model of steady inflation and no shocks ($\sigma_\theta = \sigma_x = 0$), $F/K$ determines the frequency of price changes. With $F/K = 0.00015$, firms change prices every five quarters under steady 3 percent inflation and every two quarters under steady 12 percent inflation. Microeconomic evidence suggests that actual intervals between price changes typically average two years or more. Thus our baseline value of $F/K$ is *conservative*. We certainly do not assume menu costs that are too large to be consistent with price setting in actual economies.[31]

To pick a value for $\sigma_\theta$, we use the fact that $\sigma_\theta$ equals the standard deviation of movements in profit-maximizing prices, the $p_i^*$s, across firms. This leads us to use data on relative price variability to gauge plausible values of $\sigma_\theta$. Vining and Elwertowski report a 4 to 5 percent standard deviation of annual relative price movements across highly disaggregate (eight-digit) components of the U.S. consumer price index; this is consistent with our assumption of $\sigma_\theta = 3$ percent.[32]

Finally, there is little quantitative evidence concerning the size of $v$, the elasticity of profit-maximizing relative prices with respect to aggregate output. However, our choice of a small elasticity, 0.1, is consistent with the common view that relative prices vary little in response to aggregate fluctuations. Our baseline parameters are therefore $F/K = 0.00015$, $\sigma_\theta = 3$ percent, and $v = 0.1$.

**Results** Table 1 shows the effects of average inflation, $g - \mu$, and the variability of demand, $\sigma_x$, when $F/K$, $\sigma_\theta$, and $v$ equal their baseline values. For wide ranges of $g - \mu$ and $\sigma_x$, the table shows two figures. The first is the percentage effect of a 1 percent change in demand on real output six months later. A value of zero would mean that prices adjust fully to the shock; a value of one would mean that prices do not adjust at all. We refer to this figure as simply the real effect of a shock. The figure in parentheses is the equilibrium interval between price changes, $\lambda$, in weeks. As we explain

**Table 1**
Effect of a nominal shock on real output and the equilibrium interval between price changes

| Average inflation rate, $g - \mu$ (percent) | Demand variability, $\sigma_x$ (percent) | | | | | |
|---|---|---|---|---|---|---|
| | 0 | 1 | 3 | 5 | 10 | 20 |
| 0 | 0.560 | 0.540 | 0.495 | 0.424 | 0.250 | 0.078 |
| | (31) | (30) | (28) | (25) | (17) | (10) |
| 2 | 0.519 | 0.519 | 0.470 | 0.405 | 0.250 | 0.078 |
| | (29) | (29) | (27) | (24) | (17) | (10) |
| 5 | 0.424 | 0.424 | 0.405 | 0.366 | 0.224 | 0.078 |
| | (25) | (25) | (24) | (22) | (16) | (10) |
| 10 | 0.322 | 0.322 | 0.299 | 0.299 | 0.199 | 0.078 |
| | (20) | (20) | (19) | (19) | (15) | (10) |
| 20 | 0.174 | 0.174 | 0.174 | 0.174 | 0.124 | 0.057 |
| | (14) | (14) | (14) | (14) | (12) | (9) |
| 50 | 0.057 | 0.057 | 0.057 | 0.057 | 0.039 | 0.023 |
| | (9) | (9) | (9) | (9) | (8) | (7) |
| 100 | 0.012 | 0.012 | 0.012 | 0.012 | 0.012 | 0.012 |
| | (6) | (6) | (6) | (6) | (6) | (6) |
| 250 | 0.001 | 0.001 | 0.001 | 0.001 | 0.001 | 0.001 |
| | (4) | (4) | (4) | (4) | (4) | (4) |

Source: Authors' calculations. See text description.
Notes: The table shows the effects of changing values of $g - \mu$ and $\sigma_x$ when $F/K$, $\sigma_\theta$, and $v$ equal their baseline values. $F/K$ is the ratio of the cost of changing prices to minus the second derivative of the profit function; $\sigma_\theta$ is the standard deviation of firm-specific shocks; and $v$ is the elasticity of a firm's profit-maximizing real price with respect to aggregate output. Baseline values: $F/K = 0.00015$. $\sigma_\theta = 3$ percent; and $v = 0.1$. For each entry in the table, the first number is the percentage effect of a 1 percent nominal shock on real output after six months: the number in parentheses is the equilibrium interval between price changes, $\lambda$, in weeks.

above, inflation and demand variability influence the real effects of shocks through their effects on $\lambda$.

Table 1 shows that realistic increases in average inflation have quantitatively important effects. With $\sigma_\theta = 3$ percent, roughly the standard deviation of nominal GNP growth for the postwar United States, the interval between price changes is 28 weeks if $g - \mu = 0$, but falls to 19 weeks if $g - \mu = 10$ percent and 6 weeks if $g - \mu = 100$ percent. As a result, the real effect of a shock is 0.50 for $g - \mu = 0$, 0.30 for $g - \mu = 10$ percent, and 0.01 for $g - \mu = 100$ percent.

Table 1 shows that increases in $\sigma_x$ also have important effects. With average inflation of 5 percent, raising $\sigma_x$ from 3 percent to 10 percent reduces the interval between price changes from 24 to 16 weeks and the real effect of a shock from 0.41 to 0.22. These effects are similar to the effects of raising average inflation from 5 percent to 15 percent.

**Table 2**
The effects of changes in $F/K$, $v$, and $\sigma_\theta$ on the slope of the Phillips curve and the equilibrium interval between price changes

| Parameter values | | | Average inflation rate,[a] $g - \mu$ | |
|---|---|---|---|---|
| $F/K$ | $v$ | $\sigma_\theta$ (%) | 5% | 20% |
| 0.00015 | 0.1 | 3 | 0.405 (24) | 0.174 (14) |
| 0.0003 | 0.1 | 3 | 0.519 (29) | 0.274 (18) |
| 0.00015 | 0.2 | 3 | 0.273 (24) | 0.080 (14) |
| 0.00015 | 0.1 | 6 | 0.174 (14) | 0.100 (11) |
| 0.00045 | 0.1 | 6 | 0.405 (24) | 0.274 (18) |
| 0.0003 | 0.285 | 3 | 0.406 (32) | 0.104 (18) |
| 0.00015 | 0.0295 | 6 | 0.403 (15) | 0.367 (12) |

Source: Authors' calculations. See text description.
a. For various combinations of $F/K$, $v$, and $\sigma_\theta$, the table shows the real effect of a nominal shock and the interval between price changes: for each entry in the last two columns of the table, the first number is the percentage effect of a 1 percent nominal shock on real output after six months, the number in parentheses is the equilibrium interval between price changes, $\lambda$, in weeks. Demand variability, $\sigma_x$, is set to 3 percent.

Table 2 shows the effects of varying $F/K$, $\sigma_\theta$, and $v$. For various combinations of these parameters, we show the real effect of a shock and the interval between price changes for $g - \mu = 5$ percent and $g - \mu = 20$ percent, assuming $\sigma_x = 3$ percent in both cases. The first line reproduces the results for the baseline parameters, and each of the following three lines shows the effects of doubling one parameter while holding the others constant. An increase in $F/K$ raises the real effect of a shock, and an increase in $\sigma_\theta$ or $v$ reduces it. But for all combinations of $F/K$, $\sigma_\theta$, and $v$, our central result holds: higher average inflation reduces the real effect of a shock. The remaining three lines of the table show the effects of combinations of changes that leave the real effect of a shock unchanged for $g - \mu = 5$ percent. These lines show how the parameters affect the strength of the link between average inflation and the real effect of a shock.

### Robustness

Traditional Keynesian models, such as textbook models of price adjustment or the staggered contracts models of Fischer and Taylor, do not share the key predictions of our model.[33] These older theories treat the degree of nominal rigidity (for example, the length of labor contracts or the adjustment speed of the price level) as fixed parameters; thus they rule out the channel through which average inflation affects the output-inflation trade-off. On the other hand, our central results appear to be robust implications of Keynesian theories in which the degree of rigidity is endogenous. The intuition for the effects of inflation on the frequency of price adjustment, and of this frequency on the size of nonneutralities, is not tied to the specific assumptions of our model.

One assumption of our model that requires attention is that the interval between price changes is constant over time. This assumption is ad hoc: given our other assumptions, firms could increase profits by varying the interval based on the realizations of shocks. In addition, the assumption is unrealistic, because firms in actual economies do not always change prices at fixed intervals.

We now consider the alternative assumption that firms can freely vary the timing of price changes. This assumption of complete flexibility is also far from realistic. Most wages are adjusted at constant intervals of a year. There appears to be greater flexibility in the timing of price changes, but the limited evidence suggests that it is not complete. Mail order companies change prices at fixed times during the year, even though they issue catalogs much more frequently than they change prices, and thus could vary the dates of adjustments without issuing extra catalogs. In addition, a broad range of industries appears to have a preferred time of the year, often January, for price changes.[34]

It is not yet possible to solve a model like ours with flexible timing, but suggestive results are available for simpler models. In particular, a literature beginning with Sheshinski and Weiss presents partial-equilibrium models in which a firm chooses to follow an "Ss" rule for adjusting its price: whenever inflation pushes its real price outside some bounds, it adjusts its nominal price to return the real price to a target level. These models reproduce a crucial implication of our model: higher average inflation leads to more frequent price changes. High inflation causes a firm's real price to change rapidly, so, for given Ss bounds, the price hits the bounds more often. High inflation also causes the firm to widen its bounds, which reduces the frequency of price changes, but does not fully offset the first effect.[35]

For our main argument to hold, the more frequent changes in individual prices that result from higher inflation must lead in turn to faster adjustment of the aggregate price level. Intuition clearly suggests a link between the frequency of individual adjustment and the speed of aggregate adjustment, but the difficulty of studying general equilibrium with flexible timing precludes a definitive proof. Indeed, in one prominent special case, the link does not exist. Andrew Caplin and Daniel Spulber show that if we *assume* that firms follow Ss rules with constant bounds, and if aggregate demand is nondecreasing, then the aggregate price level adjusts immediately to nominal shocks—nominal shocks are neutral. Because aggregate adjustment is always instantaneous, its speed is obviously independent of the frequency of individual price changes.[36]

Current research suggests that the Caplin-Spulber result does not hold under realistic conditions. There exist examples in which firms do *not* follow Ss rules with constant bounds, and so a shock to the money supply is not neutral, either if there is some persistence to inflation or if firms' optimal nominal prices sometimes fall. And when nonneutralities exist, it appears plausible that their size depends on the frequency of individual price adjustment. Thus, overall, models of price adjustment with flexible timing appear consistent with the predictions of our model.[37]

Another robustness issue concerns the nature of the friction that prevents nominal flexibility. In our model, the friction is a fixed cost of price adjustment. An alternative view is that the technological costs of making prices highly flexible are negligible but that for some reason, such as convenience, the desire to avoid computation costs, or habit, price setters nonetheless follow rules that focus on nominal prices.[38] Without a theory that predicts the particular rules of thumb that price setters follow, theories of this type do not make precise predictions concerning the relationship between average inflation and the degree of price flexibility. But it appears that under reasonable interpretations these theories imply that higher inflation increases nominal flexibility. As average inflation rises, so does the cost of following a rule-of-thumb pricing policy stated in nominal terms, as does the evidence that keeping a fixed nominal price is not equivalent to keeping a fixed real price. Although price setters may continue to follow rules of thumb, they will increasingly think in terms of real rather than nominal magnitudes. Nominal price flexibility will thus increase.

### The predictions of new classical theories

The prediction of Keynesian models that average inflation affects the output-inflation trade-off is important because it is inconsistent with alternative macroeconomic models in the new classical tradition. We now review the predictions of new classical models, focusing on Lucas's imperfect information theory. Like Keynesian models of nominal rigidity, Lucas's model is designed to explain the effects of nominal shocks on output, that is, to generate a short-run Phillips curve. But Lucas's model has different implications about what determines the size of the effects.

In Lucas's model, agents wish to change their output in response to changes in their relative prices, but not in response to changes in the aggregate price level. When an agent observes a change in his price, however, he cannot tell whether it results from a relative or an aggregate movement. He acts upon his best guess, which is that part of the change comes from each source. Since agents interpret any price change as partly relative, changes that in fact result from a nominal shock have effects on output.

In Lucas's model, the size of the effects of nominal shocks depends on the relative magnitudes of nominal and idiosyncratic real shocks. In particular, if nominal shocks are large, agents attribute most of the movements in their prices to nominal shocks, and respond little. Thus a large variance of nominal aggregate demand leads to a steep Phillips curve. Lucas presents cross-country evidence supporting this prediction in his famous 1973 paper. We show, however, that Keynesian models make the same prediction, although the reason—a large variance of aggregate demand causes more frequent price changes—is very different. Because both Keynesian and new classical theories explain Lucas's results, his test does not help to distinguish between them.

The effect of average inflation on the output-inflation trade-off *does* distinguish Keynesian and new classical models. Theories of nominal rigidities predict that high inflation makes the Phillips curve steeper. In Lucas's imperfect information model, average inflation is irrelevant to the output-inflation trade-off, because only the variances of random variables, not the means, affect the uncertainty that agents face. This difference between the theories is the basis for our empirical work. (A *simple* correlation between average inflation and the slope of the Phillips curve is consistent with Lucas's model, because average inflation is correlated with the variance of demand, which affects the slope. The issue is whether there is a relation between average inflation and the slope after we control for the variance of demand.)

Another difference between the predictions of Keynesian and new classical theories concerns the effects of idiosyncratic shocks. According to Lucas, a large variance of relative price shocks increases the real effects of nominal shocks, because it raises the proportion of these shocks that agents misperceive as real. Our model predicts that a large variance of idiosyncratic shocks, like a large variance of aggregate shocks, leads to more frequent price changes and thus *reduces* the effects of nominal shocks. If one could construct a measure of the variance of firm-specific shocks, which we do not attempt in this paper, then estimating the relation between this variable and the slope of the Phillips curve would be another test between the two competing theories.

The leading new classical alternative to Lucas's imperfect information model is real business-cycle theory.[39] This theory attributes all fluctuations in output to real disturbances and assumes that nominal disturbances are simply passed into prices. Because nominal shocks have no causal role in output fluctuations, it is difficult for the theory to explain the observed positive correlations of real and nominal variables, much less the effect of average inflation on the strength of these correlations. King and Plosser have devised a real business-cycle model in which output moves with nominal money through reverse causality: the banking system creates inside money in anticipation of output movements. But as Mankiw points out, the model predicts that the aggregate price level *falls* when output rises.[40] Thus real business-cycle models do not appear to provide an alternative explanation of the results that we report below.

## International Evidence

We examine here how the trade-off between output and inflation varies across countries. Our goal is to test the theoretical results discussed in the previous section. In particular, we wish to examine whether in countries with high rates of inflation, changes in aggregate demand have relatively small effects on output and instead are reflected quickly in prices.

Our analysis is divided into two parts. First we describe the data and present the basic results. We estimate the output-inflation trade-off for 43 industrialized countries and examine the relationship between the trade-off and average inflation and demand variability. Then we consider econometric issues raised by our procedure and examine variations on our basic test.

### Data and basic results

The data we examine, originally from *International Financial Statistics* of the International Monetary Fund, are from the IMF databank of Data Resources, Inc. All the data are annual. Depending on the country, output is real GNP or real GDP, whichever is available. We denote the log of output as $y$ and the log of the corresponding nominal quantity as $x$. The log of the price level is then $p = x - y$.

We wanted the most extensive possible sample of large, industrialized, free market economies. We used the following five criteria for choosing the sample of countries: the population had to be at least one million; at least 10 percent of output had to be in manufacturing; not more than 30 percent of output could be in agriculture; data had to be available at least back to 1963; the economy had to be largely unplanned. Information on the first three criteria was taken from the IMF's *Yearbook of National Account Statistics* and the *International Financial Statistics Yearbooks*; data for the year 1965 were used for these criteria. The fifth criterion is obviously open to interpretation. It led us to exclude such countries as Czechoslovakia, East Germany, and Yugoslavia.

The countries are listed in table 3, together with the period of time for which data are available. We present here some sample statistics for each country: the mean and standard deviation for real growth, inflation, and the

**Table 3**
Descriptive statistics on inflation and output for various countries and selected periods, 1948–1986

| Country | Sample period | Real growth | | Inflation | | Nominal growth | |
|---|---|---|---|---|---|---|---|
| | | Mean | Standard deviation | Mean | Standard deviation | Mean | Standard deviation |
| Argentina | 1963–1981 | 0.0262 | 0.04253 | 0.5439 | 0.42064 | 0.5702 | 0.40685 |
| Australia | 1949–1985 | 0.0416 | 0.02446 | 0.0677 | 0.05043 | 0.1094 | 0.04880 |
| Austria | 1950–1986 | 0.0396 | 0.02615 | 0.0526 | 0.04745 | 0.0923 | 0.04329 |
| Belgium | 1950–1985 | 0.0329 | 0.02238 | 0.0424 | 0.03028 | 0.0754 | 0.03343 |
| Bolivia | 1958–1983 | 0.0376 | 0.03839 | 0.2012 | 0.29272 | 0.2388 | 0.26608 |
| Brazil | 1963–1984 | 0.0633 | 0.05500 | 0.4237 | 0.25825 | 0.4871 | 0.23597 |
| Canada | 1948–1985 | 0.0436 | 0.02605 | 0.0480 | 0.03296 | 0.0917 | 0.03696 |
| Colombia | 1950–1985 | 0.0465 | 0.01881 | 0.1371 | 0.06849 | 0.1836 | 0.06394 |
| Costa Rica | 1960–1986 | 0.0459 | 0.03809 | 0.1241 | 0.13105 | 0.1701 | 0.10563 |
| Denmark | 1950–1985 | 0.0318 | 0.02451 | 0.0634 | 0.02869 | 0.0953 | 0.02812 |
| Dominican Republic | 1950–1986 | 0.0493 | 0.05084 | 0.0534 | 0.07553 | 0.1028 | 0.09106 |
| Ecuador | 1950–1985 | 0.0569 | 0.04195 | 0.0877 | 0.10082 | 0.1447 | 0.09687 |
| El Salvador | 1951–1986 | 0.0328 | 0.04140 | 0.0507 | 0.08044 | 0.0837 | 0.07675 |
| Finland | 1950–1985 | 0.0429 | 0.03339 | 0.0749 | 0.05648 | 0.1178 | 0.06088 |
| France | 1950–1985 | 0.0415 | 0.01987 | 0.0675 | 0.03798 | 0.1091 | 0.03118 |
| Germany | 1950–1986 | 0.0455 | 0.03548 | 0.0374 | 0.02125 | 0.0830 | 0.03705 |
| Greece | 1948–1986 | 0.0549 | 0.03872 | 0.0915 | 0.06568 | 0.1465 | 0.05949 |
| Guatemala | 1950–1983 | 0.0425 | 0.02802 | 0.0374 | 0.05120 | 0.0799 | 0.05812 |
| Iceland | 1948–1985 | 0.0353 | 0.05647 | 0.1977 | 0.14758 | 0.2331 | 0.13415 |
| Iran | 1959–1985 | 0.0575 | 0.08270 | 0.0937 | 0.12213 | 0.1514 | 0.13114 |
| Ireland | 1948–1985 | 0.0319 | 0.02375 | 0.0741 | 0.05432 | 0.1061 | 0.06096 |
| Israel | 1953–1982 | 0.0745 | 0.04307 | 0.2119 | 0.24465 | 0.2865 | 0.22193 |
| Italy | 1950–1985 | 0.0433 | 0.02775 | 0.0796 | 0.05715 | 0.1229 | 0.04683 |
| Jamaica | 1960–1985 | 0.0153 | 0.04616 | 0.1113 | 0.08769 | 0.1267 | 0.06723 |
| Japan | 1952–1985 | 0.0716 | 0.03642 | 0.0472 | 0.03772 | 0.1189 | 0.04482 |

**Table 3** (continued)

| Country | Sample period | Real growth | | Inflation | | Nominal growth | |
|---|---|---|---|---|---|---|---|
| | | Mean | Standard deviation | Mean | Standard deviation | Mean | Standard deviation |
| Mexico | 1948–1985 | 0.0577 | 0.03069 | 0.1392 | 0.15016 | 0.1969 | 0.13479 |
| Netherlands | 1950–1985 | 0.0388 | 0.02918 | 0.0493 | 0.03399 | 0.0882 | 0.03779 |
| Nicaragua | 1960–1983 | 0.0377 | 0.08672 | 0.0806 | 0.09377 | 0.1184 | 0.09897 |
| Norway | 1950–1986 | 0.0416 | 0.01618 | 0.0564 | 0.05166 | 0.0982 | 0.04576 |
| Panama | 1950–1986 | 0.0537 | 0.03315 | 0.0299 | 0.03548 | 0.0837 | 0.04613 |
| Peru | 1960–1984 | 0.0354 | 0.04342 | 0.2554 | 0.22662 | 0.2909 | 0.20236 |
| Philippines | 1948–1986 | 0.0484 | 0.03216 | 0.0720 | 0.08221 | 0.1205 | 0.06948 |
| Portugal | 1953–1982 | 0.0510 | 0.02771 | 0.0739 | 0.07211 | 0.1250 | 0.06844 |
| Singapore | 1960–1984 | 0.0861 | 0.04680 | 0.0356 | 0.04768 | 0.1218 | 0.05245 |
| South Africa | 1948–1986 | 0.0383 | 0.02279 | 0.0718 | 0.05457 | 0.1102 | 0.05012 |
| Spain | 1954–1984 | 0.0455 | 0.03085 | 0.0992 | 0.04698 | 0.1448 | 0.04393 |
| Sweden | 1950–1986 | 0.0301 | 0.01795 | 0.0635 | 0.03776 | 0.0937 | 0.03169 |
| Switzerland | 1948–1986 | 0.0286 | 0.03415 | 0.0387 | 0.02672 | 0.0674 | 0.03217 |
| Tunisia | 1960–1983 | 0.0621 | 0.04424 | 0.0596 | 0.05795 | 0.1217 | 0.05419 |
| United Kingdom | 1948–1986 | 0.0243 | 0.01890 | 0.0664 | 0.04984 | 0.0909 | 0.04202 |
| United States | 1948–1986 | 0.0315 | 0.02676 | 0.0415 | 0.02529 | 0.0731 | 0.03252 |
| Venezuela | 1950–1985 | 0.0459 | 0.03757 | 0.0526 | 0.08237 | 0.0985 | 0.07665 |
| Zaire | 1950–1984 | 0.0334 | 0.04248 | 0.2002 | 0.22374 | 0.2338 | 0.21167 |
| Across-country values | | | | | | | |
| Mean | | 0.0441 | 0.03591 | 0.1048 | 0.09393 | 0.1489 | 0.08881 |
| Standard deviation | | 0.0138 | 0.0147 | 0.0999 | 0.0843 | 0.1003 | 0.0776 |

Source: Authors' calculations with data from International Monetary Fund. *International Financial Statistics.* The data were obtained from the IMF data bank of Data Resources, Inc. All data are annual. Depending on the country, output is real GNP or real GDP, whichever is available. Growth rates are computed as differences in logarithms with the log of real output as $y$ and the log of nominal output as $x$: the log of the price level is $p = x - y$. For information on the selection of countries in the sample, see the text description.

growth in nominal demand. We see from this table that there is substantial variation in the macroeconomic experiences of these countries. For example, Panama had the lowest average inflation rate, less than 3 percent a year, while Argentina and Brazil each had average inflation exceeding 40 percent a year.

**Estimating the output-inflation trade-off**   We express the short-run output-inflation trade-off by estimating the following equation:

$$y_t = \text{constant} + \tau \Delta x_t + \lambda y_{t-1} + \gamma \text{time}$$

The log of real GNP is regressed on its own lag, a time trend, and the change in nominal GNP. This sort of equation has been used widely, both by new classical macroeconomists such as Robert Lucas and by Keynesian macroeconomists such as Charles Schultze.[41] Equation 14 is the empirical counterpart of equation 11 of our theoretical model. It differs from equation 11 by the use of discrete rather than continuous time and by summarizing the effects of past demand movements through the term in lagged real output. We discuss this specification of the output-inflation trade-off further in the second part of this section.

The coefficient of the change in nominal demand, $\tau$, is the parameter of central interest. It tells us how much of a shock to nominal GNP shows up in output in the first year. If $\tau = 1$, then all of the change in nominal GNP shows up in real GNP; if $\tau = 0$, then all the change in nominal GNP shows up in prices.

Table 4 presents the estimated value of $\tau$ for the 43 countries, together with the estimated standard errors. For each country, the entire available time series is used in the estimation. Table 4 also presents the estimated value of $\tau$ for two subsamples. We use 1972/1973 as the cutoff between the two subsamples. The early 1970s are often considered a time of major structural change; certainly many empirical macroeconomic relationships broke down. We therefore wanted to see whether the trade-off parameter $\tau$ changed and, if so, whether the changes could be explained.

Table 4 shows substantial variation in the output-inflation trade-off across countries. The mean value of $\tau$ for our 43 countries is 0.242 and the standard deviation is 0.272. The trade-off parameter for the United States is 0.671, which is 1.6 standard deviations above the mean. Hence, relative to the typical country in our sample, the United States exhibits large effects of aggregate demand on output.

**Table 4**
Estimates of the output-inflation trade-off for various countries and selected periods, 1948–1986

| Country | Sample period | Full sample | | Data through 1972 | | Data after 1972 | |
|---|---|---|---|---|---|---|---|
| | | Trade-off parameter, τ | Standard error | Trade-off parameter, τ | Standard error | Trade-off parameter, τ | Standard error |
| Argentina | 1963–1981 | −0.0047 | 0.0335 | −0.1179 | 0.1140 | −0.0021 | 0.0322 |
| Australia | 1949–1985 | 0.1383 | 0.0862 | 0.3029 | 0.0858 | 0.3196 | 0.1937 |
| Austria | 1950–1986 | 0.0196 | 0.1069 | 0.0830 | 0.1219 | 0.6823 | 0.2058 |
| Belgium | 1950–1985 | 0.4967 | 0.1035 | 0.3897 | 0.1036 | 0.2081 | 0.2950 |
| Bolivia | 1958–1983 | −0.0525 | 0.0424 | 0.1418 | 0.1567 | −0.0621 | 0.0276 |
| Brazil | 1963–1984 | −0.0951 | 0.1037 | −0.1999 | 0.2111 | 0.0770 | 0.1478 |
| Canada | 1948–1985 | 0.4731 | 0.0899 | 0.5052 | 0.1151 | 0.4619 | 0.2333 |
| Colombia | 1950–1985 | 0.0550 | 0.0879 | −0.0233 | 0.0919 | 0.2089 | 0.2151 |
| Costa Rica | 1960–1986 | −0.2302 | 0.0911 | 0.4041 | 0.1937 | −0.2912 | 0.0722 |
| Denmark | 1950–1985 | 0.8486 | 0.1385 | 0.6762 | 0.1491 | 1.0091 | 0.5805 |
| Dominican Republic | 1950–1986 | 0.3993 | 0.0750 | 0.5689 | 0.0591 | −0.1173 | 0.0733 |
| Ecuador | 1950–1985 | 0.1976 | 0.1148 | 0.4903 | 0.2042 | −0.2062 | 0.1226 |
| El Salvador | 1951–1986 | 0.3432 | 0.0822 | 0.4368 | 0.1162 | 0.3230 | 0.1127 |
| Finland | 1950–1985 | 0.2417 | 0.0823 | 0.2242 | 0.1000 | 0.5835 | 0.1139 |
| France | 1950–1985 | −0.0648 | 0.0899 | 0.1046 | 0.0765 | 0.3858 | 0.3129 |
| Germany | 1950–1986 | 0.6137 | 0.1005 | 0.6182 | 0.1369 | 1.0761 | 0.1333 |
| Greece | 1948–1986 | 0.2577 | 0.0974 | 0.4528 | 0.0644 | 0.4583 | 0.2869 |
| Guatemala | 1950–1983 | 0.3966 | 0.0772 | 0.3705 | 0.1036 | 0.5021 | 0.1377 |
| Iceland | 1948–1985 | 0.0154 | 0.1173 | 0.3892 | 0.1978 | −0.2487 | 0.2236 |
| Iran | 1959–1985 | 0.3785 | 0.1097 | 0.1081 | 0.0834 | 0.5018 | 0.2084 |
| Ireland | 1948–1985 | 0.2731 | 0.0710 | 0.3767 | 0.1074 | 0.1306 | 0.1733 |
| Israel | 1953–1982 | 0.0015 | 0.0847 | 0.4082 | 0.0928 | 0.0901 | 0.0372 |
| Italy | 1950–1985 | 0.2035 | 0.1007 | 0.5279 | 0.1363 | 0.5470 | 0.1276 |
| Jamaica | 1960–1985 | 0.1399 | 0.1591 | −0.0977 | 0.3055 | 0.2389 | 0.1169 |
| Japan | 1952–1985 | 0.5065 | 0.1524 | 0.4812 | 0.1363 | 0.4119 | 0.2441 |

**Table 4** (continued)

| Country | Sample period | Full sample | | Data through 1972 | | Data after 1972 | |
|---|---|---|---|---|---|---|---|
| | | Trade-off parameter, $\tau$ | Standard error | Trade-off parameter, $\tau$ | Standard error | Trade-off parameter, $\tau$ | Standard error |
| Mexico | 1948–1985 | −0.1095 | 0.0530 | 0.3139 | 0.0491 | −0.4304 | 0.0997 |
| Netherlands | 1950–1985 | 0.4546 | 0.1244 | 0.3245 | 0.1802 | 0.5214 | 0.3035 |
| Nicaragua | 1960–1983 | 0.5834 | 0.1551 | 0.8431 | 0.1833 | 0.6332 | 0.4505 |
| Norway | 1950–1986 | −0.0448 | 0.0625 | −0.0875 | 0.0719 | 0.0402 | 0.1748 |
| Panama | 1950–1986 | 0.5969 | 0.0858 | 0.5775 | 0.0900 | 0.6592 | 0.0811 |
| Peru | 1960–1984 | −0.0713 | 0.1171 | 0.1116 | 0.1696 | 0.0419 | 0.2337 |
| Philippines | 1948–1986 | 0.0424 | 0.0762 | 0.2202 | 0.1069 | −0.2266 | 0.0721 |
| Portugal | 1953–1982 | 0.1769 | 0.1692 | 0.3533 | 0.2599 | 0.3291 | 0.2994 |
| Singapore | 1960–1984 | 0.6022 | 0.1369 | 1.0316 | 0.3661 | 0.3166 | 0.0477 |
| South Africa | 1948–1986 | 0.2071 | 0.0763 | 0.2615 | 0.0914 | 0.3203 | 0.1317 |
| Spain | 1954–1984 | 0.3507 | 0.1255 | 0.5020 | 0.0945 | 0.3289 | 0.0699 |
| Sweden | 1950–1986 | 0.0067 | 0.0971 | 0.1648 | 0.1015 | 0.4184 | 0.1732 |
| Switzerland | 1948–1986 | 0.8264 | 0.1137 | 0.7475 | 0.1254 | 0.7940 | 0.1693 |
| Tunisia | 1960–1983 | 0.5251 | 0.1703 | 0.7856 | 0.2896 | 0.1342 | 0.1536 |
| United Kingdom | 1948–1986 | −0.0199 | 0.0958 | 0.0793 | 0.1293 | −0.0766 | 0.2197 |
| United States | 1948–1986 | 0.6714 | 0.0771 | 0.7229 | 0.0598 | 0.8486 | 0.1915 |
| Venezuela | 1950–1985 | 0.1146 | 0.0623 | 0.3252 | 0.1239 | −0.0240 | 0.0784 |
| Zaire | 1950–1984 | 0.0160 | 0.0414 | −0.0188 | 0.0419 | −0.0502 | 0.0984 |
| Across-country values | | | | | | | |
| Mean | | 0.2419 | 0.0985 | 0.3422 | 0.1348 | 0.2761 | 0.1739 |
| Standard deviation | | 0.2719 | 0.0326 | 0.2796 | 0.0695 | 0.3463 | 0.1089 |

Source: Authors' estimates using equation 14. The data used in the estimation are from IMF, *International Financial Statistics*.
Notes: The dependent variable is the log of real output, $y_t$. The output-inflation trade-off parameter, $\tau$, is the coefficient of the change in nominal demand, expressed as differences in logarithms.

Table 4 shows that the trade-off parameter sometimes changes substantially from the period through 1972 to the period after 1972. For the United States, there is little change in the estimate. But in 63 percent of the countries, one can reject the hypothesis of no change in $\tau$ at the 5 percent level. Across countries, the correlation between $\tau$ estimated with the earlier data and the $\tau$ estimated with the later data is 0.36. It appears that there can be substantial change in the output-inflation trade-off over time.

**The determinants of the trade-off: cross-section results**   We now wish to see whether the cross-country variation in the estimated trade-off $\tau$ can be explained. Our theoretical model suggests that $\tau$ should be low in countries where the variability of aggregate demand is high and in countries where the average level of inflation is high. Our primary attention is on these two hypotheses.

Figures 1 and 2 present scatterplots of the trade-off parameter $\tau$ against the mean level of inflation $\bar{\pi}$, the log of the mean level of inflation, and the standard deviation of the change in aggregate demand $\sigma_x$. Both pictures display the negative relation predicted by theory.

Figure 1 also suggests that the relation between the trade-off parameter and mean inflation is nonlinear. This result should not be surprising. As the rate of inflation grows larger, the trade-off parameter should decline. But we do not expect $\tau$ to decline below zero. The relation between $\bar{\pi}$ and $\tau$ should be convex. An increase in inflation from 5 percent to 10 percent should have a larger effect on $\tau$ than an increase from 10 percent to 15 percent. When we turn to formal estimation, therefore, a linear specification is likely to be inadequate.

Because our sample includes a few countries with extremely high inflation rates, it is difficult to gauge the relationship between the estimated trade-off and mean inflation among low- and moderate-inflation countries from the top portion of figure 1. The bottom portion therefore presents a scatterplot of $\tau$ against the log of mean inflation. That portion shows that the inverse relation between $\tau$ and $\bar{\pi}$ holds at both low and high inflation rates.

Figure 3, a scatterplot of mean inflation and the standard deviation of nominal GNP growth, shows a strong positive relation. This figure thus reestablishes the well-known fact that countries with high levels of inflation tend to have unstable aggregate demand. The correlation between these two variables is 0.92. We will see below, however, that multiple regression

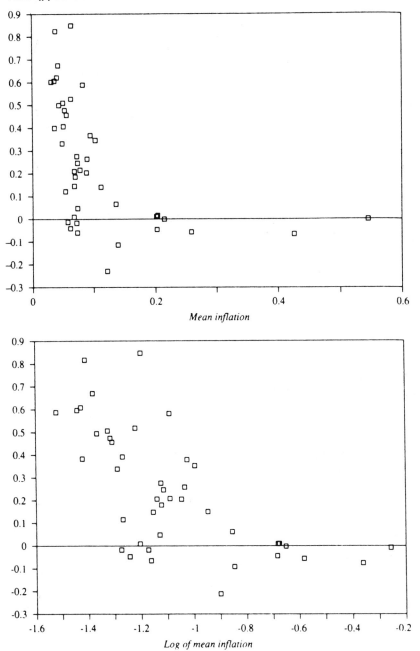

**Figure 1**
Mean inflation and the trade-off between output and inflation. The parameter $\tau$, the trade-off between output and inflation, is from table 4. Mean inflation is from table 3.

*Trade-off parameter*

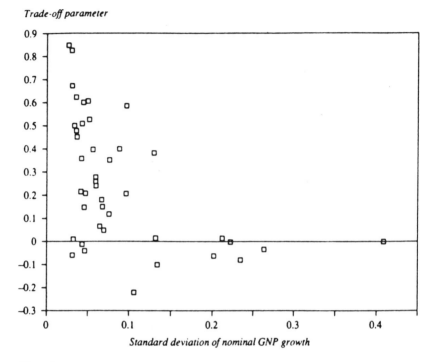

Standard deviation of nominal GNP growth

**Figure 2**
The variability of demand and the trade-off between output and inflation. The parameter $\tau$, the trade-off between output and inflation, is from table 4. Standard deviation of nominal GNP growth is from table 3.

is able to identify separate effects of these two variables on the output-inflation trade-off.

Table 5 presents cross-sectional regressions of the estimated values of the trade-off parameter $\tau$ on the mean of inflation $\bar{\pi}$ and the standard deviation of aggregate demand growth $\sigma_x$. To account for the nonlinearity, the squares of these variables are also included in some regressions.[42] The last column is the most general specification; it includes both variables and allows both to enter nonlinearly. As expected, the second-order term in mean inflation is statistically significant.[43]

The estimates in table 5 suggest that mean inflation is a statistically significant determinant of the inflation-output trade-off, but that demand variability is not. The hypothesis that inflation and inflation squared do not enter regression 5.6 is rejected at the 5 percent level. The hypothesis

*Mean inflation*

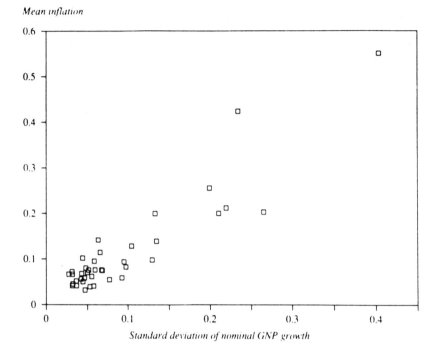

Standard deviation of nominal GNP growth

**Figure 3**
Mean inflation and the variability of demand. The source of the data is table 3.

that the standard deviation of aggregate demand and its square do not enter is not rejected even at the 20 percent level. An examination of the substantive implications of regression 5.6 also shows that only mean inflation is important. For example, an increase in mean inflation from 5 percent to 10 percent, as might be plausible for the United States, would reduce the trade-off by 0.22. An increase in $\sigma_x$ from 5 percent to 10 percent increases the trade-off by 0.04. Hence, only the effects of inflation on the trade-off are substantively important.

Note that the estimated effect of aggregate demand variability on the trade-off is positive, not negative as predicted by theory. This result is not obtained when mean inflation and its square are left out of the regression. Yet when all the variables are included, the variability coefficients, although small and statistically insignificant, have the wrong sign. This result is puzzling, and we have no definite explanation (but see the discussion below).

**Table 5**
Determinants of the output-inflation trade-off, full sample period

| Independent variable | Equation | | | | | |
|---|---|---|---|---|---|---|
| | 5.1 | 5.2 | 5.3 | 5.4 | 5.5 | 5.6 |
| Constant | 0.384 | 0.388 | 0.389 | 0.600 | 0.516 | 0.589 |
| | (0.053) | (0.057) | (0.057) | (0.079) | (0.089) | (0.086) |
| Mean inflation | −1.347 | | −1.119 | −4.835 | | −5.729 |
| | (0.368) | | (0.919) | (1.074) | | (1.973) |
| Square of mean inflation | | | | 7.118 | | 8.406 |
| | | | | (2.088) | | (3.849) |
| Standard deviation of nominal GNP growth | | −1.639 | −0.322 | | −4.242 | 1.241 |
| | | (0.482) | (1.183) | | (1.512) | (2.467) |
| Square of standard deviation of nominal GNP growth | | | | | 7.455 | −2.380 |
| | | | | | (4.118) | (7.062) |
| Summary statistic | | | | | | |
| $\bar{R}^2$ | 0.228 | 0.201 | 0.210 | 0.388 | 0.243 | 0.359 |
| Standard error | 0.241 | 0.245 | 0.244 | 0.215 | 0.239 | 0.219 |

Source: Authors' calculations.
Notes: The dependent variable is the output-inflation trade-off parameter, $\tau$ (estimated in table 4). Numbers in parentheses are standard errors.

Tables 6 and 7 present the same regressions for the data ending in 1972 and the data beginning in 1973. In both subsamples we find similar results. In high-inflation countries, aggregate demand has a smaller effect on output.

To make clear the implications of our regression results, table 8 presents the predicted values of $\tau$ for various inflation rates. We present results for each of our samples, in each case using the most general specification (regressions 5.6, 6.6, and 7.6) and assuming $\sigma_x = 3$ percent. The results show that the effects of average inflation are large. At a zero rate of inflation, fluctuations in aggregate demand are in the first year reflected two-thirds in output and one-third in prices. At a 5 percent rate of inflation, the first-year impact on output is between one-third and one-half. At a 20 percent rate of inflation, the estimated first-year impact on output is small and sometimes negative.

**The determinants of the trade-off: time-series cross-section results**   Table 9 presents cross-country regressions of the change in the trade-off from the

**Table 6**
Determinants of the output-inflation trade-off, through 1972

| Independent variable | Equation | | | | | |
|---|---|---|---|---|---|---|
| | 6.1 | 6.2 | 6.3 | 6.4 | 6.5 | 6.6 |
| Constant | 0.501 | 0.518 | 0.519 | 0.595 | 0.539 | 0.575 |
| | (0.053) | (0.075) | (0.069) | (0.085) | (0.165) | (0.175) |
| Mean inflation | −3.051 | | −2.783 | −6.081 | | −5.803 |
| | (0.730) | | (0.979) | (2.287) | | (2.417) |
| Square of mean inflation | | | | 12.145 | | 11.939 |
| | | | | (8.696) | | (8.946) |
| Standard deviation of nominal GNP growth | | −3.589 | −0.654 | | −4.295 | 0.583 |
| | | (1.281) | (1.570) | | (4.958) | (4.959) |
| Square of standard deviation of nominal GNP growth | | | | | 3.845 | −6.605 |
| | | | | | (26.066) | (24.440) |
| Summary statistic | | | | | | |
| $\bar{R}^2$ | 0.281 | 0.140 | 0.267 | 0.298 | 0.119 | 0.266 |
| Standard error | 0.239 | 0.262 | 0.242 | 0.237 | 0.266 | 0.242 |

Source: Authors' calculations.
Notes: The equations are specified exactly as in table 5 but are estimated with data only through 1972. Numbers in parentheses are standard errors.

first to the second subsample on the change in the mean level of inflation and the change in variability. These regressions test Keynesian and new classical theories by examining the differences across countries, not in the level of the output-inflation trade-off, but in the change in the trade-off over time. These regressions have the advantage of correcting for any fixed country effects. For example, the extent of wage and price rigidity and thus the output-inflation trade-off may depend on various country-specific institutions, such as the laws governing labor negotiation. If such institutions do not change substantially from our first to our second subsample, then they will not introduce a bias in these regressions, even if they do introduce a bias in the regressions in levels.[44]

The results in table 9 are qualitatively the same as those for the level regressions above, but the estimated effects are somewhat smaller. For example, regression 5.6 implies that an increase in inflation from 5 percent to 10 percent reduces the trade-off by 0.22. In contrast, regression 9.6 implies that such an increase in inflation reduces the trade-off by only 0.12.

**Table 7**
Determinants of the output-inflation trade-off, after 1972

| Independent variable | Equation | | | | | |
|---|---|---|---|---|---|---|
| | 7.1 | 7.2 | 7.3 | 7.4 | 7.5 | 7.6 |
| Constant | 0.458 (0.071) | 0.431 (0.069) | 0.459 (0.072) | 0.683 (0.099) | 0.629 (0.103) | 0.731 (0.107) |
| Mean inflation | −1.025 (0.296) | | −0.888 (0.629) | −3.307 (0.809) | | −2.571 (1.162) |
| Square of mean inflation | | | | 3.144 (1.051) | | 2.043 (1.390) |
| Standard deviation of nominal GNP growth | | −1.852 (0.599) | −0.308 (1.244) | | −6.564 (1.952) | −2.808 (2.550) |
| Square of standard deviation of nominal GNP growth | | | | | 14.375 (5.700) | 8.827 (7.192) |
| Summary statistic | | | | | | |
| $\bar{R}^2$ | 0.207 | 0.169 | 0.189 | 0.336 | 0.265 | 0.328 |
| Standard error | 0.312 | 0.319 | 0.316 | 0.286 | 0.300 | 0.287 |

Source: Authors' calculations.
Notes: The equations are specified exactly as in table 5 but are estimated using data after 1972. Numbers in parentheses are standard errors.

**Table 8**
Predicted output-inflation trade-off at various inflation rates

| Mean inflation (%) | Regression | | |
|---|---|---|---|
| | 5.6 | 6.6 | 7.6 |
| 0 | 0.62 | 0.59 | 0.65 |
| 5 | 0.36 | 0.33 | 0.53 |
| 10 | 0.14 | 0.13 | 0.42 |
| 15 | −0.05 | −0.02 | 0.32 |
| 20 | −0.19 | −0.10 | 0.22 |

Source: Author's calculations based on regression equations 5.6, 6.6, and 7.6 from tables 5, 6, and 7.
Note: These figures assume the standard deviation of nominal GNP growth, $\sigma_t$, is 3 percent.

**Table 9**
Explaining the change in the output-inflation trade-off

| Independent variable | Equation | | | | | |
|---|---|---|---|---|---|---|
| | 9.1 | 9.2 | 9.3 | 9.4 | 9.5 | 9.6 |
| Constant | 0.009 (0.078) | −0.037 (0.062) | 0.009 (0.085) | 0.172 (0.091) | −0.012 (0.059) | 0.154 (0.104) |
| Change in mean inflation | −0.595 (0.442) | | −0.603 (0.773) | −3.174 (0.968) | | −2.619 (1.458) |
| Change in the square of mean inflation | | | | 3.094 (1.054) | | 1.895 (1.608) |
| Change in the standard deviation of nominal GNP growth | | −0.852 (0.787) | 0.016 (1.366) | | −5.820 (2.095) | −2.384 (3.046) |
| Change in the square of standard deviation of nominal GNP growth | | | | | 14.392 (5.678) | 9.094 (8.589) |
| Summary statistic | | | | | | |
| $\bar{R}^2$ | 0.019 | 0.004 | −0.005 | 0.173 | 0.121 | 0.158 |
| Standard error | 0.359 | 0.362 | 0.364 | 0.329 | 0.340 | 0.333 |

Source: Authors' calculations.
Notes: The dependent variable is $\tau_{late} - \tau_{early}$, where $\tau_{late}$ is the estimate of $\tau$ using data after 1972 and $\tau_{early}$ is the estimate of $\tau$ using data through 1972. Numbers in parentheses are standard errors.

This finding may be due to the possibility of bias in the regression in levels discussed above.

There are two other reasons why the regression for the change in the trade-off might produce smaller effects of mean inflation, one statistical and one economic. The statistical reason is that the change in the sample mean inflation might be a very noisy estimator of the change in the true mean inflation. Such sampling error would tend to bias downward the coefficients. This downward bias is probably smaller in the levels regression, because the "signal to noise" ratio is greater. The noise is less because the sampling error for the level of inflation is less than it is for the change in inflation; the signal is greater because the variation in the level of mean inflation across countries is plausibly larger than the variation in the change in mean inflation across countries. Hence, measurement error in mean inflation due to sampling error is probably a more important problem for the regressions in table 9 than for those in tables 5, 6, and 7.

The economic reason is that the frequency with which prices are adjusted might not change immediately with changes in the mean level of inflation. For example, a company that issues a catalog once a year might not switch to issuing a catalog twice a year unless it were certain that the change in mean inflation were permanent. Hence, changes in mean inflation observed between our two subsamples might have been perceived as partly transitory and may have evoked smaller changes in price-setting behavior.

### Econometric issues and robustness

Having estimated the output-inflation trade-offs for different countries using standard specifications, we next discuss econometric issues raised by those specifications and examine a series of variations on our basic test. Our central finding, that the effect of nominal demand movements on real output falls as average inflation rises, is robust.

**Supply shocks**   In both the theoretical model of equations 5 to 13 and the preceding empirical work, we assume that all aggregate shocks are demand shocks. In actual economies, of course, output movements result from supply as well as demand shocks. The residual of equation 14 reflects these supply shocks. We now investigate the effects of supply shocks on our results.

The presence of supply shocks can in principle cause several distinct problems. As we explain below, our estimates of the trade-off parameter $\tau$ are biased if changes in nominal GNP are correlated with supply shocks, as can occur either if aggregate demand is not unit elastic or if supply and demand shocks are correlated. Most important, supply shocks can bias our estimates of the key relationship between $\tau$ and average inflation. This is the case if average inflation is correlated with bias in the estimated $\tau$s.

Before considering these separate problems, we perform a simple check of their overall importance by examining whether the results change when we restrict our attention to the period through 1972, when supply shocks are generally thought to have been less significant. Comparison of tables 5 and 6 shows that ending the sample in 1972 has essentially no effect on the results. Focusing on the period after 1972, on the other hand, leads to weaker results, suggesting that if supply shocks have any effect on our results, it is to obscure the phenomenon for which we are testing.

We now turn to the specific problems caused by supply shocks, beginning with bias in the estimates of $\tau$. This parameter gives the output effects of demand shocks, as measured by $\Delta x$. Supply shocks can be viewed as variables left out of the output equation, and so they cause bias if they are correlated with $\Delta x$. Supply shocks directly affect $\Delta x$ as long as the aggregate demand curve is not unit elastic; only with unit elastic demand do the movements in $p$ and $y$ caused by supply shocks have exactly offsetting effects on $x$.[45] In addition, even if demand is unit elastic, so $\Delta x$ reflects only demand shocks, movements in demand and supply may be correlated. This is the case, for example, if monetary policy accommodates supply shocks.[46]

The importance of these problems is questionable. Available evidence suggests that an elasticity of aggregate demand of roughly one is realistic.[47] And the endogeneity of monetary policy can *reduce* bias: policymakers may respond to supply shocks in a way that eliminates the effects on nominal GNP. In any case, we empirically investigate the importance of biases in $\hat{t}$ in two ways. First, note that if aggregate demand has elasticity of $a \neq 1$, a supply shock affects $x = p + y$ but leaves $ap + y$ unchanged. The same is true if policymakers target $ap + y$ rather than $p + y$. If supply shocks leave $ap + y$ unaffected, the effect of aggregate demand movements can be estimated by regressing $y_t$ on $\Delta(ap_t + y_t)$ rather than $\Delta x_t$.[48] The estimated coefficients can then be regressed on average inflation and the standard deviation of changes in $ap + y$. Thus a check for bias caused by supply shocks is to posit a range of values of $a$ and examine whether the results are robust to the choice of $a$. We consider four values for $a$ ranging from 0.5 to 2. For $a = 0.5$ the second-stage regression (with quadratic terms included) yields

$$\hat{t}_{a=0.5} = 0.812 - 6.397\bar{\pi} + 10.935\bar{\pi}^2 + 8.630\sigma_{0.5p+y} - 58.140\sigma^2_{0.5p+y},$$
$$\quad\quad\; (0.110) \;\; (1.628) \quad\; (3.671) \quad\;\; (4.704) \quad\quad\quad (30.706)$$

$\bar{R}^2 = 0.421$ \quad standard error $= 0.231,$

where $\hat{t}_{a=0.5}$ denotes the coefficient on $\Delta(ap_t + y_t)$ with $a = 0.5$ from the first-stage regression (standard errors are in parentheses). For $a = 2$,

$$\hat{t}_{a=2} = 0.211 - 2.632\bar{\pi} + 3.569\bar{\pi}^2 + 0.167\sigma_{2p+y} + 0.116\sigma^2_{2p+y},$$
$$\quad\quad\; (0.038) \;\; (0.995) \;\; (1.851) \quad\; (0.585) \quad\quad (0.792)$$

$\bar{R}^2 = 0.333$ \quad standard error $= 0.100.$

The results are similar to those for our baseline case: the coefficients on the average inflation variables are of the predicted sign, quantitatively large, and statistically significant; the coefficients on the variability measures are small, wrong-signed, and insignificant. (Because the units of $\sigma_{ap+y}$ and $\tau_a$ depend on $a$, the magnitudes of the coefficients from different regressions are not directly comparable.) The results for $a = 0.67$ and $a = 1.5$ are also similar.

A second approach to reducing bias in the estimates of $\tau$ is to include measures of supply shocks in our equation for the output-inflation trade-off—that is, to add the left-out variable. We focus on oil price changes, which are the most easily identifiable and perhaps the largest supply shocks during our sample period. We do this by including a dummy variable in our estimation of the output-inflation trade-off (equation 14) that is equal to $+1$ in the years of major oil-price increases (1974, 1979, and 1980) and $-1$ in the one year of a major price decrease (1986). (The natural alternative of entering a separate dummy for each of these years is equivalent to simply discarding these years from the sample, and would thus be similar to the previous strategy of stopping the sample in 1972.) Including the dummy has little effect on the results: the correlation of the $\tau$s estimated with and without the dummies is 0.98, and the regressions of the estimated $\tau$s on average inflation and the variability of demand growth are little changed; in fact, the magnitude and significance of the effect of average inflation are slightly larger.

So far we have addressed the problem of supply shocks by attempting to reduce the possible bias in the estimates of $\tau$. We now turn to the implications of any remaining bias for our estimates of the cross-country relation between $\tau$ and average inflation. Bias in these estimates arises from biases in $\hat{\tau}$ only if the latter are correlated with average inflation. This correlation could occur if the variance of supply shocks or the degree to which they are accommodated, which affects the bias in $\hat{\tau}$, is correlated with average inflation.[49] But there is no strong reason to expect this. For example, suppose that one country expands aggregate demand in response to un-favorable supply shocks and contracts in response to favorable shocks (so that shocks fall mainly on prices), while another country does the reverse. The estimates of $\tau$ are biased in different directions for the two countries, but the bias is not correlated with average inflation because neither country is pursuing a systematically more expansionary policy. On the other hand, if one country always pursues more expansionary policies, stimulating de-mand after both favorable and unfavorable shocks, then the countries have different average inflation, but $\hat{t}$ is not biased because nominal growth and supply shocks are uncorrelated.

Although we do not think it likely that bias in $\tau$ caused by supply shocks is correlated with average inflation, we check for such a problem. The effects of supply shocks on the cross-country regression can be reduced by controlling for differences in the size of these shocks. We experiment with two types of measures of the size of supply shocks. The first are country characteristics. Specifically, we use the degree of industrialization, measured by manufacturing output as a fraction of total output in 1965, and the degree of openness, measured by the ratio of imports to output in 1965.[50] Both variables probably affect a country's susceptibility to supply shocks. (Both could also affect the output-inflation trade-off in ways unrelated to supply shocks.) When these variables are included in regression 5.6, however, their coefficients are small and highly insignificant; more important, the coefficients on the remaining variables are virtually unchanged.

The second type of variable that we add to the cross-section regression is a crude measure of the magnitude of supply shocks. Since the residual of equation 14 reflects supply shocks, we use the variance of the residual, $\sigma_\epsilon^2$, as a measure of the variance of supply shocks. We measure the variance of demand shocks by the variance of nominal GNP growth, $\sigma_x^2$; thus $\sigma_\epsilon^2/\sigma_x^2$ is a crude proxy for the relative magnitudes of supply and demand shocks. Adding this ratio to our cross-section regression yields

$$\hat{t} = 0.163 - 5.421\bar{\pi} + 7.833\bar{\pi}^2 + 3.451\sigma_x - 5.317\sigma_x^2 + 1.339(\sigma_\epsilon^2/\sigma_x^2),$$
$$\quad (0.143) \quad (1.731) \quad (3.377) \quad (2.251) \quad (6.245) \quad (0.379)$$

$$\bar{R}^2 = 0.508 \qquad \text{standard error} = 0.192.$$

The coefficient on $\sigma_\epsilon^2/\sigma_x^2$ is positive and significant. This could occur if supply shocks fall mainly on output rather than prices, thereby causing a positive bias in $\hat{t}$, with the size of the bias increasing in the relative size of supply shocks. In any case, the coefficients on the variables of central interest, $\bar{\pi}$ and $\bar{\pi}^2$, are essentially unchanged. The effect of demand variability remains wrong-signed and insignificant but is now somewhat larger than before.

In sum, a wide variety of tests fails to provide any evidence that supply shocks have an important effect on our results.

**Specification of the cross-country regression**  Another issue concerning our specification, which is related to the possibility of supply shocks discussed above, is how to measure aggregate variability. Since the only aggregate shocks in our theoretical model are demand shocks, the model implies that the variance of nominal GNP growth is the appropriate measure. But if the model were extended to include aggregate supply shocks, the variance of inflation might be a better measure. The frequency of price changes, and hence $\tau$, would depend on the variances of both shocks. And while $\sigma_x^2$ might capture only the variance of demand shocks (for example, if demand is unit elastic), $\sigma_\pi^2$ would reflect both variances.

Replacing $\sigma_x$ with $\sigma_\pi$ in our cross-country regression leads to

$$\hat{\tau} = 0.616 - 3.221\bar{\pi} + 4.072\bar{\pi}^2 - 2.235\sigma_\pi + 5.513\sigma_\pi^2,$$
$$\quad\ (0.085)\quad (2.254)\quad (4.098)\quad (2.572)\quad (6.708)$$

$$\bar{R}^2 = 0.367 \qquad \text{standard error} = 0.218.$$

Inflation and inflation squared are now not statistically significant. The point estimates, however, continue to suggest that average inflation has a large effect on the output-inflation trade-off; for example, an increase in $\bar{\pi}$ from 5 percent to 10 percent reduces $\tau$ by 0.13. In addition, the estimated effects of variability, although highly imprecise, are now in the direction predicted by our model and are quantitatively reasonable; they imply that an increase in $\sigma_\pi$ from 5 percent to 10 percent reduces $\tau$ by 0.07. It may be that the puzzling results in our basic specification concerning the effects of variability result from an inappropriate variability measure.

It might appear that a natural extension of this consideration of alternative variability measures is to include both $\sigma_x$ and $\sigma_\pi$ in the cross-country regression. But this specification is unlikely to provide useful information: it is likely to produce small coefficients on average inflation regardless of whether average inflation truly affects $\tau$. To see why, suppose that the correct model is

$$\Delta y = \tau \Delta x + \epsilon, \tag{15}$$

where $\epsilon$ is a supply shock that is uncorrelated with $\Delta x$. Then, since $\pi = \Delta x - \Delta y$, $\sigma_\pi^2 = (1 - \tau)^2 \sigma_x^2 + \sigma_\epsilon^2$, and so

$$(1 - \tau)^2 = \frac{\sigma_\pi^2}{\sigma_x^2} - \frac{\sigma_\epsilon^2}{\sigma_x^2}. \tag{16}$$

Expression 16 is an identity and thus holds regardless of how $\tau$ is determined. Regressing $\tau$ on $\sigma_x$ and $\sigma_\pi$ would fail to produce a perfect fit only because of cross-country variation in $\sigma_\epsilon$ and because the functional form of equation 16 is not linear. Adding average inflation to an equation that is almost an identity does not yield a valid test of the importance of this variable. For a given variance of supply shocks, the variance of inflation is determined completely by the variance of demand shocks ($\sigma_x^2$) and the proportion of each shock that is reflected in inflation $(1 - \tau)$. Thus regressing any one of $\tau$, $\sigma_x^2$, and $\sigma_\pi^2$ on the other two should provide an excellent fit and leave little room for other explanatory variables. Again, this is true regardless of whether our theory of the determinants of $\tau$ is correct.

We conclude that if there were a theory that suggested that $\tau$ was a function of both $\sigma_x$ and $\sigma_\pi$, the type of test that we employ would be unable to discriminate between such a model and our model. We know of no such theory, however.[51]

**Specification of the output-inflation trade-off**  In the first part of this section, following Lucas and others, we estimated the short-run output-inflation trade-off by regressing real output on the change in nominal GNP and other variables. Our model, however, predicts that real output in the current period will depend on the innovation in nominal GNP in the current period and on lagged innovations (see equation 12). Thus the theory suggests a specification of form

$$y_t = \tau(x_t - E_{t-1}x_t) + \sum_i \alpha_i(x_{t-i} - E_{t-(i+1)}x_{t-i}) + \beta'Z_t, \tag{17}$$

where $E_t$ denotes an expectation at time $t$, $x$ is nominal demand, and $Z$ is a vector of other variables that affect output.

The equation that we use to estimate $\tau$, equation 14, differs from equation 17 by omitting past innovations and by employing the change in nominal GNP rather than the current innovation. Because $x_t - E_{t-1}x_t$ reflects information learned in period $t$ and is thus uncorrelated with all variables known at time $t - 1$, the omission of past innovations does not bias the estimate of $\tau$. The use of $\Delta x_t$ in place of the current innovation also poses no difficulties. A natural way to estimate equation 17 would be to employ a two-stage procedure, first regressing $x_t$ on a set of variables known at time $t - 1$ and then using the fitted values from this regression as an estimate of $E_{t-1}x_t$ in equation 17.[52] Estimating equation 14, however, is numerically identical to first regressing $\Delta x_t$ on the other right-hand-side variables and then using the residuals from this regression rather than $\Delta x_t$ in equation 14. Thus equation 14 can be thought of as a simple one-step way of implementing the two-stage procedure, with the right-hand-side variables for the first regression the same as the control variables in the second stage.

While our regression is in principle equivalent to a two-stage procedure, one could argue that our specification in equation 14 includes too few control variables to capture expected movements in demand. Specifically, in countries where expected inflation varies considerably over time, a large part of the variation in $\Delta x$ will be predictable (on the basis of lagged $\Delta x$, for example), but cannot be predicted using only the other right-hand-side variables of equation 14. We have also estimated more elaborate versions of equation 14 in which output depends on two lags of output, current and two lagged values of nominal GNP, and a time trend. This specification appears to be rich enough for the residuals from regressing nominal GNP on the other-hand-side variables to largely represent innovations; for example, the residuals do not exhibit serial correlation. For approximately half of the countries, one can reject the restrictions imposed by equation 14 in favor of the more general equation. Yet the estimate of the coefficient on nominal GNP, which is our main interest, is not substantially affected by these restrictions. For the United States, for example, one can reject the restrictions in favor of the more general equation at the 1 percent level; yet the estimate of $\tau$ changes only from 0.642 to 0.656. Across the 43 countries, the correlation between the $\tau$ estimated from equation 14 and the $\tau$ estimated from the more general equation is 0.88. Moreover, using the $\tau$s from the more elaborate equation for the cross-section regression has only minor effects on the results. We thus conclude that the simpler equation is sufficient for our purposes.

The parsimony of our equation also has an important statistical advantage. When we divide the time series in half and estimate the inflation-output trade-off for data both through and after 1972, we are sometimes left with very short times series: less than a dozen years. The simpler equation, even if rejected by the data for the overall sample, may be preferred because it conserves on the scarce degrees of freedom.[53]

**The sample**    To examine the effects of restricting the sample of countries, we limit the sample in two ways. First, to check whether our results depend crucially on a few extreme observations, we examine the effects of excluding countries with extreme average inflation and extreme variability of demand growth. Specifically, we drop from the sample the six countries with average inflation rates and standard deviations of nominal GNP growth greater than 20 percent (Argentina, Bolivia, Brazil, Israel, Peru, and Zaire). Second, because there may be systematic differences between the major industrialized countries and the remaining countries in our sample that influence both the output-inflation trade-off and average inflation or nominal demand variability, we consider the effects of restricting the sample to OECD countries.[54] One of these countries, Iceland, has both average inflation and standard deviation of nominal GNP growth that are nearly double those of any of the other OECD countries; we therefore consider the results both with and without Iceland. Of course, restrictions on the sample have the disadvantage of discarding some of the variation in the right-hand-side variables, which could make the relationships for which we are testing more difficult to detect.

When we estimate the cross-country regression with the six countries with high inflation and high demand variability excluded, we find that

$$\hat{t} = 1.042 - 10.563\bar{\pi} + 28.998\bar{\pi}^2 - 5.933\sigma_x + 40.634\sigma_x^2,$$
$$\quad (0.253) \quad (4.485) \quad (21.968) \quad (7.032) \quad (45.214)$$

$$\bar{R}^2 = 0.306 \qquad \text{standard error} = 0.225.$$

The results are similar to those for the full sample of countries: average inflation has a large and statistically significant effect on the output-inflation trade-off (inflation and inflation squared are jointly significant at the 1 percent level), while variability has a small and insignificant impact on the trade-off.

As before, we also regress the change in the trade-off between the period ending in 1972 and the period beginning in 1973 on the changes in average inflation and aggregate demand variability. This yields

$$\Delta\hat{t} = 0.189 - 3.089\Delta\bar{\pi} - 0.514\Delta\bar{\pi}^2 - 12.163\Delta\sigma_x + 80.887\Delta\sigma_x^2,$$
$$\quad (0.126) \quad (2.554) \quad (5.522) \quad (5.113) \quad (32.505)$$

$$\bar{R}^2 = 0.324 \qquad \text{standard error} = 0.315.$$

The change in average inflation has an important effect on the change in the trade-off; the null hypothesis that the coefficients on $\Delta\bar{\pi}$ and $\Delta\bar{\pi}^2$ are zero is rejected at the 5 percent level. The estimated relationship is essentially linear. Changes in variability also have an important effect on the trade-off. As $\sigma_x$ rises, increases in $\sigma_x$ first lower and then raise $\tau$.

Table 10 presents the results for OECD countries. We estimate the cross-country equation for our entire sample of years and for the two

**Table 10**
Determinants of the output-inflation trade-off for OECD countries

| Independent variable | Equation | | | | | |
|---|---|---|---|---|---|---|
| | Iceland included | | | Iceland excluded | | |
| | Trade-off full sample | Trade-off through 1972 | Trade-off after 1972 | Trade-off full sample | Trade-off through 1972 | Trade-off after 1972 |
| Constant | 1.073 (0.413) | 0.840 (0.673) | 1.124 (0.532) | 4.369 (1.082) | 1.470 (0.955) | 2.215 (0.832) |
| Mean inflation | −21.831 (17.608) | −19.665 (14.220) | −6.450 (4.941) | −68.672 (20.279) | −47.146 (32.716) | −17.881 (8.361) |
| Square of mean inflation | 118.022 (126.624) | 144.447 (101.199) | 20.284 (21.167) | 477.128 (150.937) | 460.137 (353.076) | 76.422 (39.482) |
| Standard deviation of nominal GNP growth | 9.020 (30.008) | 7.343 (28.282) | 1.485 (40.461) | −77.961 (36.209) | 4.061 (28.613) | −37.254 (45.024) |
| Square of standard deviation of nominal GNP growth | −140.708 (298.452) | −117.567 (320.871) | −258.212 (575.272) | 804.893 (379.404) | −79.342 (324.757) | 326.317 (651.012) |
| Summary statistic | | | | | | |
| $R^2$ | 0.147 | −0.036 | 0.453 | 0.457 | 0.008 | 0.395 |
| Standard error | 0.264 | 0.243 | 0.246 | 0.210 | 0.244 | 0.235 |

Source: Authors' calculations. See text description.
Notes: The dependent variable is the output-inflation trade-off parameter, $\tau$, estimated in table 4. Numbers in parentheses are standard errors.

subsamples. In all cases, the inflation coefficients have the predicted signs and are large. As expected, however, they are estimated much less precisely than for the larger sample of countries. Consequently, the results are often not statistically significant. For the entire sample of years, the inflation coefficients are jointly significant only when Iceland is excluded (column 4). This regression implies that an increase in inflation from 4.5 percent to 7.9 percent, which is from one standard deviation below the mean to one standard deviation above the mean, reduces the trade-off parameter $\tau$ by 0.32.

Finally, we estimate the determinants of the change in the trade-off for OECD countries. The results are little affected by the inclusion of quadratic terms or by whether Iceland is included in the sample. We therefore focus on the linear specification with Iceland included. We find that

$$\Delta\hat{\tau} = 0.192 - 2.580\Delta\bar{\pi} - 7.428\Delta\sigma_x,$$
$$\phantom{\Delta\hat{\tau} = } (0.068) \quad (0.792) \qquad (2.779)$$

$$\bar{R}^2 = 0.583 \qquad \text{standard error} = 0.189.$$

Both coefficients have the expected sign and are large and statistically significant, and the fit is excellent.

**Output variability**   If higher average inflation reduces the real effects of nominal disturbances, it also reduces the variability of output. In our theoretical model, equation 12 shows that the variance of $y$ falls when $1 - w(\cdot)$ falls. Thus another test of Keynesian theory is to examine the link between average inflation and output variability. As before, new classical theories, because they attribute fluctuations to unanticipated nominal disturbances and to real shocks, predict no role for average inflation.

In estimating the relation between output variability and average inflation, it is of course necessary to control for the variance of nominal GNP growth. Both Keynesian theories and Lucas's imperfect information theory predict that an increase in the size of nominal shocks will increase the variance of output (in both Lucas's theory and our model, the direct effect of increased shocks is only partially offset by a smaller responsiveness of output to shocks). Because the variance of nominal GNP growth is highly correlated with average inflation, omitting this variable could cause severe bias.

Table 11 reports the results.[55] Output variability is measured by the standard deviation of real GNP growth $\sigma_y$. The first two columns show that the variability of output growth is positively correlated with both

**Table 11**
Determinants of output variability

| Independent variable | Equation | | | | | |
|---|---|---|---|---|---|---|
| | 11.1 | 11.2 | 11.3 | 11.4 | 11.5 | 11.6 |
| Constant | 0.0315 | 0.0290 | 0.0290 | 0.0270 | 0.0174 | 0.0202 |
| | (0.0032) | (0.0032) | (0.0031) | (0.0053) | (0.0047) | (0.0044) |
| Mean inflation | 0.0418 | | −0.0817 | 0.1150 | | −0.3254 |
| | (0.0220) | | (0.0507) | (0.0719) | | (0.1009) |
| Square of mean inflation | | | | −0.1494 | | 0.6294 |
| | | | | (0.1398) | | (0.1967) |
| Standard deviation of nominal GNP growth | | 0.0777 | 0.1740 | | 0.3143 | 0.6581 |
| | | (0.0270) | (0.0653) | | (0.0786) | (0.1261) |
| Square of standard deviation of nominal GNP growth | | | | | −0.6779 | −1.572 |
| | | | | | (0.2140) | (0.361) |
| Summary statistic | | | | | | |
| $\bar{R}^2$ | 0.058 | 0.148 | 0.180 | 0.062 | 0.302 | 0.429 |
| Standard error | 0.0144 | 0.0137 | 0.0135 | 0.0144 | 0.0124 | 0.0112 |

Source: Authors' calculations. See text description.
Notes: Dependent variable is output variability, measured by the standard deviation of real GNP growth, $\sigma_y$. Numbers in parentheses are standard errors.

mean inflation and demand variability. Regression 11.3 shows the effects of including both variables on the right-hand side. The estimated effect of $\bar{\pi}$ is negative and that of $\sigma_x$ positive. As before, there are reasons to expect nonlinearities: the negative impact of mean inflation should diminish as mean inflation rises, and the positive impact of variability should also fall as variability rises. The final column of table 11 reports the results with quadratic terms included. All four variables have the signs predicted by Keynesian theory, and all of the $t$-statistics exceed 3. The implied effects are large: an increase in mean inflation from 5 percent to 10 percent reduces the standard deviation of output growth, $\sigma_y$, by 1.2 percentage points, while an increase in the standard deviation of nominal growth from 5 percent to 10 percent increases $\sigma_y$ by 2.1 percentage points. This finding of a strong inverse link between mean inflation and output variability confirms the predictions of Keynesian theories and contradicts those of new classical theories.[56]

**Reexamining previous evidence.** Numerous studies have examined Lucas's proposition that the variability of aggregate demand affects the output-inflation trade-off. Here we reexamine several such studies and show that the evidence provided by other authors largely supports our claim that average inflation is an important determinant of the trade-off.

Lucas originally examined 18 countries with data from 1952 to 1967.[57] Our cross-country regression using the trade-offs estimated by Lucas and his sample statistics yields

$$\hat{\tau} = 0.929 - 6.034\bar{\pi} + 19.641\bar{\pi}^2 - 8.397\sigma_x + 32.369\sigma_x^2,$$
$$(0.304) \quad (5.698) \quad (24.967) \quad (9.435) \quad (43.212)$$

$$\bar{R}^2 = 0.446 \qquad \text{standard error} = 0.185.$$

Alberro redid Lucas's study with a sample of 49 countries.[58] The cross-country regression estimated with Alberro's figures is

$$\hat{\tau} = 0.752 - 6.620\bar{\pi} + 14.763\bar{\pi}^2 - 0.158\sigma_x + 5.230\sigma_x^2,$$
$$(0.089) \quad (2.021) \quad (7.150) \quad (1.875) \quad (4.325)$$

$$\bar{R}^2 = 0.418 \qquad \text{standard error} = 0.242.$$

Both Lucas's and Alberro's estimates provide strong support for our hypothesis that high rates of inflation reduce the real impact of nominal demand. The estimated effects of average inflation are large. An increase in average inflation from 5 percent to 10 percent implies a fall in $\tau$ of 0.15 when Lucas's figures are used and of 0.22 when Alberro's figures are used. These results are quite similar to those we obtained in table 8, even though the periods of time and samples of countries are substantially different. Hence, the results of Lucas and Alberro provide support for new Keynesian rather than new classical theories of the business cycle.

We have also examined the evidence of Kormendi and Meguire on the output effects of unanticipated money.[59] A cross-country regression of their estimate of the impact of unanticipated changes in the money supply, which they call $\chi$, on their estimate of the variance of unanticipated money and on the average rate of inflation yields

$$\chi = 0.906 - 3.508\bar{\pi} + 19.422\bar{\pi}^2 - 15.908\sigma_{um} + 94.093\sigma_{um}^2,$$
$$(0.230) \quad (5.390) \quad (33.844) \quad (6.055) \quad (47.834)$$

$$\bar{R}^2 = 0.303 \qquad \text{standard error} = 0.140.$$

(Since Kormendi and Meguire do not provide the average rate of inflation, we obtain it from our sample. We restrict the regression to the 26 countries for which we can match their sample period exactly.)

In contrast to the results of Lucas and Alberro, the estimates of Kormendi and Meguire do not provide support for our hypothesis. Inflation has little effect on $\chi$, while the variance of unanticipated money appears an important determinant. There are a variety of ways to reconcile this finding with the previous results.

One possibility is that money is measured with error and that the extent of measurement error varies across countries. Greater measurement error in the money supply would tend to reduce the estimate of $\chi$ while increasing the variability of unanticipated money. Measurement error would also make it more difficult to isolate the effect of inflation on the trade-off.

A second possibility is that money may be a bad measure of aggregate demand. If different countries follow different policies regarding the extent to which they offset exogenous demand shocks, such as changes in monetary velocity, then $\chi$ will again be a noisy measure.

An examination of the estimated $\chi$ suggests it is not a good measure of the real impact of aggregate demand. In particular, the correlation between the estimates of $\chi$ provided by Kormendi and Meguire and the estimates of $\tau$ we obtain for the same 26 countries over the same time samples is only 0.38. Moreover, the United States appears a very unusual country. The estimated $\chi$ for the United States is 0.96, the largest in the sample. The second biggest $\chi$ is 0.38 for Belgium. Since it seems implausible that the United States is such an extreme outlier, we conclude that $\chi$ is probably not a good measure of the output-inflation trade-off.

A third possibility is that high average inflation, by increasing price flexibility, reduces the effects of aggregate demand on output but *increases* the effect of money on aggregate demand. In this case, the influence of average inflation on the net effect of money on output is ambiguous. De Long and Summers present a model in which price flexibility increases the effect of monetary shocks on demand by increasing the variability of expected inflation.[60] Future research might use cross-country data to untangle the effects of price flexibility on the money-demand and demand-output links.

## Conclusion

We have examined the short-run trade-off between output and inflation using international data. A robust finding is that this trade-off is affected by the average rate of inflation. In countries with low inflation, the short-run Phillips curve is relatively flat—fluctuations in nominal aggregate demand have large effects on output. In countries with high inflation, the Phillips curve is steep—fluctuations in demand are reflected quickly in the price level. The same finding emerges when we examine the change in the trade-off over time. Countries that experience an increase in average inflation also typically experience an increased responsiveness of prices to aggregate demand.

Our finding has three important implications. First, it provides evidence against new classical theories of the output-inflation trade-off. In his classic study, Lucas found that international differences in the trade-off were related to differences in the variability of aggregate demand and interpreted his finding as evidence for the imperfect information theory of the business cycle. This theory, however, predicts that the trade-off should not be related to average inflation. It is therefore inconsistent with our empirical results.

Second, our finding supports new Keynesian theories of the business cycle that derive nominal rigidities from optimizing behavior. Our theoretical model of price adjustment shows that macroeconomic effects of the sort we observe can result from empirically plausible microeconomic parameters. In particular, average inflation can strongly influence the output-inflation trade-off through its effects on the frequency of price changes.

Third, our finding implies that the trade-off faced by macroeconomic policymakers depends on the average rate of inflation and that it changes when the average rate of inflation changes. This effect is substantial even for moderate rates of inflation. Our estimates using the entire sample imply that the real impact of aggregate demand is twice as great at 5 percent inflation as at 10 percent inflation. Perhaps the short-run Phillips curve Alan Greenspan is facing today is not the same one that Paul Volcker faced a decade age.

## Appendix

This appendix describes how we solve our model of nominal rigidity.

### The behavior of $p(t)$ for a given $\lambda$

The first step is to derive the behavior of the aggregate price level for a given interval between price changes, $\lambda$. Substituting the formula for a firm's profit-maximizing price, equation 5, into the price-setting rule, equation 7, yields,

$$p_i = \frac{1}{\lambda} \int_{s=0}^{\lambda} E_t\{p(t+s) + v[y(t+s) - \bar{y}(t+s)]\}\, ds + \theta_i(t). \tag{A1}$$

Let $Q(t)$ be the average of all prices that are *set* at $t$. Equation A1 implies

$$Q(t) = \frac{1}{\lambda} \int_{s=0}^{\lambda} E_t\{p(t+s) + v[y(t+s) - \bar{y}(t+s)]\}\, ds, \tag{A2}$$

where the $\theta_i$s average to zero because they are uncorrelated across firms. Using the facts that $y(t) = x(t) - p(t)$, $E_t x(t+s) = x(t) + gs$ (because $x$ follows a random walk with drift), and $\bar{y}(t) = \mu t$, we can rewrite equation A2 as

$$Q(t) = (1 - v)\frac{1}{\lambda} \int_{s=0}^{\lambda} E_t p(t+s)\, ds$$

$$+ vx(t) + v\frac{g\lambda}{2} - v\mu\left(t + \frac{\lambda}{2}\right). \tag{A3}$$

The aggregate price level, $p(t)$, is the average of prices in effect at $t$. With our assumption of staggered price setting, this means that $p(t)$ is the average of prices set from $t - \lambda$ to $\lambda$:

$$p(t) = \frac{1}{\lambda} \int_{s=0}^{\lambda} Q(t-s)\, ds \tag{A4}$$

Substituting equation A4 into equation A3 yields

$$Q(t) = (1 - v)\frac{1}{\lambda} \int_{s=0}^{\lambda} E_t \frac{1}{\lambda} \int_{s=0}^{\lambda} Q(t+s-r)\, dr\, ds$$

$$+ vx(t) + v\frac{gs}{2} - v\mu\left(t + \frac{\lambda}{2}\right)$$

$$= (1 - v)\frac{1}{\lambda^2}\left[\int_{s=0}^{\lambda} (\lambda - s)Q(t-s)\, ds\right.$$

$$\left. + \int_{s=0}^{\lambda} (\lambda - s)E_t Q(t+s)\, ds\right]$$

$$+ vx(t) + v\frac{g\lambda}{2} - v\mu\left(t + \frac{\lambda}{2}\right). \tag{A5}$$

According to equation A4, prices set at $t$ depend on prices set between $t - \lambda$ and $t$, which are still in effect, and on expectations of prices set between $t$ and $t + \lambda$, the period when prices set at $t$ are in effect.

Equation A4 gives an expression for $Q$ in terms of its own past and expected future values. Our goal is to solve for $Q$ as a function of the underlying demand disturbances. To do this we use the method of undetermined coefficients. That is, we posit a solution of form

$$Q(t) = A + Bt + \int_{s=0}^{\infty} q(s; \lambda) \, dZ(t - s) \tag{A6}$$

and then solve for $A$, $B$, and $q(\cdot)$. The term $q(s; \lambda)$ is the fraction of a nominal shock at $t - s$ that is passed into newly set prices at $t$. Substituting equation A6 into equation A5 and simplifying, we obtain

$$A + Bt + \int_{s=0}^{\infty} q(s; \lambda) \, dZ(t - s)$$

$$= (1 - v)A + (1 - v)Bt$$

$$+ (1 - v)\frac{1}{\lambda^2} \int_{s=0}^{\infty} \left[ \int_{r=0}^{\min(s, \lambda)} (\lambda - r)q(s - r; \lambda) \, dr \right.$$

$$+ \left. \int_{r=0}^{\lambda} (\lambda - r)q(s + r; \lambda) \, dr \right] dZ(t - s)$$

$$+ vgt + v \int_{s=0}^{\infty} dZ(t - s) + \frac{vg\lambda}{2} - v\mu\left(t + \frac{\lambda}{2}\right). \tag{A7}$$

For equation A7 to hold, the constant terms, the coefficients on $t$, and the coefficients on $dZ(t - s)$ on the two sides of the equation must be equal. Setting them equal leads to

$$A = (g - \mu)(\lambda/2)$$

$$B = g - \mu$$

$$q(s; \lambda) = v + (1 - v)\frac{1}{\lambda^2}\left[ \int_{r=0}^{\min(s, \lambda)} (\lambda - r)q(s - r; \lambda) \, dr \right.$$

$$+ \left. \int_{r=0}^{\lambda} (\lambda - r)q(s + r; \lambda) \, dr \right]. \tag{A8}$$

The last equation in equation A8 defines $q(\cdot; \lambda)$ implicitly. We cannot find a closed-form solution for $q(\cdot; \lambda)$.[61] Finding $q(\cdot)$ numerically, however, is straightforward. We do this by making an initial guess of $q(\cdot; \lambda)$, substituting this guess of the function into the right-hand side of equation A7 (approximating the integrals numerically), thereby obtaining a new $q(\cdot; \lambda)$, and then iterating this procedure until $q(\cdot; \lambda)$ converges.[62]

All that remains to describe the behavior of the economy for a given $\lambda$ is to translate the results concerning the behavior of newly set prices into a description of the behavior of the price level. Substituting equation A6 and the solutions for A and B into equation A4 leads to

$$p(t) = (g - \mu)t + \int_{s=0}^{\infty} w(s; \lambda) \, dZ(t - s)$$

$$w(s; \lambda) = \int_{r=0}^{\min(s, \lambda)} q(s - r; \lambda) \, dr. \tag{A9}$$

The first line in equation A9 is the formula for the aggregate price level in the text (equation 10). We compute $w(\cdot)$ using the second line.[63]

As described in the text, the solution for $p(t)$ leads directly to a solution for the real effects of nominal shocks.

### The equilibrium $\lambda$

We now describe how we solve for the equilibrium interval between price changes, $\lambda^E$. Recall that $\lambda^E$ is the solution to equation 13,

$$\left. \frac{\partial L(\lambda_i, \lambda^E)}{\partial \lambda_i} \right|_{\lambda_i = \lambda^E} = 0,$$

where $L(\lambda_i, \lambda)$ gives firm $i$'s loss as a function of its interval between price changes and the common interval of other firms. Using the formula for the loss function, equation 6, and assuming without loss of generality that $p_i$ is set at time zero, we can write $L(\lambda_i, \lambda)$ as

$$L(\lambda_i, \lambda) = \frac{F}{\lambda_i} + \frac{1}{\lambda_i} \frac{1}{2} K \int_{s=0}^{\lambda_i} E[p_i^*(s) - p_i]^2 \, ds. \tag{A10}$$

Differentiating equation A10 with respect to $\lambda_i$ and evaluating at $\lambda_i = \lambda$, we find

$$\frac{\partial L(\lambda_i, \lambda)}{\partial \lambda_i}\bigg|_{\lambda_i = \lambda} = -\frac{F}{\lambda^2} - \frac{1}{\lambda^2}\frac{1}{2}K\int_{s=0}^{\lambda} E[p_i^*(s) - p_i]^2 \, ds$$

$$+ \frac{1}{\lambda}\frac{1}{2}KE[p_i^*(\lambda) - p_i]^2. \qquad (A11)$$

(The Envelope Theorem allows us to eliminate the term

$$\frac{1}{\lambda_i}\frac{1}{2}K\frac{\partial}{\partial p_i}\left\{\int_{s=0}^{\lambda_i} E[p_i^*(s) - p_i]^2 \, ds\right\}\frac{\partial p_i}{\partial \lambda_i} \quad \text{from} \quad \frac{\partial L(\lambda_i, \lambda)}{\partial \lambda_i},$$

because the firm optimally chooses $p_i$ given $\lambda_i$, the effect of the marginal change in $p_i$ when $\lambda_i$ changes on the objective function is zero.)

Evaluating equation A11 requires that we find $E[p_i^*(s) - p_i]^2$ for $0 \leq s \leq \lambda$. Equations A1 and A2 imply that the deviation of $p_i$ from $Q(0)$, the average of prices set at the same time as $p_i$, is $\theta_i(0)$. Thus, using the solution for $Q(t)$ (equations A6 and A8), we obtain

$$p_i = (g - \mu)(\lambda/2) + \int_{r=0}^{\infty} q(r; \lambda) \, dZ(-r) + \theta_i(0). \qquad (A12)$$

Substituting the solution for $p(t)$, equation A9, the process for $x(t)$, equation 8, and the identity $y = x - p$ into the formula for $p_i^*$, equation 5, we obtain

$$p_i^*(s) = (g - \mu)s + \int_{r=0}^{\infty} [v + (1 - v)w(r; \lambda)] \, dZ(s - r) + \theta_i(s). \qquad (A13)$$

Finally, equations A12 and A13 lead to

$$E[p_i^*(s) - p_i]^2 = (g - \mu)(s - \lambda/2)^2 + s\sigma_\theta^2$$

$$+ \sigma_x^2\left\{\int_{r=0}^{s} [v + (1 - v)w(r; \lambda)]^2 \, dr\right.$$

$$\left. + \int_{r=s}^{\infty} [v + (1 - v)w(r; \lambda) - q(r - s; \lambda)]^2 \, dr\right\}, \qquad (A14)$$

where we have used the fact that changes in $Z$ and in $\theta_i$ are uncorrelated both over time and with each other.

We can now solve numerically for the equilibrium value of $\lambda$. We begin by guessing a value of $\lambda$. After finding $q(\cdot; \lambda)$ and $w(\cdot; \lambda)$ as described above, we evaluate equation A14 numerically for $s$ between 0 and $\lambda$. We then use these results to evaluate the derivative in equation A11. If the derivative is negative, so the representative firm can reduce its loss by increasing its interval between price changes, we raise our guess of $\lambda$; if the derivative is positive, we reduce $\lambda$. We continue until the derivative converges to zero.[64]

## Acknowledgments

We thank Toshiki Jinushi, David Johnson, and David Weil for research assistance; Ray Fair, Paul Wachtel, and members of the Brookings Panel for helpful discussions; and the National Science Foundation for financial support.

## Notes

1. Keynesian models of wage and price adjustment based on Phillips curves provided poor fits to the data of the early to mid 1970s. But subsequent modifications of the models, such as the addition of supply shocks, have led to fairly good performances. See the discussions in Olivier J. Blanchard, "Why Does Money Affect Output? A Survey," working paper 2285 (National Bureau of Economic Research, June 1987), and Robert J. Gordon, "Postwar Developments in Business Cycle Theory: An Unabashedly New-Keynesian Perspective," Keynote Lecture, 18th CIRET Conference, Zurich, September 1987.

2. For disequilibrium models, see Robert J. Barro and Herschel I. Grossman, "A General Disequilibrium Model of Income and Employment," *American Economic Review*, vol. 61 (March 1971), pp. 82–93; and E. Malinvaud, *The Theory of Unemployment Reconsidered* (Basil Blackwell, 1977). For contract models, see Stanley Fischer, "Long-Term Contracts, Rational Expectations and the Optimal Money Supply Rule," *Journal of Political Economy*, vol. 85 (February 1977), pp. 191–205; and Jo Anna Gray, "On Indexation and Contract Length," *Journal of Political Economy*, vol. 86 (February 1978), pp. 1–18.

3. Lawrence H. Summers, "Should Keynesian Economics Dispense with the Phillips Curve?" in Rod Cross, ed., *Unemployment, Hysteresis, and the Natural Rate Hypothesis* (Basil Blackwell, 1988), p. 12.

4. Robert E. Lucas, Jr., "Expectations and the Neutrality of Money," *Journal of Economic Theory*, vol. 4 (April 1972), pp. 103–124; Lucas, "Some International Evidence on Output-Inflation Tradeoffs," *American Economic Review*, vol. 63 (June 1973), pp. 326–334.

5. Some of the ideas of this literature are discussed informally by earlier Keynesian authors. To cite just two examples, see the discussion of asynchronized timing of price changes in Robert J. Gordon, "Output Fluctuations and Gradual Price Adjustment." *Journal of Economic Literature*, vol. 19 (June 1981), pp. 493–530, and the discussion of externalities from nominal rigidity in Charles L. Schultze, "Microeconomic Efficiency and Nominal Wage Stickiness," *American Economic Review*, vol. 75 (March 1985), pp. 1–15.

6. N. Gregory Mankiw, "Small Menu Costs and Large Business Cycles: A Macroeconomic Model of Monopoly," *Quarterly Journal of Economics*, vol. 100 (May 1985), pp. 529–537; George A. Akerlof and Janet L. Yellen, "A Near-Rational Model of the Business Cycle, with Wage and Price Inertia," *Quarterly Journal of Economics*, vol. 100 (1985, Supplement), pp. 823–838; Olivier Jean Blanchard and Nobuhiro Kiyotaki, "Monopolistic Competition and the Effects of Aggregate Demand," *American Economic Review*, vol. 77 (September 1987), pp. 647–666; Laurence Ball and David Romer, "Are Prices Too Sticky?" working paper 2171 (NBER, February 1987).

7. The only essential feature of equation 3 is the negative relation between $Y$ and $P$. We can interpret $M$ as simply a shift term in the aggregate demand equation. Thus, as we discuss below, the results in recent papers concern the effects of any shock to aggregate demand, not just changes in the money stock.

8. Ball and Romer, "Are Prices Too Sticky?"

9. Laurence Ball and David Romer, "Real Rigidities and the Non-neutrality of Money," working paper 2476 (NBER, December 1987).

10. John B. Taylor, "Staggered Wage Setting in a Macro Model," *American Economic Review*, vol. 69 (May 1979, *Papers and Proceedings, 1978*), pp. 108–113; Taylor, "Aggregate Dynamics and Staggered Contracts," *Journal of Political Economy*, vol. 88 (February 1980), pp. 1–23; Olivier J. Blanchard. "Price Asynchronization and Price Level Inertia," in Rudiger Dornbusch and Mario Henrique Simonsen, eds., *Inflation, Debt, and Indexation* (MIT Press, 1983), pp. 3–24; Olivier J. Blanchard, "The Wage Price Spiral," *Quarterly Journal of Economics*, vol. 101 (August 1986), pp. 543–565.

11. A natural question is why firms change prices at different times if this exacerbates aggregate fluctuations. One obvious answer is that different firms receive shocks at different times and face different costs of price adjustment. Laurence Ball and David Romer, "The Equilibrium and Optimal Timing of Price Changes," working paper 2412 (NBER, October 1987), show that, because of externalities from staggering, idiosyncratic shocks can lead to staggering even if synchronized price setting is Pareto superior. But idiosyncratic shocks cannot explain all staggering. For example, some firms with two-year labor contracts set wages in even years and some set them in odd years, and this does not correspond to deterministic two-year cycles in the arrival of shocks. Another explanation for staggering is that it arises from firms' efforts to gain information. This source of staggering is discussed in Arthur M. Okun, *Prices and Quantities: A Macroeconomic Analysis* (Brookings, 1981), and formalized in Laurence Ball and Stephen G. Cecchetti, "Imperfect Information and Staggered Price Setting," working paper 2201 (NBER, April 1987). For example, a firm wants to set wages in line with the wages of other firms. If all wages are set simultaneously, each firm is unsure of what wage to set because it does not know what others will do. This gives each firm an incentive to set its wage shortly after the others. The desire of each firm to "bat last," as Okun puts it, can lead in equilibrium to a uniform distribution of signing dates.

12. Blanchard, "Price Asynchronization."

13. Timur Kuran shows that asymmetries in firms' profit functions, which many menu cost models ignore, can lead to asymmetric price rigidity. But the asymmetries appear small. See Timur Kuran, "Asymmetric Price Rigidity and Inflationary Bias," *American Economic Review*, vol. 73 (June 1983), pp. 373–382; Kuran, "Price Adjustment Costs, Anticipated Inflation, and Output," *Quarterly Journal of Economics*, vol. 101 (May 1986), pp. 407–418.

14. See, for example, Kenneth J. Arrow, "Toward a Theory of Price Adjustment," in Moses Abramovitz and others, eds., *The Allocation of Economic Resources: Essays in Honor of Bernard Francis Haley* (Stanford University Press, 1959), pp. 41–51.

15. Fischer, "Long-Term Contracts," and Gray, "On Indexation."

16. Of course economists worry that low unemployment may be inflationary. But sticky-price models with perfect competition imply that low unemployment is undesirable per se.

17. Robert E. Hall, "Market Structure and Macroeconomic Fluctuations," *BPEA*, 2 (1986), pp. 285–322; Julio J. Rotemberg and Garth Saloner, "A Supergame-Theoretic Model of Price Wars during Booms," *American Economic Review*, vol. 76 (June 1986), pp. 390–407; Mark Bils, "Cyclical Pricing of Durable Luxuries," working paper 83 (University of Rochester Center for Economic Research, May 1987).

18. Early expositions of this idea appear in Martin Neil Baily, "Wages and Employment under Uncertain Demand," *Review of Economic Studies*, vol. 41 (January 1974), pp. 37–50;

Costas Azariadis, "Implicit Contracts and Underemployment Equilibria," *Journal of Political Economy*, vol. 83 (December 1975), pp. 1183–1202; and Robert E. Hall, "The Rigidity of Wages and the Persistence of Unemployment," *BPEA*, 2 (1975), pp. 301–335.

19. Robert J. Barro, "Output Effects of Government Purchases," *Journal of Political Economy*, vol. 89 (December 1981), pp. 1086–1121.

20. Olivier J. Blanchard and Lawrence Summers, "Hysteresis and the European Unemployment Problem," in Stanley Fischer, ed., *NBER Macroeconomics Annual, 1986* (MIT Press, 1986), pp. 15–78.

21. Stephen G. Cecchetti, "The Frequency of Price Adjustment: A Study of the Newsstand Prices of Magazines," *Journal of Econometrics*, vol. 31 (August 1986), pp. 255–274. The cost of reducing nominal wage rigidity may be significant if rigidity is reduced through shorter labor contracts, which require more frequent negotiations between unions and management. But wage rigidity can also be reduced through greater indexation or by having the nominal wage change more often over the life of a contract, neither of which appears to have large costs.

22. Bennett T. McCallum, "On 'Real' and 'Sticky-Price' Theories of the Business Cycle," *Journal of Money, Credit, and Banking*, vol. 18 (November 1986), pp. 397–414.

23. Akerlof and Yellen, "A Near-Rational Model."

24. The speed of adjustment is also endogenous in Laurence Ball, "Externalities from Contract Length," *American Economic Review*, vol. 77 (September 1987), pp. 615–629.

25. Taylor, "Staggered Wage Setting" and "Aggregate Dynamics and Staggered Contracts"; and Blanchard, "Price Asynchronization" and "Wage Price Spiral."

26. As an example of foundations for equation 5, suppose that firm $i$'s demand equation is $y_i = y - \epsilon(p_i - p)$ (demand depends on aggregate spending and the firm's relative price), and that its log costs are $\gamma y_i + (1 - \epsilon + \epsilon\gamma)\theta_i$. This implies equation 5 with $v = (\gamma - 1)/(1 - \epsilon + \epsilon\gamma)$ and $\bar{y} = [1/(\gamma - 1)]\ln[(\epsilon - 1)/\epsilon\gamma]$ (the coefficient on $\theta_i$ in the cost function is chosen to satisfy the normalization that the coefficient on $\theta_i$ in equation 5 is one). For deeper microfoundations, see Ball and Romer, "Equilibrium and Optimal Timing of Price Changes," where a price-setting rule like equation 5 is derived from utility and production functions.

27. We assume that price setting is staggered so that inflation is smooth. If all firms changed prices at the same times, the aggregate price level would remain constant between adjustments and then jump discretely. We do not model the sources of staggering explicitly; for explanations of staggering, see the references in note 11.

28. More precisely, we assume that $\theta_i$ follows a stationary process and consider the limit as this process approaches a random walk. (If $\theta_i$ is a random walk, its mean is undefined, which contradicts our earlier assumption that its mean is zero.)

29. If $v > 1$, firms want to adjust their prices more than one-for-one with real output. As a result, in this case the approach to full adjustment is oscillatory. The response is again slower when the frequency of price adjustment is lower.

30. Solving for the equilibrium interval between price changes is different from the common exercise of solving for the socially optimal interval. See, for example, Gray. "On Indexation" (which focuses on the interval between wage changes—that is, the length of labor contracts). The equilibrium and optimal intervals differ because, as we stress in the first section, firms' choices of the frequency of price adjustment have externalities. See Ball, "Externalities from Contract Length," for a further discussion of this point.

31. For microeconomic evidence on price behavior, see Cecchetti, "The Frequency of Price Adjustment"; Anil K. Kashyap, "Sticky Prices: New Evidence from Retail Catalogs" (MIT, November 1987); and W. A. H. Godley and C. Gillion, "Pricing Behavior in Manufacturing Industry," *National Institute Economic Review*, no. 33 (August 1965), pp. 43–47.

32. Daniel R. Vining, Jr., and Thomas C. Elwertowski, "The Relationship between Relative Prices and the General Price Level," *American Economic Review*, vol. 66 (September 1976), pp. 699–708. As a measure of $\sigma_\theta$, Vining and Elwertowski's figure has both an upward and a downward bias. The upward bias occurs because staggered price adjustment causes actual prices, the $p_i$s, to vary across firms even when profit-maximizing prices, the $p_i^*$s, do not. As a result, the standard deviation of $p_i$, which Vining and Elwertowski measure, is greater than the standard deviation of $p_i^*$, which equals $\sigma_\theta$. The negative bias in that variation across components of the CPI, even if these are highly disaggregated, is less than variation across individual prices. It is difficult to tell the relative magnitudes of these biases.

33. For a textbook model, see Rudiger Dornbusch and Stanley Fischer, *Macroeconomics*, 4th ed. (McGraw-Hill, 1987).

34. For evidence on mail order catalogs, see Kashyap, "Sticky Prices." For evidence on industries' preferred months for price changes, see Julio J. Rotemberg and Garth Saloner, "A 'January Effect' in the Pricing of Goods" (MIT, 1988).

35. The link between inflation and the frequency of adjustment is established for the case of constant inflation in Eytan Sheshinski and Yoram Weiss, "Inflation and Costs of Price Adjustment," *Review of Economic Studies*, vol. 44 (June 1977), pp. 287–303. An extension to the case of stochastic inflation is presented by Andrew S. Caplin and Eytan Sheshinski, "Optimality of (s, S) Pricing Policies" (Princeton University, 1987).

36. Andrew S. Caplin and Daniel F. Spulber. "Menu Costs and the Neutrality of Money," *Quarterly Journal of Economics*, vol. 102 (November 1987), pp. 703–725.

37. For the implications of persistent inflation, see Daniel Tsiddon, "On the Stubbornness of Sticky Prices" (Columbia University, July 1987). For the implications of falling optimal prices, see Blanchard, "Why Does Money Affect Output?" and Tsiddon, "The (Mis)behavior of the Aggregate Price Level" (Columbia University, 1987). These authors establish results for the special case in which a firm's optimal price moves one-for-one with aggregate demand and is independent of the price level ($v = 1$ in our notation).

38. See Akerlof and Yellen, "A Near-Rational Model."

39. For a recent real business-cycle model, see Edward C. Prescott, "Theory Ahead of Business Cycle Measurement," *Federal Reserve Bank of Minneapolis Quarterly Review*, vol. 10 (Fall 1986), pp. 9–22.

40. Robert G. King and Charles I. Plosser, "Money, Credit, and Prices in a Real Business Cycle," *American Economic Review*, vol. 74 (June 1984), pp. 363–380; N. Gregory Mankiw, "Real Business Cycles: A Neo-Keynesian Perspective," *Journal of Economic Perspectives* 3 (summer 1989): 79–90.

41. Lucas, "Some International Evidence"; Charles L. Schultze, "Cross-Country and Cross-Temporal Differences in Inflation Responsiveness," *American Economic Review*, vol. 74 (May 1984, *Papers and Proceedings, 1983*), pp. 160–165.

42. Including an interaction term does not affect the results.

43. Our measures of the short-run output-inflation trade-offs for the countries in our sample are estimates. Because $\tau$ is the dependent variable in our cross-section regressions, this measurement error does not cause bias. But because the measurement errors are of different sizes, they cause heteroskedasticity in the cross-section regression. Using the estimated variances of the errors (from the standard errors of the estimated trade-offs), we can correct for the heteroskedasticity and therefore obtain more efficient estimates. Our estimates imply, however, that less than a quarter of the average variance of the residuals in the cross-section regression is due to the errors in estimating the $\tau$s. As a result, accounting for the heteroskedasticity has virtually no effect on the results.

44. For these fixed country effects to bias the regressions in levels, the fixed effects must for some reason be correlated with the average level of inflation.

45. See Marcelle Arak, "Some International Evidence on Output-Inflation Tradeoffs: Comment," *American Economic Review*, vol. 67 (September 1977), pp. 728–730.

46. This discussion suggests that instrumental variables estimation is unlikely to be useful here. Appropriate instruments are variables that affect nominal GNP growth and are uncorrelated with supply shocks. If monetary and fiscal policies respond to supply shocks, measures of the stance of these policies are not valid instruments. Both for this reason and because of data limitations, we do not pursue use of instrumental variables.

47. For example, the values that Mankiw and Summers suggest for the relevant parameters of the *IS* and *LM* curves imply an elasticity of the aggregate demand curve of slightly less than one. N. Gregory Mankiw and Lawrence H. Summers, "Money Demand and the Effects of Fiscal Policies," *Journal of Money, Credit and Banking*, vol. 18 (November 1986), pp. 415–429.

48. As in our main regressions, we also include a constant, a trend, and $y_{t-1}$.

49. Indeed, a correlation between the variance of supply shocks and average inflation causes bias even if $\hat{\tau}$ is unbiased: the size of supply shocks is a left-out variable in the equation for $\tau$ because a large variance of supply (like a large variance of demand) reduces the frequency of price adjustment.

50. We are unable to obtain data on manufacturing output for Switzerland and Iceland; we therefore exclude these countries from the regression.

51. Our discussants consider the simple model that inflation and output growth are governed by independent processes and are therefore uncorrelated. This model is quite implausible. Simple real business cycle theories, for example, suggest that real output and nominal demand are determined independently, which implies that real growth and inflation are negatively correlated. More important, the discussants' model does *not* suggest a specification in which $\sigma_\pi$ and $\sigma_x$ are entered separately. Instead it predicts that the estimated $\tau$ should equal $1 - \sigma_\pi^2/\sigma_x^2$. When $\tau$ is regressed on this ratio, average inflation, and average inflation squared, the coefficients on the average inflation variables have the signs predicted by our theory and are significant at the 1 percent level. When the discussants, appealing to their simple model, regress $\tau$ on $\bar{\pi}$, $\sigma_\pi$, and $\sigma_x$ and their squares (which, as we explain above, is not the specification implied by the model), they find, as we expect, a positive effect of $\sigma_x$, a negative effect of $\sigma_\pi$, and a small effect of $\bar{\pi}$.

52. See Robert J. Barro, "Unanticipated Money, Output, and the Price Level in the United States," *Journal of Political Economy*, vol. 86 (August 1978), pp. 549–580.

53. If the theory were extended to allow demand to follow a process other than a random walk, it appears that it would imply that information about future changes in demand would also affect current output. Indeed, for most of the countries in our sample, changes in nominal GNP are positively serially correlated rather than white noise; moreover, the degree of serial correlation is positively correlated with average inflation. Thus a conceivable alternative explanation of our finding of an inverse link between the estimated $\tau$s and average inflation is that nominal GNP changes are more persistent in high-inflation countries and that they therefore lead to larger short-run price responses even though the frequency of price adjustment is constant across countries. We find this explanation implausible: a rough calculation using a discrete-time staggering model with persistent demand changes suggests that the magnitude of this effect is much too small, and testing this explanation directly by adding to the cross-section regression an estimate of the extent to which the current change in nominal GNP helps to predict future changes given information previously available leaves the results essentially unchanged.

54. There are 21 OECD countries in our sample: Australia, Austria, Belgium, Canada, Denmark, Finland, France, Germany, Greece, Iceland, Ireland, Italy, Japan, Netherlands, Norway, Portugal, Spain, Sweden, Switzerland, United Kingdom, and United States.

55. The links between output variability, average inflation, and demand variability are also examined in Lawrence H. Summers and Sushil B. Wadhwani, "Some International Evidence on Labour Cost Flexibility and Output Variability," working paper 981 (Centre for Labour Economics, June 1987).

56. The results for the two subperiods and for the change between the two subperiods point in the same direction as the results for the full sample but are less clear-cut. Both for the period through 1972 and for the change between the two subperiods the point estimates imply large negative effects of inflation on output variability. The estimates are highly imprecise, however; the null hypothesis of no effect cannot be rejected in either case. For the post-1972 period the point estimates imply that the effect of average inflation on output variability is not monotonic: it is negative at low inflation rates but becomes positive near the sample mean.

57. Lucas, "Some International Evidence."

58. Jose Alberro, "The Lucas Hypothesis and the Phillips Curve: Further International Evidence," *Journal of Monetary Economics*, vol. 7 (March 1981), pp. 239–250.

59. Roger C. Kormendi and Philip G. Meguire, "Cross-Regime Evidence of Macroeconomic Rationality," *Journal of Political Economy*, vol. 92 (October 1984), pp. 875–908.

60. J. Bradford De Long and Lawrence H. Summers, "Is Increased Price Flexibility Stabilizing?" *American Economic Review*, vol. 76 (December 1986), pp. 1031–1044.

61. Because $q(s; \lambda)$ equals a constant plus a weighted sum of values of values of $q(\cdot; \lambda)$ with sum of weights less than one, a solution to equation A7 exists and is unique.

62. The specifics of the algorithm are as follows. Since we know that $q(\cdot; \lambda)$ converges to one as $s$ approaches infinity, we assume that $q(\cdot; \lambda) = 1$ for $s \geq T$, $T = 9$ (time is measured in years). We then consider $q(s; \lambda)$ for $s = 0, h, 2h, \ldots, T - 2h, T - h$, where $h = 1/52$; thus we divide time into periods of a week. We begin by setting all of these $q(s; \lambda)$'s to one. New values are found by substituting this initial guess into the right-hand side of equation A7. An integral from $r = 0$ to $r = nh$ is approximated by averaging the values of the integral for $r = h, 2h, \ldots,$ $(n - 1)h$ and then multiplying by $nh$. (As described below, we consider only values of $\lambda$ that are integral multiples of $h$.) The new $q(s; \lambda)$'s are then substituted back into equation A7, and another set of values is computed. We continue this process until the mean of the absolute changes in the $q(s; \lambda)$'s from one iteration to the next is less than $\delta$, $\delta = 0.00002$. In all cases the algorithm appeared to converge to the solution without difficulty.

63. We approximate the integral using the procedure described in note 62.

64. We find $E[p_i^*(s) - p_i]^2$ for $s = 0, h, 2h, \ldots, \lambda - h, \lambda$, where, as before, $h = 1/52$. Since we assume $q(r; \lambda) = 1$ for $r \geq T$, and thus $w(r; \lambda) = 1$ for $r \geq T + \lambda$, we truncate the second integral in equation A14 at $r = T + \lambda$. Otherwise the integrals in equation A14 and equation A11 are approximated as described above. We stop when we find an $n$ such that equation A11 is negative for $\lambda = nh$ and positive for $\lambda = (n + 1)h$; we then set $\lambda$ at whichever value yielded the smaller absolute value of equation A11. All of the functions involved appeared to be well behaved, and convergence occurred without difficulty.

# II THE STAGGERING OF WAGES AND PRICES

# 7 Long-Term Contracts, Rational Expectations, and the Optimal Money Supply Rule

Stanley Fischer

This paper is concerned with the role of monetary policy in affecting real output and argues that activist monetary policy can affect the short-run behavior of real output, rational expectations notwithstanding. Recent contributions have suggested that the behavior of real output is invariant to the money supply rule chosen by the monetary authority if expectations are formed rationally.[1] The argument to the contrary advanced below turns on the existence of long-term contracts in the economy and makes the empirically reasonable assumption that economic agents contract in nominal terms for periods longer than the time it takes the monetary authority to react to changing economic circumstances—in this paper the relevant contracts are labor contracts.

The literature on the policy implications of rational expectations is relatively technical. It is therefore worthwhile to set the issue in recent historical perspective. Since the discovery of the Phillips curve in 1958,[2] the logic of the evolution of professional views on the ability of monetary policy to affect real output has tended toward a position similar to the empirically based early postwar Keynesian view that monetary policy can play no significant role in determining the behavior of output.

The Phillips curve was originally seen as a stable long-run relationship providing those combinations of unemployment and inflation rates among which policymakers could choose in accord with their preferences. The theoretical rationalization due to Lipsey (1960), based on the "law of supply and demand" in the labor market, did not affect that particular view of the curve.[3]

The famous "Phillips loops" around the long-run relationship, discussed in the original Phillips article, suggested that the short-run trade-off differed from the long-run relationship. The distinction between the short- and long-run trade-offs formed the basis for the originally startling natural-rate hypothesis of Friedman (1968) and Phelps (1967), which argued that while there was a short-run Phillips trade-off, there was in the long run a natural unemployment rate independent of the steady state rate of inflation. More dramatically, the natural-rate hypothesis implies that the long-run Phillips curve is vertical.

*Journal of Political Economy* 85 (1977), no. 1: 191–205. Copyright © 1977 by The University of Chicago. All rights reserved. Reprinted with permission.

The arguments rested on the point that the short-run trade-off was the result of expectational errors by economic agents. In Friedman's version, suppliers of labor at the beginning of an inflationary period underestimate the price level that will prevail over the period of the work contract, accordingly overestimate the real wage, and offer a greater supply of labor at the prevailing nominal wage than they would if expectations were correct. The result is employment in excess of the equilibrium level and a trade-off between output and unanticipated inflation.[4] However, the expectational errors cannot persist, so that employment returns to its equilibrium level —and unemployment returns to its natural rate—as expectations adjust to reality. Subsequent work by Phelps and others (1970) provided a better-worked-out theoretical foundation for the short-run trade-off.[5]

The dependence of the short-run trade-off on expectational errors did not by itself preclude any effects of monetary policy on output provided the monetary authority could produce a rate of inflation that was not anticipated. Indeed, the widespread use of adaptive expectations suggested that an ever accelerating rate of inflation could maintain an unemployment rate below the natural rate—hence, adherents of the natural rate hypothesis were for a time known as accelerationists. The accelerationist version of the natural-rate hypothesis had two important consequences. First, by making the short-run trade-off depend on expectational errors, it brought to the fore the question of the optimality of the natural rate.[6]

Second, the reliance of the accelerationist hypothesis on expectational errors made it possible that some mechanism of expectations other than adaptive expectations would imply that there is no trade-off usable by policymakers. Rational expectations is that hypothesis.[7]

Briefly, rational expectations as applied in the context of economic models is the hypothesis that expectations are the predictions implied by the model itself, contingent on the information economic agents are assumed to have.[8] In particular, if economic agents are assumed to know the policy rule being followed by the monetary authority, that rule itself will affect expectations. For instance, consider the consequences for the expected price level of a current price level that is higher than had been expected. Adaptive expectations implies that the price level currently expected for next period will be higher than the price level that was expected last period to prevail in this period. Under rational expectations, the expected price level will change in a manner dependent on the money supply rule: if monetary policy accommodates inflationary shocks, the expected price level will rise; if monetary policy counteracts inflationary shocks, the expected price level may be lower than the level expected for this period.

Now consider the implications of the rational expectations hypothesis for the effects on output of alternative preannounced monetary rules in an economy that has an expectational Phillips curve of the Lucas form:[9]

$$Y_t = \alpha + \beta(P_t - {}_{t-1}P_t) + u_t, \qquad \beta > 0, \tag{1}$$

where $\alpha$ and $\beta$ are constant parameters, $Y_t$ the level of output, $P_t$ the logarithm of the price level, and ${}_{t-1}P_t$ the expectation taken at the end of period $(t - 1)$ of $P_t$, and $u_t$ is a stochastic disturbance term.

The only way in which monetary policy can affect output, given (1), is by creating a difference between the actual price level and the expected price level. However, if the money supply rule is known to economic agents and is based on the same information as those agents have (for example, the money supply may be adjusted on the basis of lagged values of prices and output), then the predictable effects of the money supply on prices are embodied in ${}_{t-1}P_t$, and monetary policy can affect output only by doing the unexpected. Alternatively, if the monetary authority has superior information to private economic agents, say because it receives data more rapidly than they do, it can affect the behavior of output.[10] Superior information is, however, a weak reed on which to base the argument for the effectiveness of monetary policy because useful information has a habit of becoming available, perhaps through inference based on the actions of the monetary authority.

The argument made in this paper for the effectiveness of monetary policy depends instead on the existence of nominal long-term contracts in the economy. The aggregate supply equation (1) implies that the only expectation relevant to the behavior of output is the expectation formed one period earlier. The length of the period is not specified, but for the result to be interesting, one supposes that it is a year or less. Since there are contracts that are made for more than a year, expectations of $P_t$ made in periods earlier than $(t - 1)$ are likely to be relevant to the behavior of output.

In this paper I construct a model similar in spirit to the simple rational expectations models such as that of Sargent and Wallace (1975) (SW) and assume that expectations are formed rationally. If all contracts in the model economy are made for one period, the SW result on the irrelevance of the money supply rule for the behavior of output obtains; if there are some longer-term nominal contracts, then even fully anticipated monetary policy affects the behavior of output and there is room for a stabilizing monetary policy. The use of longer-term nominal contracts puts an element of stickiness into the nominal wage which is responsible for the effectiveness of monetary policy.

The paper does not provide a microeconomic basis for the existence of long-term nominal contracts, though the transaction costs of frequent price setting and wage negotiations must be part of the explanation. It will be seen below that the essential element needed for the effectiveness of monetary policy in this paper is that long-term contracts not be written in such a way as to duplicate the effects of a succession of single-period contracts, or the use of spot markets. It is reasonable to conjecture that the costs of wage setting lead to the use of long-term contracts and that the difficulties of contract writing prevent the emergence of contracts that are equivalent to the use of spot markets.

Section 1 introduces the model and demonstrates the fundamental rational expectations result on the irrelevance of monetary policy in a world where all contracts are made for only one period. Section 2 presents a model with overlapping labor contracts in which all labor contracts are made for two periods and in which at any one time half the firms are operating in the first year of a two-year contract and the other half in the second year of a contract. In this model monetary policy can affect the behavior of output. Section 3 considers various indexed labor contracts. Conclusions and further discussion are contained in section 4.

## 1   The Model with One-Period Contracts

The model used to study monetary policy in this paper has three elements: wage setting behavior, an output supply equation, and an aggregate demand equation. The economy is stationary in that the analysis abstracts from growth in the capital stock and an increasing price level though the latter is readily included. A potential role for stabilization policy is created by the assumption that the economy is subjected to random disturbances —real supply disturbances and nominal demand disturbances—that affect output and the price level in each period. Depending on the details of wage setting, monetary policy may be able to offset some of the effects of these disturbances on real output.

First we consider wage-setting behavior. The nominal wage is treated as predetermined throughout the paper in that it is known at the beginning of the period while output and the price level adjust during the period. The assumption that the wage is predetermined is based on the empirical observation that wages are usually set in advance of employment.

It is assumed that the nominal wage is set to try to maintain constancy of the real wage, which is equivalent in this model to maintaining constancy of employment and/or labor income; this assumption is based on recent work on the labor contract.[11] However, it should be emphasized that no substantive results of the paper would be affected if a nominal-wage *schedule* (e.g., specifying overtime payments) were to be negotiated, rather than simply a nominal-wage *rate*.[12]

If labor contracts are made every period, and assuming that the goal of nominal wage setting is to maintain constancy to the real wage,

$$_{t-1}W_t = \gamma + {}_{t-1}P_t, \tag{2}$$

where $_{t-1}W_t$ is the logarithm of the wage set at the end of period $t - 1$ for period $t$, $\gamma$ is a scale factor in the determination of the real wage and will be set at zero for convenience.

Second, the supply of output is assumed to be a decreasing function of the real wage:

$$Y_t^s = \alpha + (P_t - W_t) + u_t, \tag{3}$$

where, again, the coefficient $\beta$ of (1) has been set equal to unity for convenience, and where $\alpha$ will be taken to be zero; $P_t$ is the logarithm of the price level and $Y_t$ the level of output. It is assumed that firms operate on their demand curves for labor, that is, that the level of employment is determined by demand. If we substitute from (2) into (3),[13]

$$Y_t^s = (P_t - {}_{t-1}P_t) + u_t. \tag{4}$$

This is similar to the standard rational expectations supply function (1). The form of the aggregate supply function is essentially unaffected if the firm faces a nominal wage schedule in which the wage rises as labor input is increased.[14] The term $u_t$ is a stochastic "real" disturbance that impinges on production in each period; its properties will be specified below.

It remains now to close the model by taking demand considerations into account, and the simplest way of doing so is to specify a velocity equation,

$$Y_t = M_t - P_t - v_t, \tag{5}$$

where $M_t$ is the logarithm of the money stock in period $t$ and $v_t$ is a disturbance term.[15]

Disturbances aside, this very simple macro model would be assumed in equilibrium to have the real wage set at its full employment level, would imply the neutrality of money, and would obviously have no role for monetary policy in affecting the level of output. Note again that (2) implies that all wages are set each period—there are only one-period labor contracts. A potential role for monetary policy is created by the presence of the disturbances $u_t$ and $v_t$ that are assumed to affect the level of output each period. Each of the disturbances is assumed to follow a first-order autoregressive scheme:

$$u_t = \rho_1 u_{t-1} + \epsilon_t, \qquad |\rho_1| < 1, \tag{6}$$

$$v_t = \rho_2 v_{t-1} + \eta_t, \qquad |\rho_2| < 1, \tag{7}$$

where $\epsilon_t$ and $\eta_t$ are mutually and serially uncorrelated stochastic terms with expectation zero and finite variances $\sigma_\epsilon^2$ and $\sigma_\eta^2$, respectively.

We shall assume that expectations are formed rationally. Eliminating $Y_t$ between (4) and (5)—which is equivalent to assuming the price level adjusts each period to equate aggregate supply and demand—we get

$$2P_t = M_t + {}_{t-1}P_t - (u_t + v_t). \tag{8}$$

Now taking expectations as of the end of $(t-1)$ in (8) and noting that $E_{t-1}({}_{t-1}P_t) = {}_{t-1}P_t$,

$${}_{t-1}P_t = {}_{t-1}M_t - {}_{t-1}(u_t + v_t), \tag{9}$$

where ${}_{t-1}X_t$ is the expectation of $X_t$ conditional on information available at the end of $(t-1)$.

Assume the monetary rule is set on the basis of disturbances which have occurred up to and including period $(t-1)$. Then

$$M_t = \sum_{i=1}^{\infty} a_i u_{t-i} + \sum_{i=1}^{\infty} b_i v_{t-i}. \tag{10}$$

The disturbances can be identified ex post so that there is no difficulty for the monetary authority in following such a rule as (10) or for the public in calculating the next period's money supply. From (10) it follows that

$${}_{t-1}M_t = M_t \tag{11}$$

and thus that

$$P_t - {}_{t-1}P_t = \frac{M_t}{2} - \frac{{}_{t-1}P_t}{2} - \frac{u_t + v_t}{2}$$

$$= \frac{{}_{t-1}(u_t + v_t)}{2} - \frac{u_t + v_t}{2}$$

$$= \tfrac{1}{2}[\rho_1 u_{t-1} + \rho_2 v_{t-1} - (\rho_1 u_{t-1} + \epsilon_t + \rho_2 v_{t-1} + \eta_t)]$$

$$= -\tfrac{1}{2}(\epsilon_t + \eta_t). \tag{12}$$

The disturbances in (12) are current shocks that can be predicted by neither the monetary authority nor the public and thus cannot be offset by monetary policy.

By substitution of (12) into (4), it becomes clear that the parameters $a_i$ and $b_i$ of (10) have no effect on the behavior of output. Of course, as SW note, the monetary rule does affect the behavior of the price level, but since that is not at issue, there is no point in exploring the relationship further. The explanation for the irrelevance of the money supply rule for the behavior of output in this model is simple: money is neutral, and economic agents know each period what next period's money supply will be. In their wage setting they aim only to obtain a specified real wage, and the nominal wage is accordingly adjusted to reflect the expected price level.

Thus, the model with only one-period contracts confirms the SW result of the irrelevance of the monetary rule for the behavior of output.

## 2 The Model with Two-Period Nonindexed Labor Contracts

We now proceed to inject an element of stickiness into the behavior of the nominal wage. Suppose that all labor contracts run for two periods and that the contract drawn up at the end of period $t$ specifies nominal wages for periods $(t + 1)$ and $(t + 2)$.[16] Assuming again that contracts are drawn up to maintain constancy of the real wage, we specify

$$_{t-i}W_t = {}_{t-i}P_t, \qquad i = 1, 2, \tag{13}$$

where $_{t-i}W_t$ is the wage to be paid in period $t$ as specified in contracts drawn up at $(t - i)$, and $_{t-i}P_t$ is the expectation of $P_t$ evaluated at the end of $(t - i)$. To prevent misunderstanding it should be noted that the use of a one-period, and not a two-period, labor contract is optimal from the viewpoint of minimizing the variance of the real wage. As discussed in the introduction, there must be reasons other than stability of the real wage, such as the costs of frequent contract negotiations and/or wage setting, for the existence of longer-term contracts.

In period $t$, half the firms are operating in the first year of a labor contract drawn up at the end of $(t - 1)$, and the other half in the second year of a contract drawn up at the end of $(t - 2)$. There is only a single price for output.[17] Given that the wage is predetermined for each firm, the aggregate supply of output is given by

$$Y_t^s = \frac{1}{2} \sum_{i=1}^{2} (P_t - {}_{t-i}W_t) + u_t \tag{14}$$

$$Y_t^s = \frac{1}{2} \sum_{i=1}^{2} (P_t - {}_{t-i}P_t) + u_t. \tag{14'}$$

Now, using rational expectations again, by combining (14') and (5) and noting that $E_{t-2}({}_{t-1}P_t) = {}_{t-2}P_t$,

$${}_{t-2}P_t = {}_{t-2}M_t - {}_{t-2}(u_t + v_t) \tag{15}$$

$${}_{t-1}P_t = \tfrac{2}{3}{}_{t-1}M_t + \tfrac{1}{3}{}_{t-2}M_t - \tfrac{1}{3}{}_{t-2}(u_t + v_t) - \tfrac{2}{3}{}_{t-1}(u_t + v_t). \tag{16}$$

Note that since, by assumption, $M_t$ is a function only of information available up to the end of period $(t - 1)$, ${}_{t-1}M_t = M_t$.

Accordingly,

$$2P_t = \tfrac{4}{3}M_t + \tfrac{2}{3}{}_{t-2}M_t$$
$$- (u_t + v_t) - \tfrac{1}{3}{}_{t-1}(u_t + v_t) - \tfrac{2}{3}{}_{t-2}(u_t + v_t) \tag{17}$$

and

$$Y_t = \frac{M_t - {}_{t-2}M_t}{3}$$
$$+ \tfrac{1}{2}(u_t - v_t) + \tfrac{1}{6}{}_{t-1}(u_t + v_t) + \tfrac{1}{3}{}_{t-2}(u_t + v_t). \tag{18}$$

Let the money supply again be determined by the rule of equation (10), so that

$${}_{t-2}M_t = a_1 \rho_1 u_{t-2} + \sum_{i=2}^{\infty} a_i u_{t-1} + b_1 \rho_2 v_{t-2} + \sum_{i=2}^{\infty} b_i v_{t-i} \tag{19}$$

and

$$M_t - {}_{t-2}M_t = a_1(u_{t-1} - \rho_1 u_{t-2}) + b_1(v_{t-1} - \rho_2 v_{t-2})$$

$$= a_1 \epsilon_{t-1} + b_1 \eta_{t-1}. \tag{20}$$

The difference between the actual money stock in period $t$ and that stock as predicted two periods earlier arises from the reactions of the monetary authority to the disturbances $\epsilon_{t-1}$ and $\eta_{t-1}$ occurring in the interim. It is precisely these disturbances that cannot influence the nominal wage for the second period of wage contracts entered into at $(t-2)$.

By substitution of (20) and (10) into (18) it becomes clear that the parameters $a_i$ and $b_i$ of the money supply rule for $i \geq 2$ have no effect on the behavior of output, and for purposes of this paper can set at zero.[18] Thus,

$$Y_t = \tfrac{1}{3}[a_1(u_{t-1} - \rho_1 u_{t-2}) + b_1(v_{t-1} - \rho_2 v_{t-2})]$$

$$+ \tfrac{1}{2}(u_t - v_t) + \tfrac{1}{6}{}_{t-1}(u_t + v_t) + \tfrac{1}{3}{}_{t-2}(u_t + v_t)$$

$$= \tfrac{1}{2}(\epsilon_t - \eta_t) + \tfrac{1}{3}[\epsilon_{t-1}(a_1 + 2\rho_1) + \eta_{t-1}(b_1 - \rho_2)] + \rho_1^2 u_{t-2}. \tag{21}$$

Before we examine the variance of output as a function of the parameters $a_1$ and $b_1$, it is worth explaining why the values of those parameters affect the behavior of output, even when the parameters are fully known. The essential reason is that between the time the two-year contract is drawn up and the last year of operation of that contract, there is time for the monetary authority to react to new information about recent economic disturbances. Given the negotiated second-period nominal wage, the way the monetary authority reacts to disturbances will affect the real wage for the second period of the contract and thus output.

Calculating the asymptotic variance of $Y$ from (21) we obtain

$$\sigma_Y^2 = \sigma_\epsilon^2 \left[ \tfrac{1}{4} + \tfrac{4}{9}\rho_1^2 + \frac{\rho_1^4}{1 - \rho_1^2} + \frac{a_1(4\rho_1 + a_1)}{9} \right]$$

$$+ \sigma_\eta^2 \left[ \tfrac{1}{4} + \tfrac{1}{9}\rho_2^2 - \frac{b_1}{9}(2\rho_2 - b_1) \right]. \tag{22}$$

The variance minimizing values of $a_1$ and $b_1$ are accordingly

$$a_1 = -2\rho_1 \quad \text{and} \quad b_1 = \rho_2, \tag{23}$$

which yield an output variance of

$$\sigma_\gamma^2 = \sigma_\epsilon^2 \left[ \frac{1}{4} + \frac{\rho_1^4}{1 - \rho_1^2} \right] + \tfrac{1}{4}\sigma_\eta^2. \tag{24}$$

To interpret the monetary rule, examine the second equality in (21). It can be seen there that the level of output is affected by current disturbances that cannot be offset by monetary policy ($\epsilon_t - \eta_t$), by disturbances that have occurred since the signing of the older of the existing labor contracts ($\epsilon_{t-1}$ and $\eta_{t-1}$), and by a lagged real disturbance ($u_{t-2}$). The disturbances $\epsilon_{t-1}$ and $\eta_{t-1}$ can be wholly offset by monetary policy, and that is precisely what (23) indicates. The $u_{t-2}$ disturbance, on the other hand, was known when the older labor contract was drawn up and cannot be offset by monetary policy because it is taken into account in wage setting. Note, however, that the stabilization is achieved by affecting the real wage of those in the second year of labor contracts and thus should not be expected to be available to attain arbitrary levels of output—the use of too active a policy would lead to a change in the structure of contracts.

For a more general interpretation of the monetary rule, note from (17) that $u$, the real disturbance, and $v$, the nominal disturbance, both tend to reduce the price level. Accordingly, the rule is to accommodate real disturbances that tend to increase the price level and to counteract nominal disturbances which tend to increase the price level. Such an argument has been made by Gordon (1975).

The monetary rule can alternately be expressed in terms of observable variables as

$$M_t = \rho_2 M_{t-1} + (2\rho_1 - \rho_2)P_{t-1} - (2\rho_1 + \rho_2)Y_{t-1}$$

$$- \rho_1({}_{t-2}W_{t-1} + {}_{t-3}W_{t-1}) \tag{25}$$

and it is also possible to substitute out for the wage rates in (25) to obtain a money supply rule solely in terms of lagged values of the money stock, prices, and income.

## 3   Indexed Contracts

The only way in which monetary policy can lose its effectiveness when there are long-term labor contracts is for the wage to be indexed in a way which duplicates the effects of one-period contracts. However, it will be seen in

(28) below that such indexing is not of the type generally encountered. Other types of indexing do allow monetary policy that can affect output.

If the wage is set such that

$$_{t-i}W_t = {}_{t-1}P_t, \qquad i = 1, 2, \ldots, \tag{26}$$

then the results of section 1 above obtain, and in particular, output is given by

$$Y_t = \tfrac{1}{2}(\epsilon_t - \eta_t) + \rho_1 u_{t-1}. \tag{27}$$

However, the indexing formula implied by (26) is unlike anything seen in practice. It is

$$W_t = -\rho_2 M + (\rho_1 + \rho_2)P_{t-1} + (\rho_2 - \rho_1)Y_{t-1} - \rho_1 W_{t-1}, \tag{28}$$

where $M_t$ is assumed constant at $M$, since the monetary rule is of no consequence for the behavior of output. For $\rho_1 < 0$ (a negative serial correlation of real disturbances) and $\rho_1 + \rho_2 > 0$, the above formula could be similar to a wage contract which specifies both indexation to the price level and profit sharing, but it is certainly not in general the type of contract which is found. Probably the major reason such contracts are not seen in practice is that calculation of their terms would be difficult since industry and firm-specific factors omitted from this simple model are relevant to contracts that duplicate the effects of a full set of spot markets.

The variance of output obtaining with the general indexing formula (28) for wage determination is

$$\sigma_Y^2 = \sigma_\epsilon^2 \left( \frac{1}{4} + \frac{\rho_1^2}{1 - \rho_1^2} \right) + \tfrac{1}{4}\sigma_\eta^2. \tag{29}$$

This exceeds the variance of output with optimal monetary policy in the nonindexed economy with two-period contracts. This is because the criterion for wage setting, which attempts to maintain constancy of the real wage, is not equivalent to the criterion of minimizing the variance of output. This result may be part of the explanation for the continued hostility of stabilization authorities to indexation.

If any indexation formula for wages other than (28) is used, and there are contracts that last more than one period, there is again room for stabilizing monetary policy. For instance, consider a wage indexed to the price level so that

$$_{t-i}W_t = {}_{t-i}W_{t-i+1} + P_{t-1} - P_{t-i}, \tag{30}$$

in which the wage paid in period $t$ on a contract made at the end of $(t - i)$ is the wage specified for the first year of the contract adjusted for inflation over the intervening period. We also specify that

$$_{t-i}W_{t-i+1} = {}_{t-i}P_{t-i+1}, \tag{31}$$

that is, that the wage for the first year of the contract minimizes the variance of the real wage in that period.

Assuming two-year real contracts, the supply equation (14), the velocity equation (5), and rational expectations in determining the expected price level in (31), one obtains, using the lag operator $L$,

$$Y_t(6 - 4L + 2L^2) = 2M_t(1 - L)^2 + \mu_t[3 - (1 - \rho_1)L + \rho_1 L^2]$$
$$- v_t[3 - (3 + \rho_2)L + (2 - \rho_2)L^2], \tag{32}$$

where use has been made of the fact that $M_t = {}_{t-1}M_t$.

Since $M_t$ enters the output equation, it is clear that monetary policy does have an effect on the behavior of output. In this case it is actually possible for monetary policy to offset the effects of all lagged disturbances by using the rule

$$M_t = Lu_t[-(1 + 4\rho_1) + (1 + \rho_1)L - \rho_1 L^2][2(1 - L)^2]^{-1}$$
$$- Lv_t[(1 - 2\rho_2) + (-1 + 3\rho_2)L - \rho_2 L^2][2(1 - L)^2]^{-1}, \tag{33}$$

which leaves

$$\sigma_y^2 = \frac{\sigma_\epsilon^2}{4} + \frac{\sigma_\eta^2}{4}. \tag{34}$$

In the face of real disturbances, the monetary rule (33) destabilizes the real wage relative to its behavior under the optimal monetary policy in the nonindexed two-period contract model and a fortiori relative to its behavior when there are single-period contracts. Given that the assumed aim of labor is to have stable real wages, an indexed contract like (30) would be less attractive to labor than the nonindexed contracts of section 2.

## 4 Conclusions

The argument of this paper about active monetary policy turns on the revealed preference of economic agents for long-term contracts. The only long-term contracts discussed here are labor contracts, which generally provide a Keynesian-like element of temporary wage rigidity that provides a stabilizing role for monetary policy even when that policy is fully anticipated.[19] Monetary policy loses its effectiveness only if long-term contracts are indexed in an elaborate way that duplicates the effects of single-period contracts, as indicated at the beginning of section 3—and it should not be doubted that the labor contract of equation (28) is a very simplified version of the long-term contract that would in practice be needed to duplicate the effects of contracts negotiated each period.

The effectiveness of monetary policy does not require anyone to be fooled. In the model of section 2, with two-period contracts, monetary policy is fully anticipated, but because it is based on information that becomes available after the labor contract is made, it can affect output. If the monetary authority wants to stabilize output, it can do so; in the model of section 2 its optimal policy for stabilizing output is to accommodate real disturbances that tend to increase the price level and to counteract nominal disturbances that tend to increase the price level. Stabilization of output in the face of real disturbances implies a less stable real wage than would obtain with one-period contracts, while output stabilization in the face of nominal disturbances implies a real wage as stable as that obtained with one-period contracts.

Despite the different implications of this model from that of SW for the effectiveness of monetary policy in affecting output, the implied aggregate-supply functions are only subtly different. An aggregate-supply function, such as that used by Lucas (1973), in which monetary policy cannot affect the behavior of output can be written

$$Y_t = \sum_{i=0}^{\infty} \gamma_i (P_{t-i} - {}_{t-i-1}P_{t-i}) + u_t. \tag{35}$$

That is, output is determined as a distributed lag on one-period forecast errors of the price level. A general aggregate supply function implying the potential effectiveness of monetary policy would be

$$Y_t = \sum_{i=0}^{\infty} \theta_i (P_t - {}_{t-i}P_t) + u_t. \tag{36}$$

In this case output is determined as a function of one and more period forecast errors of the price level.[20] The two formulations could be difficult to distinguish empirically.

Before concluding, we should note that there is no dispute that monetary policy can affect price-level behavior. To the extent that price changes are costly, it would be desirable to maintain price stability. In the face of autocorrelated disturbances of the sort discussed in this paper, and even if all contracts are one period, an activist monetary policy would be needed to maintain stable prices. Thus an argument for the desirability of an activist monetary policy could be constructed even if there were no potential role for monetary policy in affecting output.

While this paper argues that an active monetary policy can affect the behavior of output if there are long-term contracts and is desirable in order to foster long-term contracts, one of the important lessons of the rational expectations literature should not be overlooked: the structure of the economy adjusts as policy changes.[21] An attempt by the monetary authority to exploit the existing structure of contrasts to produce behavior far different from that envisaged when contracts were signed would likely lead to the reopening of the contracts and, if the new behavior of the monetary authority were persisted in, a new structure of contracts. But given a structure of contracts, there is some room for maneuver by the monetary authorities—which is to say that their policies can be stabilizing though they will not necessarily be so.

## Acknowledgments

I am indebted to Rudiger Dornbusch for extensive discussions, to Edmund Phelps for a suggestive discussion some years age and for his comments on the first draft of this paper, and to Robert Barro, Benjamin Friedman, and Thomas Sargent for comments. An argument similar to the thesis of this paper is contained in an independent paper by Phelps and Taylor (1977); the details are sufficiently different that the two papers should be regarded as complementary. Note 19 below discusses the relationship between the two papers. Research support from the National Science Foundation is gratefully acknowledged.

## Notes

1. Notably the contribution of Sargent and Wallace (1975); this paper is henceforth referred to as SW.

2. Despite Fisher's (1926) earlier discovery of the unemployment-inflation relationship, it was not until the publication of Phillips's 1958 article that the relationship began to play a central role in policy discussions.

3. However, Harry Johnson in his inflation survey (1969) expressed doubts as to the ability of policymakers to exploit the Phillips tradeoff (see pp. 132–133).

4. The level of employment and the rate of unemployment move inversely in Friedman's exposition.

5. These developments are summarized by Gordon (1976).

6. This issue, among others, was analyzed by Tobin (1972); it is taken up by Prescott (1975).

7. The fundamental application of the rational expectations hypothesis in a Phillips curve context is by Lucas (1972); see also Lucas (1973) and SW.

8. See Barro and Fischer (1976) for an extended discussion of rational expectations.

9. This is similar to the aggregate supply function of SW and also Lucas (1973).

10. SW examine a case in which the monetary authority has superior information; see also Barro (1976).

11. See Azariadis (1975), Baily (1974), and Grossman (1975); Gordon (1976) discusses these contributions.

12. The derivation of the aggregate supply function (4) below for the case of a nominal wage schedule is available from the author on request. The function has the same form as (4) but with different coefficients; no subsequent argument is affected by those differences.

13. By setting $\alpha$ in (3) at zero, we appear to make negative levels of output possible. Any reader worried by that possibility should either set $\alpha$ to a positive value or else view (4) as a relationship that applies to deviations of output from a specified level. Note also that (3) can be viewed as a markup equation with the markup dependent on the level of output.

14. See n. 12 above.

15. SW are interested in the question of the optimal monetary instrument and thus specify two additional equations: an aggregate-demand or $IS$ equation and a portfolio-balance or $LM$ equation. I use the single equation (5) to avoid unnecessary detail. A model with overlapping labor contracts and separate goods and money markets is presented in the appendix to Fischer (1977).

16. Akerlof (1969) uses a model with overlapping labor contracts, in which prices charged differ among firms.

17. The extreme assumption is made here that labor is attached to a particular set of firms and that the state of excess supply or demand for labor in firms operating in midcontract does not affect the starting wage in the new contracts of the remaining firms. Some labor mobility between firms could be incorporated in the analysis without affecting the results so long as mobility is not sufficiently great to eliminate all wage differentials between the two types of firms in a given period.

18. From the viewpoint of the behavior of the price level it might be desirable to have nonzero values of those parameters, but we are focusing strictly on the behavior of output.

19. The major difference between this paper and that of Phelps and Taylor (1977) (PT) is that in most of PT it is price rigidity, rather than wage rigidity, that provides the element of nominal stickiness from which monetary policy derives its effectiveness. At the end of their paper, PT do present a model with (single-period) price and wage stickiness. Persistence effects in the present paper arise from the overlapping contracts and serial correlation of disturbances, while in PT, inventory accumulation produces persistence of past disturbances.

20. Obviously, a more general form of (36) could involve terms like

$$\sum_{j=0}^{\infty} \phi_j \sum_{i=0}^{\infty} \theta_i (P_{t-j} - {}_{t-i-j}P_{t-j}).$$

21. Lucas (1976).

# References

Akerlof, George A. "Relative Wages and the Rate of Inflation." *Q.J.E.* 83, no. 3 (August 1969): 353–374.

Azariadis, Costas. "Implicit Contracts and Underemployment Equilibria." *J.P.E.* 83, no. 6 (December 1975): 1183–1202.

Baily, Martin N. "Wages and Employment under Uncertain Demand." *Rev. Econ. Studies* 41, no. 1 (January 1974): 37–50.

Barro, Robert J. "Rational Expectations and the Role of Monetary Policy." *J. Monetary Econ.*, vol. 2 (1976).

Barro, Robert J., and Fischer, Stanley. "Recent Developments in Monetary Theory." *J. Monetary Econ.* 2, no. 2 (April 1976): 133–168.

Fischer, Stanley. "Wage Indexation and Macro-economic Stability." *J. Monetary Econ.* 5 (1977), supp. series.

Fisher, Irving. "A Statistical Relation between Unemployment and Price Changes." *International Labor Review* (June 1926), reprinted in *J.P.E.* 81, no. 2 (March–April 1973): 496–502.

Friedman, Milton. "The Role of Monetary Policy." *A.E.R.* 58, no. 1 (March 1968): 1–17.

Gordon, Robert J. "Alternative Responses of Policy to External Supply Shocks." *Brookings Papers on Economic Activity*, no. 1 (1975), pp. 183–206.

Gordon, Robert J. "Recent Developments in the Theory of Inflation and Unemployment." *J. Monetary Econ.* 2, no. 2 (April 1976): 185–220.

Grossman, Herschel I. "The Nature of Optimal Labor Contracts: Towards a Theory of Wage and Employment Adjustment." Unpublished paper, Brown University, 1975.

Johnson, Harry G. "A Survey of Theories of Inflation." In *Essays in Monetary Economics*, by H. G. Johnson. 2d ed. Cambridge: Harvard Univ. Press, 1969.

Lipsey, Richard G. "The Relation between Unemployment and the Rate of Money Wage Changes in the United Kingdom, 1862–1957: A Further Analysis." *Economica* 27, no. 105 (February 1960): 1–31.

Lucas, Robert E. "Expectations and the Neutrality of Money." *J. Econ. Theory* 4, no. 2 (April 1972): 103–124.

Lucas, Robert E. "Some International Evidence on Output-Inflation Trade-offs." *A.E.R.* 63, no. 3 (June 1973): 326–334.

Lucas, Robert E. "Econometric Policy Evaluation: A Critique." In *The Phillips Curve and Labor Markets*, edited by Karl Brunner and Allan H. Meltzer. *J. Monetary Econ.*, suppl. (1976), pp. 19–46.

Phelps, Edmund S. "Phillips Curves, Expectations of Inflation, and Optimal Unemployment over Time." *Economica* 34, no. 135 (August 1967): 254–281.

Phelps, Edmund S., and Taylor, John B. "Stabilizing Powers of Monetary Policy under Rational Expectations." *J.P.E.* 85, no. 1 (February 1977): 163–190.

Phelps, Edmund S., et al. *Microeconomic Foundations of Employment and Inflation Theory.* New York: Norton, 1970.

Phillips, A. W. "The Relation between Unemployment and the Rate of Change of Money Wage Rates in the United Kingdom, 1862–1957." *Economica* 25, no. 100 (November 1958): 283–299.

Prescott, Edward C. "Efficiency of the Natural Rate." *J.P.E.* 83, no. 6 (December 1975): 1229–1236.

Sargent, Thomas J., and Wallace, Neil. "'Rational' Expectations, the Optimal Monetary Instrument, and the Optimal Money Supply Rule." *J.P.E.* 83, no. 2 (April 1975): 241–254.

Tobin, James. "Inflation and Unemployment." *A.E.R.* 62, no. 1 (March 1972): 1–18.

# 8 Staggered Wage Setting in a Macro Model

**John B. Taylor**

Few economists now question the validity of the Friedman-Phelps accelerationist hypothesis that the Phillips curve is vertical in the long run, at least as a first-order approximation. Indeed, the once controversial hypothesis is now embodied in basic textbook macro models (see Dornbusch and Fischer 1978 and Gordon 1978, for example). This new accelerationist consensus, however, has done little to settle the ongoing debate over aggregate demand policy, where the crucial issues appear to depend on the *short-run* Phillips curve and its dynamic properties. The accelerationist theory provided an elegant and concise representation of the inflationary process for the long run. However, it has proved distressingly unspecific as a framework for the development of short-run dynamics.

Two sources of this incomplete specification have stimulated extensive research in recent years. The first, about which little will be said here, is that the accelerationist theory was not specific about the process of expectation formation. According to the theory, the expected inflation rate $\pi^*$ should be added to the right-hand side of the Phillips equation. Hence the expectation process determining $\pi^*$ matters greatly for short-run dynamics. For example, if expectations are formed rationally, then as Thomas Sargent and Neil Wallace have shown (using the Robert Lucas supply model), the Phillips curve will be vertical in the short run as well as the long run from the point of view of aggregate demand policy. On the other hand, if expectations are adaptive, either by assumption or by derivation from a learning model, then the short-run slope might be very flat. But, if this were the only source of ambiguity in the accelerationist model, then it is likely that the controversy over the short-run properties would have been settled quickly: the attractiveness of rational expectations, again as a first-order approximation, has become increasingly evident in theoretical and empirical work.

The second source of imprecision is more troublesome and is unlikely to be resolved quickly. It involves the microeconomic details of wage and price adjustment which are just as much a part of the famous macro expectations adjustment as the expection-formation mechanism itself. While an extremely literal reading of the accelerationist theories would interpret $\pi^*$

*American Economic Review* 69 (May 1979): 108–113. Copyright © 1979 by the American Economic Association. Reprinted with permission.

as a pure forecast of inflation independent of the dynamics of wage and price contracts, a more practical reading would suggest that $\pi^*$ represents the persistence of inflation due to the gradual adjustments of outstanding wage and price contracts to new economic information. Some modeling of this phenomenon can be found in Edmund Phelps (1970), especially his appendix 1, and in Arthur Okun's contract-based inflation model with accelerationist implications (1975). Empirical work on price and wage equations by Philip Cagan (1974) and Michael Wachter (1976) has emphasized the dynamic implications of both contracts and expectations. Policy-oriented studies by William Fellner (1978) and George Perry (1978) have also taken this view of the accelerationist theory, though with widely differing policy suggestions.

The impact of aggregate demand on inflation and employment is crucially dependent on whether the contract mechanism or the expectation mechanism dominates the persistence effects commonly represented by $\pi^*$. Hence, a resolution of the current macroeconomic controversy requires some explicit models to disentangle the two mechanisms theoretically, if not empirically, and to determine how contract length and adjustment speeds affect aggregate demand.

The purpose of this paper is to discuss one such model, which focuses on contracts and staggered wage setting with rational expectations. The model is based on some of my recent research (see my 1978, 1979 papers) but is generalized here to permit alternative mixes of expectation and contract effects in the wage equations.

## 1  Staggered Wage Setting

A property of wage and price contracts that has not typically been emphasized in microeconomic analyses but which is important from the viewpoint of macroeconomics is that contract decisions are staggered: all contract decisions in the economy are not made at the same point in time. While some months are more popular than others for adjusting wage contracts, these adjustment decisions are generally staggered throughout the year. This property of contract formation is the central feature in the model discussed below.

To make things simple suppose that *wage* contracts last one year and that decision dates are evenly staggered: half the contracts are set in January and half in July. If we let six-month (semiannual) intervals be the period of measurement and $x_t$ be the *log* of the contract wage for periods $t$ and $t + 1$ set at the start of period $t$, then a simple model of contract wage determination is given by

$$x_t = bx_{t-1} + d\hat{x}_{t+1} + \gamma(b\hat{y}_t + d\hat{y}_{t+1}) + \epsilon_t, \tag{1}$$

where $y_t$ is a measure of excess demand in period $t$, $\epsilon_t$ is a random shock, and $b, d$, and $\gamma$ are positive parameters. The "hat" over a variable represents its conditional expectation, based on period $t - 1$ information. Equation (1) states the assumption that the contract wage set at the start of each semiannual period depends on three factors: the contract wage set in the previous period, the contract wage expected to be set in the next period, and a weighted average of excess demand expected during the next two periods. Since, by assumption, $x_t$ will prevail for two periods, firms and/or unions contemplating a wage adjustment in period $t$ will be concerned with wage rates which will be in effect during periods $t$ and $t + 1$. Hence both $x_{t-1}$ and $\hat{x}_{t+1}$ are included in the equation. Note that contracts set before period $t - 1$ and after period $t + 1$ are not included in the equation. Such contracts do not overlap with the current contract and are therefore not part of the relative wage structure.

The $b$ and $d$ coefficients in equation (1) represent the elasticity of the current contract decision is homogeneous of degree 1 in these lag and lead contracts. If $b = d = 1/2$ then the lag and lead distribution is symmetric. current contract decision is homogeneous of degree 1 in these lag and lead contracts. If $b = d = 1/2$, then the lag and lead distribution is symmetric. This has been the parametric assumption used in my previous work and reflects the plausible assumption that current negotiations weight other contracts according to the number of periods that they overlap with the current contract. In this sense, when $b$ and $d$ are equal to $1/2$, contract decisions are unbiased. Wage setters look forward to the same degree they look backward. However, I will allow for the possibility of biased weights in this paper by permitting $b$ and $d$ to differ from $1/2$. This permits a spectrum of contract-determination hypotheses between the extremes of pure backward looking ($b = 1$) and pure forward looking ($d = 1$). As will be demonstrated below, the size of $b$ versus $d$ is important for the dynamic behavior of contracts and for the sensitivity of wage behavior to excess demand. This importance of forward looking versus backward looking has been emphasized in a recent paper by Perry (1978) in analyzing an hypothesis set forth by Fellner (1976).

To derive a dynamic representation for the behavior of the contract wage from equation (1), it is necessary to solve for $\hat{y}_t$, $\hat{y}_{t+1}$, and $\hat{x}_{t+1}$. This involves specifying an aggregate demand relationship and a policy rule. Assume that the excess demand variable $y_t$ is the percentage output gap (that is, the deviation of the *log* of real output from trend) and that the demand for money is given by $m_t = y_t + w_t - v_t$, where the variables $m_t$, $w_t$, and $v_t$ are the *logs* of the aggregate wage level, the money supply, and a shock, all measured as deviations from trend. Note that this money-demand equation is simply the quantity equation with the wage substituted for the price level. This approximation saves one equation and can easily be modified. If the policy rule for the money supply is the *log*-linear form $m_t = gw_t$, we can derive the simple aggregate demand relation

$$y_t = -\beta w_t + v_t, \tag{2}$$

where $\beta = 1 - g$. Note that $\beta$ is a policy parameter indicating the degree of accommodation of aggregate demand to wage changes. The model is closed by noting that $w_t$ is an aggregate of the contract wages $x_t$ and $x_{t-1}$ outstanding at time $t$. If we use the geometric average, then

$$w_t = .5(x_t + x_{t-1}) \tag{3}$$

By substituting equations (3) and (2) into (1) and taking expectations conditional on $t - 1$ information, we have that

$$b\hat{x}_{t-1} - c\hat{x}_t + d\hat{x}_{t+1} = 0, \tag{4}$$

where $c = (1 + .5\gamma\beta)/(1 - .5\gamma\beta)$. Assuming that $x_t$ is stable yields a solution for $x_t$ of the form

$$x_t = \alpha x_{t-1} + \epsilon_t, \tag{5}$$

where $\quad \alpha = \dfrac{c - [c^2 - 4d(1 - d)]^{1/2}}{2d}.$

An equation for the average wage $w_t$ can readily be derived from (5) using (3) and is given by

$$w_t = \alpha w_{t-1} + .5(\epsilon_t + \epsilon_{t-1}). \tag{6}$$

Equations (6) and (2) can be used to address a number of the issues raised above. From the parameter $\alpha$ we can determine how the wage dynamics depend on aggregate demand policy ($\beta$), on the sensitivity of wage change to excess demand ($\gamma$), and on the degree of forward-looking ($d$).

Note, however, that in this model we cannot identify the two parameters $\gamma$ and $d$ from a time series on $w_t$ and $y_t$ without further assumptions. Given such time-series, we could easily estimate $\beta$ and $\alpha$ from equations (2) and (6). However, from the definition of $\alpha$, these estimates would not determine $d$ and $\gamma$ uniquely. Of course, this identification problem could be surmounted by making additional assumptions or by looking for shifts in policy. For example, additional identifying constraints arise when contracts last for more than two periods. Nevertheless, this potential identification problem should be kept in mind when attempting to estimate the degree of forward-looking using aggregate time-series data.

## 2 Forward-Looking Contracts and Aggregate Wage Dynamics

The parameter $\alpha$ in equation (5) characterizes the degree of persistence in aggregate wage behavior. Clearly the persistence will depend on how accommodative aggregate-demand policy is to wage-contract adjustments that are "too inflationary." This dependence is captured in the model by the relationship between $\alpha$ and $\beta$. The higher $\beta$ is (i.e., the less accommodative policy is) the lower $\alpha$ is (i.e., the less persistent wage fluctuations are). Hence, by choosing $\beta$ large enough, policy can achieve high degrees of stability in the path of aggregate wages. However, since higher values of $\beta$ result in larger fluctuations in the output gap (see equation (2)), this wage stability must be traded off against real output and employment stability. This stability trade-off defines the inflation/unemployment dilemma in this model.

In order to distinguish between the impact of contract effects and expectations effects on this trade-off, the parameter $d$ can be varied over its range between 0 and 1. Recall that the lower $d$ is the more backward looking contract determination is and the less important expectations are. For certain values of $\beta$ and $\gamma$, figure 1 illustrates how the wage dynamics depend on $d$. As one would expect, smaller values of $d$ are associated with larger values of $\alpha$. That is, more backward-looking wage determination increases the persistence or the inertia of aggregate wages. The shape of this negative relationship shows that increasing forward-looking ($d$) from 40 to 50 percent would reduce persistence substantially. Increasing $d$ from 10 to 20 percent would only reduce persistence slightly, however.

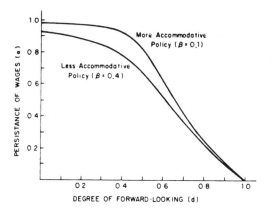

**Figure 1**
The effect of forward-looking contracts on the persistence of wages ($\gamma = .2$)

It can also be shown that the wage-output stability trade-off depends on $d$. Because forward-looking increases the demand effects on wages, higher values of $d$ improve the trade-off. This corresponds to the intuitive notion that more forward-looking contract determination increases the impact of aggregate-demand policy on wages. Hence, inflation-stabilizing fluctuations in aggregate demand can be smaller and need not last as long.

## 3   Contract Length, Empirical Regularities, and Micro Foundations

The wage and output dynamics generated by this model share a number of features with the actual behavior of these series, and this lends some support to the idea that contract formation as well as expectations is an important part of wage and price dynamics. Two features are worth mentioning here. (For further details see Taylor 1978.)

First, the serial-correlation structure for the output gap (or unemployment) in this model is hump shaped: the impact of shocks on output rises before diminishing toward zero. This hump-shaped property is also present in the actual process for output or unemployment in the United States and a number of other countries. Hence, the model is capable of explaining not only the serial persistence of unemployment but also the shape of the persistence.

Second, a striking aspect of the *U.S.* quarterly data is that the hump shape reaches a peak at about one year; this corresponds to contract lengths in the model of about the same length. Hence, relatively short contracts (much shorter than the frequently cited three-year union contracts) are capable of displaying empirically observed serial persistence. Although other models might explain these correlations just as well, this type of model with relatively short contracts appears to be consistent with the data.

Whether the model is consistent with a rigorous micro theory is more difficult to determine. Unfortunately, the assumed contract-formation behavior is not explicitly derived from a utility-maximization model (see Robert Barro 1977). While significant gains have been made in our understanding of contracts through the work by Costas Azariadis (1975), Martin Baily (1974), and D. F. Gordon (1976), the micro foundations of the staggered-contract model presented here are far from complete. I think there are important information reasons for contracts to be staggered (without an auctioneer some staggering is necessary for firms to obtain information about the relative wage structure), but these are yet to be laid out rigorously. For this reason such models should be used cautiously since contract length is not a datum, and the optimal length of contracts may change with changes of policy. By way of comparison, the information-based theories of aggregate dynamics that have been developed by Lucas also have problems with micro foundations. For example, disparate information is imposed on such models with little discussion of how stabilization policy might affect mobility or communication between markets, which would alter this information structure.

The theoretical approach to micro foundations has proved difficult and is likely to remain so. But there is also an empirical approach that has received little attention. An early example of this approach is the study of compensation policy made by Richard Lester (1948). His aim was to investigate (through a survey of firms) a number of alternative wage-setting procedures: whether firms use wage surveys in determining their wage scales, whether firms try to anticipate future wage developments, and whether tight labor markets influence wage policy. While far from conclusive, the study is suggestive of what might be done using modern techniques. For example, although wage surveys are now used almost universally by firms in determining wage scales, there is very little information available concerning how firms use these surveys. Such information would appear to be invaluable in modeling the macroeconomics of wage behavior.

## 4   Concluding Remarks

The theme of this paper has been that the inflation dynamics typically associated with the "expectations-augmented" Phillips curve are significantly influenced by the interaction of staggered contracts as well as by expectations effects. While these ideas are implicit in much accelerationist research, the aim here has been to make them explicit in order that alternative hypotheses concerning the inflation process can be stated more clearly. The overlapping contract model described in the paper is closely related to a number of other models. (See Akerlof 1969; Baily 1976; Fischer 1977; Phelps 1978, forthcoming; Ross and Wachter 1973; and Rowley and Wilton 1973; for example.) While the micro foundations of such models need to be developed more rigorously, they seem capable of improving our understanding of the dynamics of the inflationary process within a reasonable well-specified rational setting.

## Acknowledgments

This research is being supported by the National Science Foundation. This paper was completed while I was a consultant to the Federal Reserve Bank of Philadelphia, which does not necessarily endorse the views expressed. I wish to thank Martin Baily, Philip Cagan, Guillermo Calvo, and Edmund Phelps for useful comments.

## References

G. Akerlof, "Relative Wages and the Rate of Inflation," *Quart. J. Econ.*, Aug. 1969, 83, 353–374.

C. Azariadis, "Implicit Contracts and Unemployment Equilibria," *J. Polit. Econ.*, Dec. 1975, 83, 1183–1202.

M. N. Baily, "Contract Theory and the Moderation of Inflation by Recession and Controls," *Brookings Papers*, Washington 1976, 3, 585–622.

M. N. Baily, "Wages and Employment under Uncertain Demand," *Rev. Econ. Statist.*, Jan. 1974, 41, 37–50.

R. J. Barro, "Long-Term Contracting, Sticky Prices, and Monetary Policy," *J. Monet. Econ.*, July 1977, 3, 305–316.

Philip Cagan, *The Hydra-Headed Monster: The Problem of Inflation in the United States*, Washington, 1974.

Rudiger Dornbusch and Stanley Fischer, *Macroeconomics*, New York, 1978.

William J. Fellner, *Towards a Reconstruction of Macroeconomics: Problems of Theory and Policy*, Washington, 1976.

William J. Fellner, "The Core of the Controversy about Reducing Inflation: An Introductory Analysis," in his *Contemporary Economic Problems*, Washington, 1978.

S. Fischer, "Long-Term Contracts, Rational Expectations, and the Optimal Money Supply Rule," *J. Polit. Econ.*, Feb. 1977, 85, 191–205.

M. Friedman, "The Role of Monetary Policy," *Amer. Econ. Rev.*, Mar. 1968, 58, 1–17.

D. F. Gordon, "A Neo-Classical Theory of Keynesian Unemployment," in Karl Brunner, and Allan H. Meltzer, eds., *The Phillips Curves and Labor Markets*, Amsterdam, 1976, 65–97.

Robert J. Gordon, *Macroeconomics*, Boston, 1978.

Richard A. Lester, *Company Wage Policies*, Princeton, 1948.

R. E. Lucas, "Some International Evidence on Output Inflation Trade-offs," *Amer. Econ. Rev.*, June 1973, 63, 326–334.

A. M. Okun, "Inflation: Its Mechanism and Welfare Costs," *Brookings Papers*, Washington, 1975, 2, 351–401.

G. L. Perry, "Slowing the Wage-Price Spiral: The Macroeconomic View," *Brookings Papers*, Washington, 1978, 2, 259–291.

E. S. Phelps, "Phillips Curves, Expectations of Inflation, and Optimal Employment over Time," *Economica*, Aug. 1967, 34, 254–281.

E. S. Phelps, "Money Wage Dynamics and Labor Market Equilibrium," in Edmund S. Phelps et al., *Microeconomic Foundations of Employment and Inflation Theory*, New York, 1970.

E. S. Phelps, "Introduction: Developments in Non-Walrasian Theory," in his *Studies in Macroeconomic Theory: Employment and Inflation*, New York, 1978.

E. S. Phelps, "Disinflation without Recession: Adaptive Guideposts and Monetary Policy," *Weltwirtsch. Arch.*, 1978, 114, 783–809.

S. A. Ross and M. L. Wachter, "Wage Determination, Inflation, and the Industrial Structure," *Amer. Econ. Rev.*, Sept. 1973, 63, 675–694.

J. C. Rowley and D. A. Wilton, "Quarterly Models of Wage Determination: Some New Efficient Estimates," *Amer. Econ. Rev.*, June 1973, 63, 380–389.

T. J. Sargent and N. Wallace, "'Rational' Expectations, the Optimal Monetary Instrument, and the Optimal Money Supply Rule," *J. Polit. Econ.*, Apr. 1975, 83, 241–254.

J. B. Taylor, "Aggregate Dynamics and Staggered Contracts," unpublished paper, Columbia Univ., 1978.

J. B. Taylor, "Estimation and Control of a Macroeconomic Model with Rational Expectations," *Econometrica*, 1979.

M. L. Wachter, "The Changing Cyclical Responsiveness of Wage Inflation," *Brookings Papers*, Washington, 1976, 1, 115–159.

# 9 Price Asynchronization and Price-Level Inertia

Olivier J. Blanchard

## 1 Introduction

It is often informally argued that because of the complexity of the price system, and the inherent problems of coordination, the apparent inertia of the price level should come as no surprise.[1] A rather appealing argument along these lines is the following: when a nominal disturbance requires a change in the price level, what is required is not a change of a single price but of a complex structure of final good, intermediate good, and input prices. Price decisions for each of these goods are not taken continuously, and, price decisions across goods are not likely to be perfectly synchronized. The process of adjustment of all prices to a new nominal level will therefore imply movements of relative prices along the way. If prices setters do not want large changes in relative prices, the path of adjustment of all prices may be slow, in other words, the price level may adjust slowly.

The purpose of this chapter is to formalize this argument and to see whether and how it survives formalization. We focus on three sets of questions. First, can asynchronization of individual price decisions generate "substantial" price inertia? It is obvious that with so many price decisions the price level will not adjust overnight to changes in aggregate demand; the question is whether, if each price is set for a relatively short period of time, say a month or two at most, asynchronization can generate the degree of price inertia we appear to have in the United States. The answer is that this is indeed possible.

The second set of questions addresses whether the price level inertia so generated coincides with the usual notion of inertia or "stickiness." Does price-level inertia, for example, imply that decreases in money or decelerations in money growth necessarily lead to recessions? The answer is mixed. In general, movements in money will lead to movements in real money balances and economic activity. There are, however, paths of monetary deceleration that lead to disinflation with no output loss. These paths are reasonable and, apart from issues of credibility, easy to implement.

The third set of questions considers the implications of asynchronization for the relations between disturbances, the price level, and the structure of relative prices. This is of interest both in itself and because it provides a way of differentiating this theory of price inertia from other theories and potentially testing it.[2] Asynchronization implies snake effects, movements in factor prices slowly transmitted to intermediate and final good prices. It also implies more variability of profits and prices for primary inputs than for intermediate goods, for intermediate goods than for final goods; these implications seem to be in accordance with facts.

This chapter therefore suggests that asynchronization of price decisions is capable of generating price level inertia. If price level inertia is indeed partly due to asynchronization, the prospects for reducing it are not good. Given the time structure of price decisions, each price setter chooses its price optimally and frequently. Reducing inertia requires better overall synchronization of price decisions; this may be difficult to achieve by agents or by policy.

## 2  The Model

To focus later on the effects of asynchronization, I start with an economy in which all price decisions are perfectly synchronized.

### Equilibrium with synchronized prices

The economy is characterized by its technology and a specification of input supply and output demand.

Final output is produced in $n$ stages, each carried under constant returns to scale by competitive firms. *Technology* is given by $n$ relations:

$$y_i = y_{i-1} + \theta_i, \qquad i = 1, \ldots, n, \tag{1}$$

where $y_i$ denotes good $i$, so that $y_0$ denotes the primary input and $y_n$ the final output. All variables in this chapter are in logarithms. The $\theta_i$ are constants. They are unimportant for our purposes and will be deleted in what follows. Production is instantaneous, and to avoid issues of inventories, all goods are perishable.[3]

Competitive zero-profit equilibrium implies that if $p_i$ is (the log of) the price of good $i$, the following relations hold (forgetting the $\theta_i$):

$$p_i = p_{i-1}, \qquad i = 1, \ldots, n \Rightarrow p_n = p_0 \tag{2}$$

Increasing the number of production stages, $n$, keeping the sum of $\theta_i$s constant allows us to increase the number of price decisions while leaving the technology unchanged.[4] In this economy with synchronized prices, the number of price decisions is clearly irrelevant: $y_n$ is always equal to $y_0$ and $p_n$ to $p_0$.

The model is closed by a specification of *input supply* and *output demand*:

$$y_0 = \beta(p_0 - p_n) + \xi, \qquad \beta \geq 0, \tag{3}$$

$$y_n = m - p_n. \tag{4}$$

Input supply is an increasing function of its real price and of a disturbance $\xi$.[5] Output demand depends positively on real money balances.[6]

Equilibrium is characterized by the price relations given by (2) and equilibrium in the primary input market; the derived demand for the primary input must equal the supply:

$$\beta(p_0 - p_n) + \xi = m - p_n. \tag{5}$$

Combining (2) and (5) gives $y_n = y_0 = \xi$ and $p_n = \cdots = p_i = \cdots = p_0 = m - \xi$.

Money is neutral and affects only the level of all prices. Supply disturbances increase output, decrease all nominal prices, and leave relative prices unchanged.

**Price asynchronization**

I now relax the assumption that price decisions are taken every period and are perfectly synchronized. All price decisions are now taken every two periods. The basic period is presumably short and can be thought of as a month at most.[7] Price decisions are not all taken at the same time. Half of them are taken every period in the following way: firms at the same stage of production take decisions at the same time for two periods. At even stages ($i$ even) firms take decisions at $t$, $t + 2$, and so on; at odd stages ($i$ odd) firms take decisions at $t - 1$, $t + 1$, and so on. For convenience, $n$ is assumed to be even, so that firms producing $y_n$ take decisions at $t$, $t + 2$, ..., firms producing $y_{n-1}$ take decisions at $t - 1$, $t + 1$, ..., and suppliers of the primary input take decisions at $t$, $t + 2$, ....

Firms choosing $p_i$ at time $t$ for periods $t$ and $t + 1$ face two possibly different input prices for $t$ and $t + 1$. The competitive zero profit condition (2) is now replaced by an expected zero profit condition over the two periods. This is formalized by (6).[8]

$$p_{it} = \tfrac{1}{2}[p_{i-1\,t-1} + E(p_{i-1\,t+1}|t)], \qquad i = 2, 4, \ldots, n \tag{6}$$

$E(\cdot\,|t)$ denotes the expectation conditional on information available at time $t$; $p_{i-1\,t-1}$ is the current input price in period $t$, which was set in period $t-1$, and $E(p_{i-1\,t+1}|t)$ the expected input price for period $t+1$. A corresponding formula holds for $i$ odd at time $t-1$ or $t+1$.

Since nominal prices are fixed at each stage for two periods, they may not clear the market in both periods, and an assumption must be made about quantity determination. I assume the outcome to be demand determined: when a firm fixes its price for two periods, it stands ready to supply on demand. This is feasible as production is instantaneous and all input suppliers also supply on demand. Demand for the final good determines the demand for intermediate inputs and for the primary input.[9]

Prices in the primary input market are set in period $t$ at the average expected market-clearing levels over periods $t$ and $t+1$. For convenience, I assume $m$ and $\xi$ to move only every two periods, so that $m_t = m_{t+1}$ and $\xi_t = \xi_{t+1}$. As $p_{n\,t} = p_{n\,t+1}$, the derived demand and the supply of the primary input are the same in periods $t$ and $t+1$. The primary input price for $t$ and $t+1$ is therefore given by (7).[10]

$$\beta(p_{0t} - p_{nt}) + \xi_t = m_t - p_{nt}. \tag{7}$$

To summarize, all firms choose their relative price every two periods. Their price decision depends on current and expected input prices for the next two periods. Half of the prices change every period.

The only deviation from the flexible-price world is the presence of asynchronization: other sources of price inertia are excluded in order to isolate the effects of asynchronization. In particular, this excludes such elements as labor contracts with nominal wages predetermined for long periods of time.[11] As a result, it is not clear whether the primary input should be thought of as labor or as a raw material. If thought of as labor, its price has probably more inertia than formalized in equation (7).

### Equilibrium with asynchronized prices

Equilibrium is now characterized by equations (6) and (7). Input market equilibrium, equation (7), gives us a first relation between $p_{0t}$ and $p_{n\,t}$, given $m_t$ and $\xi_t$. The other relation between $p_{n\,t}$ and $p_{0t}$ follows from the set of pricing relations given by (6). We now derive it by recursive substitution.

Starting from $i = n$, equation (6) gives

$$p_{nt} = \tfrac{1}{2}[p_{n-1\,t-1} + E(p_{n-1\,t+1}|t)].$$ (8)

For $i = n - 1$, it gives for $t - 1$ and $t + 1$

$$p_{n-1\,t-1} = \tfrac{1}{2}[p_{n-2\,t-2} + E(p_{n-2\,t}|t - 1)],$$

$$p_{n-1\,t+1} = \tfrac{1}{2}[p_{n-2\,t} + E(p_{n-2\,t+2}|t + 1)].$$

Assuming rational expectations, taking expectations of $p_{n-1\,t+1}$ at time $t$, using iterated expectations, and replacing in equation (8) give

$$p_{nt} = (\tfrac{1}{2})^2[p_{n-2\,t-2} + E(p_{n-2\,t}|t - 1) + p_{n-2\,t} + E(p_{n-2\,t+2}|t)].$$ (9)

By induction we can express $p_n$ as a function of $p_0$:

$$p_{nt} = 2^{-n}\left[\sum_{i=1}^{n/2}\sum_{j=0}^{(n/2)-i} b_{n\,j} E\left(p_{0\,t-2i}\bigg| t - \frac{n}{2} - i + j\right)\right.$$

$$+ \sum_{j=0}^{n/2} b_{n\,j} E\left(p_{0\,t}\bigg| t - \frac{n}{2} + j\right)$$

$$\left. + \sum_{i=1}^{n/2}\sum_{j=0}^{(n/2)-i} b_{n\,j} E\left(p_{0\,t+2i}\bigg| t - \frac{n}{2} + i + j\right)\right],$$ (10)

with

$$b_{n\,j} \equiv \binom{n}{j} - \binom{n}{j-1}, \qquad b_{n\,0} \equiv 1.$$

This formula is quite formidable but has a simple structure. Consider first the case of perfect foresight, so that expectations are equal to actual values. This gives

$$p_{nt} = 2^{-n}\left[\sum_{i=1}^{n/2}\binom{n}{(n/2) - i}p_{0\,t-2i} + \binom{n}{n/2}p_{0\,t} + \sum_{i=1}^{n/2}\binom{n}{(n/2) - i}p_{0\,t+2i}\right].$$ (11)

This shows the first effect of asynchronization: the price level depends on input prices up to $n$ periods in the past and $n$ periods in the future. The weights are simply the coefficients of a binomial expansion normalized by their sum, $2^n$.

When we relax the assumption of perfect foresight and allow for uncertainty, actual values of input prices in (11) are replaced by expectations.

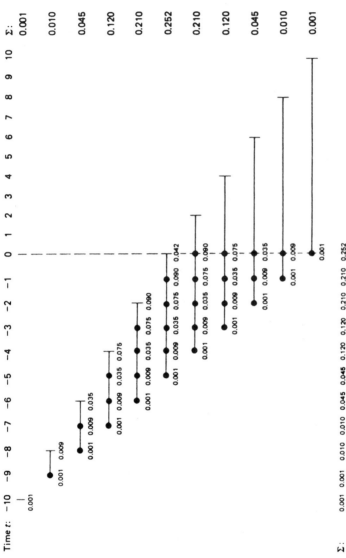

**Figure 1**
Weights on the primary input price for $n = 10$

The price level depends, then, on three sets of terms. The first double sum involves past input prices, both actual and expected; the term in $p_{0\,t-2i}$, for example, includes both the actual value of $p_{0\,t-2i}$ and the values of $p_{0\,t-2i}$ expected prior to $t - 2i$, from $t - (n/2) - i$ to $t - 2i - 1$. The second sum involves both the actual value and past expectations of the current input price. The third involves both past and current expectations of future input prices. Note, and we shall return to this later, that many terms in this last double sum are past expectations of future prices and thus are predetermined at time $t$. Thus the symmetry between the effects of the future and the past which obtains under perfect foresight (equation (11)) does not obtain under uncertainty and rational expectations.

A visually more explicit representation of (1) is given in figure 1 for $n = 10$. Each line represents a set of terms in equation (10). The right end of a line indicates for what period the expectation of $p_0$ is held. The dots on each line indicate when these expectations were formed. The numbers under the dots are the relative weights, $2^{-n}b_{n\,j}$. All elements strictly to the left of the vertical line $t = 0$ are predetermined at time $t$.

## 3 Price Level Inertia and the Number of Price Decisions

### A simple measure of inertia

Producers of the final good freely choose their own nominal price, the price level, every two periods and would not characterize it as sluggish. Their price decision, however, depends directly and indirectly on past input prices, and in a well-defined sense the price level is sluggish. Looking at equation (10), we can usefully think of the price level as the sum of $2^n$ components, some determined in the past and thus predetermined at time $t$, some free to move at time $t$.

This suggests a simple measure of price level inertia, namely, the ratio of the number of predetermined components to the number of nonpredetermined components in (10). From equation (10), this ratio, $R$, is:[12]

$$R = 1 - 2^{-n}\binom{n}{n/2},$$

which gives 0.5 for $n = 2$, 0.75 for $n = 10$, and 0.92 for $n = 100$. Thus this ratio is higher than the proportion of prices, which are not free to adjust at any given time—one half—and is increasing with the number of price decisions. If $n$ is large, most of the elements that compose the price level are predetermined.

As $n$ increases, asynchronization implies a dependence of the price level on input prices further in the past and expected further in the future that is quite intuitive. That as $n$ increases, the degree of predetermination increases is less intuitive. Figure 2 helps us understand why by showing how the price level depends on input prices as we go down the chain of production. Any element below the line is predetermined and thus can only depend in turn on predetermined elements. Any element above the line is not predetermined and may in turn depend both on predetermined and nonpredetermined elements. $p_{nt}$ depends on predetermined $p_{n-1\,t-1}$ and nonpredetermined $E(p_{n-1\,t+1}|t)$. $E(p_{n-1\,t+1}|t)$, however, depends on partly predetermined elements such as $p_{n-3\,t-1}$. As we extend the graph to the right, more and more elements go below the line: the ratio, $R$, of predetermined to nonpredetermined elements increases and tends to 1 as $n$ gets large.

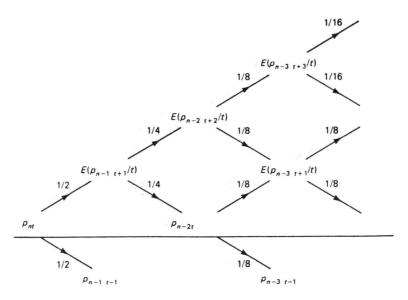

**Figure 2**
The degree of predetermination of the price level $p_n$

This measure of price level inertia is a bit crude: it tells us how much of the price level is predetermined and cannot change in response to disturbances in the current period but tells us nothing about the path of price level adjustment thereafter. We now look at the complete path; this requires solving the model.

### The effects of an increase in money

As characterized by (10), the effect of the input price, actual or expected, on the price level is unambiguously positive. The effect of the price level on the input price is however ambiguous, as shown in (7). An increase in the price level decreases real balances, aggregate demand, the derived input demand, and thus the equilibrium real input price: the net effect of a higher price level and a lower real price is ambiguous. If $\beta = 1$, the net effect is zero, and the input price does not depend on the price level. The system is then recursive, the price level depending on the input price and the input price on money and the supply disturbance. We start with this case; the general case will be analyzed in the next section. If $\beta = 1$, replacing $p_{0\,t}$ from (7) in (10) gives

$$
p_{n\,t} = 2^{-n}\left[\sum_{i=1}^{n/2}\sum_{j=0}^{(n/2)-i} b_{nj}E\left(\psi_{t-2i}\left|t-\frac{n}{2}-i+j\right.\right) + \sum_{j=0}^{n/2} E\left(\psi_t\left|t-\frac{n}{2}+j\right.\right)\right.
$$
$$
\left. + \sum_{i=1}^{n/2}\sum_{j=0}^{(n/2)-i} b_{nj}E\left(\psi_{t+2i}\left|t-\frac{n}{2}+i+j\right.\right)\right],
\tag{12}
$$

with $\psi_t \equiv m_t - \xi_t$.

Consider a permanent unanticipated increase in money at time $t_0$. Because of the long-run neutrality of money in this model, the long-run elasticity of the price level with respect to money is unity. We can derive from (12) incremental and cumulative price level elasticities over time. Denoting the proportional increase in money by $dm$, we get

$$
\begin{aligned}
p_{n\,t_0+2i} - p_{n\,t_0+2i-2} &= 0 && \text{if } i < 0, \\[6pt]
&= \binom{n}{n/2}dm && \text{if } i = 0, \\[6pt]
&= 2\binom{n}{(n/2)-i}dm && \text{if } i = 1,\dots,n/2, \\[6pt]
&= 0 && \text{if } i > n/2.
\end{aligned}
$$

Tables 1 and 2 give incremental and cumulative elasticities of $p_n$ over time for different values of $n$. They show a monotonic adjustment with the rate of adjustment increasing initially before decreasing later.

The adjustment of the price to its higher level takes exactly $n$ periods. The adjustment is, however, substantially complete before that: if we assume the period to be a month, the adjustment after a year is 99 percent complete if $n = 20$, 90 percent complete if $n = 50$, and 75 percent complete if $n = 100$. Values of $n$ of 100 may therefore generate the amount of price inertia we observe in the United States. Given the highly idealized nature of the model, it is difficult to decide whether such values for $n$ are or are not reasonable.

There is an interesting distinction between demand disturbances, $m$, and supply disturbances, $\xi$. Note from equation (12) that they have an identical dynamic effect on the price level. Demand disturbances, however, affect demand and production along the chain of production and thus are immediately perceived by all producers. The assumption made above about the change in money being immediately known by all is therefore reasonable. Supply disturbances, on the other hand, have no direct effect on demand (this results from the assumption of demand determination). Thus producers of $y_i$, $i = 2, \ldots, n$, will perceive no change in their demand or input price at time $t_0$. If their information included only the demand they face and the input price they pay, they would not revise expectations. In this case the increase in the primary input price would slowly be transmitted to the structure of prices. $p_n$ would not be given by equation (12) but by $p_{nt} = p_{0\,t-n}$, which implies substantially more inertia.

### The effects of money deceleration

Characterizing the effects of a change in the level of money is a useful first step, but the experiment lacks empirical relevance. Of more direct relevance are the effects of money deceleration. Suppose that money and prices are both growing at rate $g$ per period and that this rate of inflation is considered too high by policymakers. What are the effects on real output of a sudden deceleration, say, sudden zero growth of money?[13] The effects differ, depending on whether this change is anticipated or not. Let's first assume that the policy is announced at time $t_0$ to take place at time $t_0 + n$: the rate of money growth remains equal to $g$ until $t_0 + n$ and is equal to zero thereafter. From (12), real money balances from $t_0$ on are given by

**Table 1**
Effects of an unanticipated increase in money at time $t_0$: incremental effects on $p_n$

| $n$ | | $t_0$ | $t_0 + 2$ | $t_0 + 4$ | $t_0 + 6$ | $\ldots$ | $t_0 + 10$ | $\ldots$ | $t_0 + 20$ | $\ldots$ | $t_0 + 50$ |
|---|---|---|---|---|---|---|---|---|---|---|---|
| 2 | $p_2$ | 0.5 | 0.5 | 0 | | | | | | | |
| 4 | $p_4$ | 0.375 | 0.5 | 0.125 | 0 | $\ldots$ | | | | | |
| 6 | $p_6$ | 0.312 | 0.468 | 0.187 | 0.031 | $\ldots$ | 0 | | | | |
| 10 | $p_{10}$ | 0.247 | 0.410 | 0.234 | 0.086 | $\ldots$ | 0 | | | | |
| 20 | $p_{20}$ | 0.176 | 0.322 | 0.240 | 0.148 | $\ldots$ | 0.028 | $\ldots$ | 0 | | |
| 50 | $p_{50}$ | 0.113 | 0.214 | 0.192 | 0.158 | $\ldots$ | 0.084 | $\ldots$ | 0.004 | $\ldots$ | 0 |
| 100 | $p_{100}$ | 0.079 | 0.156 | 0.148 | 0.132 | $\ldots$ | 0.098 | $\ldots$ | 0.022 | $\ldots$ | 0 |
| 500 | $p_{500}$ | 0.035 | 0.072 | 0.070 | 0.068 | $\ldots$ | 0.064 | $\ldots$ | 0.048 | $\ldots$ | 0.006 |

**Table 2**
Effects of an unanticipated increase in money at time $t_0$: cumulative effects on $p_n$

| $n$ | $f_n$ | $t_0$ | $t_0+2$ | $t_0+4$ | $t_0+6$ | ... | $t_0+10$ | ... | $t_0+20$ | ... | $t_0+50$ |
|---|---|---|---|---|---|---|---|---|---|---|---|
| 2 | $p_2$ | 0.5 | 1.0 | | | | | | | | |
| 4 | $p_4$ | 0.375 | 0.875 | 1.0 | | | | | | | |
| 6 | $p_6$ | 0.312 | 0.770 | 0.957 | 0.988 | ... | 1.0 | | | | |
| 10 | $p_{10}$ | 0.247 | 0.547 | 0.891 | 0.977 | ... | 1.0 | | | | |
| 20 | $p_{20}$ | 0.176 | 0.498 | 0.738 | 0.886 | ... | 0.988 | | | | |
| 50 | $p_{50}$ | 0.113 | 0.327 | 0.519 | 0.677 | ... | 0.881 | ... | 0.997 | ... | |
| 100 | $p_{100}$ | 0.079 | 0.235 | 0.383 | 0.515 | ... | 0.730 | ... | 0.966 | ... | 0.999 |
| 500 | $p_{500}$ | 0.035 | 0.107 | 0.177 | 0.245 | ... | 0.378 | ... | 0.654 | ... | 0.998 |

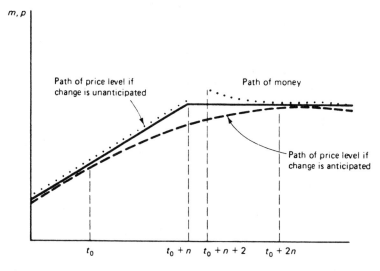

**Figure 3**
The effects of money deceleration

$$(m - p)_{t_0+2i} = (2^{n-1}g) \sum_{j=0}^{i-1} (i-j)\binom{n}{j}, \qquad \text{for } i = 1, \dots, \frac{n}{2},$$

$$= (2^{n-1}g) \sum_{j=0}^{i-1} \left(\frac{n}{2} - j\right)\binom{n}{j}, \qquad \text{for } i = \frac{n}{2}, \dots, n.$$

The paths of money and prices are plotted in figure 3. Real money balances, and therefore output, increase slowly after the announcement. They reach their maximum value at $t_0 + n$, when money growth stops. If, for example, $n = 50$ and $g = 1$ percent, which corresponds, if the basic period is a month, to 12 percent annually, real money balances are higher by 1.3 percent at time $t_0 + 50$. They decrease thereafter and return to their normal level at $t_0 + 2n$. Thus deflation is achieved not with a recession but with a mild expansion!

What is this due to? The announcement of a lower money growth leads price setters to slow down their rate of increase of prices before money deceleration takes place. When zero money growth actually takes place, real money balances are higher but progressively return to their normal level as prices keep increasing until $t_0 + 2n$. This is a very general feature of the "new" models of price inertia and holds, for example, also in the

Taylor-Phelps (Taylor (1980), Phelps (1979)) model of overlapping labor contracts.[14] What is required, however, is a decrease in inflation before the decrease in money growth. For this to happen, the announcement of the future change in policy must be credible. In practice, the lack of credibility is probably what makes this result unlikely to occur. If, for example, agents do not believe zero money growth before it is actually implemented, this deceleration leads to a temporary loss in output. The path of prices in this case is also plotted in figure 3.

## 4  Price-Level Inertia and the Elasticity of Input Supply

In traditional empirical macroeconometric models prices are approximately markups over wages. Wages in turn depend on labor market conditions; of central importance for price inertia and the effects of money on real activity is the elasticity of nominal wages to the unempolyment rate, the slope of the short-run Phillips curve. These models have, however, been criticized for their formalization of expectations. The critique is that expectations of inflation should be included in the Phillips curve and that with rational expectations, anticipated movements in money will have no effect on output, independently of the slope of the short-run Phillips curve.

This section shows that if prices are asynchronized, the slope of the short-run Phillips curve is, even with rational expectation, an important determinant of the degree of price inertia. More precisely, it shows that the flatter the input supply, the slower the price level will adjust and the larger the effect of money on real output will be.

The case $n = 2$ can be solved analytically. Since $\beta$ is not necessarily equal to unity, the model is no longer recursive and is a little more difficult to solve. To focus on the effects of demand disturbances, $\xi$ is put equal to zero. Replacing (7) in (9) gives us an equation in $p_{nt}$:

$$p_{nt} = \frac{1 - \beta^{-1}}{4} [p_{nt-2} + E(p_{nt}|t-2) + p_{nt} + E(p_{nt+2}|t)]$$

$$+ \frac{\beta^{-1}}{4} [m_{t-2} + E(m_t|t-2) + m_t + E(m_{t+2}|t)]. \tag{13}$$

Taking expectations at time $t - 2$, denoting $E(\cdot|t-2)$ by a hat, and defining $\hat{\phi}_t \equiv \beta^{-1}(\hat{m}_{t-2} + 2\hat{m}_t + \hat{m}_{t+2})$,

$$(1 - \beta^{-1})\hat{p}_{n\,t+2} - 2(1 + \beta^{-1})\hat{p}_{n\,t} + (1 - \beta^{-1})\hat{p}_{n\,t-2} = -\hat{\phi}_t. \tag{14}$$

Equation (14) can be solved by factorization to give

$$\hat{p}_{n\,t} = \lambda\hat{p}_{n\,t-2} + \lambda(1 - \beta^{-1})^{-1} \sum_{i=0}^{\infty} \lambda^i\hat{\phi}_{t+2i}, \tag{15}$$

with $\lambda \equiv (1 - \beta^{-1/2})^2(1 - \beta^{-1})^{-1}$.

$\lambda$ gives the direct dependence of $\hat{p}_{nt}$ on $\hat{p}_{n\,t-2}$; it is an increasing function of $\beta$. For $\beta = 1$ (the value assumed in the previous section), taking limits appropriately, $\lambda = 0$ and equation (15) reduces to the equation of the previous section. If input supply is relatively inelastic, that is, for $\beta$ between 0 and 1, $\lambda$ is negative and tends to $-1$ as $\beta$ tends to zero. If input supply is relatively elastic, that is, for $\beta$ greater than 1, $\lambda$ is positive and tends to 1 as $\beta$ tends to infinity. Thus the flatter input supply, the larger the direct dependence of the price level on the past.

What we want, however, is not $\hat{p}_{n\,t}$ but the actual value of $p_{n\,t}$. Consider as in the previous section an unanticipated permanent increase in money at time $t_0$, and assume for notational convenience that the increase is from zero to unity. Since there are no unanticipated movements in money or prices after $t_0$, equation (15), together with the assumed path of money, implies in this case

$$p_{n\,t+2} = \lambda p_{n\,t} + (1 - \lambda), \qquad t \geq t_0. \tag{16}$$

Thus, given $p_{n\,t_0}$, we can solve for the sequence of prices after $t_0$. Equation (13) and the assumptions about the path of money give us another relation between $p_{n\,t_0+2}$ and $p_{n\,t_0}$ and thus the initial condition we need:

$$p_{n\,t_0} = \frac{1 - \beta^{-1}}{4}(p_{n\,t_0} + p_{n\,t_0+2}) + \frac{\beta^{-1}}{2}. \tag{17}$$

Equations (16) and (17) allow us to solve for the path of prices at and after $t_0$.

Table 3 gives the path of prices for different values of $\beta$. It shows in particular that if real input prices are insensitive to market conditions, that is, if $\beta$ is large, the price level reacts less and adjusts more slowly to changes in money: money has larger and more lasting effects on output. If we think of the input as labor, this shows the importance of the short-run Phillips curve slope, even in an economy with rational expectations.

Extending the analysis to values of $n$ larger than 2 presents no particular difficulty, and the method is sketched in the appendix. Results for $n = 10$

**Table 3**
Cumulative effects of a permanent unanticipated increase in money at time $t$

| | $\beta = 10.0$ | $\beta = 2.0$ | $\beta = 1.25$ | $\beta = 1.0$ | $\beta = 0.80$ | $\beta = 0.66$ | $\beta = 0.50$ | $\beta = 0.10$ |
|---|---|---|---|---|---|---|---|---|
| $n = 2$ | | | | | | | | |
| $p_t$ | 0.24 | 0.41 | 0.47 | 0.50 | 0.52 | 0.55 | 0.58 | 0.76 |
| $p_{t+2}$ | 0.73 | 0.90 | 0.97 | 1.00 | 1.02 | 1.05 | 1.07 | 1.12 |
| $p_{t+4}$ | 0.86 | 0.98 | 0.99 | 1.00 | 0.99 | 0.99 | 0.99 | 0.93 |
| $p_{t+6}$ | 0.92 | 1.00 | 1.00 | 1.00 | 1.00 | 1.00 | 1.00 | 1.03 |
| $n = 10$ | | | | | | | | |
| $p_t$ | | 0.19 | 0.23 | 0.25 | 0.26 | 0.27 | 0.30 | |
| $p_{t+2}$ | | 0.55 | 0.62 | 0.66 | 0.68 | 0.72 | 0.77 | |
| $p_{t+4}$ | | 0.77 | 0.85 | 0.89 | 0.92 | 0.95 | 0.99 | |
| $p_{t+6}$ | | 0.90 | 0.96 | 0.98 | 0.99 | 1.01 | 1.03 | |
| $p_{t+8}$ | | 0.95 | 0.99 | 1.00 | 1.00 | 1.01 | 0.99 | |
| $p_{t+10}$ | | 0.98 | 1.00 | 1.00 | 1.00 | 1.00 | 1.00 | |

and different values of $\beta$ are presented in table 3. The conclusions are the same. Since the analysis is substantially simpler when $\beta = 1$, the last section makes this assumption; this section has shown how the results would be modified if the assumption were relaxed.

## 5   Variability of Relative Prices and Profits

Asynchronization of price decisions has implications not only for the dynamics of the price level but for the dynamics of the structure of relative prices. The equation giving the behavior of any nominal price $p_k$ is, if $k$ is even, the same equation as for $p_n$, that is, equation (10) with $n$ replaced by $k$. The formula for odd $k$ is slightly different but as there are no particular insights to be obtained from it, we will limit our attention to prices for which $k$ is even.

### Snake effects

To see the effects of a permanent increase in money on the structure of prices, we can return to tables 1 and 2: they can also be interpreted as giving the cross-section time series of prices. The first column gives the values of $p_{k\,t}$ for values of $k$ ranging from 2 to 500, the second column the values of $p_{k\,t+2}$ for the same values of $k$, and so on.

Table 2 shows how the increase in money twists the structure of prices. Prices early in the chain of production move more and adjust faster; prices farther in the chain move less and adjust more slowly. If we measure profit rates by $(p_k - p_{k-2})$ for sector $k$, it also appears that profit rates move more for low values of $k$.[15] These results would be unchanged if we were looking at a supply disturbance, $\xi$, instead of a demand disturbance, $m$.

### Variance of prices and profits

Instead of looking at effects of once-and-for-all changes in $m$ or $\xi$, we may look at the stochastic behavior of prices for a given process for $m$ or $\xi$. Assume, for example, that $\xi$ and $m$ are white and for convenience that for $t$ even realizations of $\xi$ and $m$ are the same for $t$ and $t + 1$. If, as before, we define $\psi_t$ as $m_t - \xi_t$, the behavior of $p_{kt}$ is, from (10),

$$p_{k\,t} = 2^{-k}\left[\sum_{i=0}^{k/2} b_{k,(k/2)} - i\,\psi_{t-2i}\right]. \tag{18}$$

Thus the standard deviations of nominal prices, real prices, and profit rates are given by

$$\sigma(p_k) = 2^{-k} \left[ \sum_{i=0}^{k/2} (b_{k,(k/2)-i})^2 \right]^{1/2} \sigma_\psi,$$

$$\sigma(p_k - p_n) = \left[ \sum_{i=0}^{n/2} (2^{-k}b_{k,(k/2)-i} - 2^{-n}b_{n,(n/2)-i})^2 \right]^{1/2} \sigma_\psi, \quad b_{kj} = 0 \text{ if } j < 0,$$

$$\sigma(p_k - p_{k-2}) = 2^{-k} \left[ \sum_{i=0}^{k/2} (b_{k,(k/2)-i} - 4b_{k-2,(k/2)-i})^2 \right]^{1/2} \sigma_\psi, \quad b_{kj} = 0 \text{ if } j < 0.$$

Using identities associated with the hypergeometric distribution (Feller 1950, 62), the first expression can be rewritten as

$$\sigma(p_k) = 2^{-k} \left( \binom{2k}{k} - \binom{2k}{k-1} \right)^{1/2} \sigma_\psi.$$

The values of these standard deviations, for $n = 10$ and $k = 0, \ldots, 10$, are reported in table 4. The standard deviations of nominal prices, real prices, and profit rates are all decreasing in $k$. This ordering is again independent of whether the economy is affected by supply or demand disturbances.

This result is fairly robust, being due to asynchronization rather than to the other assumptions of the model. There are two ways to potentially reverse it. The first is to relax the assumptions of constant returns and no inventory. In this case, faced for example with a temporary increase in demand, a firm may decrease its price, decumulate inventory, and not change its derived demand; it would therefore not transmit the disturbance

**Table 4**
Standard deviations of prices and profits

| Sector | Nominal prices | Real prices | Profits |
|---|---|---|---|
| $n = k = 10$ | 0.126 | 0 | 0.025 |
| $k = 8$ | 0.146 | 0.025 | 0.044 |
| $k = 6$ | 0.178 | 0.067 | 0.070 |
| $k = 4$ | 0.253 | 0.135 | 0.153 |
| $k = 2$ | 0.353 | 0.276 | 0.790 |
| $k = 0$ | 1.00 | 0.966 | — |

Note: $\sigma_\psi^2 = \sigma_\xi^2 + \sigma_m^2$ is normalized to unity.

farther down the chain of production. Its price may then vary more than prices farther down the chain. The second is to allow for disturbances to the technology itself, for example, to allow the $\theta_i$ in equation (1) to be stochastic. In this case, sectors affected by large technological disturbances may experience more price variability than the others.

If we think of the primary input as raw materials—there are clearly other factors at work in the labor market—the result is in accordance with facts. In the United States the variance in raw material prices is larger than the variance in intermediate product prices, which is itself larger than the variance in the WPI, both for periods dominated by demand disturbances and periods dominated by supply disturbances.[16]

## 6   Conclusions and Extensions

This chapter has shown that asynchronization of individual price decisions generates both inertia for the price level and movements in relative prices which appear in accordance with the facts.

It is time to return to the assumptions and face the questions addressed to other models of price inertia. Are there obvious opportunities for profit left unused? Is every agent acting optimally? There are two crucial assumptions in the model.

The first is that price setters choose the same nominal price for two periods rather than different nominal prices for both periods or allow the second-period price to be contingent. We have purposefully chosen a basic period short enough for such schemes to have costs that outweigh their benefits. Indexation of the second-period price on the price level is clearly unfeasible if the basic period is short: there may well be no reliable price-level index.

The second is the structure of timing decisions. Given the timing decisions of others, does an agent have an incentive to maintain his own timing decision? In our model the answer is that he has an incentive to change it: each producer has an incentive to synchronize his price decisions with those of his supplier. This feature is, however, a characteristic of the simple structure of the model and is easily removed: if, for example, each producer uses two inputs, the prices of which change at different times, he cannot achieve synchronization with both. It is easy to construct such structures of timing decisions that no price setter has an incentive to change his own timing, given the timing of others. With such structures, asynchronization and the implied inertia for the price level will remain: no agent has an incentive to change his timing or behavior.

This model can be seen as an alternative to the model of overlapping labor contracts developed by Akerlof (1969), Phelps (1979), and Taylor (1980). Both explanations of price inertia are, however, probably empirically relevant. The comparative advantage of this model is twofold. The first is that it is more explicitly grounded in maximizing behavior; this allows for an easier treatment of normative aspects of policies. The second, and more important, is that it derives the complete structure of prices together with the price level. Thus it is well adapted to analyze questions involving both nominal and relative prices. It can, for example, easily be used to look at the desirability of exchange rate indexation under various sources of disturbances, a question analyzed by Dornbusch (1982) using the Taylor model.

## Appendix: Price Solution for Arbitrary $n$ and $\beta$

Replacing equation (7) with $\xi_t \equiv 0$ in equation (10) gives

$$
\begin{aligned}
p_{nt} = 2^{-n} \Bigg\{ & \sum_{i=1}^{n/2} \sum_{j=0}^{(n/2)-i} b_{nj} E\left[ (1 - \beta^{-1})p_{n\,t-2i} - \beta^{-1}m_{t-2i} \middle| t - \frac{n}{2} - i + j \right] \\
& + \sum_{j=0}^{(n/2)-i} b_{nj} E\left[ (1 - \beta^{-1})p_{nt} - \beta^{-1}m_t \middle| t - \frac{n}{2} + j \right] \\
& + \sum_{i=1}^{n/2} \sum_{j=0}^{(n/2)-i} b_{nj} E\left[ (1 - \beta^{-1})p_{n\,t+2i} - \beta^{-1}m_{t+2i} \middle| t - \frac{n}{2} + i + j \right] \Bigg\}. \quad \text{(A1)}
\end{aligned}
$$

We proceed in two steps. The first is to derive the behavior of $E(p_{nt}|t - n)$. Taking expectations in (A1) at time $t - n$ and denoting them with a hat,

$$
\hat{p}_{nt} = 2^{-n}(1 - \beta^{-1})A(L)\hat{p}_{nt} + 2^{-n}\beta^{-1}A(L)\hat{m}_t, \tag{A2}
$$

with $L: Lx_t = x_{t-2}$ and

$$
A(L) \equiv \sum_{i=-n/2}^{n/2} \binom{n}{(n/2) + i} L^i.
$$

Consider the polynomial $1 - 2^{-n}(1 - \beta^{-1})A(L)$ associated with the homogenous part of this difference equation. It is symmetric, so that if $\lambda$ is a root,

$\lambda^{-1}$ is also a root. Thus it can be factorized as $1 - 2^{-n}(1 - \beta^{-1})A(L) = \sigma B(L)B(L^{-1})$, where $\sigma$ is a scalar and $B(L) = 1 + b_1 L + \cdots + b_{n/2} L^{n/2}$ has all roots inside the unit circle.

This implies that $E(p_{nt}|t - n)$ follows

$$B(L)\hat{p}_{nt} = 2^{-n}\beta^{-1}\sigma^{-1}[B(L^{-1})]^{-1}A(L)\hat{m}_t. \tag{A3}$$

The second step is to solve for the actual value of $p_{nt}$. This is easily done for any specific path of, or process for, money. In the case of a permanent unanticipated increase in money at time $t_0$ from zero to unity, it is derived as follows.

Since there are no unanticipated movements of money or prices after $t_0$, equation (A3) implies for $t \geq t_0 + n$,

$$B(L)p_{nt} = 2^{-n}\beta^{-1}\sigma^{-1}[B(L^{-1})]^{-1}A(L)\hat{m}_t.$$

The path of money considered here is such that all values of $m_t$ on the right hand side are equal to unity. Thus

$$B(L)p_{nt} = 2^{-n}\beta^{-1}\sigma^{-1}[B(1)]^{-1}A(1)$$

$$\Rightarrow B(L)p_{nt} = [\beta\sigma B(1)]^{-1} \quad \text{as } 2^{-n}A(1) = 1 \tag{A4}$$

For $t = t_0 + n, \ldots, t_0 + 2n - 2$ this gives a system of $n/2$ equations in $n$ unknowns, $p_{0t_0+2n-2}, \ldots, p_{0t_0}$. In turn, equation (A1) gives, for $t = t_0, \ldots, t_0 + n - 2$ and, given the path of money, $n/2$ equations in the same unknowns. This gives a system of $n$ equations in $n$ unknowns. Once this system is solved, values of $p_{0t}$ for $t \geq t_0 + 2n$ can be derived using (A4). This is the method used to construct the second part of table 3.

## Acknowledgments

I thank Stanley Fischer, Danny Quah, and Jose Scheinkman for comments and suggestions. Financial assistance from the National Science Foundation and the Sloan Foundation is gratefully acknowledged.

## Notes

1. Many arguments along this line are presented in Gordon (1981).

2. The implications of various theories for the relation between disturbances, the price level and relative prices are presented in Fischer (1981).

3. It is sometimes argued that a source of price inertia is the length of the production process (for example, Coutts et al. 1978). The argument is that if price is based on historical cost, a longer production process will lead to longer lags in price adjustment. Although this argument seems to have some empirical success, it appears difficult to reconcile with rational behavior on the part of firms.

4. An alternative formalization, which would extend work by Akerlof (1969), would postulate a large number of imperfectly substitutable final outputs produced under monopolistic competition. An increase in the number of price decisions would be obtained by increasing the number of products. The problem for our purposes is that the "technology" would not remain invariant as the number of price decisions increased. Otherwise, results are very similar. Another alternative is to formalize production as iterations of an input-output matrix. This turns out to be difficult to analyze.

5. The supply disturbance $\xi$ does not affect the technology. It would be easy to allow for technological disturbances as well, by letting the $\theta_i$ be stochastic in equation (1).

6. It is well known that this relation can either be seen as a velocity equation or as a reduced form IS-LM. Allowing for an interest rate would complicate the analysis but bring few insights. The unitary elasticity of output with respect to money balances assumption can be easily relaxed.

7. Although we do not derive the decision about period length from an optimization problem, this can be done by equalizing the marginal cost of more frequent changes to the marginal benefit of more accurate relative prices. This analysis has been pursued by Sheshinski and Weiss (for example, 1981).

8. This voluntarily abstracts from issues of monopoly power which may arise with asynchronized price setting. Condition (6) differs in two minor ways from the correct expected zero-profit condition: it neglects the fact that the second-period expected profit should be discounted by the interest rate; equivalently, it assumes the real interest rate to be equal to zero. It assumes that the firm sells the same quantities in both periods, so that the weights on profit rates in period $t$ $(p_{i\,t} - p_{i-1\,t-1})$ and period $t + 1$ $(p_{i\,t} - E(p_{i-1\,t+1}|t))$ are equal. Both shortcuts simplify the analysis considerably and are not the source of its main results.

9. In a more realistic model, firms would have the choice of supplying demand out of production or inventories. The initial effect of an increase in aggregate demand on the derived demand for the primary input would in general be smaller.

10. Using the terminology of fixed-price equilibrium, our model allows for overemployment or underemployment of the primary input but not for unemployment since the input market is always in equilibrium. If we allowed for changes in $m$ and $\xi$ every period, the price would not necessarily clear the market in both periods, and there could be unemployment.

11. The nominal rigidity of labor contracts is of a different nature from the rigidities considered in this chapter. It is usually of much longer duration, and the assumption of demand determination is certainly more questionable.

12. All the expressions in this chapter are computed using binomial distribution tables (Aiken 1955). These give $F(n, r, p) = \text{Prob}(x > r)$ if $x$ follows an $n$-binomial distribution with probability $p$. Then

$$2^{-n}\binom{n}{r} = F(n, r, 1/2) - F(n, r + 1, 1/2).$$

13. The usual caveat about policy invariance of the structure applies. Such a drastic change may lead price setters to change price decisions more often or to try to achieve better synchronization.

14. In his 1979 paper Phelps considers a slightly different question. The question is whether, starting from steady inflation, there is a path of money such that inflation disappears over

time and there is no change, positive or negative, in output. Phelps shows that there is such a path in his model but that the path is unappealing, involving oscillations in the rate of inflation along the way. Our model also has such a path, with the same unappealing features for $n > 2$.

15. This is more precisely the profit rate of the consolidated sector $(k, k - 1)$. We use this definition to avoid having to introduce $p_k$ for odd $k$. The change in definition does not affect any of the conclusions.

16. This statement is based on comparisons of standard deviations of residuals from regressions on a quadratic trend, for subsamples of 47-1 to 80-1, for the following three series: "finished goods" producer price index (WPISOP3000NS in the DRI U.S. price bank), "intermediate materials, supplies and components" index (WPISOP2000NS), and "crude materials for further processing" index (WPISOP1000NS).

# References

Aiken, H. *Tables of the Cumulative Binomial Probability Distribution.* Harvard University Press, Cambridge, 1955.

Akerlof, G. "Relative Wages and the Rate of Inflation." *Quarterly Journal of Economics,* August 1969: 353–374.

Coutts, K., W. Godley, and W. Nordhaus. *Industrial Pricing in the United Kingdom.* Cambridge University Press, Cambridge, 1978.

Dornbusch, R. "PPP Exchange Rate Rules and Macroeconomic Stability." *Journal of Political Economy,* February 1982: 158–165.

Feller, W. *An Introduction to Probability Theory and Its Applications.* Vol. 1. 2d ed. Wiley, New York, 1957.

Fischer, S. "Relative Shocks, Relative Price Variability and Inflation." *Brookings Papers on Economic Activity* 2 (1981): 381–442.

Gordon, R. "Output Fluctuations and Gradual Price Adjustment," *Journal of Economic Literature,* June 1981: 493–530.

Phelps, E. "Disinflation without Recession: Adaptive Guideposts and Monetary Policy." *Studies in Macroeconomic Theory.* Academic Press, New York, 1979.

Sheshinski, E., and Y. Weiss. "Optimum Pricing Policy under Stochastic Inflation." Mimeograph, October 1981.

Taylor, J.: "Aggregate Dynamics and Staggered Contracts." *Journal of Political Economy,* February 1980: 1–23.

# 10 Will Wage Setters Ever Stagger Decisions?

Gary Fethke and Andrew Policano

## 1 Introduction

Models featuring the implications of long-term contracts typically impose the pattern of negotiation and then develop the implications of this particular structure with no analysis of whether the structure is optimal or stable. Recent work, however, focuses on the choice of the timing of wage negotiations across sectors.[1] In Fethke and Policano (1984) we develop a two-sector model in which each sector is subject to both aggregate and relative disturbances. The main result is that whenever the variability of relative disturbances exceeds the weighted variability of aggregate disturbances, a uniformly staggered pattern of negotiation represents a symmetric noncooperative Nash solution. The two-sector case has special properties. First, the benefit associated with staggered negotiation apparently depends on the existence of large negotiating sectors in the economy. Second, symmetry of relative disturbances in the two-sector case leads to the unusual equivalence of the noncooperative and the joint-optimization solutions to the problem of determining the optimal negotiation pattern.

One natural question concerns whether the incentive to stagger negotiation dates will diminish as the number of sectors increases. In this paper we develop the three-sector case in detail and then generalize the analysis to any number of sectors. The results indicate that the more significant are relative disturbances, the larger is the number of sectors that will be supported by a stable Nash equilibrium with uniformly staggered negotiation dates. In an economy characterized by atomistic sectors, the incentive to stagger negotiation dates disappears. We also compare the joint-optimization solution with the Nash solution and find that when there are more than two sectors, the requirement for uniform staggering to be optimal is more difficult to satisfy under joint optimization than under the Nash strategy. This divergence creates the possibility that individual sectors may choose to stagger their negotiation dates when a synchronized pattern of negotiation is jointly optimal. Finally, we briefly consider the effects on the negotiation pattern of introducing price-setting behavior. Here the optimality of staggered negotiation depends not only on the importance of

*Quarterly Journal of Economics* 101 (November 1986): 867–877. Copyright © 1986 by the President and Fellows of Harvard College. Reprinted by permission of John Wiley & Sons.

relative and aggregate shocks but also on the elasticity of aggregate demand with respect to real balances. We show that if demand is characterized by the quantity equation, then the results under perfect competition continue to hold under monopolistic competition.

## 2  The Model

The economy consists of $n$ sectors, defined as separate negotiating units. Each sector produces the same product, which is sold in a competitive market; the case of monopolistic competition is discussed in section 4. The nominal wage for each sector is set at the beginning of each contract negotiation date for $\tau$ periods, where $\tau$ is identical and fixed for all sectors. While contract length is fixed, the negotiation dates and thus the information incorporated into the wage contracts need not correspond. Once the nominal wage is set, employment over the contract is determined by labor demand. Labor is assumed to be immobile after the contract is negotiated.

The production function and employment rule for each sector are given by

$$y_{kt} = \alpha l_{kt} + z_{kt} + u_t, \qquad 0 < \alpha < 1, \tag{1}$$

and

$$l_{kt} = \eta[(p_t - {}_hp_t) + (u_t - {}_hu_t) + (z_{kt} - {}_hz_{kt})], \qquad \eta > 0. \tag{2}$$

Here $y_{kt}$ is the logarithm of output for sector $k$ at time $t$; $l_{kt}$ is the logarithm of employment for sector $k$; $p_t$ is the logarithm of the price of output; ${}_hp_t = E[p_t|I_h]$, where $E$ denotes the mathematical expectation operator and $I_h$ is the information set possessed at the point of negotiation; $z_{kt}$ is a relative productivity disturbance that nets out across the $n$ sectors each period; and $u_t$ is a common disturbance to productivity. Constants are suppressed for convenience. The information set $I_h$ includes current and past values of all variables, the forms of the various decision rules, and all parameters of the system. One specification leading to equation (2) assumes that the wage is set to equate the expected demand and supply of labor in each sector over the $\tau$-period contract. If labor is inelastically supplied, then $-\eta$ equals the elasticity of demand for labor with respect to the real wage (see Fethke and Policano 1984, p. 153).

Supply of output depends on the timing of the contract negotiation dates. For ease of exposition, initially assume that there are three sectors with the following negotiation pattern: sector 3 negotiates at $t = 0$ and next at $t = \tau$; sector 1 negotiates at $t = b$ and next at $t = b + \tau$; and sector 2 negotiates at $t = a$ and $t = a + \tau$, with $0 \leq b \leq a < \tau$. Synchronized negotiation occurs when $a = b = 0$, while uniformly staggered negotiation occurs when $b = \tau/3$ and $a = 2\tau/3$. Employing this pattern, we can derive supply by substituting equation (2) into equation (1) and summing across the three sectors; each sector receives one third of the weight in total output:

$$y_t^s = (1 + \phi)u_t + \phi p_t - \phi/3[(_h p_t + {}_i p_t + {}_j p_t)$$

$$+ (_h u_t + {}_i u_t + {}_j u_t) + (_h z_{1t} + {}_i z_{2t} + {}_j z_{3t})], \qquad \phi \equiv \alpha\eta > 0. \tag{3}$$

Since aggregate supply depends on the information set used by each sector at its most recent negotiation date, the function differs across the subintervals of the contract period. Specifically, in equation (3), $h = b - \tau$, $i = a - \tau$, and $j = 0$ when $0 \leq t < b$; $h = b$, $i = a - \tau$, and $j = 0$ when $b \leq t < a$; and $h = b$, $i = a$, and $j = 0$ when $a \leq t < \tau$.

Demand for the product is given by

$$y_t^d = m_t - p_t, \tag{4}$$

where $m_t$ is a stochastic process that is distributed independently from $u_t$ and $z_{kt}$. The unitary price elasticity of demand significantly simplifies the analysis without affecting the results.[2] Specifically, the distribution of any $m_t$ disturbance between output and price will depend entirely on the supply schedule.[3]

Each sector negotiates a contract of length $\tau$. Given the negotiation dates of the other sectors, sector $k$ chooses its point of negotiation to minimize an expected cost per cycle, $\psi_k$, which consists of an efficiency loss plus a fixed cost per negotiation, $c$. Specifically,

$$\psi_k = \frac{1}{\tau}\left\{\theta\left(\int_0^b E(l_{kt} - \tilde{l}_{kt})^2 \, dt + \int_b^a E(l_{kt} - \tilde{l}_{kt})^2 \, dt\right.\right.$$

$$\left.\left. + \int_a^\tau E(l_{kt} - \tilde{l}_{kt})^2 \, dt\right) + c\right\}, \tag{5}$$

where $\theta = (1/\eta)^2$. The expression $\theta E(l_{2t} - \tilde{l}_{2t})^2$ is the (weighted) mean-square discrepancy between actual employment $l_{kt}$ and full information employment $\tilde{l}_{kt}$ and depends on the wage rate set by sector $k$ at its point of negotiation. The full-information level of employment is determined from equation (2) by setting the expectations $_h p_t$, $_h u_t$, and $_h z_{k\,t}$ equal to their actual values; here $\tilde{l}_{k\,t} = 0$.

We are able to obtain a closed-form expression for equation (5) when it is assumed that $u_t$, $m_t$, and $z_{k\,t}$ are (continuous-time equivalent) random-walk processes with forecast variances $\sigma_u^2 t$, $\sigma_m^2 t$, and $\sigma_z^2 t$, respectively. The innovations in $u_t$, $m_t$, and $z_{k\,t}$ are uncorrelated. When $n = 3$, the symmetry underlying the framework implies that the correlation between any pair of relative productivity innovations is equal to minus one-half.

Using equation (2), we can express the employment deviations as a function of orthogonal error terms. In the appendix the error terms in the price level are derived for the three-sector case as follows: first, aggregate demand $y_t^d$ is equated to aggregate supply $y_t^s$, to determine the equilibrium price level as a function of $_h p_t$, $_i p_t$, $_j p_t$ and the realizations and expectations of all disturbances. Second, the market-clearing expression for the price level is used by each sector to form expectations of $p_t$ conditional on the information sets $I_j$, $I_i$, and $I_h$, respectively. Finally, the market-clearing price level and the relevant expectations are used to compute the orthogonal forecast errors in the price level. As shown in the appendix, these forecast errors are used to form the mean-square employment deviations over each interval of the contract for each sector, using equation (2) and the timing pattern described above. To determine the optimal timing of contract negotiation, each sector is assumed to select its negotiation date to minimize the expected resource cost per cycle, given the negotiation dates of the other sectors.

## 3   The Pattern of Contract Negotiation

The condition for staggered negotiation to be optimal in the $n$-sector case is given by

$$\left[1 - \left(\frac{n}{n + \phi}\right)^2\right]\sigma_z^2 > \left[\left(\frac{n}{n + \phi}\right)^2 - \left(\frac{1}{1 + \phi}\right)^2\right]\sigma_m^2, \tag{6}$$

with $\phi \equiv \alpha\eta > 0$.

If there are no relative disturbances, $\sigma_z^2 = 0$, then synchronized negotiation is optimal. Alternatively, if there are no aggregate disturbances, $\sigma_m^2 = 0$, with $\sigma_z^2 > 0$, then uniformly staggered negotiation is optimal. The essential idea here is that when contract negotiation dates are staggered, the negotiation by one sector transmits an externality, via the price level, to the sectors that are locked into a previously negotiated contract; this externality is beneficial when disturbances derive primarily from relative sources but is detrimental when disturbances derive primarily from aggregate sources.

To illustrate the implications of condition (6), consider the two-sector case and assume first that there is only an aggregate shock and then only a relative shock at the midpoint of the contract interval. Consider a positive shock to aggregate demand. If contract dates are synchronized, then neither sector negotiates at the midpoint of the contract interval, and employment rises in each sector in response to a decline in the real wage. If contract dates are staggered, with sector 2 negotiating at the midpoint of sector 1's contract, employment in sector 2 remains fixed, and there is a greater price response than in the synchronized case. With the nominal wage in sector 1 predetermined, this larger price effect implies greater employment disequilibrium in sector 1. Alternatively, consider a relative shock that increases labor demand in sector 2 at the midpoint of sector 1's contract. In the synchronized case neither sector adjusts its nominal wage rate, and employment rises in sector 2 and falls in sector 1 with no aggregate effects. If, alternatively, sector 2 negotiates at this time, then, since the full information level of employment is not altered by the shock, $l_{2t}$ will remain fixed. In this case the price level rises, and the negotiation by sector 2 thereby transmits a beneficial externality in sector 1, where employment will increase back toward its original level. Thus, if disturbances derive primarily from relative sources, the Nash equilibrium with be characterized by a uniformly staggered pattern of negotiation.

If the economy consists of a larger number of small sectors, condition (6) implies that staggered negotiation will not be optimal; the effect on the aggregate price level of the actions by any one sector is negligible, and the beneficial externality associated with staggered negotiation is too small to have an effect. More generally, consider an economy that consists of a large but finite number of sectors. Using (6), we see that the maximum number of sectors that will be supported by a stable Nash solution with staggered negotiation dates satisfies

$$\frac{n}{n + \phi} = \frac{\sigma_z^2 + (1/(1 + \phi))^2 \sigma_m^2}{\sigma_z^2 + \sigma_m^2}. \tag{7}$$

Here $n$ is increasing in $\sigma_z^2$, decreasing in $\sigma_m^2$, and increasing in $\phi \equiv \alpha \eta$. In the special case where $-\eta \equiv (\alpha - 1)^{-1}$ is the elasticity of demand for labor, as labor demand becomes more elastic, the number of sectors consistent with staggered negotiation rises rapidly for given values of $\sigma_z^2$ and $\sigma_m^2$.

An important issue concerns whether bargaining units will benefit by abandoning noncooperative strategies and jointly choosing the timing of negotiations. To consider the Pareto optimal solution, we select the pattern of negotiation to minimize $\psi = \sum \psi_i$. In the two-sector case the impact of a relative shock must be symmetrical, and the Pareto optimal solution will coincide with the Nash solution (see Fethke and Policano 1984). This is not the case when there are more than two sectors, because the possibility arises that the relative shocks are distributed asymmetrically.

The three-sector case is developed in the appendix. Here, while the joint-cost minimization and Nash solution do not coincide, both solutions are characterized by synchronization if $\sigma_z^2 = 0$ and by uniform staggered negotiation if $\sigma_m^2 = 0$. The difference between the Nash solution and the joint-cost solution derives from the asymmetric distribution of relative shocks across the three sectors. For example, assume that sector 1 negotiates in the current period and that sectors 2 and 3 are locked into a previously negotiated contract. A relative shock can be distributed across the sectors in three ways. Assume an adverse relative shock in sector 1, and note that sectors 2 and 3 either both face a positive shock, or one sector faces a positive shock, while the other faces an adverse shock. In the first case the negotiation by sector 1 implies a decrease in the price level that is beneficial to both of the noncontracting sectors. For the second and third cases, only one of the noncontracting sectors benefits, while the other sector is harmed. Under the Nash solution neither the benefits nor the costs imposed on the noncontracting sectors are considered by the contracting sector when it selects the location point. In general, the joint-cost requirement for contracts to be staggered is more difficult to satisfy than the analogous requirement for the noncooperative solutions; thus the possibility exists that the noncooperative outcome is characterized by uniform staggering of negotiation dates when, in fact, synchronized negotiaton minimizes joint costs.

## 4  Extensions and Conclusions

Since our analysis assumes perfect competition in the product market, an important consideration concerns the effect of price-setting behavior on the negotiation pattern. Under perfect competition, the results derive from the effect of one sector's negotiation on the real wage in the sectors under contract. Under monopolistic competition the firm's demand for labor depends not only on the real wage but also positively on real money balances (see Ball 1986). Here the results concerning the timing of negotiations will depend both on the importance of aggregate and relative shocks and on the relative sensitivity of labor demand to movements in real balances versus movements in the real wage. For example, consider the two-sector case. When there is a positive disturbance to the money supply and both sectors are under contract, employment increases because real balances rise and real wages fall. Under staggered negotiation, if sector 2 negotiates, there will be a larger price increase than in the synchronized case. While this larger price increase acts, through the effect on the real wage, to exacerbate the disequilibrium in sector 1, it will also have an equilibrating effect in sector 1 by reducing real balances. The net effect on the deviation in employment, and thus the optimality of staggered versus synchronized negotiation, will depend on the net effect of these two forces. In response to a relative productivity shock that increases labor demand in sector 2, the price level will rise when negotiation dates are staggered. The corresponding reduction in the real wage will reduce the disequilibrium in sector 1, but the decrease in real balances will exacerbate the disequilibrium in sector 1. Thus if labor demand is very responsive to aggregate demand shocks, our results under the perfectly competitive case can be reversed: staggered negotiation will be optimal if aggregate demand disturbances are dominant, while synchronized negotiation can occur if relative shocks are dominant.

It is straightforward to show that if aggregate demand is characterized by the quantity equation, then the results under perfect competition will continue to hold under imperfect competition. Under monopolistic competition, demand for sector $k$'s product as a share of aggregate demand depends on the relative price,

$$y_{kt}^d - y_t^d = -\epsilon(p_{kt} - p_t), \qquad \epsilon > 1, \tag{8}$$

where $\epsilon$ is determined by the substitutability of the products of the different sectors. Given the nominal wage, which is set at contract negotiation points, the price in each sector is determined so as to equate marginal revenue with marginal cost, under the assumption that the price set by any single firm in each sector has no perceived impact on the aggregate price level. Staggered negotiation is optimal if the following condition holds:

$$\left(\frac{\epsilon - 1}{\phi + \epsilon}\right)^2 \left[ 1 - \left(\frac{n(\phi + \epsilon)}{\phi + \epsilon(\eta + \phi)}\right)^2 \right] \sigma_z^2$$

$$> \left(\frac{1}{1 + \phi}\right)^2 \times \left[ \left(\frac{n\epsilon(1 + \phi)}{\phi + \epsilon(\eta + \phi)}\right)^2 - 1 \right] \sigma_m^2. \tag{9}$$

The more elastic is product demand, the greater is the number of sectors consistent with staggered negotiation. As $\epsilon \to \infty$, condition (9) reduces to the case of competitive product markets, as given by condition (6). Again, the results depend on the importance of relative shocks as compared with aggregate shocks. Thus, under a reasonable characterization of aggregate demand, our results remain unaffected by the introduction of price-setting behavior.

The main conclusion of this paper concerns the relation between the number of contracting sectors and the timing of wage negotiations. Staggered negotiation is optimal in the presence of significant relative disturbances because at negotiation points the price level transmits beneficial impacts into the sectors that are currently locked into previously negotiated contracts. As the number of sectors increases, given $\sigma_z^2$, the correlation between innovations in relative disturbances falls, and the effect on the price level of any one negotiating sector diminishes: thus it becomes less likely that staggered negotiation will be optimal. This argument assumes, however, that there is only one relative disturbance term in the system that affects all sectors. If, plausibly, the relative shock faced by any individual sector is correlated with the relative shocks faced by only a small number of other sectors, then it will be optimal for these sectors to choose the timing of their contracts relative to one another. In this case the condition for staggered negotiation may not depend on the number of sectors.

## Appendix: The Expected Cost per Contract Cycle in the Three-Sector Case

The equilibrium price level is obtained from equations (3) and (4) in the text and is given by the following expression:

$$p_t = (1/(1 + \phi))[m_t - (1 + \phi)u_t + (\phi/3)$$

$$((_h p_t + _i p_t + _j p_t) + (_h u_t + _i u_t + _j u_t) + (_h z_{1t} + _i z_{2t} + _j z_{3t}))], \tag{A1}$$

where $h$, $i$, and $j$ have the same pattern over the contract subintervals as that associated with aggregate supply, equation (3). Using equation (A1), we represent the orthogonal errors in $p_t$ over each subinterval of the contract by

$$p_t - {}_hp_t = [1/(1 + \phi)](m_t - {}_hm_t) - (u_t - {}_hu_t), \tag{A2}$$

$$
\begin{aligned}
{}_hp_t - {}_ip_t &= (3/(3 + 2\phi))({}_hm_t - {}_im_t) - ({}_hu_t - {}_iu_t) \\
&\quad + (\phi/(3 + 2\phi))({}_hz_{kt} - {}_iz_{kt}),
\end{aligned} \tag{A3}
$$

$$
\begin{aligned}
{}_ip_t - {}_jp_t &= (3/(3 + \phi))({}_im_t - {}_jm_t) - ({}_iu_t - {}_ju_t) \\
&\quad + (\phi/(3 + \phi))({}_iz_{lt} - {}_jz_{lt}),
\end{aligned} \tag{A4}
$$

where $h = 0$, $i = a - \tau$, $j = b - \tau$, $k = 3$, and $l = 1$ when $0 \le t < b$; $h = b$, $i = 0$, $j = a - \tau$, $k = 1$, and $l = 2$ when $b \le t < a$; and $h = a$, $i = b$, $j = 0$, $k = 2$, and $l = 3$ when $a \le t < \tau$.

The employment deviation for each sector over each subinterval of the contract can be derived using equations (2) and (A2)–(A4). For example, the employment deviations for sector 2 are given by the following: For $0 \le t < b$,

$$
\begin{aligned}
l_{2t} - \tilde{l}_{2t} = \eta\Bigg[ &\frac{1}{1 + \phi}(m_t - {}_0m_t) + \frac{3}{3 + 2\phi}({}_0m_t - {}_{a-\tau}m_t) \\
&+ \frac{1}{3 + 2\phi}({}_0z_{3t} - {}_{a-\tau}z_{3t}) + (z_{2t} - {}_{a-\tau}z_{2t}) \Bigg].
\end{aligned} \tag{A5}
$$

For $b \le t < a$,

$$
\begin{aligned}
l_{2t} - \tilde{l}_{2t} = \eta\Bigg[ &\frac{1}{1 + \phi}(m_t - {}_bm_t) + \frac{3}{3 + 2\phi}({}_bm_t - {}_0m_t) \\
&+ \frac{3}{3 + \phi}({}_0m_t - {}_{a-\tau}m_t) + (z_{2t} - {}_{a-\tau}z_{2t}) \\
&+ \frac{\phi}{3 + 2\phi}({}_bz_{1t} - {}_0z_{1t}) + \frac{\phi}{3 + \phi}({}_0z_{2t} - {}_{a-\tau}z_{2t}) \Bigg].
\end{aligned} \tag{A6}
$$

For $a \le t < \tau$,

$$l_{2t} - \tilde{l}_{2t} = \eta[(1/(1 + \phi))(m_t - {}_am_t) + (z_{2t} - {}_az_{2t})]. \tag{A7}$$

Similar expressions can be derived for sectors 1 and 3.

Using equation (5) and (A5)–(A7) and the properties of the exogenous processes, we can express the expected cost function for sector 2 as follows:

$$\psi_2 = \Pi_0 + (\Pi_1 - \Pi_2)(b^2 - b\tau)/\tau$$
$$+ (\Pi_1 - \Pi_3)(a^2 + b\tau - a\tau - ab)/\tau, \tag{A8}$$

where

$$\Pi_0 = \Pi_1 \tau/2 + c/\tau,$$

$$\Pi_1 = (1/(1 + \phi))\sigma_m^2 + \sigma_z^2,$$

$$\Pi_2 = (3/(3 + 2\phi))^2 \, [\sigma_m^2 + (1 + \phi(1 + (\phi/3)))\sigma_z^2],$$

$$\Pi_3 = (3/(3 + \phi))^2 \, [\sigma_m^2 + \sigma_z^2].$$

Following an analogous procedure for sectors 1 and 3, we obtain

$$\psi_1 = \Pi_0 + (\Pi_1 - \Pi_2)(a^2 - a\tau)/\tau$$
$$+ (\Pi_1 - \Pi_3)(b^2 - ab)/\tau, \tag{A9}$$

and

$$\psi_3 = \Pi_0 + (\Pi_1 - \Pi_2)(a^2 - a\tau + b^2 + ab)/\tau$$
$$+ (\Pi_2 - \Pi_3)(ab - b\tau)/\tau. \tag{A10}$$

The Nash solution for the three-sector case is given by

$$a^* = b^* = 0, \quad \text{when } \Pi_1 < \Pi_3, \tag{A11}$$

and

$$a^* = 2\tau/3, b^* = \tau/3, \quad \text{when } \Pi_1 > \Pi_3. \tag{A12}$$

The condition $\Pi_1 > \Pi_3$ can be written as

$$\left[1 - \left(\frac{3}{3 + \phi}\right)^2\right]\sigma_z^2 > \left[\left(\frac{3}{3 + \phi}\right)^2 - \left(\frac{1}{1 + \phi}\right)^2\right]\sigma_m^2. \tag{A13}$$

Condition (A13) generalizes to condition (6).

To consider the joint-cost minimization problem, we minimize $\psi = \sum_1^3 \psi_i$ formed from equations (A8)–(A10). We obtain

$$a^* = b^* = 0, \quad \text{when } \Pi_1 < \Pi_3 + (2/3)(\Pi_2 - \Pi_3), \tag{A14}$$

and

$$a^* = 2\tau/3 \quad \text{and} \quad b^* = \tau/3, \quad \text{when } \Pi_1 > \Pi_3 + 2/3(\Pi_2 - \Pi_3). \quad (A15)$$

## Acknowledgments

We wish to thank Jo Anna Gray for discussions concerning the relationship between the number of contracting sectors and the timing of wage negotiations. The comments of Olivier Blanchard, who suggested that we consider the monopolistic competitive case, are also appreicated.

## Notes

1. Fischer (1977), Taylor (1980), and Blanchard (1983) impose the pattern of negotiation from the outset. Fethke and Policano (1984), Matsukawa (1983), and Hosios (1983) attempt to endogenize the timing pattern.

2. As discussed in section 4, the elasticity of aggregate demand becomes important under imperfect competition in the product market. Our results concerning the pattern of negotiation hold under perfect competition regardless of the size of this elasticity.

3. With unitary elasticity of aggregate demand and an inelastic supply of labor, the price response to an aggregate productivity shock exactly clears the labor market under any pattern of negotiation. The effect of these two conditions is to eliminate the impact of $u_t$ on employment. The case where labor supply is not perfectly inelastic considerably complicates the algebra, but the main results of the analysis are not affected.

## References

Ball, L., "Externalities from Contract Length," mimeo, 1986.

Blanchard, O. J., "Inflexible Relative Prices and Price Level Inertia," National Bureau of Economic Research, working paper no. 1147, 1983.

Fethke, G., and A. Policano, "Wage Contingencies, the Pattern of Negotiation and Aggregate Implications of Alternative Contract Structures," *Journal of Monetary Economics* 14 (1984), 151–170.

Fischer, S., "Long-Term Contracts, Rational Expectations and the Optimal Money Supply Rule," *Journal of Political Economy* 85 (1977), 191–205.

Hosios, A. J., "Staggered Employment Contracts," mimeo, 1983.

Matsukawa, S., "The Equilibrium Distribution of Wage Settlements and Economic Stability," mimeo, 1983.

Taylor, J., "Aggregate Dynamics and Staggered Contracts," *Journal of Political Economy* 88 (1980), 1–23.

# 11 Imperfect Information and Staggered Price Setting

## Laurence Ball and Stephen G. Cecchetti

In many Keynesian models of the business cycle, firms change prices at different times. Even if individual prices change frequently, this "staggered" price setting leads to inertia in the aggregate price level, which causes nominal disturbances to have large and long-lasting real effects (see Blanchard 1983, 1986; Taylor 1980). A frequent criticism of this research is that the timing of price changes is treated as exogenous. The models show that staggering has important macroeconomic effects, but they do not explain why staggering occurs. In fact, if the firms in these models are allowed to choose when to change prices, all firms change them simultaneously.[1]

This paper attempts to strengthen the foundations of Keynesian models by presenting an explanation for staggered price setting. We develop a model in which firms have imperfect knowledge of the current state of the economy and gain information by observing the prices set by others. This gives each firm an incentive to set its price shortly after other firms set theirs. Staggering can be the equilbrium outcome.[2]

The argument that imperfect information can lead to staggered price setting is an old one. Arthur Okun (1981), for example, argues that firms' concern for relative wages combined with their ignorance of one another's plans leads to staggering. Okun describes a hypothetical economy in which all firms set wages on January 1 of each year. He then speculates,

The inability of firms to assess relative wage prospects would destabilize the synchronized situation. Every employer would like to make a decision in full light of decisions that others had made, but would also like to respond promptly. So an employer would want to move a bit behind the schedule followed by the others. As a result, some employer would decide to shift the wage adjustment date to February 1, in order to observe what all the other employers had done. Others would also want to make such a move, but obviously everyone cannot exercise the preference to bat last. The likely result of this "time-location" problem is analogous to that of some spatial location problems. It generates a tendency to spread the distribution of wage-adjustment dates around the calendar. (p. 95)

While Okun discusses wages, his point applies equally well to price setting in general. Similar discussions of imperfect information and staggering appear in recent macroeconomics textbooks (for example, Hall and Taylor 1988, chap. 15).

*American Economic Review* 78 (December 1988): 999–1018. Copyright © 1988 by the American Economic Association. Reprinted with permission.

Despite their popularity, these explanations for staggering have never been formalized. This paper shows that adding imperfect information to Blanchard's (1986) model of monopolistically competitive price setters can create endogenous staggering. In our model, each firm's desired price depends separately on local and aggregate demand shocks, but the firm observes only their sum. As a result, if all firms change prices at the same times, each faces a version of Robert Lucas's (1973) signal extraction problem. But when price decisions are staggered, a price setter observes prices set recently by other firms. These provide information about the previous price setters' estimates of the underlying shocks, and this information improves the current firm's estimates.

We use the model to address two questions. First, when does imperfect information lead to staggering? We characterize the conditions under which staggering and synchronization are stable Nash equilibria. Second, can staggering be socially optimal? When information considerations are absent, staggering is Pareto-inferior to synchronization because it leads to price-level inertia, which exacerbates business cycles. But in our model, staggered price setting helps firms set prices closer to full-information levels and may lead to a net improvement in welfare.

Much of our analysis, including our welfare results, depends only on the presence of a firm-specific and an aggregate demand shock that price setters cannot distinguish. It turns out, however, that these two shocks are *not* sufficient to make staggering a stable decentralized equilibrium. Stable staggering arises only when we assume that each firm belongs to a small "neighborhood" of firms, an industry or geographic area, and that there is a third demand shock that is common to neighbors. Throughout we compare the implications of the model with and without neighborhood shocks.[3]

The remainder of the paper consists of six sections. Section 1 presents the model, and section 2 describes the information gains from staggering. Section 3 derives the behavior of the aggregate price level under staggering and synchronization. As in previous work, staggering leads to price-level inertia. Section 4 uses the results of the earlier sections to determine which of the two regimes is socially optimal, and section 5 determines when each is a stable decentralized equilibrium. Finally, section 6 discusses generalizations and offers conclusions.

Our results illustrate the complementarity of new classical and new Keynesian macroeconomic models. Lucas's framework of imperfect information provides a foundation for Blanchard's model of staggered price setting. At the same time, the possibility of staggering makes more plausible the idea that information imperfections are an important source of aggregate fluctuations. In actual economies these imperfections appear short-lived. For example, data on the U.S. price level are available with approximately a one-month lag. Short information lags can lead to staggering, however, and staggering causes nominal shocks to have long-lasting real effects.

## 1 The Model

Our model combines elements of the models in Blanchard 1986, Blanchard and Nobuhiro Kiyotaki 1987, and Blanchard and Stanley Fischer 1988. The economy contains a large number of firms that sell differentiated products. Each firm fixes its nominal price for two periods. Departing from previous work, we assume that each firm chooses the timing of its price changes; that is, it chooses whether to set its price in even- or odd-numbered periods. In addition, a firm faces several demand shocks and cannot fully distinguish between them.

Part A of this section describes tastes, technology, and price setting. Here, the only departure from previous papers is the addition of product-specific taste shocks to utility: these taste shocks are the source of local demand shocks. Part B describes the structure of shocks and agents' information, which are the crucial parts of the model.

### A Tastes, technology, and price setting

The economy consists of $N$ agents, where $N$ is a large number. Each agent is a producer-consumer: he uses his own labor to produce a differentiated good and then sells this product and purchases the products of all other agents. Agents take one another's prices as given. With these assumptions, we suppress the labor market and focus on price setting in the goods market. (In future sections we generally refer to agents as "firms."[4])

Omitting time subscripts, agent $i$'s utility function is

$$U_i = C_i - \frac{\epsilon \gamma}{\epsilon - 1} L_i^\gamma, \qquad C_i = N \left[ \frac{1}{N} \sum_{j=1}^{N} (\phi_j C_{ij})^{(\epsilon-1)/\epsilon} \right]^{\epsilon/(\epsilon-1)}, \tag{1}$$

where $C_{ij}$ is agent $i$'s consumption of agent $j$'s product, $C_i$ is an index of agent $i$'s total consumption, $L_i$ is agent $i$'s labor supply, $\phi_j$ is a shock to tastes for agent $j$'s product, $\epsilon$ is the elasticity of substitution between any two goods ($\epsilon > 1$), and $\gamma$ measures the degree of increasing marginal disutility of labor ($\gamma > 1$). The coefficient multiplying $L_i$ is chosen for convenience.

Agent $i$ has a linear production function

$$Y_i = L_i, \tag{2}$$

where $Y_i$ is agent $i$'s output. A money demand function determines the relation between real balances and total spending on goods:

$$Y = M/P, \tag{3}$$

where

$$Y = \frac{1}{N} \sum_{j=1}^{N} \frac{P_j Y_j}{P}$$

and

$$P = \left[ \frac{1}{N} \sum_{j=1}^{N} (P_j/\phi_j)^{1-\epsilon} \right]^{1/(1-\epsilon)}.$$

$M$ is the money stock, $P_j$ is the price of agent $j$'s product, and $P$ is the price index for consumption (agent $i$ must spend $P$ to obtain one unit of $C_i$).[5]

The utility function determines the demand for agent $i$'s product as a fraction of aggregate spending. Writing this relation in logs,

$$y_i - y = -\epsilon(p_i - p) + u_i, \tag{4}$$

where $y = \ln(Y)$, $p = \ln(P)$, and $u = (\epsilon - 1)\ln(\phi)$.[6] Combining (3) and (4) yields product demand:

$$y_i = (m - p) - \epsilon(p_i - p) + u_i, \tag{5}$$

where $m = \ln(M)$. According to (5), demand for agent $i$'s product depends on three variables: real money, which determines aggregate demand; the agent's relative price (with an elasticity determined by the substitutability of goods); and a shock determined by tastes for the agent's product. (Below we assume that the shock $u_i$ has both firm-specific and "neighborhood" components.)

If agent $i$ set his price every period with full information, he would choose the price that maximizes utility, (1), subject to (2), (5), and the constraint that his consumption spending equal his revenue ($PC_i = P_i Y_i$). In logs, the utility-maximizing price is

$$p_i^* = v(m + u_i) + (1 - v)p, \qquad v = \frac{\gamma - 1}{1 + \gamma\epsilon - \epsilon}. \tag{6}$$

We assume, however, that agent $i$ fixes his price for two periods. If he sets a price at $t$, it is in effect at $t$ and $t + 1$. This assumption captures the idea that costs of price adjustment lead agents to change prices less frequently than shocks arrive. In principle, we could make the adjustment cost explicit and assume that agents optimize over the frequency of price changes as well as the timing (as in Ball 1987). But adding another choice variable would complicate the analysis tremendously, and so we treat the frequency of adjustment as exogenous.[7]

Substituting the production function and product demand into (1) yields agent $i$'s utility in terms of his price and the other variables that affect demand ($p, m$, and $u_i$). For simplicity, in the analysis below we approximate this indirect utility function with $-(p_i - p_i^*)^2$; that is, we assume that the agent minimizes the squared deviations of his price from the utility-maximizing level. (Because demand is loglinear, $(p_i - p_i^*)^2$ is proportional to $(y_i - y_i^*)^2$, the squared deviation of the agent's output from the utility-maximizing level.)[8]

In choosing a price for $t$ and $t + 1$, agent $i$ uses all information available at the end of $t - 1$. Thus, ignoring discounting, the agent minimizes the loss function

$$\mathcal{L}_i = E_{t-1}^i\{(x_{it} - p_{it}^*)^2 + (x_{it} - p_{it+1}^*)^2\}, \tag{7}$$

where $x_{it}$ is the log of agent $i$'s price for $t$ and $t + 1$ and $E_{t-1}^i$ is the expectation conditional on his information at the end of $t - 1$. Minimization of (7) implies the simple price-setting rule

$$x_{it} = \tfrac{1}{2}\{E_{t-1}^i p_{it}^* + E_{t-1}^i p_{it+1}^*\}. \tag{8}$$

Finally, to simplify aggregation, we approximate the log of the price index in (3) with (9).[9]

$$p_t \simeq \frac{1}{N} \sum_{j=1}^{N} p_{jt}. \tag{9}$$

## B    The structure of shocks and agents' information

For realism, we now refer to the model's producers-consumers as "firms."

Both the money stock and local demand are stochastic. $m_t$ follows a random walk:

$$m_t = m_{t-1} + \delta_t, \qquad \delta_t \sim N(0, \sigma_m^2). \tag{10}$$

The local demand shock $u_i$ contains both a firm-specific component and a component that is common to firms within a neighborhood. Specifically, assume that each firm belongs to a neighborhood of $n$ firms, where $n$ is a *small* number. The economy contains a large number of neighborhoods. If firm $i$ is a member of neighborhood $I$, then

$$u_{it} = \theta_{It} + \theta_{It-1} + \eta_{it}, \tag{11}$$

where $\theta_I$ is common to firms within a neighborhood but uncorrelated across neighborhoods, and $\eta_i$ is uncorrelated across all firms. The neighborhood shock $\theta$ and the firm-specific shock $\eta$ are both white noise with mean zero and variances $\sigma_\theta^2$ and $\sigma_\eta^2$. Equation (11) implies that the neighborhood shock affects $u_i$ for two periods.[10]

A neighborhood can be interpreted as an industry or geographic area. The neighborhood shock captures the realistic idea that a firm's demand is more highly correlated with the demand of "neighbors" than with the demand of other firms. This will mean that a firm learns more by observing neighbors' prices than by observing prices in the rest of the economy. The presence of neighborhood shocks and the persistence of their effects prove essential to the result, in section 5, that staggered price setting can be a stable decentralized equilibrium. But much of our analysis holds for the special case in which $u_i$ contains only a firm-specific component ($\sigma_\theta^2 = 0$). Since this case is relatively simple, we emphasize it throughout.

Our central assumption is that agents have imperfect imformation. Firms observe one another's prices when they are set, but the demand shocks $\theta$ and $\eta$ and the money stock (which should be interpreted as nominal aggregate demand) are observed with a lag. Specifically, assume that all shocks are revealed, for example through announcements by the government or trade associations, with a two-period lag. Firms set $x_{it}$ based on information revealed through $t - 1$, so they have full information about shocks two periods earlier, at $t - 3$. Assuming that shocks are revealed with a two-period lag, rather than a longer one, simplifies the analysis but is not crucial. As will be clear below, a shorter lag would eliminate the information gains from staggering, which are the focus of the paper.[11]

## 2 The Information Gains from Staggering

### A Overview

The remainder of the paper studies the economy described in section 1. We focus on two price-setting regimes: synchronization, in which all firms set prices in even periods, and uniform staggering, in which half set prices in even periods and half in odd periods. When neighborhood shocks are present ($\sigma_\theta^2 > 0$) and price setting is staggered, we assume that each neighborhood is split equally between even and odd periods.[12] This section describes the price-setting problem facing a firm in each regime to show that there are information gains from staggering. Later sections build on this analysis to determine when synchronization and staggering are socially optimal and when each is a stable decentralized equilbrium.

To understand the benefits from staggering, consider the information available to a firm when it sets $x_{it}$. As we specified above, the firm observes the underlying demand shocks ($m$, $\theta$, and $\eta$) only through $t - 3$ but observes all prices, and hence the aggregate price level, through $t - 1$. The demand equation, (5), shows that the firm can infer the sum of its demand shocks, ($m + u_i$), from its own price and sales and the aggregate price level. Since the firm always knows its own price and sales, ($m + u_i$) is observed through $t - 1$.

If price setting is synchronized, ($m + u_i$) is firm $i$'s only information about shocks since $t - 3$. But if price setting is staggered, prices set at $t - 1$ reveal further information. As we show below, prices set at $t - 1$ depend on ($m_{t-2} + u_{i\,t-2}$), the last composite shock before $t - 1$. The local shock $u_i$ averages to zero over the many $t - 1$ price setters, so the average of $t - 1$ prices reveals $m_{t-2}$.[13] Thus a firm setting $x_{it}$ under staggering knows the money stock through $t - 2$ even though $m$ is directly observed only through $t - 3$. (In contrast, under synchronization, firms observe prices in effect at $t - 1$, but these were all set at $t - 2$ based on information about $t - 3$. Since $t - 3$ shocks are directly observed, the prices reveal nothing new.)

Staggering yields this information gain regardless of whether the local shock is purely firm-specific ($\sigma_\theta^2 = 0$) or includes a neighborhood component. With neighborhood shocks, staggering has an additional benefit: by observing prices set by neighbors at $t - 1$, a firm gains information about its $t - 2$ neighborhood shock, $\theta_{i\,t-2}$. This proves useful both in distinguishing $m$ from $u_i$ and in distinguishing the two components of $u_i$. The complicated details are described below.

The rest of this section formally describes a firm's price-setting problem and its information set. We begin with the simple model without neighborhood shocks and then consider the general model. In each case we compare the synchronized and uniformly staggered regimes.

## B    The simple model

**The synchronized regime**    If all firms change prices at $t, t + 2$, and so on, the aggregate price level does not change in alternate periods. This means that $p_t = p_{t+1}$ and $E^i_{t-1}p_t = E^i_{t-1}p_{t+1}$. Since the money stock follows a random walk, $E^i_{t-1}m_{t+1} = E^i_{t-1}m_t = E^i_{t-1}m_{t-1}$. Finally, since $u_i = \eta_i$ in the simple model and $\eta_i$ is serially uncorrelated, $E^i_{t-1}u_{it} = 0$. Combining these results with firm $i$'s price-setting rule, (8), and the expression for the firm's desired price, (6), leads to

$$x^S_{it} = vE^i_{t-1}m_{t-1} + (1 - v)E^i_{t-1}p_t, \tag{12}$$

where $x^S_{it}$ is firm $i$'s price in the synchronized regime.

Equation (12) shows that $x^S_{it}$ depends on firm $i$'s estimates of $m_{t-1}$ and $p_t$. Since $m_{t-3}$ is announced, estimation of $m_{t-1}$ reduces to estimation of the last two innovations in the money stock, $(\delta_{t-1} + \delta_{t-2})$. As noted above, firm $i$'s sales at $t - 1$ and $t - 2$ reveal $(m_{t-2} + u_{it-2})$ and $(m_{t-1} + u_{it-1})$. In the simple model these signals equal $(m_{t-2} + \eta_{it-2})$ and $(m_{t-1} + \eta_{it-1})$. Along with $m_{t-3}$, they reveal two pieces of information useful in estimating $(\delta_{t-1} + \delta_{t-2})$:

$$z_1 = \delta_{t-1} + \delta_{t-2} + \eta_{it-1} \tag{13}$$

$$z_2 = \delta_{t-2} + \eta_{it-2}. \tag{14}$$

When price setting is synchronized, the firm has no additional information.

Since the $\delta$s are normally distributed, the expectation of their sum conditional on $z_1$ and $z_2$ is given by the linear projection

$$E^i_{t-1}(\delta_{t-1} + \delta_{t-2}) = a_1 z_1 + a_2 z_2,$$

where

$$a_1 = \frac{\sigma^2_m + 2\sigma^2_\eta}{\sigma^2_m + 3\sigma^2_\eta + (\sigma^2_\eta)^2/\sigma^2_m} \quad \text{and} \quad a_2 = \frac{\sigma^2_\eta}{\sigma^2_m + 3\sigma^2_\eta + (\sigma^2_\eta)^2/\sigma^2_m}.$$

The expectation of $m_{t-1}$ follows immediately:

$$E_{t-1}^i m_{t-1} = m_{t-3} + a_1 z_1 + a_2 z_2. \tag{16}$$

According to (16), expected money depends on the last announced money stock, $m_{t-3}$, and the noisy information about recent changes in money.

Below we substitute (16) into firm $i$'s price-setting rule to solve for the aggregate price level. But first we turn to price setting and information in the staggered regime.

**The uniformly staggered regime**  When half of the firms change prices in each period, $p_t$ does not equal $p_{t-1}$. Instead of (12), the price-setting rule implied by (6) and (8) is

$$x_{it}^U = v E_{t-1}^i m_{t-1} + \frac{1-v}{2}(E_{t-1}^i p_t + E_{t-1}^i p_{t+1}), \tag{17}$$

where $x_{it}^U$ is firm $i$'s price in the uniformly staggered regime.

Once again, a firm's price depends on its estimate of $m_{t-1}$. Crucially, this estimate is better under staggering than under synchronization. As noted above, firms in the staggered regime infer $m_{t-2}$ from prices set at $t-1$. Thus estimation of $m_{t-1}$ reduces to estimation of the single shock $\delta_{t-1}$, not $(\delta_{t-1} + \delta_{t-2})$, as in the synchronized regime.

Formally, we assume that staggered firms observe $m_{t-2}$ and then verify this after solving for the price level. It turns out that each price set at $t-1$ is a linear combination of prices set at $t-2$ and shocks at $t-2$ and $t-3$. Since local shocks average to zero across the economy, the average of prices set at $t-1$ depends only on prices set at $t-2$ and the money stock at $t-2$ and $t-3$. When firm $i$ sets $x_{it}^U$, it knows prices at $t-2$ and the money stock at $t-3$ (which has been announced). Therefore, the average of prices set at $t-1$ reveals the money stock at $t-2$.

To estimate $\delta_{t-1}$, the unknown part of $m_{t-1}$, firm $i$ uses

$$z_3 = \delta_{t-1} + \eta_{it-1}, \tag{18}$$

which it infers from its $t-1$ sales. Projection of $\delta_{t-1}$ onto $z_3$ leads to

$$E_{t-1}^i m_{t-1} = m_{t-2} + b z_3, \quad \text{where} \quad b = \frac{\sigma_m^2}{\sigma_m^2 + \sigma_\eta^2}. \tag{19}$$

Not suprisingly, a comparison of (16) and (19) shows that the error in estimating $m_{t-1}$ has smaller variance under staggering than under synchronization. In the simple model this is the information gain from staggering.

### C   The neighborhood model

When the local shock $u_i$ contains a neighborhood component, the price-setting problem facing firms is more complicated. In addition, there is a second information gain from staggering. This will be important for the result that staggering can be a stable equilibrium. We again consider synchronization and uniform staggering in turn.

**The synchronized regime**   In the neighborhood model the price-setting rule for synchronized firms implied by (6) and (8) is

$$x_{it}^S = vE_{t-1}^i m_{t-1} + (1 - v)E_{t-1}^i p_t^S + \frac{v}{2}E_{t-1}^i \theta_{It-1}. \tag{20}$$

$x_{it}^S$ depends on firm $i$'s estimates of both the aggregate and the neighborhood shock at $t - 1$. (It depends on $\theta_{IT-1}$ but not the firm-specific shock $\eta_{it-1}$ because, by (11), only the former affects demand at $t$.) As in the simple model, the firm observes $(m_{t-1} + u_{it-1})$ and $(m_{t-2} + u_{it-2})$. Along with the announcements of $t - 3$ shocks, these reveal

$$z_1^N = \delta_{t-1} + \delta_{t-2} + \theta_{It-1} + \theta_{It-2} + \eta_{it-1} \tag{21}$$

and

$$z_2^N = \delta_{t-2} + \theta_{It-2} + \eta_{it-2}. \tag{22}$$

Firm $i$ estimates $\theta_{It-1}$ and the unknown parts of $m_{t-1}$, $\delta_{t-1}$, and $\delta_{t-2}$ by projecting them on $z_1^N$ and $z_2^N$:

$$E_{t-1}^i \delta_{t-1} = a_1^N z_1^N + a_2^N z_2^N, \tag{23}$$

$$E_{t-1}^i \delta_{t-2} = a_3^N z_1^N + a_4^N z_2^N, \tag{24}$$

$$E_{t-1}^i \theta_{It-1} = a_5^N z_1^N + a_6^N z_2^N, \tag{25}$$

where $a_1^N$ through $a_6^N$ depend on the variances of the shocks, $\sigma_m^2$, $\sigma_\theta^2$, and $\sigma_\eta^2$. (The expressions for $a_1^N$–$a_6^N$ are given in the appendix.) The firm's estimate of $m_{t-1}$ follows from (23) and (24):

$$E_{t-1}^i m_{t-1} = m_{t-3} + (a_1^N + a_3^N)z_1^N + (a_2^N + a_4^N)z_2^N. \tag{26}$$

**The uniformly staggered regime**   In the neighborhood model, the price-setting rule under staggering is

$$x_{it}^U = vE_{t-1}^i m_{t-1} + \frac{1-v}{2}(E_{t-1}^i p_t^U + E_{t-1}^i p_{t+1}^U) + \frac{v}{2}E_{t-1}^i \theta_{I\,t-1}. \tag{27}$$

Again, staggered firms infer $m_{t-2}$ from prices set at $t-1$. Thus they need only estimate $\delta_{t-1}$ and the neighborhood shock $\theta_{I\,t-1}$. As in the simple model, one relevant piece of information is

$$z_3^N = \delta_{t-1} + u_{i\,t-1} = \delta_{t-1} + \theta_{I\,t-1} + \theta_{I\,t-2} + \eta_{i\,t-1}. \tag{28}$$

But when neighborhood shocks are present, there is an additional piece of information provided by neighbors' prices. Each price set by a neighbor of firm $i$ at $t-1$, $x_{j\,t-1}$, depends on $(m_{t-2} + u_{j\,t-2})$. Since $m_{t-2}$ is known under staggering, the price reveals $u_{j\,t-2} = (\theta_{I\,t-2} + \theta_{I\,t-3} + \eta_{j\,t-2})$. Because $t-3$ shocks are announced, this means that firm $i$ knows $\theta_{I\,t-2} + \eta_{j\,t-2}$, the sum at $t-2$ of the neighborhood shock and the neighbor's firm-specific shock. Firm $i$ also infers $\theta_{I\,t-2} + \eta_{i\,t-2}$, the $t-2$ sum of the neighborhood shock and its *own* firm-specific shock, from its sales. The firm averages this information over the half of its neighborhood that set prices at $t-1$ and itself—a total of $(n/2)+1$ observations—and obtains

$$z_4^N = \theta_{I\,t-2} + \bar{\eta}_{i\,t-2}, \tag{29}$$

where $\bar{\eta}_{i\,t-2}$ is the average of the $\eta_{j\,t-2}$ and $\eta_{i\,t-2}$. The $\eta$s do not average to zero, because the neighborhood size, $n$, is small (This will be important for some of our results.)

Observation of $z_4^N$ is the second information gain from staggering. (Under synchronization, no prices are set at $t-1$, and so firms cannot construct $z_4^N$.) Intuitively, $z_4^N$ is useful as an estimate of $\theta_{I\,t-2}$. Because of the persistence of the neighborhood shock, $\theta_{I\,t-2}$ is part of $u_{i\,t-1}$. Thus information about $\theta_{I\,t-2}$ helps a firm disentangle $\delta_{t-1}$ from $u_{i\,t-1}$.

Formally, firm $i$ estimates the unknown shocks $\delta_{t-1}$ and $\theta_{I\,t-1}$ by projecting them on $z_3^N$ and $z_4^N$:

$$E_{t-1}^i \delta_{t-1} = b_1^N z_3^N + b_2^N z_4^N \tag{30}$$

and

$$E_{t-1}^i \theta_{I\,t-1} = b_3^N z_3^N + b_4^N z_4^N, \tag{31}$$

where the $b^N$s depend on the variances of the shocks and the neighborhood size, $n$ (see the appendix). The neighborhood size matters because $\bar{\eta}$ is the average of $\eta$ over $(n/2) + 1$ observations, so $\text{Var}(\bar{\eta}) = (\sigma_\eta^2/(n/2 + 1))$. An increase in $n$ reduces the variance of $\bar{\eta}$, making $z_4^N$ a better estimate of $\theta_{I\,t-2}$.

Firm $i$'s estimate of $m_{t-1}$ follows from $E_{t-1}^i \delta_{t-1}$:

$$E_{t-1}^i m_{t-1} = m_{t-2} + b_1^N z_3^N + b_2^N z_4^N. \tag{32}$$

As in the simple model, information is better under staggering than under synchronization: the errors in estimating $m_{t-1}$ and $\theta_{I\,t-1}$ have smaller variances.

## 3  The Aggregate Price Level

The next step is to solve for the behavior of the aggregate price level under synchronization and staggering. Since neighborhood shocks average to zero across the economy, the results for the simple model and the neighborhood model are similar. We describe only the general case.

### A  The synchronized regime

Let $x_t^S$ be the average across firms of $x_{i\,t}^S$. When all prices are set at $t$ (even), $x_t^S$ is the aggregate price level at $t$ and $t + 1$. Only monetary shocks affect $x_t^S$, because all other shocks average to zero. We solve for $x_t^S$ by the method of undetermined coefficients. Guess the general solution

$$p_t^S = x_t^S = m_{t-3} + \pi_1 \delta_{t-1} + \pi_2 \delta_{t-2} \qquad (t \text{ even}). \tag{33}$$

To solve for the $\pi$s, substitute (33) into the price-setting rule (20). This yields $x_{i\,t}^S$ in terms of expectations of monetary and neighborhood shocks. Evaluate the expectations using (23)–(25). Aggregating the result yields $p_t^S$ in terms of monetary shocks alone. Finally, set the coefficients on the shocks equal to the $\pi$s in (33) and solve for

$$\pi_1 = \frac{v(a_1^N + a_3^N) + \dfrac{v}{2}a_5^N + (1 - v)a_3^N \pi_2}{1 - (1 - v)a_1^N}$$

and

$$\pi_2 = \frac{v(a_2^N + a_4^N) + \dfrac{v}{2}a_6^N + [(1 - v)a_2^N + 1]\pi_1}{1 - (1 - v)a_4^N}$$

(See the appendix for details of these calculations.)

## B  The uniformly staggered regime

In the staggered regime, half the prices in effect at $t$ are set at $t$ and half are set at $t - 1$. Thus the aggregate price level is

$$p_t^U = \tfrac{1}{2}(x_t^U + x_{t-1}^U), \tag{34}$$

where $x_t^U$ is the average of prices set at $t$. To solve for $x_t^U$, guess the general solution

$$x_t^U = \lambda_0 x_{t-1}^U + \lambda_1 m_{t-1} + (1 - \lambda_0 - \lambda_1)m_{t-2}. \tag{35}$$

To find the coefficients, substitute (34) and (35) into the price-setting rule (27) and calculate expectations using (30) and (31). Aggregating and setting the coefficients in the resulting expression equal to the $\lambda$s yields

$$\lambda_0 = \frac{1 - \sqrt{v}}{1 + \sqrt{v}} \quad \text{and} \quad \lambda_1 = \frac{[4v + 2v(b_3^N/b_1^N) + (1 - v)(1 - \lambda_0)]b_1^N}{4 - b_1^N(1 - v)(2 + \lambda_0)},$$

$\lambda_0, \lambda_1 > 0$; $\lambda_0 + \lambda_1 \leq 1$.[14]
(Again, see the appendix.) Combining (34) and (35) yields the solution for the aggregate price level:

$$p_t^U = \lambda_0 p_{t-1}^U + \tfrac{1}{2}[\lambda_1 m_{t-1} + (1 - \lambda_0)m_{t-2} + (1 - \lambda_0 - \lambda_1)m_{t-3}]. \tag{36}$$

Equation (36) shows that staggering leads to price-level inertia, that is, to slow adjustment of the price level to shocks. The degree of inertia depends on $\lambda_0$. Perhaps suprisingly, it is independent of the variances of local and aggregate shocks. Inertia is greatest ($\lambda_0$ is largest) when $v$ is small. In turn, $v$ is small when $\epsilon$ is large (product demand is highly elastic) and when $\gamma$ is small (the marginal disutility of labor increases slowly).

## 4  The Optimal Timing of Price Changes

## A  The approach

This section computes a firm's loss under synchronization, $\mathscr{L}^S$, and its loss under staggering, $\mathscr{L}^U$, to determine which regime is socially optimal. Synchronization is optimal if $\mathscr{L}^S < \mathscr{L}^U$.[15] To compute each loss, we combine the price-setting rule, (20) for synchronization and (27) for staggering, with the solutions for the price level, (33) and (36), and the formula for a firm's desired price, (6). This yields expressions for $(x_{it} - p_{it}^*)$ and $(x_{it} - p_{it+1}^*)$, the deviations of a firm's price from the desired level at $t$ and $t + 1$. Squaring these results and taking expectations yields the values of the loss function, (7), in each regime. The appendix presents details of these calculations and the final expressions for $\mathscr{L}^S$ and $\mathscr{L}^U$.

## B   Results: The simple model

We first present results for the model without neighborhood shocks. In this case the relative sizes of $\mathscr{L}^S$ and $\mathscr{L}^U$ depend on two parameters: $\rho = \sigma_u/\sigma_m$ (the ratio of the standard deviations of local and aggregate shocks) and $v$. Numerical calculations determine the locus of $(v, \rho)$ pairs for which $\mathscr{L}^S = \mathscr{L}^U$. This is plotted as the top line in figure 1. Below the line, $\mathscr{L}^S < \mathscr{L}^U$, so synchronization is optimal. Above the line, staggering is optimal.

To understand this result, recall that staggering has both benefits and costs. The benefit is improved information. There are two costs: price-level inertia, which exacerbates fluctuations in real aggregate demand, and the unintended movements in relative prices that occur when some prices adjust while others are fixed. Since there are both advantages and disadvantages, it is not surprising that staggering is optimal for some parameter values but not for others.

Figure 1 shows that synchronization is optimal when either $v$ or $\rho$ is small. As noted above, $v$ is small when product demand is highly elastic ($\epsilon$ is large). Elastic product demand implies that the fluctuations in relative

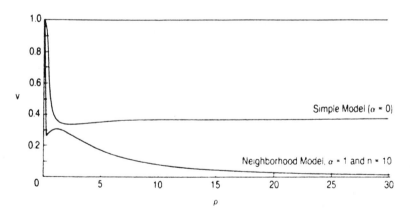

**Figure 1**
The optimal timing of price changes

prices caused by staggering are very costly. In addition, firms reduce these costly fluctuations by setting prices close to those set in the previous period: thus staggering leads to a high degree of inertia and large fluctuations in aggregate demand. These large costs imply that staggering is undesirable despite the information gains.

Turning to the role of $\rho$, note that if $\rho = 0$, so there are no local shocks, then synchronization is optimal. This case is essentially the Blanchard model. Information is perfect, and so there is no information gain from staggering. On the other hand, as long as $\rho$ is greater than one, its value is unimportant in the simple model.[16]

## C  Results: The neighborhood model

The results for the general model are complicated by the addition of two parameters: $n$ (the size of a neighborhood) and $\alpha = \sigma_\theta/\sigma_\eta$ (the relative importance of neighborhood and firm-specific shocks). (When $\alpha = 0$, the model reduces to the simple model.) For comparability with our earlier results, we fix $n$ and $\alpha$ and graph the results in terms of $v$ and $\rho$.[17] For $n = 10$ and $\alpha = 1$, the bottom line in figure 1 shows the $(v, \rho)$ locus for which $\mathscr{L}^S = \mathscr{L}^U$; staggering is optimal above the line. The results for other values of $n$ and $\alpha$ are similar, and so we omit them.

Figure 1 shows that the welfare results for the neighborhood model are broadly similar to those for the simple model. One difference is that in the neighborhood model the value of $\rho$ is important even for $\rho > 1$. In particular, as $\rho$ approaches infinity, the $\mathscr{L}^S = \mathscr{L}^U$ locus approaches the horizontal axis, so staggering is optimal for all values of $v$. As $\rho$ becomes large, monetary shocks disappear. In this case, the aggregate price level is stable, since it is unaffected by local shocks. Both of the costs of staggering—slow adjustment of the price level to monetary shocks and changes in relative prices caused by changes in the price level when some prices are fixed—are eliminated. But staggering still has benefits: even without monetary shocks, firms want to distinguish neighborhood and firm-specific shocks, and thus value the information in prices set recently by neighbors.[18]

## 5  The Equilibrium Timing of Price Changes

While it is interesting to compare welfare under synchronization and staggering, it is also important to ask when each will arise in a decentralized economy. Therefore, we now assume that each firm chooses whether to change its price in even or odd periods. This allows us to determine when synchronization and staggering are stable Nash equilibria.

## A  Synchronization

First consider synchronization. We study only the general model because the model without neighborhoods is similar. We assume that all firms set prices in even periods and ask whether a single "rebel" can gain by moving to odd periods. If not, then synchronization is a Nash equilibrium.

The rebel sets its price at $t$ and $t + 2$ (odd), while all other firms set prices at $t - 1$ and $t + 1$ (even). Since the economy is large, the rebel's behavior does not affect the aggregate price level. Only the rebel changes price at $t$, so $p_t^S = p_{t-1}^S$. Using (33),

$$p_t^S = p_{t-1}^S = m_{t-4} + \pi_1 \delta_{t-2} + \pi_2 \delta_{t-3} \qquad (t \text{ odd}). \tag{37}$$

All firms but the rebel change prices at $t + 1$, so

$$p_{t+1}^S = m_{t-2} + \pi_1 \delta_t + \pi_2 \delta_{t-1} \qquad (t \text{ odd}). \tag{38}$$

Since $p_t \neq p_{t+1}$, the rebel uses the same price-setting rule as a firm in the staggered regime, (27). The rebel's information is similar, but not identical, to that of a staggered firm. Equation (37) implies that the rebel can infer $m_{t-2}$ from prices set at $t - 1$: $p_{t-1}^S$ depends only on $m_{t-2}$ and earlier money stocks, which have been announced. Since $m_{t-2}$ is known, the rebel, like a firm under staggering, needs only estimate $\delta_{t-1}$ and $\theta_{I\,t-1}$. And the rebel has the same pieces of information, $z_3^N = \delta_{t-1} + \theta_{I\,t-1} - \theta_{I\,t-2} + \eta_{i\,t-1}$ and $z_4^N = \theta_{I\,t-2} + \bar{\eta}_{i\,t-2}$. But the results from projecting $\delta_{t-1}$ and $\theta_{I\,t-1}$ on $z_3^N$ and $z_4^N$ are different from those in the staggered regime (see the appendix). The reason is that $\bar{\eta}_{i\,t-2}$ has a smaller variance. Under staggering, $\bar{\eta}_{i\,t-2}$ is the average of the $\eta$s over firm $i$ and the $(n/2)$ neighbors who set prices at $t - 1$; thus the variance of $\bar{\eta}_{i\,t-2}$ is $\sigma_\eta^2/(n/2 + 1)$. In contrast, since the rebel is the only firm that sets its price at $t$, it observes prices set by *all* its neighbors at $t - 1$. Thus $\bar{\eta}_{i\,t-2}$ is constructed from $n$ observations and its variance is $\sigma_\eta^2/n$.

Calculations similar to the derivations of $\mathscr{L}^S$ and $\mathscr{L}^U$ lead to the rebel's loss, $\mathscr{L}^R$ (these calculations use the price-setting rule, (27); the equations for the price level, (37) and (38); and the appropriate projection formulas; again see the appendix). Synchronization is an equilibrium if $\mathscr{L}^R > \mathscr{L}^S$, that is, if the rebel loses by breaking from synchronization.[19] For the simple

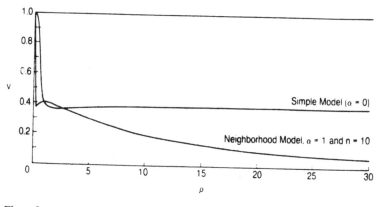

**Figure 2**
Equilibrium timing: synchronization

model ($\alpha = 0$) and for $n = 10$, $\alpha = 1$, figure 2 shows the $(v, \rho)$ combinations for which $\mathscr{L}^R = \mathscr{L}^S$. Below each line, synchronization is an equilibrium; above the line, it is not.

The explanation for these results is that there are both costs and benefits to rebelling. The rebel gains information by observing prices set recently by all other firms. On the other hand, breaking from synchronization leads to large fluctuations in the rebel's relative price. If either $v$ or $\rho$ is small—so either relative price fluctuations have large costs or the information gains from staggering are small—no one breaks from synchronization. (Below, we compare the condition for synchronization to be an equilibrium to the condition for it to socially optimal.)

## B Uniform staggering

We now consider uniform staggering. The results for the simple model are very different from those for the neighborhood model.

**The simple model** In the simple model, uniform staggering is clearly a Nash equilibrium for all parameter values. With no neighborhoods, the even- and odd-period cohorts of price setters are identical halves of the economy, and so the losses of firms in the two cohorts are the same. Further, since the economy is large, these losses do not change if a single firm switches cohorts. Thus no firm has an incentive to switch.

In the simple model, however, the staggered equilibrium is *never* stable. Stability of staggering is defined as follows: after a small perturbation in the cohort sizes away from half and half, firms in the larger group can gain by moving to the smaller one, restoring the equal size. To see whether this condition is met, we solve for the behavior of the economy when the cohorts have arbitrary sizes. (These calculations are similar in spirit to those for the special case of equal sizes; see the appendix.)[20] We compute a firm's loss as a function of the proportion of firms in its cohort, $k$, and find that the derivative of this function evaluated at $k = \frac{1}{2}$ is always negative. Thus, following a perturbation away from uniform staggering, firms in the larger cohort are better off than firms in the smaller one. All firms want to join the larger group, and so uniform staggering is unstable.

This result arises because each firm wants to minimize fluctuations in its relative price, and therefore wants to synchronize its price setting with as many firms as possible. Crucially, this incentive to join the larger cohort is *not* offset by information loss. To understand this, recall the information gain from uniform staggering in the simple model: a firm observes prices set at $t - 1$ by half of all firms, each price reveals the sum of $m_{t-2}$ and a local shock, and so the average of the prices reveals $m_{t-2}$. After a perturbation away from uniform staggering, firms in the large cohort observe prices set at $t - 1$ by 50 minus percent of all firms (the small cohort), while firms in the small cohort observe prices set by 50 plus percent. But since the economy is large, prices set by 50 plus percent and 50 minus percent of firms reveal the same information: in both cases the local shocks affecting prices average to zero, and $m_{t-2}$ is revealed.

**The neighborhood model**   In the simple model, uniform staggering is unstable because each firm wants to join the larger of two price-setting cohorts. The importance of our assumptions about neighborhoods is that they give firms an incentive to join the smaller cohort. As a brief digression, note that there are other plausible modifications of the simple model that would do the same. For example, we could assume that gathering price data is costly. Suppose that the cost of observing enough prices set at $t - 1$ to obtain a good estimate of $m_{t-2}$ grows as the $t - 1$ cohort shrinks. (A firm might need to travel farther to survey a given number of $t - 1$ price setters.) In this case, each firm has an incentive to set its price *after* as many firms as possible, that is, to join the smaller cohort.[21]

Returning to our neighborhood model, we now determine when uniform staggering is a stable equilibrium. As in the simple model, it is always an equilibrium, and so we focus on stability.[22] Recall that uniform staggering is defined as an equal split of each neighborhood into even- and odd-period price setters. We define stability as follows. Suppose that one firm in each neighborhood is moved from the odd to the even cohort, so that $((n/2) + 1)$ firms in each neighborhood set prices in even periods and $((n/2) - 1)$ set prices in odd periods. Staggering is stable if firms in the larger cohort have greater losses than firms in the smaller cohort.[23]

The appendix computes the losses of firms in the even (larger) and odd (smaller) cohorts, $\mathscr{L}^E$ and $\mathscr{L}^O$. For $\alpha = 1$ and $n = 10$, figure 3 shows the $(v, \rho)$ combinations for which $\mathscr{L}^E = \mathscr{L}^O$. Staggering is stable above the line.

Staggering can be stable because firms in the smaller cohort have better information. A firm setting its price at $t$ observes prices set at $t - 1$. As described above, these reveal $\theta_{I\,t-2} + \bar{\eta}_{i\,t-2}$, where again $\bar{\eta}_i$ is the average of $\eta$ over firm $i$ and all neighbors setting prices at $t - 1$. A firm in the smaller cohort observes more prices set at $t - 1$, and therefore $\bar{\eta}_{i\,t-2}$ has a smaller variance. $\theta_{I\,t-2} + \bar{\eta}_{i\,t-2}$ is a better estimate of $\theta_{I\,t-2}$, and so it is more useful in disentangling local and aggregate shocks. For some parameter values this information advantage outweighs the disadvantage of changing prices at the same time as less than half the firms.

It is crucial that the neighborhoods are small. A firm that observes six neighboring prices set at $t - 1$ obtains a better estimate of $\theta_{I\,t-2}$ than a firm that observes four. In contrast, if the neighborhoods were large, a firm observing prices set by 50 plus percent of its neighborhood would learn no more than a firm observing 50 minus percent. The $\eta_{j\,t-2}$'s would average to zero for both cohorts, and so all firms would observe $\theta_{I\,t-2}$ exactly.

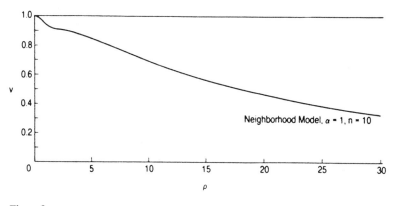

Figure 3
Equilibrium timing: staggering

## C  Comparison of equilibrium and optimum

The conditions under which synchronization and staggering are stable
equilibria differ from the conditions under which they are socially optimal.
This is shown by figure 4, which summarizes the results in figures 1–3
for the neighborhood model. In the region between the two lower lines in
figure 4, synchronization is an equilibrium even though staggering is optimal. In addition, betwee the top and bottom lines, staggering is optimal
but not a stable equilibrium. According to these results, the incentives for
an individual firm to break from synchronization or to join the smaller of
two cohorts are weaker than the incentives for a social planner to choose
staggering. Furthermore, for parameter values between the two upper lines,
there is no stable equilibrium.

The relative positions of the three lines in figure 4 do not appear robust.
To take an example discussed above, suppose that gathering price data is
costly. Let $c(k)$ be the cost of inferring $m_{t-2}$ from prices set at $t-1$, where
$k$ is the proportion of the economy in a firm's cohort. Assume that $c'(k) > 0$:
the cost of gathering price data rises as a firm's cohort grows and the $t-1$
cohort shrinks. To see the implications for the positions of the lines, recall
that the bottom line is determined by comparing $\mathscr{L}^S$ to $\mathscr{L}^U$, and the middle
line by comparing $\mathscr{L}^S$ to $\mathscr{L}^R$. This means that the relation between the two
lower lines depends on $\mathscr{L}^U$ and $\mathscr{L}^R$. The cost of gathering prices under
uniform staggering is $c(1/2)$, while the cost to the rebel is $c(0)$, because no
other firm belongs to the rebel's cohort. Since $c(1/2)$ is greater than $c(0)$,

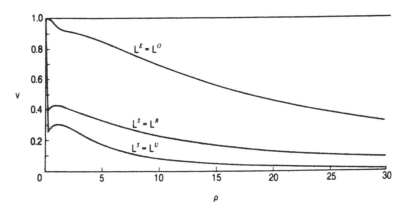

**Figure 4**
Equilibrium versus optimum

introducing the cost raises $\mathscr{L}^U$ more than it raises $\mathscr{L}^R$. One can show that this raises the bottom line relative to the middle line and that the two may switch positions. By a similar argument, the top line may move below the others. (The position of the top line depends on $c'(1/2)$, which affects the benefit from belonging to the small cohort after a perturbation away from uniform staggering.)[24]

## 6  Conclusion

Imperfect information can lead to staggered price setting. While fluctuations in relative prices are minimized when firms make decisions at the same times, a firm gains valuable information about demand if it waits to see other prices. This information gain can lead firms to break from synchronization and can make staggering a stable equilibrium. Thus staggered price adjustment, a crucial foundation of new Keynesian macroeconomic models, can arise from rational economic behavior.

Imperfect information can also make staggering socially optimal. Staggering leads to price-level inertia, which exacerbates aggregate fluctuations. However, by helping firms set prices closer to full-information levels, staggering creates efficiency gains that may outweigh the costs. Policy proposals to reduce staggering—for example, by requiring labor unions to sign contracts at the same times—could reduce welfare despite lessening inertia.

The model predicts that staggering is least likely when firms are nearly perfectly competitive and when idiosyncratic shocks are small. If the model is applied to an industry rather than the entire economy, these predictions are borne out by casual observation. In the automobile industry, products are fairly close substitutes and shocks are likely to affect all firms equally. The result is the synchronized pricing that we see. On the other hand, the drugstore on the corner and the diner next door produce goods that are poor substitutes, and they are likely to face different shocks. Thus it is not surprising that they change prices at different times.

This paper has studied a very specific model. Some results, notably the relation between the equilibrium and optimal regimes, are not likely to be robust. We doubt, however, that reasonable changes in the model would reverse the conclusion that staggering can be both optimal and a stable equilibrium if firms possess strong market power or idiosyncratic shocks are large.

A natural extension of our analysis is to alter the assumption that prices are fixed for two periods. If prices are fixed for longer, one can show that the incentive for a rebel to break from synchronization is greater. Thus the region of parameter values for which synchronization is an equilibrium is smaller. Intuitively, if prices are set for many periods, then a rebel setting its price one period after other firms is only slightly out of step. The cost in relative price fluctuations is small, while the rebel still gains the information in others' prices. Unfortunately, it is very difficult to determine how changing the frequency of price adjustment affects the socially optimal regime and the stability of uniform staggering.

Our intuition about the costs and benefits of staggering carries over to continuous time, but the model must be modified. In this paper, firms have perfect information about prices set in the most recent period. In a continuous time model, it would be unrealistic to assume that firms observe and respond to others' prices the instant they are set.[25] Instead, one might assume that firms learn about prices slowly, gaining full information after a discrete amount of time (for example, the time it takes to visit all neighboring stores). This modification of the model would complicate the analysis considerably.

## Appendix

This appendix outlines the calculations omitted from the text. A more detailed version of the appendix is available from the authors. Throughout we consider the general model with neighborhood shocks. To obtain results for the simple model, set $\sigma_\theta^2 = 0$.

### Projection coefficients

Here we present the formulas for the projection coefficients in equations (23)–(25) and (30)–(31):

$$a_1^N = \frac{1 + \rho_1^2 + \rho_2^2}{D_1}, \tag{A1}$$

$$a_2^N = \frac{-1 - \rho_1^2}{D_1}, \tag{A2}$$

$$a_3^N = \frac{\rho_2^2}{D_1}, \tag{A3}$$

$$a_4^N = \frac{1 + \rho_1^2 + \rho_2^2}{D_1}, \tag{A4}$$

$$a_5^N = \rho_1^2 a_1^N, \tag{A5}$$

$$a_6^N = \rho_1^2 a_2^N, \tag{A6}$$

$$b_1^N = \frac{\rho_1^2 + (2\rho_2^2)/(n + 2)}{D_2}, \tag{A7}$$

$$b_2^N = \frac{-\rho_1^2}{D_2}, \tag{A8}$$

$$b_3^N = \rho_1^2 b_1^N, \tag{A9}$$

$$b_4^N = \rho_1^2 b_2^N, \tag{A10}$$

where

$$\rho_1 = \sigma_\theta/\sigma_m, \quad \rho_2 = \sigma_\eta/\sigma_m,$$

$$D_1 = [2(1 + \rho_1^2) + \rho_2^2](1 + \rho_1^2 + \rho_2^2) - (1 + \rho_2^2)^2,$$

$$D_2 = (1 + 2\rho_1^2 + \rho_2^2)(\rho_1^2 + 2\rho_2^2/(n + 2)) - \rho_1^4.$$

**The aggregate price level**

Here we find the coefficients in the solutions for the price level under staggering and synchronization, (33) and (36). For synchronization, substitute (33) into (20) to obtain

$$x_{it}^S = m_{t-3} + [v + (1 - v)\pi_1]E_{t-1}^i \delta_{t-1}$$

$$+ [v + (1 - v)\pi_2]E_{t-1}^i \delta_{t-2} + \frac{v}{2} E_{t-1}^i \theta_{I\,t-1}. \tag{A11}$$

Using (23)–(25), this becomes

$$x_{it}^S = m_{t-3} + \left\{ [v + (1 - v)\pi_1]a_1^N + [v + (1 - v)\pi_2]a_3^N + \frac{v}{2} a_5^N \right\} z_1^N$$

$$+ \left\{ [v + (1 - v)\pi_1]a_2^N + [v + (1 - v)\pi_2]a_4^N + \frac{v}{2} a_6^N \right\} z_2^N. \tag{A12}$$

Aggregating (which eliminates the local components of $z_1^N$ and $z_2^N$) and matching coefficients with (33) yields the solutions for $\pi_1$ and $\pi_2$ in the text.

For staggering, substitute (34) and (35) into (27):

$$x_{it}^U = \frac{(1-v)(1-\lambda_0)^2}{4} x_{t-1}^U + \left[ v + \frac{(1-v)(1-\lambda_0+2\lambda_1+\lambda_0\lambda_1)}{4} \right] E_{t-1}^i m_{t-1}$$

$$+ \frac{(1-v)(2+\lambda_0)(1-\lambda_0-\lambda_1)}{4} m_{t-2} + \frac{v}{2} E_{t-1}^i \theta_{I\,t-1}. \tag{A13}$$

Using (30)–(31), this leads to

$$x_{it}^U = \frac{(1-v)(1-\lambda_0)^2}{4} x_{t-1}^U + \left[ v + \frac{(1-v)(\lambda_0+3)(1-\lambda_0)}{4} \right] m_{t-2}$$

$$+ \left\{ \left[ v + \frac{(1-v)(1-\lambda_0+2\lambda_1+\lambda_0\lambda_1)}{4} \right] b_1^N + \frac{v}{2} b_3^N \right\} z_3^N$$

$$+ \left\{ \left[ v + \frac{(1-v)(1-\lambda_0+2\lambda_1+\lambda_0\lambda_1)}{4} \right] b_2^N + \frac{v}{2} b_4^N \right\} z_4^N. \tag{A14}$$

Aggregating and matching coefficients with (35) yields the solutions for $\lambda_0$ and $\lambda_1$ in the text.

## Computation of $\mathcal{L}^S$ and $\mathcal{L}^U$

This section computes a firm's loss under synchronization, $\mathcal{L}^S$, and its loss under staggering, $\mathcal{L}^U$, to determine the optimal regime. To compute $\mathcal{L}^S$, recall that the coefficients on $\delta_{t-1}$ and $\delta_{t-2}$ in (A12) must equal $\pi_1$ and $\pi_2$. Thus (A12) can be written as

$$x_{it}^S = m_{t-3} + \pi_1 z_1^N + (\pi_2 - \pi_1) z_2^N$$

$$= p_t^S + \pi_1(\theta_{I\,t-1} + \theta_{I\,t-2} + \eta_{i\,t-1}) + (\pi_2 - \pi_1)(\theta_{I\,t-2} + \eta_{i\,t-2}). \tag{A15}$$

Combining (A15) with (33) and (6) yields $(x_{it}^S - p_{it}^*)$ and $(x_{it}^S - p_{it+1}^*)$ as functions of $\delta$, $\theta$, and $\eta$. Squaring these expressions and taking expectations yields

$$\mathcal{L}^S = v^2[2(1-\pi_1)^2 + 2(1-\pi_2)^2 + 3]\sigma_m^2$$

$$+ [3v^2 + (\pi_1 - v)^2 + \pi_1^2 + 2\pi_2^2]\sigma_\theta^2$$

$$+ 2[v^2 + (\pi_2 - \pi_1)^2 + \pi_1^2]\sigma_\eta^2. \tag{A16}$$

To compute $\mathcal{L}^U$, recall that the coefficients in (A14) must be consistent with the coefficients in (35). This leads to

$$x_{it}^U = x_t^U + \lambda_1(\theta_{I\,t-1} + \theta_{I\,t-2} + \eta_{i\,t-1}) + (b_2^N/b_1^N)\lambda_1(\theta_{I\,t-2} + \bar{\eta}_{i\,t-2}). \quad \text{(A17)}$$

Using (35), $x_t^U$ can be written as

$$x_t^U = \frac{(1 - \lambda_0)m_{t-1} - (1 - \lambda_0 - \lambda_1)\delta_{t-1}}{(1 - \lambda_0 B)}, \quad \text{(A18)}$$

where $B$ is the lag operator. Substituting (A18) into (A17) and combining the result with (6) and (36) leads, after considerable algebra, to $(x_{it}^U - p_{it}^*)$ and $(x_{it}^U - p_{it+1}^*)$ as functions of the shocks. Squaring and taking expectations yields

$$\mathcal{L}^U = \left[2v^2 + \beta_0 + \beta_2 + \frac{(\beta_0\lambda_0 + \beta_1)^2 + (\beta_2\lambda_0 + \beta_3)^2}{1 - \lambda_0^2}\right]\sigma_m^2$$

$$+ [3v^2 + \lambda_1^2 + (\lambda_1 - v)^2 + 2\lambda_1^2(1 + (b_2^N/b_1^N))^2]\sigma_\theta^2$$

$$+ 2\left[v^2 + \lambda_1^2 + \left(\frac{2}{n+2}\right)((b_2^N/b_1^N)\lambda_1)^2\right]\sigma_\eta^2, \quad \text{(A19)}$$

where

$$\beta_0 = \frac{\lambda_1(v+1) - 2v}{2}, \qquad \beta_1 = \frac{(1-v)(1 - \lambda_0 - \lambda_1)}{2},$$

$$\beta_2 = \frac{\lambda_1(v-1) - 2v}{2}, \qquad \beta_3 = \frac{(1+v)(\lambda_1 + \lambda_0 - 1)}{2}.$$

### The rebel

This section computes the rebel's price, $x_{it}^R$, and its projection formulas and uses these to find the rebel's loss, $\mathcal{L}^R$. Combining equations (8), (27), (37), and (38) leads to

$$x_{it}^R = m_{t-2} + \frac{1-v}{2}[(\pi_1 - 1)\delta_{t-2} + (\pi_2 - 1)\delta_{t-3}]$$

$$+ \left[v + \frac{1-v}{2}\pi_2\right]E_{t-1}^i\delta_{t-1} + \frac{v}{2}E_{t-1}^i\theta_{I\,t-1}. \quad \text{(A20)}$$

As explained in the text, the rebel knows, $m_{t-2}$ and, like a firm in the staggered regime, uses $z_3^N$ and $z_4^N$ to estimate $\delta_{t-1}$ and $\theta_{I\,t-1}$. But the variance of $\bar{\eta}_{i\,t-2}$ is now $\sigma_\eta^2/n$. The rebel's projection equations are

$$E_{t-1}^i \delta_{t-1} = c_1^N z_3^N + c_2^N z_4^N \tag{A21}$$

and

$$E_{t-1}^i \theta_{I\,t-1} = c_3^N z_3^N + c_4^N z_4^N \tag{A22}$$

where the $c^N$s are formed from the $b^N$s defined above by replacing $(n/2) + 1$ with $n$.

Substituting (A21) and (A22) into (A20) and combining the result with (6), (37), and (38) leads to $(x_{it}^R - p_{it}^*)$ and $(x_{it}^R - p_{it-1}^*)$. Squaring and taking expectations yields the rebel's loss:

$$\mathscr{L}^R = [2v^2 + 2\alpha_1^2 + 2\alpha_2^2 + \alpha_3^2 + (\alpha_0 - v)^2 + (\alpha_0 - \alpha_4)^2]\sigma_m^2$$

$$+ [3v^2 + (\alpha_0 - v)^2 + \alpha_0^2 + 2(\alpha_0 + \alpha_6)^2]\sigma_\theta^2 + 2\left[v^2 + \alpha_0^2 + \frac{\alpha_6^2}{n}\right]\sigma_\eta^2,$$

$$\tag{A23}$$

where

$$\alpha_0 = Ac_1^N, \qquad\qquad \alpha_1 = \frac{1-v}{2}(\pi_1 - 1),$$

$$\alpha_2 = \frac{1-v}{2}(\pi_2 - 1), \qquad \alpha_3 = v + (1-v)\pi_1,$$

$$\alpha_4 = v + (1-v)\pi_2, \qquad \alpha_5 = \alpha_0 - \alpha_4,$$

$$\alpha_6 = Ac_2^N, \qquad\qquad A = \left[v + \frac{1-v}{2}\pi_2 + \frac{\rho_1^2 v}{2}\right].$$

### Is uniform staggering stable?

This section studies the neighborhood model when an arbitrary proportion of each neighborhood, $k$, belongs to the even cohort. We use the results to determine when uniform staggering is a stable equilibrium.

Let $p_t^E$ be the price level at an even $t$, and let $p_{t+1}^O$ be the price level at $t + 1$ (odd). From the definition of the aggregate price level,

$$p_t^E = kx_t^E + (1 - k)x_{t-1}^O;$$

$$p_{t+1}^O = (1 - k)x_{t+1}^O + kx_t^E. \tag{A24}$$

Combining (A24) with (6) and (8) yields price-setting rules for firms in the even and odd cohorts:

$$x_{it}^E = v E_{t-1}^i m_{t-1} + \frac{v}{2} E_{t-1}^i \theta_{I\,t-1}$$

$$+ \frac{1-v}{2} [(1-k) E_{t-1}^i x_{t+1}^O + 2k E_{t-1}^i x_t^E + (1-k) x_{t-1}^O] \tag{A25}$$

and

$$x_{it+1}^O = v E_t^i m_t + \frac{v}{2} E_t^i \theta_{I\,t}$$

$$+ \frac{1-v}{2} [k E_t^i x_{t+2}^E + 2(1-k) E_t^i x_{t+1}^O + k x_t^E]. \tag{A26}$$

Firms in both the even and odd cohorts use $z_3^N$ and $z_4^N$ to estimate $\delta_{t-1}$ and $\theta_{I\,t-1}$. However, the projection equations for the two cohorts differ because $\bar{\eta}_{it-2}$ has different variances: $\text{Var}(\bar{\eta}_{it-2}) = \sigma_\eta^2/[(1-k)n+1]$ for the even cohort and $\text{Var}(\bar{\eta}_{it-2}) = \sigma_\eta^2/(kn+1)$ for the odd cohort. The estimates of firms in the even cohort are given by (30) and (31) with the $b^N$s replaced by $b^E$s, which are formed by replacing $(n/2)+1$ with $(1-k)n+1$ in (A7) to (A10). The estimates for the odd cohort are given by the estimates for the even cohort with $k$ replaced by $1-k$.

The price-setting rules (A21) and (A22) imply solutions for $x_t^E$ and $x_{t+1}^O$ of the form

$$x_t^E = \lambda_0^E x_{t-1}^O + \lambda_1^E m_{t-1} + (1 - \lambda_0^E - \lambda_1^E) m_{t-2} \tag{A27}$$

and

$$x_{t+1}^O = \lambda_0^O x_t^E + \lambda_1^O m_t + (1 - \lambda_0^O - \lambda_1^O) m_{t-1}. \tag{A28}$$

To solve for the $\lambda$s, first use the projection equations to find the expectation of (A27). Use this result and the projection equations again to find the expectation of (A28). Substitute the two results into (A25), aggregate, and set the coefficients on $x_{t-1}^O$ and $m_{t-1}$ equal to $\lambda_0^E$ and $\lambda_1^E$. Symmetry yields similar expressions for $\lambda_0^O$ and $\lambda_1^O$. Finally, combining these four expressions yields

$$\lambda_0^E = \frac{(v+k-vk)}{k(1-v)}$$

$$- \frac{\sqrt{(v+k-vk)^2 - [(v+k-vk)(1-k)k(1-v)^2]/(1-k+vk)}}{k(1-v)}$$

$$\tag{A29}$$

and

$$\lambda_1^E = \frac{b_1^E[v(2 + \rho_1) - (1 - v)(1 - k)(1 - \lambda_0^O)]}{2 - b_1^E(1 - v)(2k + (1 - k)\lambda_0^O)}. \tag{A30}$$

The solutions for $\lambda_0^O$ and $\lambda_1^O$ are obtained by replacing $k$ with $1 - k$ in (A29) and (A30).

By reasoning analogous to the derivation of (A17), we can write $x_{it}^E$ as

$$x_{it}^E = x_t^E + \lambda_1^E(\theta_{I\,t-1} + \theta_{I\,t-2} + \eta_{i\,t-1}) + (b_2^E/b_1^E)\lambda_1^E(\theta_{I\,t-2} + \bar{\eta}_{i\,t-2}). \tag{A31}$$

Combining this with (6) and (A24) leads to $(x_{it}^E - p_{it}^*)$ and $(x_{it}^E - p_{it+1}^*)$. Squaring and taking expectations yields the loss of a firm in the even cohort:

$$\mathscr{L}^E = \left\{2v^2 + \gamma_0^2 + \gamma_3^2 + \frac{\gamma_1^2 + \gamma_4^2 + (\gamma_0\lambda_0^E\lambda_0^O + \gamma_2)^2 + (\gamma_3\lambda_0^E\lambda_0^O + \gamma_5)^2}{1 - (\lambda_0^E\lambda_0^O)^2}\right\}\sigma_m^2$$

$$+ \left\{3v^2 + (\lambda_1^E - v)^2 + (\lambda_1^E)^2 + 2\left[\lambda_1^E\left(1 + \frac{b_2^E}{b_1^E}\right)\right]^2\right\}\sigma_\theta^2$$

$$+ 2\left\{v^2 + (\lambda_1^E)^2 + \left[\frac{1}{(1 - k)n + 1}\right]\left[\lambda_1^E\frac{b_2^E}{b_1^E}\right]^2\right\}\sigma_\eta^2, \tag{A32}$$

where

$$\gamma_0 = (1 - k + vk)\lambda_1^E - v,$$

$$\gamma_1 = (1 - \lambda_1^O)[(1 - k + vk)(1 - \lambda_0^E) - v],$$

$$\gamma_2 = (1 - v)(1 - k)\lambda_0^O(1 - \lambda_0^E - \lambda_1^E),$$

$$\gamma_3 = -[v + (1 - v)(1 - k)\lambda_1^O],$$

$$\gamma_4 = \gamma_0 - (1 - v)(1 - k)(1 - \lambda_0^O + \lambda_1^E\lambda_0^O),$$

$$\gamma_5 = \gamma_1 - (1 - v)(1 - k)(1 - \lambda_0^O - \lambda_1^E\lambda_0^O) + v\lambda_0^E\lambda_0^O.$$

To find the loss of a firm in the odd cohort, replace $(1 - k)$ with $k$, replace the $b^E$s with the corresponding coefficients for the odd cohort, and switch all $\lambda^E$s and $\lambda^O$s. As explained in the text, uniform staggering is stable if $\mathscr{L}^E > \mathscr{L}^O$ when $(n/2) + 1$ firms in each neighborhood belong to the even cohort (that is, when $k = 1/2 + (1/n)$).

## Acknowledgments

This is a revised version of National Bureau of Economic Research working paper no. 2201, April 1987. We are grateful for many helpful suggestions from Olivier Blanchard, Larry Jones, David Romer, Julio Rotemberg, Matthew Shapiro, Michael Whinston, the referees, and seminar participants at Columbia, North Carolina State, Ohio State, and the Federal Reserve Bank of Kansas City.

## Notes

1. The result that synchronization is the equilibrium timing is apparently a long-standing folk theorem. It is demonstrated formally for the Blanchard model in this paper and in Laurence Ball and David Romer (1987b).

2. Other explanations for staggering are presented by Gary Fethke and Andrew Policano (1984, 1986), Eric Maskin and Jean Tirole (1985), Michael Parkin (1986), and Ball and Romer (1987b). One prominent informal explanation is that firms change prices at different times simply because they face different shocks and different costs of price adjustment. If this were the entire explanation, however, a large enough nominal shock would cause all prices to adjust immediately. Only moderate shocks would have real effects.

3. The presence of shocks specific to sectors of the economy is also crucial in Fethke and Policano's (1984, 1986) models of staggering. In their work, however, the sectors must be large, and price setting is synchronized within sectors (for example, all manufacturing firms change prices in even periods and all service firms in odd periods). In our model, the economy contains many small sectors, and (as we show below) price setting can be staggered within sectors. We view our model as more realistic. Note also that the source of staggering in Fethke and Policano is very different from the source in this paper. In their models, staggered wage setting arises because adjustment of one sector's wage when other wages are fixed causes beneficial changes in relative wages. In our model, by contrast, the relative price movements caused by staggering are undesirable (again, we believe that this is realistic). Most important, in our model the benefit from staggering is that firms learn about the current values of demand shocks by observing one another's prices. This benefit is not present in Fethke and Policano, because there firms have complete information about current shocks.

4. Our model of producer-consumers is a simplification of Blanchard and Kiyotaki (1987), which contains both goods and labor markets. Ball and Romer (1987a, 1987b) study a similar economy of producer-consumers.

5. Our qualitative results are robust to natural modifications of (1)–(3). For example, we can introduce decreasing returns in production (this has the same effects as increasing the taste parameter $\gamma$): we can add real money balances to the utility function (as in Blanchard and Kiyotaki 1987) rather than simply assuming (3); or we can introduce risk aversion in consumption (as in Ball and Romer 1987a).

6. For details of the derivation of (4), see the analogous derivations in Blanchard and Fischer (1988) and in Blanchard and Kiyotaki (1987).

7. In the concluding section we discuss the implications of assuming that prices are fixed for more than two periods. Note that the cost of price adjustment need not be large for firms to fix prices for two or more periods, because a "period" can be short. As we emphasize throughout the paper, staggering causes nominal shocks to have large real effects even if individual prices change frequently.

8. Similar quadratic objective functions appear in Gray (1976), Parkin (1986), Ball (1987), and many other papers. Ball and Romer (1987b, appendix) study a model of staggered price setting without making this paper's approximation to utility.

9. This is a first-order approximation used by Blanchard and Fischer (1988) and many others. The taste shocks in (3) drop out of the first-order approximation because, as we specify below, the mean of the log taste shocks is zero. Again, see Ball and Romer (1987b, appendix) for the implications of foregoing the approximation.

10. Our qualitative results are robust to other specifications of the stochastic processes of the shocks. The only essential assumptions are that the aggregate, neighborhood, and firm-specific shocks follow different processes and that the first two are not white noise.

11. In the United States the money stock is announced with a very short lag. But if we interpret $m_t$ as nominal aggregate demand (money times velocity), it is realistic to assume a significant lag.

12. One can show that no other pattern of price setting is ever a stable equilibrium.

13. A firm's local shock is correlated with that of its neighbors because it contains a neighborhood component, $\theta$. But the shock still averages to zero over all $t - 1$ price setters because the economy contains a large number of neighborhoods.

14. There are two solutions for $x_t^U$. We choose the stable one, $0 < \lambda_0 < 1$. Note that $x_{t-1}^U$ depends on $x_{t-2}^U, m_{t-2}$, and $m_{t-3}$. Since a firm setting $x_{it}^U$ observes $x_{t-2}^U$ and $m_{t-3}$, this verifies our claim that the firm can infer $m_{t-2}$ from $x_{t-1}^U$.

15. Recall from section 1 that "firms" are producer-consumers and that minus the loss function is an approximation to an indirect utility function. Thus, finding the regime that minimizes the loss function is (approximately) the same as finding the one that maximizes utility of producer-consumers. Since the producer-consumers are the only agents in the model, it is natural to define the optimal regime as the one that maximizes their utility. (Although we refer to agents as firms, they are economy's workers and consumers as well as its sellers; it is not the case that there are other agents whose utility we neglect.)

16. According to figure 1, the effect of $\rho$ on the relative sizes of $\mathcal{L}^S$ and $\mathcal{L}^U$ is not monotonic. We have no explanation for this result.

17. Recall that $\rho = \sigma_u / \sigma_m$. From (11), $\sigma_u^2 = 2\sigma_\theta^2 + \sigma_\eta^2$.

18. As Lucas (1977) emphasizes, aggregate shocks are responsible for only a small part of the uncertainty facing firms in actual economies. Thus it seems realistic to assume that $\rho$ is large and hence that staggering is optimal for a wide range of $v$.

19. More precisely, synchronization is an equilibrium if $\mathcal{L}^R \geq \mathcal{L}^S$, but it is a stable equilibrium only if $\mathcal{L}^R > \mathcal{L}^S$.

20. We derive price-setting rules for each cohort, aggregate to determine the behavior of the price level, and then combine these results to find the losses of firms in each cohort. The appendix presents these calculations for the neighborhood model; the corresponding expressions for the simple model are obtained by setting a (which measures the importance of neighborhood shocks) to zero.

21. Alternatively, one could assume that a firm observes only a small subset of other firms' prices. In this case the firm obtains an imperfect estimate of $x_{t-1}$. When the prices observed by the firm include many set at $t - 1$, the estimate of $x_{t-1}$ is more precise and therefore provides more information about $m_{t-2}$. This is an incentive for the firm to join the smaller cohort.

22. The equilibrium question is more subtle than in the simple model. Uniform staggering is a Nash equilibrium if no firm has an incentive to move from one of its neighborhood's cohorts to the other, given that all other neighborhoods remain equally divided. One can show that a firm that switches loses information because it synchronizes its price setting with more of its

neighbors. There is no offsetting gain, because the firm still changes prices with 50 percent of the economy and therefore experiences the same fluctuations in its relative price. No firm wants to switch, and so staggering is an equilibrium.

23. There are other reasonable definitions of stability based on different perturbations. For example, we could move one firm in a single neighborhood from the odd to the even cohort while leaving the other neighborhoods unchanged and compare the losses of the two cohorts in the perturbed neighborhood. By this weak definition, the condition for stability is the same as the condition for staggering to be a Nash equilibrium, and it always holds (see n. 22). Alternatively, we could perturb a small but nonnegligible proportion of the neighborhoods while leaving the others unchanged. With this definition, we conjecture that staggering is stable for a wider range of parameter values than in the text.

24. We also suspect that changing assumptions about the timing of announcements or the stochastic processes followed by shocks could change the relative positions of the lines.

25. For example, if the length of labor contract negotiations is given, one union's wage can influence another's only if the first union signs its contract significantly earlier.

# References

Ball, Laurence, "Externalities from Contract Length," *American Economic Review*, September 1987, 77, 615–629.

Ball, Laurence, and Romer, David, "Are Prices Too Sticky?" NBER, working paper no. 2171, January 1987a.

Ball, Laurence, and Romer, David, "The Equilibrium and Optimal Timing of Price Changes," NBER working paper no. 2412, October 1987b.

Blanchard, Olivier J., "Price Asynchronization and Price Level Inertia," in R. Dornbusch and M. Simonsen, eds., *Inflation, Debt and Indexation*, Cambridge: MIT Press, 1983, 3–24.

Blanchard, Olivier J., "The Wage-Price Spiral," *Quarterly Journal of Economics*, August 1986, 101, 543–65.

Blanchard, Olivier J., and Kiyotaki, Nobuhiro, "Monopolistic Competition and the Effects of Aggregate Demand," *American Economic Review*, September 1987, 77, 647–666.

Blanchard, Olivier J., and Fischer, Stanley, *Macroeconomics*, mimeo., Cambridge: MIT, 1988, chap. 9.

Fethke, Gary, and Policano, Andrew, "Wage Contingencies, the Pattern of Negotiaton, and Aggregate Implications of Alternative Contract Structures," *Journal of Monetary Econmics*, September 1984, 14, 151–170.

Fethke, Gary, and Policano, Andrew, "Will Wage Setters Ever Stagger Decisions?" *Quarterly Journal of Economics*, November 1986, 101, 867–877.

Gray, Jo Anna, "Wage Indexation: A Macroeconomic Approach," *Journal of Monetary Economics*, April 1976, 3, 221–235.

Hall, Robert E., and Taylor, John B., *Macroeconomics*, 2nd ed., New York: W. W. Norton, 1988.

Lucas, Robert E., Jr., "Some International Evidence on Output-Inflation Tradeoffs," *American Economic Review*, June 1973, 63, 326–334.

Lucas, Robert E., Jr., "Understanding Business Cycles," in K. Brunner and A. Meltzer, eds., *Stabilization of the Domestic and International Economy*, Carnegie-Rochester Conference on Public Policy, 1977, 5, 7–29.

Maskin, Eric S. and Tirole, Jean, "Models of Dynamic Oligopoly. II: Competition through Prices," MIT Department of Economics working paper no. 373, 1985.

Okun, Arthur M., *Prices and Quantities*, Washington, D.C.: Brookings Institution, 1981.

Parkin, Michael, "The Output-Inflation Trade-Off When Prices Are Costly to Change," *Journal of Political Economy*, February 1986, 84, 200–224.

Taylor, John B., "Aggregate Dynamics and Staggered Contracts," *Journal of Political Economy*, February 1980, 88, 1–23.

# III IMPERFECT COMPETITION

# 12 A Model of Imperfect Competition with Keynesian Features

Oliver Hart

## 1 Introduction

In the last few years, a considerable amount of work has been done under the general heading of "the reappraisal of Keynesian economics." This work has taken as its starting point Clower's observation (1965) that, away from a Walrasian equilibrium, effective demands and supplies rather than their notional counterparts will govern the behavior of the economic system. This has led a number of economists to study non-Walrasian equilibria," in which prices are fixed and effective demands and supplies are equilibrated through the adjustment of quantities and rationing (for a survey of this work, see Grandmont 1977).

While this reappraisal has undoubtedly led to more rigorously formulated Keynesian models than existed previously, the fixed-price approach would seem to have a major shortcoming. In particular, it lacks a theory of how prices are determined. More specifically, the fixed price approach does not explain why, if prices are at non-Walrasian levels, it does not pay a rationed seller (respectively, buyer) to reduce (respectively, increase) his price by a small amount in order to increase sales (respectively, purchases). In other words, the fixed price approach does not explain how a non-Walrasian equilibrium can be sustained once one allows agents to change prices.

One way around this difficulty is to drop the commonly made assumption that agents are perfect competitors, i.e., that they face perfectly elastic demand or supply curves.[1] This is the approach adopted here. We shall show that the equilibrium of an economy in which prices are fully flexible but where agents are imperfectly competitive exhibits a number of non-Walrasian or Keynesian features. In such an economy an agent who would like, say, to sell more at the going price than he is able to may not find it in his interest to reduce price because the consequent increase in demand may not offset the loss in his revenue.

The imperfect competition that we analyze in this paper will be of a particular variety. Specifically, we shall assume that each agent is negligible relative to the aggregate economy, but we shall permit some agents to be of

*Quarterly Journal of Economics* 97 (February 1982): 109–138. Copyright © 1982 by the President and Fellows of Harvard College. Reprinted by permission of John Wiley & Sons.

significant size relative to the particular markets in which they operate. Thus, the imperfect competition that we shall deal with is close to monopolistic competition in the sense of Chamberlin (1933), although product differentiation will not be emphasized in our analysis. In the model that we study, workers (through the formation of syndicates or unions) have monopoly power in the labor market, and firms have monopoly power in the product market (there is no bilateral monopoly). Workers and firms are assumed to set wages and prices optimally, given the demand curves facing them. The position of these demand curves will turn out to depend on the level of per capita income in the economy. Given our assumption that each agent is negligible relative to the aggregate economy, per capita income is a variable that no agent by himself can affect. Thus each agent takes this variable as given. Per capita income is, however, determined endogenously in equilibrium as a consequence of the optimizing activities of agents. We shall show that an imperfectly competitive economy of this type exhibits the following Keynesian features:

• In equilibrium the economy will in general operate at too low a level of activity, and there will be underemployment.

• An exogenous increase in demand for current consumption will increase employment and output, the latter by more than the initial increase in demand, i.e., there is a multiplier greater than unity.

• Changes in demand, which in the Walrasian model cause price changes but not output changes, may under imperfect competition lead to output changes and no price changes.

• There is a role for simple balanced budget fiscal policy to increase employment.

This paper is not the first attempt to develop a model of imperfect competition with Keynesian features.[2] One important difference between the present approach and most previous approaches is that we shall assume that agents maximize utility or profit, knowing the objective demand curves facing them, where these demand curves are, in the case of firms (respectively, workers), based on the Cournot-Nash assumption that other firms' production plans (respectively, other workers' supplies of labor) are fixed. One advantage of the Cournot-Nash approach is that it makes the amount of monopoly power possessed by each agent endogenous to the model. If an agent is small relative to his market, he will have little monopoly power and will behave approximately competitively, while if the agent is large, he will have substantial monopoly power, and there will be a significant deviation from the competitive outcome. Thus in particular, the Cournot-Nash approach permits us to view the competitive outcome (more precisely, an approximately competitive outcome) as arising in situations where agents set prices optimally (as opposed to taking prices as given) but where each agent is very small relative to his market. (Our approach is therefore consistent with a number of recent papers on noncooperative approaches to perfect competition; see *Symposium in Journal of Economic Theory* 1980.)[3]

Unfortunately, as is well-known by now, the Cournot-Nash assumption introduces a serious nonexistence problem (see Roberts and Sonnenschein 1977). We avoid this by considering a particularly simple model, and by making a number of strong assumptions about demand functions. There is no doubt, however, that generalizing the model significantly could be hard. For this reason, the analysis presented here should be considered more as an extended example than as a general model.

The paper is organized as follows. The basic model is presented in sections 2 and 3. In section 4 the multiplier and the role of fiscal policy are examined. In section 5 a number of extensions to the model are considered. Finally, concluding remarks appear in section 6.

## 2   The Model

We now develop a simple general equilibrium model of imperfect competition with Keynesian features. As noted in the introduction, a feature of the model is that all agents are negligible relative to the aggregate economy, but some agents are significant relative to the markets they operate in. In particular, workers have some monopoly power in labor markets, while firms have some monopoly power in product markets.

We shall assume that the aggregate economy consists of $N$ "identical" firms and $mN$ "identical" consumers, where $N$ is a large number (the reason for the quotation marks will become clear later). There will be assumed to be three goods: labor, a produced good, and a nonproduced good (it is natural to think of the nonproduced good as being an asset such as money, but such an interpretation may be misleading; see the remarks in section 6). Each consumer has an endowment of labor, given by $T$, an endowment of the nonproduced good, given by $\bar{k}$, and initial shareholdings in the various firms. Consumers supply labor to the firms, which use it to produce the produced good. This good is consumed by consumers, who also consume the nonproduced good. The economy is assumed to last only one period, and so there is no saving or investment.

In order to develop an appropriate model of imperfect competition, we shall assume that, for trading purposes, the economy is divided up into a large number of different labor and output markets (as we shall see below, the number of output markets will generally exceed the number of labor markets). Each market will be assumed to be a small version of the aggregate economy in the sense that the ratio of firms to consumers is $1:m$. It is assumed that agents are assigned to the various markets and cannot move between them (this is the sense in which they are not really identical). In addition, there is no trading across markets.

Consider first the product markets. We assume that these are identical and that each contains $1/\Theta$ firms and $m/\Theta$ consumers (where $1 > \Theta > 0$). We allow for the possibility that each firm is of significant size relative to its market (in particular, $1/\Theta$ can be small), but we assume that individual consumers are negligible relative to the market (i.e., $m$ is large). As a result, firms have some monopoly power in the output market, while consumers have none.

In contrast, in the case of the labor markets, it will be assumed that consumers (or workers) have monopoly power, while firms do not. All labor markets will be assumed to be identical and to contain $q$ firms and $mq$ consumers. In order to formalize the idea that workers have monopoly power, we assume that they form unions or syndicates. Each labor market will be assumed to have $1/\rho$ identical syndicates (where $1 > \rho > 0$), where each syndicate has $mq\rho$ members. We will take $q$ to be large (this justifies the assumption that firms have no monopoly power) but allow $1/\rho$ to be small (this justifies the assumption that syndicates have monopoly power).

In what follows, we take $m$ to be fixed, and consider how the equilibrium of the economy depends on $\Theta$ and $\rho$ (the equilibrium of the economy will turn out to be independent of $N$ and $q$). Note that $\Theta$, $\rho$ are measures of how monopolistic the typical product market and labor market are. In particular, as we shall see, the limiting cases $\Theta = 0$, $\rho = 0$ correspond to perfect competition in these markets.

We shall make the following additional assumptions:

A1   Any two firms in the same product market are also in the same labor market.

A2   The consumers from any given labor market are distributed uniformly across the different product markets, i.e., there are $mq/N\Theta$ consumers from a given labor market in each product market.

A3   Each consumer owns a fraction $1/mN$ of every firm.

An implication of A1 is that the number of labor markets is less than or equal to the number of product markets. The reasons for assuming A1 to A3 will become clear shortly.

The division of the economy into many subeconomies, or markets, may seem artificial. One way to think of this is that there are actually many different qualities or types of goods and labor in the economy, rather than just one type, and that different markets represent different types. If consumers and firms have differing tastes, endowments, and technologies, it is then quite natural for them to locate in different markets. (We do not, however, model the choice of which market to be in.) What is really important for our purposes is that the assumption that there are many markets allows us to capture the idea that individual agents are negligible relative to the aggregate economy, but are significant relative to the particular markets they operate in.

We shall assume that firms act as Cournot-Nash oligopolists in the product market; i.e., each firm chooses its output to maximize profits, taking as given the outputs of other firms in its market. An important implication of A2–A3 is that no firm can influence the income (or wealth) of consumers in its market. Hence, firms take the income of consumers as exogenous. In addition, since individual firms are small relative to their respective labor markets, their activities have no influence on the wage rate they face. Hence, firms also take wages as given. Finally, firms are assumed to know the true demand curves facing them (these will be described below).

Syndicates are also assumed to act as Cournot-Nash oligopolists in the labor market. For most of the paper we shall suppose that syndicate members obtain neither utility nor disutility out of work. Given this, we shall assume that each syndicate chooses its supply of labor to maximize total wage receipts, taking as given the supplies of other syndicates in its market. We shall assume that members of a syndicate are treated symmetrically in the sense that if the supply of labor by a particular syndicate is $L$, then each member supplies labor equal to $L/mq\rho$ (thus each member is underemployed to the extent of $T - L/mq\rho$—in our analysis there will be underemployment but no unemployment). Since syndicate membership is fixed, it follows that maximizing total wage receipts is equivalent to maximizing wages per member.[4] In making their supply decision, syndicates are assumed to recognize that a reduction in labor supply will drive up the wage rate and that this in turn will influence the Cournot-Nash equilibrium in the product market that their firms operate in and hence the demand for labor.

In order to complete the model, it remains to specify agents' tastes and production possibilities. Each firm will be assumed to have a production function of the form $L = C(Y)$, where $L$ is labor and $Y$ is output. In order to simplify matters, we shall assume that $L = aY^\alpha$, where $a > 0$; i.e., the elasticity of output with respect to labor is constant. We also assume that $\alpha \geq 1$; i.e., there are nonincreasing returns to scale (this assumption can be relaxed, however; see section 5). Each consumer will be assumed to have a utility function $U(k, y)$, where $k$ is consumption of the nonproduced good and $y$ is consumption of the produced good. For most of the paper we shall assume that there is no disutility of work (however, see section 5). We make the following assumptions about $U$:

A4  $U$ is nondecreasing in $k$ and $y$ and is increasing in $k$ and $y$ when $k$, $y > 0$.[5]

A5  $U$ is continuous, homothetic, and strictly quasi-concave.

A6  $U$ is differentiable if $k > 0$, $y > 0$, and $\partial U(0, y)/\partial k$ is defined and equal to infinity for all $y > 0$.

The homotheticity of $U$ makes it easy to compute the demand for the produced good in a particular product market. Let $I$ be the total income (or wealth), i.e., wages plus profits plus value of the endowment of the nonproduced good, of all the consumers in this market. Then total demand in the market is simply the solution to max $U(k, y)$ subject to $k + py \leq I$ and $k, y \geq 0$, where $p$ is the price of the produced good and the price of the nonproduced good is normalized to be 1.

We may write the solution to the above problem as $y = h(p)I$. Clearly $h$ is nonincreasing in $p$ (all goods are normal under homothetic preferences). Let $\bar{p} = \inf\{p > 0 \,|\, h(p) = 0\}$, where we set $\bar{p} = \infty$ if $h(p) > 0$ for all $p > 0$. In other words, $\bar{p}$ is the lowest price at which demand for the produced good becomes zero. We shall assume that $h$ is twice differentiable for $0 < p < \bar{p}$, differentiable to the left at $p = \bar{p}$ if $\bar{p} < \infty$, and that $h' < 0$ for all $0 < p < \bar{p}$. The following additional properties of $h(p)$, which will turn out to be useful, are implied by the assumption of utility-maximizing behavior:

$$ph(p) < 1 \quad \text{for all } p > 0; \tag{1}$$

$$\lim_{p \to 0} h(p) = \infty, \qquad \lim_{p \to \infty} h(p) = 0; \tag{2}$$

the term $h(p)/(1 - ph(p))$ is decreasing in $p$ for $0 < p < \bar{p}$, and hence

$$h'(p) + h^2(p) \leq 0 \text{ for all } 0 < p < \bar{p}. \tag{3}$$

Equation (1) follows from A6 and the fact that expenditure on the produced good cannot exceed income. The second part of (2) follows from the same consideration. The first part of (2) is a consequence of A4. Finally, (3) follows from A6 and the fact that, since preferences are homothetic, $y/k = h(p)/(1 - ph(p))$ is a nonincreasing function of the price ratio $p$.

## 3 The Determination of Equilibrium

We now compute the equilibrium of the economy. In what follows, we shall confine our attention to symmetric equilibria in which income, prices, etc., in each market are the same.

**Equilibrium in a typical product market**

Consider a typical product market. By A2 and A3, the income of consumers in this market comes (almost) entirely from wages and profits earned in other markets, and from endowment of the nonproduced good. Therefore, no firm has any influence on the income in its product market.[6] As above, denote this income by $I$. Then firms face a demand curve given by $h(p)I$, where $I$ is exogenous. By assumption, each firm maximizes profit, taking the *outputs* of other firms in its market and the wage rate as given. Let $Y$ be the output of a typical firm and $Y'$ the total output of all other firms in the market. Then if $w > 0$ is the wage rate, the equilibrium price $p$ must maximize

$$p\{h(p)I - Y'\} - wC(h(p)I - Y'). \tag{4}$$

For if this expression is higher at $\tilde{p} \neq p$, then by selecting the output level $(h(\tilde{p})I - Y')$, the typical firm can increase its profits under the Cournot-Nash assumption. Equation (4) yields the first-order condition

$$[ph'(p) + h(p)]I - Y' \geq wC'(h(p)I - Y')h'(p)I, \tag{5}$$

with equality if $Y + Y' = h(p)I > 0$, i.e., if $p < \bar{p}$.

Since the left-hand side of (5) is decreasing in $Y'$ and the right-hand side is nondecreasing in $Y'$ (recall that $h' < 0$), there cannot be two different $Y'$s satisfying (5). This shows that every Cournot-Nash equilibrium is symmetric: all firms choose the same output. Hence, since there are $1/\Theta$ firms, $Y = \Theta h(p)I$, and $Y' = (1 - \Theta)h(p)I$. Therefore, (5) simplifies to

$$p\left(1 + \frac{\Theta}{\eta(p)}\right) \leq wC'(\Theta h(p)I) = wa\Theta^{\alpha-1}h(p)^{\alpha-1}I^{\alpha-1}, \tag{6}$$

with equality if $p < \bar{p}$, where

$$\eta(p) \equiv \frac{h'(p)p}{h(p)} < 0$$

is the price elasticity of demand.

Equation (6) is simply the formula marginal revenue equals marginal cost for each firm. The condition can also be expressed in quantities rather than prices. Let $f \equiv h^{-1}$ be the inverse of the demand function $h$. Then, $Y = \Theta h(p)I$ implies that $p = f(Y/\Theta I)$, and so, using the fact that $f' = 1/h'$, we may rewite (6) as

$$f\left(\frac{Y}{\Theta I}\right) + \Theta\left[\frac{Y}{\Theta I}f'\left(\frac{Y}{\Theta I}\right)\right] = wC'(Y) \tag{7}$$

as long as the output of each firm $Y > 0$.

Equation (6) (or (7)) is a necessary condition for a Cournot-Nash equilibrium to be achieved at price $p$ (or output $Y$), but it is not generally sufficient, because it guarantees only that each firm's profits are at a stationary point. We now make an assumption which ensures that (6) (or (7)) is necessary and sufficient. In particular, we assume that marginal revenue is decreasing in output or increasing in price.

A7   The function $\gamma(p) \equiv p(1 + \Theta/\eta(p))$ is an increasing function of $p$ for $p$ satisfying $0 < p < \bar{p}$. In addition, $\gamma(p) > 0$ for $0 < p < \bar{p}$.

We make this assumption for the purely pragmatic reason that in its absence the analysis becomes much more complicated. See section 5, remark D.[7]

LEMMA 1   Assume A1–A7. Then, given $w > 0, I > 0$, there is a unique solution to (6), which we denote $p(w, I)$. Furthermore, there is a Cournot-Nash equilibrium in which the price of the produced good is $p(w, I)$ and each firm

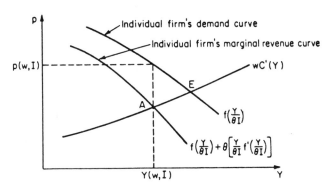

**Figure 1**

supplies $Y(w, I) = \Theta h(p(w, I))I$ (where $Y(w, I)$ is the unique solution to (7)). Finally, if $h(p(w, I)) > 0$, this Cournot-Nash equilibrium is unique.

*Proof*   See appendix.

The Cournot-Nash equilibrium is illustrated in figure 1 at $A$. It is clear from the diagram that each firm underproduces relative to the Walrasian equilibrium $E$. It is also clear that if we increase the size of a typical product market while keeping per capita income constant, that is—if we reduce $\Theta$ and increase $I$ so that $\Theta I$ remains constant—then the marginal-revenue curve in figure 1 moves upward, $Y(w, I)$ increases, and $p(w, I)$ decreases. Thus a reduction in $\Theta$ corresponds to a reduction in monopoly power. In the limit as $\Theta \to 0$ ($\Theta I$ constant), $A$ converges to $E$, so that perfect competition arises as a special case of the model where $\Theta = 0$.

**Equilibrium in a typical labor market**

We have shown how equilibrium is determined in the product market for fixed $w$ and $I$. We turn now to a consideration of equilibrium in the labor market.

By assumption A1, each labor market contains the firms from $q\Theta$ different product markets. Given the wage rate $w$ in a particular labor market, a Cournot-Nash equilibrium in each of these product markets will be determined according to (6). The demand for labor at wage $w$ in a labor market is therefore given by

$$L(w, I) = qC(\Theta h(p(w, I))I). \qquad (8)$$

It is easy to see that A7 implies that $p(w, I)$ is increasing in $w$ (see also figure 1). Therefore, the demand for labor is a *decreasing* function of the wage rate for each $I$.

As noted previously, we assume that there are $1/\rho$ identical syndicates in each labor market and that each syndicate makes the Cournot-Nash assumption that the total supply of labor by other syndicates is fixed. In addition, by A2 and A3, no syndicate has any influence on the income in the product markets in which the firms it works for operate, and so $I$ is also taken as fixed. Each syndicate maximizes wage receipts,

$$w\tilde{L}(w, \ldots),\tag{9}$$

where $\tilde{L}(w, \ldots)$ is the demand curve it faces. In view of the Cournot-Nash assumption, $\tilde{L}(w, \ldots) = L(w, I) - L'$, where $L'$ is the supply of all other syndicates in the particular labor market. Since $L(w, I)$ is decreasing in $w$, the choice for syndicates is between high wages and low employment and low wages and high employment.

A parallel argument to that of equations (4)–(6) yields the first-order condition

$$\left(w\left(1 + \frac{\rho}{\epsilon(w, I)}\right)\right) \geq 0,\tag{10}$$

with equality if there is underemployment, i.e., if $L(w, I) < mqT$, where

$$\epsilon(w, I) = \frac{\partial L(w, I)}{\partial w}\frac{w}{L(w, I)}\tag{11}$$

is the elasticity of demand for labor with respect to the wage. Equation (10) is simply the condition that marginal revenue equals marginal cost for syndicates. In the absence of disutility of work, the marginal cost of providing labor is zero up to full employment and infinite thereafter.

Again, (10) can be expressed in terms of quantities rather than prices. Invert (8) to write the wage rate in a typical labor market as $w = g((L/q), I)$, where $L$ is total labor supply by all syndicates. Let $l = L/mq$ be the labor supply of each individual worker. Then we can rewrite (10) as

$$g(ml, I) + \rho ml \frac{\partial g}{\partial(ml)}(ml, I) \geq 0,\tag{12}$$

with equality if $l < T$. Condition (12) is illustrated in figure 2. The solution to (12) is at $l = \hat{l}$ and the corresponding wage is $w = \hat{w}$.

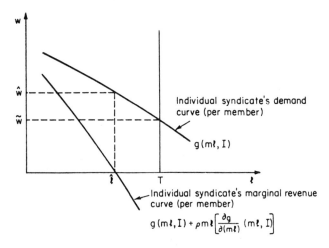

**Figure 2**

As in the case of the product market, (10) (or (12)) is a necessary but not sufficient condition for Cournot-Nash equilibrium in the labor market. Below we make an assumption that ensures that (10) (or (12)) is necessary and sufficient. This assumption says essentially that the left-hand side of (12) is decreasing in $l$. Given this it is clear from figure 2 that a decrease in $\rho$, i.e., a reduction in monopoly power in the labor market, moves the marginal revenue curve up and hence increases $\hat{l}$ and reduces $\hat{w}$. It is also clear that as $\rho \to 0$, the marginal revenue curve eventually cuts the $l$ axis to the right of $l = T$, in which case the solution to (12) is $l = T$, $w = \hat{w}$. In other words, when the labor market is close to being perfectly competitive, Cournot-Nash equilibrium in the labor market will involve full employment (competition between syndicates will bid down the wage until any underemployment is eliminated). However, when $\rho$ is not close to zero, the equilibrium will generally be a point $l < T$ and will involve underemployment.

Returning to (10), we may use (6) and (8) to express the elasticity of demand for labor, $\epsilon(w, I)$, in terms of the elasticity of demand for output $\eta(p)$. Define $z(p) = (d\gamma(p)/dp)(p/\gamma(p))$, where $\gamma(p)$ is as in A7. In the appendix we show that if $p(w, I) < \bar{p}$,

$$\epsilon(w, I) = \alpha \left/ \left[ \frac{z(p(w, I))}{\eta(p(w, I))} - (\alpha - 1) \right] \right. . \tag{13}$$

Therefore, using the fact that $w = 0$ is not optimal for a syndicate, we may rewrite (10) as

$$\delta(p) \equiv \left(1 + \frac{\rho}{\alpha}\left[\frac{z(p)}{\eta(p)} - (\alpha - 1)\right]\right) = 1 + \frac{\rho}{\epsilon(w, I)} \geq 0, \tag{14}$$

with equality if there is underemployment.[8]

We now make an assumption which ensures that (14) is a sufficient as well as necessary condition for Cournot-Nash equilibrium in the labor market. The assumption is a slightly weaker version of decreasing marginal revenue for syndicates.

A8  If $\delta(p') = 0$ for some $0 < p' < \bar{p}$, then $\delta(p) > 0$ for $\bar{p} > p > p'$ and $\delta(p) < 0$ for $0 < p < p'$.

A8 implies that, if $\delta(p) = 0$ has a solution in the range $0 < p < \bar{p}$, then the solution is unique. Denote this solution by $\hat{p}$. If no solution exists, set $\hat{p} = 0$.[9] The $\delta(p)$ curve is illustrated in figure 3.

LEMMA 2   Assume A1–A8. Then, given $I$, there is a unique Cournot-Nash equilibrium in the labor market, denoted by $p(I)$, $w(I)$. This equilibrium will satisfy $p(I) = \hat{p}$, i.e., $\delta(p(I)) = 0$, as long as $(1/m)C(\Theta h(\hat{p})I) < T$. In this case, there will be underemployment in equilibrium. On the other hand, if $(1/m)C(\Theta h(\hat{p})I) > T$, then $p(I)$ satisfies $(1/m)C(\Theta h(p)I) = T$, and there will be full employment. In both cases $w(I)$ satisfies (6) with equality.

*Proof*   See appendix.

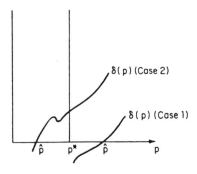

Figure 3

Lemma 2 tells us that if there is underemployment in equilibrium, syndicates will choose the wage rate so that the price of the produced good in output markets is $\hat{p}$; i.e., they will set $w$ so that $\gamma(\hat{p}) = wC'(\Theta h(\hat{p})I)$. That is, it is as if the syndicates controlled the price of the produced good directly. On the other hand, if at price $\hat{p}$ there is overemployment of labor, the syndicates raise the wage until full employment is established.

**Determination of an overall imperfectly competitive equilibrium**

So far we have taken $I$ to be exogenous. We now proceed to the determination of an overall equilibrium for the economy in which $I$ is endogenous. The demand function for the produced good is $h(p)I$. Therefore, from the budget constraint, we know that each consumer demands $y$ and $k$ in the ratio

$$y/k = h(p)/(1 - ph(p)). \tag{15}$$

Hence, in equilibrium,

$$Y/m\bar{k} = h(p)/(1 - ph(p)), \tag{16}$$

where $Y$ is the output of each firm and $\bar{k}$ is the per capita endowment of the nonproduced good. The right-hand side of (16) is decreasing in $p$ (see (3)). Let $p^*$ be the unique solution of

$$\frac{1}{m} C\left(\frac{h(p)m\bar{k}}{1 - ph(p)}\right) = T. \tag{17}$$

Then $p^*$ is that price for the produced good relative to the nonproduced good which generates the level of demand consistent with full employment. If $p > p^*$, there will be underemployment. On the other hand, $p < p^*$ is infeasible.

We know from lemma 2 that the imperfectly competitive equilibrium must be one of two types. Either there is underemployment, in which case $\delta(p) = 0$ and $p = \hat{p}$, or there is full employment, in which case $p = p^*$. The two possibilities are illustrated in figure 3 (drawn according to A8). If $\delta(p^*) < 0$, then $\hat{p} > p^*$, and the equilibrium occurs at $\hat{p}$ (case 1). Since

$$\frac{1}{m} C\left(\frac{h(\hat{p})m\bar{k}}{1 - \hat{p}h(\hat{p})}\right),$$

there will be underemployment. (In case 1, $p = p^*$ is not a possible equilibrium, since (14) is violated at $p^*$.) On the other hand, if $\delta(p^*) \geq 0$, then

$\hat{p} \leq p^*$, the equilibrium occurs at $p^*$, and there will be full employment (case 2). (In case 2, $p = \hat{p}$ would imply overemployment.)

PROPOSITION 1    Assume A1–A8. Let $p^*$, $\hat{p}$ be the solutions to (17) and $\delta(p) = 0$, respectively (if there is no solution to $\delta(p) = 0$, set $\hat{p} = 0$). Define $\tilde{p} = \max(\hat{p}, p^*)$. Then there is a unique imperfectly competitive equilibrium (ICE) for the economy, given as follows: the price of the produced good is $\tilde{p}$; each firm produces $\tilde{Y} = m\bar{k}(h(\tilde{p})/(1 - \tilde{p}h(p)))$ units of output; each consumer supplies $\tilde{l} = (1/m)C(h(\tilde{p})m\bar{k}/(1 - \tilde{p}h(\tilde{p}))\lambda$ units of labor; the wage rate $\tilde{w}$ satisfies $\gamma(\tilde{p}) = \tilde{w}C'(\tilde{Y})$; income in each product market is given by $\tilde{I} = (\tilde{Y}/\Theta h(\tilde{p}))$ and per capita income by $(\tilde{Y}/mh(\tilde{p}))$. If $\hat{p} \leq p^*$, there is full employment in equilibrium. On the other hand, if $\hat{p} > p^*$, each worker is underemployed by the amount $T - (1/m)C(h(\hat{p})m\bar{k}/(1 - \hat{p}h(\hat{p})))$.

*Proof*    See appendix.

As we have emphasized above, in order to get underemployment in equilibrium in our model, it is necessary for the labor market to be non-competitive; i.e., $\rho$ cannot be zero (or close to zero). For if $\rho = 0$, then $\delta(p) \equiv 1$, so that $0 = \hat{p} < p^*$. On other hand, underemployment is quite consistent with a competitive product market, i.e., with $\Theta = 0$. In fact, if the product market is competitive, $z(p) = 1$, and so $\delta(p) = 0$ if and only if

$$\eta(p) = \frac{1}{\alpha - 1 - (\alpha/p)}. \tag{18}$$

As long as this equation does have a solution, underemployment will occur in an ICE if $T$ is sufficiently large.[10]

Returning to the general case where the product market is imperfectly competitive, we may use the formula for $\delta(p)$ in (14) to derive simple comparative statics properties of an ICE. Clearly, an increase in $\rho$ reduces $\delta(p)$ for each $p$ (since $\epsilon(w, I) < 0$). It follows from figure 3 that $\hat{p}$ rises as $\rho$ increases. Hence, by (3), as one might expect, an increase in monopoly power in labor markets, i.e., an increase in $\rho$, raises the equilibrium level of underemployment, $T - (1/m)C(h(\hat{p})m\bar{k}/(1 - \hat{p}h(\hat{p})))$. The effect of a change in monopoly power in product markets is not so clear-cut, however, since $\Theta$ affects $\gamma$ and $z$ in a complicated way.

Note that an ICE coincides with the usual Walrasian equilibrium in the special case where $\Theta = \rho = 0$.

Finally, it is worth reviewing our assumption that firms maximize profits and that syndicates maximize wage receipts. Are these reasonable objectives given that the economy is imperfectly competitive? The answer is that they are in view of A2 and A3. For A2 implies that only a negligible fraction of workers purchase output in a market served by the firm they work for (when $N$ is large). As a result, for a majority of workers, the beneficial effects of an increase in wages will dominate any adverse effects on output prices. Similarly, A3 implies that when $N$ is large, a negligible fraction of workers' incomes comes from holding shares in the firms they work for. As a result, for the majority of workers, the beneficial effects of an increase in wages will dominate any adverse effect on profits. Finally, A3 implies that a negligible fraction of a firm's owners purchase output in a market served by the firm. As a result, for the majority of shareholders, the beneficial effects of an increase in profits will dominate any adverse effect on output prices. Thus A2 and A3 together ensure that the maximization of wage receipts is in the interest of (almost all) syndicate members and that the maximization of profits is in the interest of (almost all) firms' owners.[11]

## 4 The Multiplier

In this section we consider how the imperfectly competitive equilibrium (ICE) of the last section is affected by changes in demand conditions. We shall find that the imperfectly competitive model of sections 2–3 exhibits a number of Keynesian features.

Suppose that demand for the produced good increases for either of the following reasons: the per capita endowment of the nonproduced good $\bar{k}$ increases, or consumers' tastes change in such a way that the demand function for the produced good becomes $\lambda h(p)I$ for all $p$, where $\lambda > 1$.[12] In both cases the elasticity of demand $\eta(p)$ is not affected, and hence, $\gamma(p)$ and $\delta(p)$ aren't either. It follows that $\hat{p}$ stays the same. Therefore, if the economy is initially in underemployment equilibrium, i.e., $\tilde{p} = \hat{p} > p^*$, then a small increase in $\bar{k}$ or $\lambda$ will not affect the equilibrium price of the produced good $\tilde{p}$. Output and employment will both rise, however, since equilibrium output is given by

$$\tilde{Y} = \lambda h(\tilde{p}) m \bar{k} / (1 - \lambda \tilde{p} h(\tilde{p})), \tag{19}$$

which is an increasing function of both $\bar{k}$ and $\lambda$. Note that if demand continues to increase, then eventually full employment will be reached, and from then on an increase in demand will not affect output but will simply lead to a higher price for the produced good (relative to the nonproduced good). This is because increases in demand increase $p^*$, and so we eventually switch to the regime $\tilde{p} = p^* > \hat{p}$.

Of particular interest is the fact that increases in demand have a multiplier effect on output. Suppose that we start off in an underemployment equilibrium with $p = \hat{p}$. Let $\lambda = 1$, and write $\sigma = mh(\hat{p})\bar{k}$. Here $\sigma$ is that part of the demand for the produced good which comes from endowment income. Then, from (19) we have

$$\frac{d\tilde{Y}}{d\sigma} = \frac{1}{1 - \hat{p}h(\hat{p})}. \tag{20}$$

That is, an increase in $\bar{k}$ that initially raises demand for the produced good by one (i.e., $mh(\hat{p})d\bar{k} = d\sigma = 1$) has the final effect of increasing output by $1/(1 - \hat{p}h(\hat{p}))$. Since $\hat{p}h(\hat{p})$ is the marginal propensity to consume (in money terms), the multiplier here is just the traditional Keynesian one: the reciprocal of one minus the marginal propensity to consume.

On the other hand, consider again an underemployment equilibrium and suppose now that $\lambda$, rather than $\bar{k}$, increases. Then

$$\left.\frac{d\tilde{Y}}{d\lambda}\right|_{\lambda=1} = \frac{\tilde{Y}}{1 - \hat{p}h(\hat{p})} > \tilde{Y}. \tag{21}$$

Again, the final increase in $\tilde{Y}$ exceeds the initial increase in demand; i.e., the multiplier exceeds one.

The usual dynamic story that goes with the multiplier can also be told here. An initial increase in demand leads to expansion by firms and hence to greater employment. The price of the produced good does not change, since syndicates adjust the wage to maintain $\delta(p) = 0$. Consumers' incomes rise as a result of the expansion, and a fraction of this increase $(\hat{p}h(\hat{p}))$ is spent on greater consumption of the produced good. There is a further expansion, and so on. Of course, since we have no theory of dynamics, this is as usual no more than a story.

What determines the size of the multiplier? Consider again the case where demand increases as a result of a change in $\bar{k}$. Then the multiplier is $1/(1 - \hat{p}h(\hat{p}))$. We have seen above that a decrease in $\rho$ leads to a decrease in $\hat{p}$. In general, this can either increase or decrease $\hat{p}h(\hat{p})$. If the product market is perfectly competitive, however, it follows from (18) that $\eta(\hat{p}) +$

$1 > 0$, and so a decrease in $\hat{p}$ decreases $\hat{p}h(\hat{p})$ and decreases the multiplier. In other words, if the product market is competitive, a reduction in monopoly power in the labor market reduces the multiplier. (Note that if $\rho$ becomes small enough, we switch to the full employment regime, and the multiplier becomes zero.) The effects of a change in $\Theta$ on the multiplier do not seem to be clear-cut.

It is possible to develop something close to the traditional Keynesian national income analysis for the model presented here. What corresponds in our model to national income is output of the produced good per firm $Y$. The demand for the produced good by a typical group of $m$ consumers is given by

$$c = h(p)(mi), \tag{22}$$

where $i$ is per capita income (or wealth). Now $mi = w(ml) + (pY - w(ml)) + m\bar{k} = pY + m\bar{k}$. Therefore, we can rewrite (22) as

$$c = h(p)(pY + m\bar{k}) = ph(p)Y + mh(p)\bar{k}. \tag{23}$$

If there is underemployment in equilibrium, $p = \hat{p}$. Substituting $\sigma = mh(\hat{p})\bar{k}$ and $\tau = \hat{p}h(\hat{p})$, we obtain

$$c = \sigma + \tau Y, \tag{24}$$

which is, of course, the traditional linear consumption function, where $\tau$ is the marginal propensity to consume. The equilibrium condition (since there is no investment) is

$$Y = c = \sigma + \tau Y, \tag{25}$$

i.e.,

$$Y = \sigma/(1 - \tau), \tag{26}$$

which is, of course, just equation (19) with $\lambda = 1$.

It is instructive to compare the effects of changes in demand in the imperfectly competitive model of sections 2–3 with those in the usual Walrasian model. Suppose that $\tilde{\bar{k}}$ is stochastic, and hence so is $\tilde{\sigma} = mh(\hat{p})\tilde{\bar{k}}$. Then if $C(\tilde{\sigma}/(1 - \tau))$ never exceeds $mT$, $p$ will remain constant at $\hat{p}$, and changes in demand in the imperfectly competitive model will lead to fluctuations in output and employment but to no fluctuations in output price. In contrast, in the Walrasian model, which occurs when $\Theta = p = 0$, there will always be full employment. Hence, output and employment will be constant, and fluctuations in demand will simply cause fluctuations in the price of the produced good ($p$ will vary so as to satisfy (17)). This last conclusion is true even if the product market is imperfectly competitive, as long as the labor market is perfectly competitive. We see, then, that the presence of imperfect competition can lead to greater fluctuations in output and smaller fluctuations in price than in the usual Walrasian model.

It should also be noted that there is a role for a simple balanced budget fiscal policy in this model. Suppose that the economy is experiencing underemployment. Then the government can stimulate demand by taxing consumers' incomes and spending these incomes in such a way as to increase demand for the produced good relative to the nonproduced good. In particular, suppose that the government taxes in a lump sum fashion all the income $I$ of consumers, spends this income according to the demand function $\lambda h(p)I$, and gives the goods that it purchases to consumers. (As long as resale of the produced good by consumers can be prevented, crowding out will then not occur.) Then, in view of the results above, this will increase output and employment without changing output price until full employment is reached.[13] It should be noted that the fiscal policy which we are considering here differs from traditional fiscal policy in that both the marginal propensity to consume, $\tau$, and the average propensity to consume are affected by the government's activities. Traditional fiscal policy, which affects only the average propensity to consume, will alter the price elasticity of demand $\eta(p)$ and hence will affect $p$ even at an underemployment equilibrium.

It is worth considering finally how changes in demand affect the wage rate. We have observed that if we start at an underemployment equilibrium, a small increase in $\bar{k}$ or $\lambda$ will not change $\hat{p}$. Rewriting (6) as $\gamma(\hat{p}) = wC'(Y)$ and using the fact that $Y$ increases with demand, we see that $w$ falls when demand increases if there are decreasing returns to scale, and it stays constant if there are constant returns. The idea that increases in demand may lead to reductions in the wage may seem strange at first sight. It is, however, analogous to the result that, in the textbook Keynesian model with fixed money wages and a competitive product market, an increase in demand leads to lower *real* wages if the marginal product of labor is declining. Note that this feature of the model will disappear if we assume that there are increasing returns in production—a case that fits well into the framework of imperfect competition. Then $\gamma(p) = wC'(Y)$ implies that $w$ and $Y$ move together if $p$ stays constant.[14]

## 5   Comments and Extensions of the Basic Model

### Introducing disutility of labor

The model described above makes the strong assumption that there is no disutility of work. We now sketch how this assumption can be relaxed (a detailed exposition may be found in Hart 1980). Suppose that each consumer's utility function is $U(k, y) - d(L)$, where $L$ is labor and $d$ is increasing in $L$ on $[0, T]$. Assume also that $U$ is homogeneous of degree one in $k$, $y$. Then the utility of a worker who supplies $L$ units of labor at a wage $w$ can be written as

$$V(p)(wL + \pi + \bar{k}) - d(L), \tag{27}$$

where $V(p) \equiv \max \{U(k, y|k + py \leq 1), k \geq 0, y \geq 0\}$, $\pi$ is the worker's income from profits, and $p$ is the price of the produced good in the output market visited by the worker. A2 and A3 imply that the workers in a particular syndicate have no influence over $p$ or $\pi$. Therefore, each syndicate's objective, given that it faces the demand curve $\tilde{L}(w, \ldots)$, is to choose $w$ to maximize

$$V(p)\frac{w\tilde{L}(w, \ldots)}{qm\rho} - d\left(\frac{\tilde{L}(w, \ldots)}{qm\rho}\right). \tag{28}$$

Arguing as in section 3 and using the fact that $p(w, I) = p$ in a symmetric equilibrium yields

$$V(p)\gamma(p)\delta(p) = d'((1/m)C(\Theta h(p)I))C'(\Theta h(p)I) \tag{29}$$

as a necessary condition for equilibrium. Under an appropriate generalization of A8, this condition is also sufficient.

We also know, however, that in equilibrium

$$Y = \Theta h(p)I = (h(p)m\bar{k})/(1 - ph(p)), \tag{30}$$

where $Y$ is the output of each firm. Using (30) to solve for $I$ and substituting in (29) gives us a single equation in $p$ as our condition for equilibrium. Once this has been solved for $p$, we may find the equilibrium output of each firm from (30).

The model with disutility of labor differs from the previous model in a number of ways. First, there may be multiple imperfectly competitive equilibria (even under the generalized version of A8), i.e., (29) and (30) may have several solutions.[15] Each of these solutions can be shown to have the property that the level of employment is below the Walrasian, i.e., socially optimal, level. Second, the level of employment will be suboptimal even if the labor market is competitive, as long as the product market is non-competitive. In this case, workers equate the marginal disutility of work with the marginal utility of the real wage; however, imperfect competition in the product market makes the latter too low from a social point of view. As we have noted previously, in the no-disutility-of-work, there is full employment; i.e., the level of employment is optimal, whenever the labor market is competitive.

Third, increases in demand due to changes in $\bar{k}$ or $\lambda$ will tend to increase output price $p$ and the level of output and employment together, rather than just affecting output when there is underemployment and price when there is full employment. This reduces the size of the multiplier when there is underemployment.

Finally, it is worth noting that the case where there is disutility of work can also be interpreted as a case where there is an alternative activity to working in the unionized sector. For example, suppose that every individual has a plot of land on which he can work. Suppose that the individual divides his time between working in the unionized sector and on his plot. Assume that the individual's utility function can be written as $U(k, y) + G(T - L)$, where $G$ is consumption of the (nonmarketed) crop. Then, if we write $G(T - L) = -d(L)$, we have the same model as described above. Now imperfect competition in the unionized sector causes a misallocation between the unionized and home production sectors rather than underemployment per se. (We can equally well interpret the underemployment in the model of sections 2 and 3 as a misallocation between the unionized sector and the "leisure sector.")

### Allowing the income distribution to affect demand

In the model of sections 2 and 3 a decrease in money wages leads to a decrease in $p$ and hence to an increase in the equilibrium output of the produced good, given by $h(p)m\bar{k}/(1 - ph(p))$, and in employment. It is sometimes argued by Keynesians, however, that an overall decrease in wages may *decrease* output and employment. This possibility can be incorporated into our model by allowing demand to depend not only on aggregate income, $I$, but also on the distribution of income.[16]

We shall give an example to illustrate this. Suppose the $C(Y) = Y$, i.e., $a = \alpha = 1$. Let us drop the assumption that all consumers are identical and assume instead that the population of consumers is divided into two groups: workers who can supply labor, but do not own shares in firms, and capitalists who cannot supply labor but who own all the firms. To make matters very simple, we shall suppose that workers consume the produced good according to the demand function $h(p)I_w$, where $I_w$ is workers' income, and that capitalists consume only the nonproduced good.

Under these conditions, market demand for the produced good is given by

$$h(p)I_w. \tag{31}$$

Hence, the analysis of sections 2 and 3 applies, with $I_w$ replacing $I$. In particular, the elasticity of demand is the same for each value of $p$ as previously.

Let $\beta$ be the fraction of consumers who are workers. Then, if we assume that the endowment of the nonproduced good is distributed evenly across all consumers, the condition for equilibrium in the product market is

$$Y = h(p)I_w = h(p)(w(\beta ml) + \beta m\bar{k}). \tag{32}$$

However, since (6) holds with equality, and $C'(Y) = 1$,

$$w = \gamma(p). \tag{33}$$

Substituting this into (32), and using the fact that $Y = C(Y) = \beta ml$, we get that equilibrium output of each firm is

$$[h(p)/(1 - h(p)\gamma(p))]\beta m\bar{k}. \tag{34}$$

As before, $p$ will satisfy $\delta(p) = 0$ at an underemployment equilibrium.

Assume that initially we are at an ICE. Suppose now that money wages fall in all labor markets. Then in view of (33) and A7, $p$ will decrease. Hence, by (34), $Y$ will decrease as long as

$$\frac{d}{dp}\left[\frac{h(p)}{1 - h(p)\gamma(p)}\right] > 0, \tag{35}$$

i.e., as long as

$$h'(p) + h^2(p)\gamma'(p) > 0. \tag{36}$$

Equation (36) will certainly be satisfied if $\gamma'(p)$ is large enough, i.e., as long as marginal revenue is increasing sufficiently rapidly in $p$ at the ICE. Condition (36) ensures that a decrease in $w$ does not decrease $p$ so much as to cause the "normal demand" effect; i.e., the increase in demand due to the fact that the produced good is cheaper relative to the nonproduced good, to offset the decrease in demand caused by the shift in income distribution to the capitalists.

We see, then, that a decrease in money wages throughout the economy can *decrease* employment. However, if money wages continue to fall, then eventually employment will rise. This follows from the fact that (a) $p \to 0$ as $w \to 0$ (see (33) and result 1(3) in the appendix) and (b) $h(p) \to \infty$ as $p \to 0$ (see (2)). In other words, eventually the "normal demand" effect dominates.

Note that (36) will not be satisfied if the product market is competitive, for then $\gamma(p) = p$, and (36) is inconsistent with (3). Hence, we obtain the perhaps surprising result that a decrease in wages can lead to a decrease in output and employment only if the product market is imperfectly competitive. Note also that while we have obtained conditions for workers as a whole to face an upward-sloping demand curve for labor, this does not alter the fact that each syndicate faces a downward-sloping demand curve. The point is that no individual syndicate can affect the distribution of income and therefore for an individual syndicate the "normal demand" effect always dominates. Only a general decrease in wages can change the distribution of income in such a way as to decrease the demand for labor.

**The role of the nonproduced good**

The nonproduced good plays a central role in our model. On the one hand, there is a close relationship between the quantity of it available and the equilibrium activity level, represented by $Y$. On the other hand, "depressions" occur when demand shifts from the produced good to the nonproduced good. It is important to realize, however, that similar results can be obtained if we replace the nonproduced good by another produced good. Suppose, for example, that $k$ is produced according to the cost function $L = D(k)$, where $L$ is labor. Assume that production of $k$ takes place under competitive conditions—both in labor and product markets. Then in equilibrium labor that is withheld from the unionized sector to keep the wage there high will be diverted to the production of $k$. Thus, there will be no underemployment—only a misallocation between sectors. (This is the similar to the case discussed in the subsection "Introducing disutility of labor" above.)

Suppose now that there is a shift in demand from $Y$ to $k$. Output of $Y$ will fall, and output of $k$ will rise. However, the relative magnitudes of these changes may be quite different. In particular, if $D'(k)$ is steeply sloped in the relevant range, then an increase in demand will bring about a large increase in the price of $k$ and only a small increase in the quantity. Thus in a very real sense the increase in production of $k$ may not match the decrease in production of $Y$, and the shift in demand will cause the overall activity level of the economy to decline. (The case of the nonproduced good is simply the special case where $D(k) = 0$ for $0 \leq k \leq m\bar{N}\bar{k}$, $D(k) = \infty$ otherwise.)

**Relaxing the assumptions**

To carry out the analysis, we have made a number of strong assumptions. The most important of these are A1–A3. A1–A3 decompose the economy in such a way that, in spite of the existence of imperfect competition, there is a clear division between the variables each agent can affect and those it cannot affect. As a consequence, imperfectly competitive agents face, under the Cournot-Nash assumption, well-defined demand curves and have simple well-defined objective functions. In the absence of something like A1–A3, it becomes much harder to talk about the "true" demand curve facing an imperfectly competitive agent, since, in principle, the agent's actions have repercussions for, and hence may set off reactions from, every other agent in the economy. It is also much harder under these conditions to define an appropriate objective function for an imperfect competitor.

We have also assumed—without any justification from consumer theory —A7 and A8. In the absence of A7 and A8, unfortunately, the analysis becomes considerably more complicated. In particular, it does not seem possible to establish the existence of an ICE. The theorems by McManus (1962) and Roberts and Sonnenschein (1976) on existence of Cournot-Nash equilibria in the absence of diminishing marginal revenue do not seem to be applicable here.

It is possible that allowing different prices in different output markets would smooth things sufficiently to permit us to establish the existence of a nonsymmetric ICE. There seems little doubt, however, that analyzing properties of such an ICE—even if it could be shown to exist—would be a complicated task.

Given the difficulties of dropping A7 and A8, it would also seem hard to relax the assumption that consumers have homothetic preferences in $k$ and $y$ and the assumption that $C(Y) = aY^{\alpha}$. Without homothetic preferences and the assumption that $C(Y) = aY^{\alpha}$, $\gamma(p)$ and $\delta(p)$ will depend on quantities like $L$ and $Y$ as well as on $p$. Under these conditions, A7 and A8 may become so strong as to be never satisfied over the whole range.

## 6   Conclusions

In this paper we have argued that several features of Keynesian economics can be captured by a model which departs from the classical Walrasian model by assuming that agents are imperfect competitors rather than perfect competitors. In particular, we have shown that, under certain assumptions the following hold:

• An imperfectly competitive economy will operate at too low a level of activity; i.e., it will be depressed, and there will be underemployment.

• An increase in demand for current consumption will lead to an increase in output. Moreover, this will take place without any change in output price, and the increase in output will exceed the initial increase in demand, i.e., the multiplier exceeds 1.

• A balanced-budget fiscal policy can be used to stimulate the economy.

For most of our analysis the crucial assumption has been the existence of imperfect competition in the labor market—it is this that is responsible for the existence of underemployment in our basic model. In extensions of the basic model, however, the existence of imperfect competition in the product market also has interesting implications. For example, it can imply that workers as a whole face an upward-sloping demand curve for labor if capitalists and workers have different propensities to consume.

While the model presented here covers some of the same ground as the standard fixed-price model, it differs from the fixed price model in the following respects. First, whereas the fixed price model yields an infinite number of equilibria (for each initial price vector and each exogenously specified rationing scheme there is at least one equilibrium), the imperfectly competitive model will in general yield a small number of equilibria; in the case considered here, just one. Second, the Walrasian equilibrium is never an imperfectly competitive equilibrium (unless $\Theta = \rho = 0$), whereas it is always an equilibrium in the fixed price model.

Under imperfect competition, as under fixed prices, an agent's actions will depend not only on prices, but also on realized transactions, i.e., quantities. As Clower (1965) has emphasized, this seems to be a crucial feature of any Keynesian model. Under imperfect competition, the quantity constraints arise from the fact that at any price there is a limit to the demand for the agent's product. A consequence of this is that in an imperfectly competitive equilibrium an agent will generally want to buy or sell more at the going price. It is inappropriate, however, to describe this as "rationing" or to associate it with the nonclearing of markets. Rather, it is simply an indication of the fact that an imperfectly competitive agent is not a price-taker.

In the model we have presented, demand "failures" or depressions arise because at equilibrium prices, demand for the produced good is too low relative to that for the nonproduced good. This raises an important question about what might correspond to the nonproduced good in reality. Possible candidates are land, old masters, etc. These are straightforward. Another possible candidate for the nonproduced good is money. This is more complicated. In the static model presented here there is no reason for agents to hold money. In a model with time, cash balances might enter the (indirect) utility function as a proxy for future consumption. Note, however, that $k$ will then correspond to real, rather than nominal, cash balances (where the deflator is the price of future consumption). Thus, there is no reason to think that a change in the nominal supply of money will lead to a change in $k$.[17] In any case, the incorporation of time and money into the model is a topic for further research.

While the imperfectly competitive model considered here does have Keynesian features, it is a big step from this to the conclusion that the model captures a significant part of the ideas of Keynes or of Keynesians. Leijonhufvud (1968) has argued forcefully that Keynes believed that unemployment and depressions were a consequence of the failure of the market system to provide the right signals and could not be traced simply to the existence of large agents, such as unions or monopolists. In this respect, the model presented here may be closer to the ideas of such "pre-Keynesians" as Pigou (1933) than to those of Keynes himself. Note, however, that in the model of this paper, the imperfectly competitive agents are significant only at the "local" level, i.e., in their own markets. Each agent is negligible relative to the whole economy. In this sense, the model may not be so far removed from the atomistic world that Keynes had in mind.

It should also be noted that the imperfectly competitive equilibrium which we have studied in this paper applies equally to the short run and the long run. One consequence of this is that our model would not seem to be consistent with the view that Keynesian demand failures arise only in the short run and that in the long run the economy will achieve full employment. Rather, the imperfectly competitive model suggests that demand failures can be permanent. In this respect, the model may have a greater affinity to the work of Harrod (1939), Kalecki (1954), and some of the Marxian underconsumptionists, than it does to some neo-Keynesian thinking.

## Appendix

RESULT 1   (1) $\lim_{p \to \bar{p}} \sup \gamma(p) > 0$; (2) $\lim_{p \to \bar{p}} \sup \gamma(p) = \infty$ if $\bar{p} = \infty$; (3) $\lim_{p \to 0} \inf \gamma(p) = 0$.

*Proof*   Assume that $\lim_{p \to \bar{p}} \sup \gamma(p) \leq 0$. Then $\lim_{p \to \bar{p}} \sup(1 + \Theta/\eta(p)) \leq 0$. Choose $\epsilon$ to be a positive number less than $1 - \Theta$. Then for $p \geq$ some $p'$, $p' < \bar{p}$,

$$1 + \Theta/\eta(p) \leq \epsilon, \tag{1'}$$

$$h'(p)/h(p) \geq -\Theta/p(1 - \epsilon). \tag{2'}$$

Integrating this from $p'$ to $p$, we get

$$\log \frac{h(p)}{h'(p)} \geq -\frac{\Theta}{1 - \epsilon} \log \frac{p}{p'}. \tag{3'}$$

Therefore,

$$h(p) \geq \frac{h(p')}{(p')^{-\Theta/(1-\epsilon)}} p^{-\Theta/(1-\epsilon)}, \tag{4'}$$

from which it follows that

$$ph(p) \geq \frac{h(p')}{(p')^{-\Theta/(1-\epsilon)}} p^{(1-(\Theta/(1-\epsilon)))}. \tag{5'}$$

If $\bar{p} < \infty$, then $h(\bar{p}) = 0$, which contradicts (4'). If $\bar{p} = \infty$, then (5') is not consistent with the fact that $ph(p) < 1$ for all $p$ (recall that $\epsilon < (1 - \Theta)$). This proves (1) and that

$$\lim_{p \to \bar{p}} \sup \left( 1 + \frac{\Theta}{\eta(p)} \right) > 0.$$

Condition (2) follows from this immediately. To prove (3), one uses a similar argument to that given above to show that

$$\lim_{p \to 0} \inf \left( 1 + \frac{\Theta}{\eta(p)} \right) = \infty$$

is inconsistent with the fact that $\lim_{p \to 0} h(p) = \infty$. Therefore,

$$\lim_{p \to 0} \inf \left( 1 + \frac{\Theta}{\eta(p)} \right) < \infty,$$

which, together with the second part of (A7), implies (3).

*Proof of lemma 1* It is worth noting that lemma 1 is not proved by showing that firms' profit functions are concave. It appears that A7 is not strong enough to ensure concavity and yet is strong enough to ensure existence. We prove existence of $p(w, I)$ first. If $\bar{p} < \infty$ and (6) holds at $\bar{p}$, then $p(w, I) = \bar{p}$. Suppose now that $\bar{p} < \infty$ and (6) is violated at $\bar{p}$. By result 1, $\lim_{p \to 0} \inf \gamma(p) = 0 < \lim_{p \to 0} C'(\Theta h(p)I)$. Hence by continuity there exists $0 < p < \bar{p}$ such that (6) holds with equality. The remaining case is $\bar{p} = \infty$. But then $\lim_{p \to \infty} \sup \gamma(p) = \infty > \lim_{p \to \infty} C'(\Theta h(p)I)$. Again, by continuity, there exists $0 < p < \bar{p}$ such that (6) holds with equality. This establishes the existence of $p(w, I)$. Uniqueness follows from the fact that the left-hand side of (6) is increasing in $p$ and the right-hand side is nonincreasing in $p$.

To show that $p(w, I)$ is a Cournot-Nash equilibrium is trivial in the case where (6) holds with inequality. Hence assume equality. Since (6) holds with equality at $p(w, I)$, (5) holds with equality where $Y' = (1 - \Theta)h(p)I$. Suppose that (4) is not maximized; i.e., there exists $p'$ at which a typical firm's profits are higher. Consider first the case where $p' > \tilde{p} = p(w, I)$. Then there must be a $p' \geq p \geq \tilde{p}$, at which

$$\frac{d}{dp} \{ p[h(p)I - Y'] - wC(h(p)I - Y') \} > 0. \tag{6'}$$

But this means that

$$[ph'(p) + h(p)]I - (1 - \Theta)h(\tilde{p})I$$
$$- wC'(h(p)I - (1 - \Theta)h(\tilde{p})I)h'(p)I > 0. \tag{7'}$$

$$[p - wC'(h(p)I - (1 - \Theta)h(\tilde{p})I)]h'(p) + h(p) > h(\tilde{p}) - \Theta h(\tilde{p}). \qquad (8')$$

However, by (A7) and (6) and the fact that there are nonincreasing returns to scale,

$$p\left(1 + \frac{\Theta}{\eta(p)}\right) \geq \tilde{p}\left(1 + \frac{\Theta}{\eta(\tilde{p})}\right) = wC'(\Theta h(\tilde{p})I)$$

$$\geq wC'(h(p)I - (1 - \Theta)h(\tilde{p})I). \qquad (9')$$

Hence

$$p - wC'(h(p)I - (1 - \Theta)h(\tilde{p})I) \geq -\Theta p/\eta(p). \qquad (10')$$

Substituting into (8'), we obtain

$$-\Theta ph'(p)/\eta(p) + h(p) > h(\tilde{p}) - \Theta h(\tilde{p}); \qquad (11')$$

that is,

$$h(p)(1 - \Theta) > h(\tilde{p})(1 - \Theta), \qquad (12')$$

which contradicts $p \geq \tilde{p}$.

A similar argument works for the case $p' < \tilde{p}$. This proves that there is a Cournot-Nash equilibrium at $p = \tilde{p}$. The uniqueness of equilibrium follows from the fact that (6), which is a necessary condition for existence, has a unique solution. (Note that uniqueness does not obtain if $h(p, w)I = 0$, since then any increase in $p$ will leave the equilibrium unchanged.)

                                                                            Q.E.D.

RESULT 2

$$\epsilon(w, I) = \alpha \left/ \left(\frac{z(p(w, I))}{\eta(p(w, I))} - (\alpha - 1)\right)\right. .$$

*Proof* Write $p(w, I) = p$. Then

$$\log L(w, I) = \text{const} + \log C(\Theta h(p(w, I))I), \qquad (13')$$

which, on differentiation with respect to $\log w$, yields

$$\epsilon(w, I) = \alpha\eta(p)\frac{w}{p}\frac{\partial p}{\partial w}. \qquad (14')$$

Now

$$\log \gamma(p) = \log w + (\alpha - 1)\log h(p) + \text{const.} \tag{15'}$$

Differentiating (15') with respect to $\log p$ yields

$$\frac{w}{p}\frac{\partial p}{\partial w} = [z(p) + (1 - \alpha)\eta(p)]^{-1}. \tag{16'}$$

Combining (14') with (16') yields the desired result.

RESULT 3 $\lim_{p \to \bar{p}} \sup \delta(p) > 0.$

*Proof* We use an argument similar to that of lemma 1 to show that $(1/(\rho/\epsilon(w, I))) \leq \omega < (1 - \rho)$ is inconsistent with the fact that $wL(w, I) = wqC(\Theta h(p)I) \leq qp\Theta h(p)I \leq q\Theta I.$

*Proof of lemma 2* It follows from result 3 that either $\delta(p) > 0$ for all $0 < p < \bar{p}$ or $\delta(p) = 0$ has a unique solution $\hat{p}$ (uniqueness is implied by A8). In the former case, the unique solution of (14) is $p(I) = p^*(I)$, where $(1/m)C(\Theta h(p^*(I))I) = T.$ In the latter case, A8 implies that the unique solution of (14) is $p(I) = \max(\hat{p}, p^*(I)).$ That the solution to (14) is a Cournot-Nash equilibrium follows from an argument similar to that used in the proof of lemma 1.

*Proof of proposition 1* From lemma 2, if an ICE exists, $p = \max(\hat{p}, p^*(I)).$ But $p = p^*(I)$ implies full employment; i.e., $p = p^*.$ Hence, any ICE satisfies $\tilde{p} = \max(\hat{p}, p^*).$ To prove the existence of an ICE, set $\tilde{I} = (1/\Theta)(m\bar{k}/(1 - \tilde{p}h(\tilde{p}))),$ where $\tilde{p} = \max(\hat{p}, p^*),$ and apply lemma 2.

## Acknowledgments

I am very grateful to Frank Hahn for numerous helpful discussions. I have also benefited from the comments of Philip Dybvig, Sandy Grossman, Louis Makowski, Roy Radner, Bob Rowthorn, Steve Ross, and seminar participants at Johns Hopkins University and the University of Pennsylvania. Finally, I would like to thank an editor and two anonymous referees for helpful suggestions. All errors are, of course, my own. Research support from NSF grant SOC 790/430 is gratefully acknowledged.

## Notes

1. This is not the only approach. Other possibilities are to suppose that prices do not change in response to excess demand or supply for long-term contracting reasons (see, e.g., Azariadis 1975) or because prices are a screening device (see, e.g., Weiss 1980).

2. Other contributions in this area include Benassy (1976, 1978), Grandmont and Laroque (1976), Hahn (1978), and Negishi (1978).

3. Most of the previous contributions that model Keynesian phenomena in terms of imperfect competition assume—in the spirit of Negishi (1960)—that agents act on the basis of conjectured or perceived demand curves, which may not in any sense be the true ones (an exception to this is Hahn 1978). The conjectural approach, in contrast to the Cournot-Nash approach, does not distinguish between small and large economies. In particular, a highly monopolistic outcome can be sustained in a large economy if agents are given appropriate conjectures and a competitive outcome can be sustained in a small economy with different conjectures.

4. An alternative justification can also be given for maximizing wage income. Suppose that each worker is either fully employed or fully unemployed. Suppose also that when the wage is set, workers do not know which category they will be in. Then, if each worker is risk neutral, workers will want syndicates to maximize $(L/mq\rho)wT$, i.e., to maximize $wL$. Note that in this case we get unemployment rather than just underemployment.

5. That is, $U(k', y') \geq U(k, y)$ if $k' \geq k$, $y' \geq y$; $U(k', y) > U(k, y)$ if $k' > k > 0$, $y > 0$; $U(k, y') > U(k, y)$ if $y' > y > 0$, $k > 0$.

6. Furthermore, if a firm changes its production plan, this will have a negligible influence on income in any other market, and hence, there is no reason to expect agents in other markets to react. I am grateful to Philip Dybvig and Steve Ross for pointing out that an earlier version of A2 and A3 was not strong enough to ensure this.

7. Note that the first part of A7 will certainly be satisfied if $\Theta$ is small; i.e., if the product market is approximately perfectly competitive. It will also be satisfied if $|\eta(p)|$ is nondecreasing in $p$. It follows that the first part of A7 holds for the cases where $U(k, y)$ is Cobb-Douglas or involves constant elasticity of substitution. For general utility functions $U(k, y)$ and arbitrary $\Theta$, however, the first part of A7 may not be satisfied. The second part of A7 is made for simplicity and can easily be relaxed.

8. Equation (13) implies, as is to be expected, that the demand for labor will be more elastic the higher is the elasticity of demand for output or the less responsive is marginal revenue to price. It is interesting to note that simplified versions of (13) may be found in Pigou (1933).

9. A8 will be satisfied if the labor market is approximately competitive. Of more interest from our point of view is the fact that it will be satisfied if the product market is perfectly competitive and $|\eta(p)|$ is increasing in $p$.

10. Is this underemployment voluntary or involuntary? It is voluntary in the sense that it would disappear if workers chose not to exercise their monopoly power. On the other hand, it is involuntary in the sense that workers would be willing to work more at the going wage; i.e., the wage exceeds the reservation wage (the latter is zero). For the purpose of this analysis, the distinction between voluntary and involuntary underemployment does not seem of great importance. Of greater interest are the determinants of the equilibrium level of underemployment. Note that (18) will not have a solution if consumers' demand functions exhibit a constant elasticity of demand (unless this elasticity just happens to equal $(1/\alpha - 1 - (\alpha/\rho))$. A constant elasticity of demand everywhere, however, is inconsistent with (1) and (2), unless the constant equals $-1$, i.e., $U$ is Cobb-Douglas. In the Cobb-Douglas case, (18) has no solution (since $\rho < 1$), and so our model predicts full employment.

11. It is also worth reconsidering at this point our assumption that consumers cannot move between markets. Since prices turn out to be the same in all markets in an ICE, the reader may wonder whether this assumption is important. The answer is that it is. For while it is true that in equilibrium consumers would not wish to move, out of equilibrium they might want to. In particular, if a firm in some product market expands and as a result the price in this market falls, this will make consumers want to move from other markets. Thus, if movement is possible, the demand curve facing an individual firm will be considerably more elastic than if, as assumed, movement is not possible.

12. It is straightforward to show that there exists a homothetic utility function $U_\lambda(k, y)$ that generates the demand function $\lambda h(p)I$ as long as $\lambda p h(p) < 1$, and $h'(p) + \lambda h^2(p) < 0$ for all $p$. The latter condition ensures that the Slutsky matrix is negative semidefinite.

13. An alternative policy that the government might adopt to increase demand for the produced good is to subsidize consumption through the use of commodity subsidies.

14. If the increasing returns are mild enough, lemma 1 will continue to hold. With strongly increasing returns, however, it seems that a Cournot-Nash equilibrium may not exist in the product market.

15. Multiple equilibria may also occur in the model of sections 2 and 3 in the absence of A7 and A8. (Without A7 and A8, however, there is no guarantee that an ICE will exist at all; see remark $D$ of this section.)

16. As in, for example, Kaldor (1956).

17. To put it somewhat differently, imperfect competition by itself cannot explain the non-neutrality of money, since the marginal revenue equals marginal cost conditions are conditions about relative and not absolute prices.

# References

Azariadis, C., "Implicit Contracts and Underemployment Equilibria," *Journal of Political Economy*, 83 (1975), 1183–1202.

Benassy, J. P., "The Disequilibrium Approach to Monopolistic Price Setting and General Monopolistic Equilibrium," *Review of Economic Studies*, 43 (1976), 69–81.

Benassy, J. P., "A Neo-Keynesian Model of Price and Quantity Determination in Disequilibrium," in *Equilibrium and Disequilibrium in Economic Theory*, G. Schwodiauer, ed., proceedings of a conference held in Vienna (1978).

Chamberlin, E. H., *The Theory of Monopolistic Competition* (Cambridge: Harvard University Press, 1933).

Clower, R. W., "The Keynesian Counterrevolution: A Theoretical Appraisal," in *The Theory of Interest Rates*, Hahn and Brechling, eds. (London: Macmillan, 1965).

Grandmont, J. M., "Temporary General Equilibrium Theory," *Econometrica*, 43 (1977), 535–572.

Grandmont, J. M., and G. Laroque, "On Keynesian Temporary Equilibria," *Review of Economic Studies*, 43 (1976), 53–67.

Hahn, F. H., "On Non-Walrasian Equilibria," *Review of Economic Studies*, 45 (1978), 1–17.

Hart, O., "A Model of Imperfect Competition with Keynesian Features," Economic Theory Discussion Paper, University of Cambridge, 1980.

Harrod, R., "An Essay in Dynamic Theory," *Economic Journal*, 49 (1939), 14–33.

Kaldor, N., "Alternative Theories of Distribution," *Review of Economic Studies*, 23 (1956), 83–100.

Kalecki, M., *Theory of Economic Dynamics: An Essay on Cyclical and Long-Run Changes in a Capitalist Economy* (London: Allen and Unwin, 1954).

Leijonhufvud, A., *On Keynesian Economics and the Economics of Keynes* (London: Oxford University Press, 1968).

McManus, M., "Numbers and Size in Cournot Oligopoly," *Yorkshire Bulletin*, 14 (1962), 14–22.

Negishi, T., "Monopolistic Competition and General Equilibrium," *Review of Economic Studies*, 28 (1960), 196–201.

Negishi, T., "Existence of an Underemployment Equilibrium," in *Equilibrium and Disequilibrium in Economic Theory*, G. Schwodiauer, ed., proceedings of a conference held in Vienna (1978).

Pigou, A. C., *The Theory of Unemployment* (London: Macmillan, 1933).

Roberts, J., and H. Sonnenschein, "On the Existence of Cournot Equilibrium without Concave Profit Functions," *Journal of Economic Theory*, 13 (1976), 112–117.

Roberts, J., and H. Sonnenschein, "On the Foundations of the Theory of Monopolistic Competition," *Econometrica*, 45 (1979), 101–114.

*Symposium in Journal of Economic Theory on Noncooperative Approaches to Competitive Equilibrium* (April 1980).

Weiss, A., "Job Queues and Layoffs in Labor Markets with Flexible Wages," *Journal of Political Economy*, 88 (1980), 526–538.

# 13 Monopolistic Competition and the Effects of Aggregate Demand

Olivier Jean Blanchard and Nobuhiro Kiyotaki

Monopolistic competition provides a convenient conceptual framework in which to think about price decisions and appears to describe many markets more accurately than perfect competition. But how important is monopolistic competition for macroeconomics? In particular, how important is monopolistic competition to an understanding of the effects of aggregate demand on economic activity? This is the question we analyze in this paper.

One can ask the question at three levels. First, using perfect competition as a benchmark, can monopolistic competition by itself explain why aggregate demand movements affect output? Second, can monopolistic competition together with some other imperfection generate effects of aggregate demand in a way that perfect competition cannot? Third, if aggregate demand movements affect output, can monopolistic competition give a more accurate account of the response of the economy to aggregate demand shocks? The paper analyzes these three questions in turn.

Section 1 builds a simple general equilibrium model with goods, labor, and money, and monopolistic competition in both the goods and the labor markets. It then characterizes the equilibrium. Section 2 characterizes the inefficiency associated with monopolistic competition and shows that it is associated with an aggregate demand externality. It shows that this externality cannot, however, explain why pure aggregate demand movements affect output. In particular, it cannot explain why changes in nominal money have real effects. The answer to the first question is therefore negative. Section 3 studies the effects of "menu costs" when combined with monopolistic competition. It shows that small (second-order) costs of changing prices may lead to large (first-order) changes in output and welfare in response to changes in nominal money. It shows the close relation between this result and the aggregate demand externality identified in section 2. The answer to the second question is therefore positive. Section 4 takes as given that prices and wages do not adjust to movements in nominal money and draws the implications of monopolistic competition with fixed costs for the behavior of output, productivity, profits, and entry by new firms in response to fluctuations in aggregate demand. These implications fit the facts, and our answer to the third question is positive.

*American Economic Review* 77 (September 1987): 647–666. Copyright © 1987 by the American Economic Association. Reprinted with permission.

We conclude by discussing how the implications for entry may in turn help explain the lack of adjustment of prices and wages.

Our paper is closely related to three recent strands of research on general equilibrium implications of monopolistic competition (Hart 1982 and Weitzman 1982, in particular), on "menu costs" or "near rationality" (Mankiw, 1985, Akerlof and Yellen 1985a, 1985b), and on "coordination failures" (Cooper and John 1985, in particular). We shall point out specific relations as we proceed. Our intent is in part to show their relation and macroeconomic implications in the specific context of monopolistic competition.

## 1   A Model of Monopolistic Competition

In developing a model of monopolistic competition, we make four main choices. Because we want to focus on both wage and price decisions, we construct a model with both households and firms and with separate labor and goods markets. Both labor and goods markets are monopolistically competitive. The assumption of monopolistic competition in both sets of markets is made for symmetry and transparence rather than for realism. For some purposes, however, the model that has both wage and price setters is not the simplest, and we also occasionally focus on a special case that can be thought of as an economy of household-firms, each producing a differentiated good; in that case, there is only one set of price setters and the analysis is simplified.

The second choice follows from the need to avoid Say's Law, or the result that the supply of goods produced by the monopolistically competitive firms automatically generates its own demand. To avoid this, agents must have the choice between these goods and something else. In the standard macroeconomic model, the choice is between consumption and savings. In other models of monopolistic competition, the choice is between produced goods and a nonproduced good (Hart 1982, for example). Here, we shall assume that the choice is between buying goods and holding money. This is most simply and crudely achieved by having real money balances in the utility function. Thus, money plays the role of the nonproduced good and provides services.[1] Money is also the numeraire, so that firms and workers quote prices and wages in terms of money; this plays no role in this and the next section but will become important in section 3.

The third choice is to make assumptions about utility and technology that lead to demand and pricing relations, which are as close to traditional ones as possible, so as to allow an easy comparison with standard macroeconomic models. In effect, we follow Dixit and Stiglitz (1977) in adopting constant elasticity of substitution specifications in utility and production.[2] These specifications lead to log-linear demand and pricing functions, and rule out potentially important nonlinearities as well as a potential source of multiple equilibria.[3]

Finally, the model is static, and we leave the potentially important dynamic implications of monopolistic competition to future work.[4]

**The model**

The economy is composed of $m$ firms, each producing a specific good that is an imperfect substitute for the other goods, and $n$ consumer-workers, households for short, each of them selling a type of labor which is an imperfect substitute for the other types. As a result, each firm and each worker has some monopoly power.[5] We now describe the problem faced by each firm and each household.

*Firms* are indexed by $i$, $i = 1, \ldots, m$. Each firm $i$ has the following technology:

$$Y_i = \left( \sum_{j=1}^{n} N_{ij}^{((\sigma-1)/\sigma)} \right)^{(\sigma/(\sigma-1))(1/\alpha)}, \tag{1}$$

where $Y_i$ denotes the output of firm $i$. $N_{ij}$ denotes the quantity of labor of type $j$ used in the production of output $i$. There are $n$ different types of labor, indexed $j, j = 1, \ldots, n$. The production function is a CES production function, with all inputs entering symmetrically. Introducing fixed costs would not affect the analysis of the first three sections where we assume the number of firms to be fixed; we shall for simplicity introduce them only in the last section, where they matter.

The two parameters characterizing the technology are $\alpha$ and $\sigma$. The parameter $\sigma$ is the elasticity of substitution of inputs in production. The parameter $\alpha$ is the inverse of the degree of returns to scale; $\alpha - 1$ is the elasticity of marginal cost with respect to output, "elasticity of marginal cost" for short in what follows. To guarantee the existence of an equilibrium, we restrict $\sigma$ to be strictly greater than unity, and $\alpha$ to be equal to or greater than unity.

The firm maximizes profits. Nominal profits for firm $i$ are given by

$$V_i = P_i Y_i - \sum_{j=1}^{n} W_j N_{ij}, \tag{2}$$

where $P_i$ denotes the nominal output price of firm $i$, and $W_j$ denotes the nominal wage associated with labor type $j$. The firm maximizes (2) subject to the production function (1). It takes as given nominal wages and the prices of the other outputs. It also faces a downward-sloping demand schedule for its product, that will be derived below as a result of utility maximization by households. We assume that the number of firms is large enough that taking other prices as given is equivalent to taking the price level as given.

*Households* are indexed by $j, j = 1, \ldots, n$. Household $j$ supplies labor of type $j$. It derives utility from leisure, consumption, and real money balances. Its utility function is given by

$$U_j = (m^{1/(1-\theta)} C_j)^{\gamma} (M_j'/P)^{1-\gamma} - N_j^{\beta}, \tag{3}$$

where $\quad C_j = \left( \sum_{i=1}^{m} C_{ij}^{(\theta-1)/\theta} \right)^{(\theta/(\theta-1))} \quad$ and $\quad P = \left( \frac{1}{m} \sum_{i=1}^{m} P_i^{1-\theta} \right)^{1/(1-\theta)}.$

The first term in utility is a consumption index (basket) that gives the effect of the consumption of goods on utility. $C_{ij}$ denotes the consumption of good $i$ by household $j$, and $C_j$ is a CES function of the $C_{ij}$s. All types of consumption goods enter utility symmetrically. The parameter $\theta$ is the elasticity of substitution between goods in utility. To guarantee existence of an equilibrium, $\theta$ is restricted to be greater than unity. The constant in front of $C_j$, that depends on $\theta$ and on the number of products $m$, is a convenient normalization with the implication that an increase in the number of products does not affect marginal utility after optimization.

The second term gives the effect of real money balances on utility. $\gamma$ is a parameter between zero and one. Nominal money balances are deflated by the nominal price index associated with $C_j$. We shall refer to $P$ as the price level.

The third term in utility gives the disutility from work; $N_j$ is the amount of labor supplied by household $j$. The term $\beta - 1$ is the elasticity of marginal disutility of labor; $\beta$ is assumed to be equal to or greater than unity.[6]

Households maximize utility subject to a budget constraint. Each household takes prices and other wages as given. Again, we assume that $n$ is large enough that taking other wages as given is equivalent to taking the nominal wage level as given. It also faces a downward-sloping demand schedule for its type of labor, which will be derived as the result of profit maximization by firms. The budget constraint is given by

$$\sum_{i=1}^{m} P_i C_{ij} + M_j' = W_j N_j + M_j + \sum_{i=1}^{m} V_{ij}, \tag{4}$$

where $M_j$ denotes the initial endowment of money and $V_{ij}$ is the share of profits of firm $i$ going to household $j$.

### The equilibrium

The derivation of the equilibrium is given in the appendix. The equilibrium can be characterized by *a relation between real money balances and aggregate demand, a pair of demand functions* for goods and labor, and by *a pair of price and wage rules*.

The relation between real money balances and real aggregate consumption expenditures, which we shall call aggregate demand for short, is given by

$$Y = K(M/P), \tag{5}$$

where

$$Y \equiv \left( \sum_{j=1}^{n} \sum_{i=1}^{m} P_i C_{ij} \right) \Big/ P \tag{6}$$

and

$$P \equiv \left( (1/m) \sum_{i=1}^{m} P_i^{1-\theta} \right)^{1/(1-\theta)}.$$

The demand functions for goods and labor are given by

$$Y_i = \sum_{j=1}^{n} C_{ij} = K_c Y (P_i/P)^{-\theta} \qquad i = 1, \dots, m \tag{7}$$

$$N_j = \sum_{i=1}^{m} N_{ij} = K_n Y^{\alpha} (W_j/W)^{-\sigma} \qquad j = 1, \dots, n \tag{8}$$

where the wage index $W$ is given by

$$W = \left( \frac{1}{n} \sum_{j=1}^{n} W_j^{1-\sigma} \right)^{1/(1-\sigma)}. \tag{9}$$

The price and wage rules are given by

$$(P_i/P) = [(\theta/(\theta - 1))K_p(W/P)Y^{\alpha-1}]^{1/(1+\theta(\alpha-1))}, \quad i = 1, \ldots, m, \quad (10)$$

$$(W_j/W) = [(\sigma/(\sigma - 1))K_w(P/W)Y^{\alpha(\beta-1)}]^{1/(1+\sigma(\beta-1))}, \quad j = 1, \ldots, n. \quad (11)$$

The letters $K$, $K_c$, $K_n$, $K_p$, and $K_w$ are constants that depend on the parameters of the technology and the utility function as well as the number of firms and households.

We interpret these equations, starting with the relation between real money balances and aggregate demand. First-order conditions for households imply that desired real money balances are proportional to consumption expenditures. Aggregating over households and using the fact that in equilibrium, desired money is equal to actual money gives equation (5).

The demand for each type of good relative to aggregate demand is a function of the ratio of its nominal price to the nominal price index, the price level, with elasticity $(-\theta)$. The demand for labor by firms is a derived demand for labor; it depends on the demand for goods. The demand for each type of labor is a function of the ratio of its nominal wage to the nominal wage index, with elasticity $(-\sigma)$.

We now consider the *price rule*. Given the price level, each firm is a monopolist and decides about its real (or relative) price $P_i/P$. An increase in the real wage $(W/P)$ shifts the marginal cost curve upward, leading to an increase in the relative price. An increase in aggregate demand shifts the demand curve for each product upward; if the firm operates under decreasing returns, the marginal cost curve is upward sloping, and the relative price increases. Under constant returns, the shift in demand has no effect on the relative price.

We finally consider the *wage rule*, equation (11). We can think of households as solving their utility-maximization problem in two steps. They first solve for the allocation of their wealth, including labor income, between consumption of the different products and real money balances. After this step the assumption that utility is linearly homogeneous in consumption and real money balances implies that utility is linear in wealth and thus linear in labor income. The next step is to solve for the level of labor supply and the nominal wage. Given that utility is linear in labor income, we can think of households as monopolists maximizing the surplus from supplying labor. Formally, if $\mu$ denotes the constant marginal utility of real wealth, households solve in the second step:

$$\max \mu(W_j/P)N_j - N_j^\beta; \qquad N_j = K_n Y^\alpha(W_j/W)^{-\sigma}.$$

The real wage relevant for worker $j$ is $W_j/P$, which we can write as the product $(W_j/W)(W/P)$. The demand for labor of type $j$ is a function of the relative wage $(W_j/W)$ as well as of aggregate demand.

An increase in the aggregate real wage $(W/P)$ leads household $j$ to increase its labor supply, and to decrease its relative wage $(W_j/W)$. An increase in aggregate demand leads, if $\beta$ is strictly greater than unity, to an increase in the relative wage. If $\beta$ is equal to unity, if the marginal disutility of labor is constant, workers supply more labor at the same relative wage, in response to an increase in aggregate demand.

### Symmetric equilibrium

Equilibrium and symmetry, both across firms and across households, implies that all relative prices and all relative wages must be equal to unity. Thus, using $P_i = P$ for all $i$ and $W_j = W$ for all $j$, and substituting in equations (10) and (11) gives

$$(P/W) = (\theta/\theta - 1))K_p Y^{\alpha-1}; \tag{12}$$

$$(W/P) = (\sigma/(\sigma - 1))K_w Y^{\alpha(\beta-1)}. \tag{13}$$

Equation (12), obtained from the individual price rules and the requirement that all prices be the same, gives the price wage ratio $(P/W)$ as a function of output. If firms operate under strictly decreasing returns, the price wage ratio is an increasing function of the level of output. Equivalently, the real wage $(W/P)$ consistent with firms' behavior is a decreasing function of output. We shall refer to equation (12) as the "aggregate price rule."

Equation (13), obtained from the individual wage rules and the requirement that all wages be the same, gives the real wage $(W/P)$ as a function of output. If $\beta$ is strictly greater than unity, that is, if workers have increasing marginal disutility of work, an increase in output, that leads to an increase in the derived demand for labor, requires an increase in the real wage. The real wage consistent with households' behavior is an increasing function of output. We shall refer to equation (13) as the "aggregate wage rule."

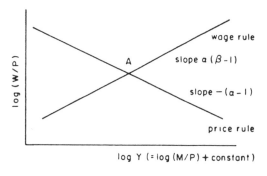

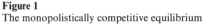

**Figure 1**
The monopolistically competitive equilibrium

Equations (12) and (13) give $(W/P)$ and $Y$. The value of $(M/P)$ follows from (5). The equilibrium is characterized graphically in figure 1. As (12) and (13) are log-linear, we measure $\log(W/P)$ on the vertical axis and $\log(Y)$ (or $\log(M/P)$ as the two are linearly related) on the horizontal axis. If $\alpha$ and $\beta$ are both strictly greater than unity, the aggregate wage rule is upward sloping, while the aggregate price rule is downward sloping. The equilibrium determines the real wage and output. Given output, we obtain the equilibrium level of real money balances, and given nominal money, we finally obtain the price level.

Figure 1 looks like the characterization of equilibrium under perfect competition with an upward-sloping labor supply curve and a downward-sloping labor demand. What is the effect of monopolistic competition? Before turning to that issue, we briefly consider a special case of the model that will be convenient later.

**A convenient special case**

In the special case of the model where the marginal utility of leisure is constant so that $\beta = 1$, the characterization of the equilibrium is much simpler. The relation between real money balances and aggregate demand is still given by equation (5). But from equation (11) and symmetry, the real wage is constant, so that the price rules are now given by

$$P_i/P = k(M/P)^{(\alpha-1)/(1+\theta(\alpha-1))}, \qquad (14)$$

where $k$ is an unimportant constant. Equations (5) and (14) characterize the equilibrium. The symmetric equilibrium is identical to that in figure 1 except for the fact that the aggregate wage rule is horizontal.

This special case is convenient as it allow us to concentrate on the interactions between price setters rather than the interactions between both price and wage setters. The assumption of constant marginal utility of leisure is unattractive, but equations (5) and (14) admit an alternative interpretation: they can also be derived as the equations characterizing the equilibrium of an economy with many household-firms, each producing a differentiated good with a constant-returns technology and increasing marginal disutility of work, and deriving utility from the consumption of all goods and money services.[7] Under that interpretation, $(\alpha - 1)$ stands for the elasticity of marginal utility of leisure.

## 2  Inefficiency and Externalities

### Comparing monopolistic competition and perfect competition

To characterize the inefficiency associated with monopolistic competition, we first compare the equilibrium to the competitive equilibrium. The competitive equilibrium is derived under the same assumptions about tastes, technology, and the number of firms and households but on the assumption that each firm (each household) takes its price (wage) as given when deciding about its output (labor).

The competitive equilibrium is very similar to the monopolistically competitive one. The demand functions for goods and labor are still given by equations (7) and (8). The price and wage rules are identical to equations (10) and (11), except for the absence of $\theta/(\theta - 1)$ in the price rules and the absence of $\sigma/(\sigma - 1)$ in the wage rules (the $K$s are the same in both equilibria). The explanation is simple. The term $\theta/(\theta - 1)$ is the excess of price over marginal cost, and reflecting the degree of monopoly power of firms in the goods market; if firms act competitively, price is instead equal to marginal cost. The same explanation applies to households.

Again, symmetry requires in equilibrium all prices and all wages to be the same; this gives equations identical to (12) and (13) but without the terms $\theta/(\theta - 1)$ and $\sigma/(\sigma - 1)$. The price-wage ratio consistent with firms' behavior is lower in the competitive case by $\theta/(\theta - 1)$ at any level of output; the real wage consistent with households' behavior is lower in the competitive case by $\sigma/(\sigma - 1)$ at any level of output. The monopolistically competitive and competitive aggregate wage and price rules are drawn in figure 2. Point $A'$ gives the competitive equilibrium; point $A$ gives the monopolistically competitive equilibrium.

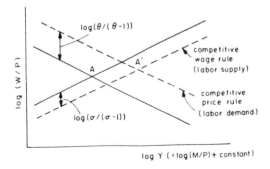

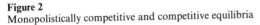

**Figure 2**
Monopolistically competitive and competitive equilibria

The equilibrium level of real money balances is lower in the monopolistic equilibrium; the price level is higher. Employment and output are lower. What happens to the real wage is ambiguous and depends on the degrees of monopoly power in the goods and the labor markets. If, for example, there is monopolistic competition in the labor market, then the real wage is unambiguously lower under monopolistic competition.

Denoting by $R$ the ratio of output in the monopolistically competitive equilibrium to output in the competitive equilibrium, $R$ is given by

$$R = \left( \frac{\sigma - 1}{\sigma} \frac{\theta - 1}{\theta} \right)^{1/(\alpha\beta - 1)} < 1,$$

where $R$ is an increasing function of $\sigma$ and $\theta$. The higher the elasticity of substitution between goods or between types of labor, the closer is the economy to the competitive equilibrium. $R$ is an increasing function of $\alpha$ and $\beta$. If $\alpha$ and $\beta$ are both close to unity, $R$ is small: the existence of monopoly power in either the goods or the labor markets can have a large effect on equilibrium output.[8]

**Aggregate demand externalities**

Under monopolistic competition, output of monopolistically produced goods is too low. We have shown above that this follows from the existence of monopoly power in price and wage setting. An alternative way of thinking about it is that it follows from an aggregate demand externality.

The argument is as follows. In the monopolistically competitive equilibrium, each price (wage) setter has, given other prices, no incentive to decrease its own price (wage) and increase its output (labor). Suppose however that all price setters decrease their prices simultaneously; this increases real money balances and aggregate demand. The increase in output reduces the initial distortion of underproduction and underemployment and increases social welfare.[9]

We now make the argument more precise. By the definition of a monopolistically competitive equilibrium, no firm has an incentive to decrease its price, and no worker has an incentive to decrease its wage, given other prices and wages. Consider now a proportional decrease in all wages and all prices, $(dP_i/P_i) = (dW_j/w_j) < 0$, for all $i$ and $j$, that leaves all relative prices unchanged but decreases the price level.

Consider first the change in the real value of firms.[10] At a given level of output and employment, the real value of each firm is unchanged. The decrease in the price level, however, increases real money balances and aggregate demand. This in turn shifts outward the demand curve faced by each firm and increases profit: an increase in demand at a given relative price increases profit as price exceeds marginal cost. Thus, the real value of each firm increases.

Consider then the effect of a proportional reduction of prices and wages on the utility of each household. Consider household $j$. We have seen that, once the household has chosen the allocation of his wealth between real money balances and consumption, we can write its utility as $U_j = \mu(I_j/P) - N_j^\beta$, where $\mu$ is the constant marginal utility of real wealth and $I_j$ is the total wealth of the $j$th household. Using the budget constraint, we can express utility as

$$U_j = [\mu(W_j/P)N_j - N_j^\beta] + \mu \sum_{i=1}^{m} V_{ij}/P + \mu(M_j/P).$$

Utility is the sum of three terms. The second is profit income in terms of utility; we have seen that each firm's profit goes up after an increase in aggregate demand. Thus this term increases. The first term is the household's surplus from supplying labor. At a given level of employment $N_j$, the proportional change in wages and prices leaves this term unchanged. But the increase in aggregate demand and the implied derived increase in employment implies that this term increases: at a given real wage, an outward shift in the demand for labor increases utility, as the real wage initially exceeds the marginal utility of leisure. The third term is the real value of the money stock, which increases with the fall in the price level. Thus utility unambiguously increases.[11]

The aggregate demand externality implies that underproduction is magnified through macroeconomic interactions. Consider the problem faced by an individual firm, with upward-sloping marginal cost and downward-sloping demand, taking as given other prices and aggregate demand. Because the marginal utility of wealth is constant under our assumption, we can measure welfare by looking at the sum of consumers' and producers' surplus. If the firm acted competitively rather than as a monopolist, the price would be lower and the surplus would be larger. This is the familiar partial-equilibrium effect. But here, in addition, if all firms acted competitively and decreased their prices, aggregate demand would be higher and the demand curve facing each firm would shift to the right, and welfare would be further increased. This is the additional general equilibrium effect present here.

Identifying the inefficiency associated with monopolistic competition as an aggregate demand externality does not, however, imply that movements in aggregate demand affect output. Aggregate-demand changes associated with changes in the demand elasticities facing firms and workers will have real effects, and these effects are likely to be different under perfect and monopolistic competition. These are not, however, the effects we want to focus on. For that reason, we shall concentrate on changes in nominal money. But then it is clear that as equations (12) and (13) are homogeneous of degree zero in $P$, $W$, and $M$, nominal money is neutral, affecting all nominal prices and wages proportionately and leaving output and employment unchanged. Thus something else is needed to obtain real effects of nominal money. We examine the effects of costs of price setting in the next section.

## 3   Menu Costs and Real Effects of Nominal Money

We now introduce small costs of setting prices, small "menu" costs. Akerlof and Yellen (1985a, 1985b) and Mankiw (1985) have shown how such small costs can lead to large welfare effects in imperfectly competitive economies.[12] We apply their argument of the specific context of monopolistic competition, derive welfare and output effects as explicit functions of the underlying parameters, and relate these effects to the externality identified earlier.

### The effects of small changes in nominal money

We start by considering the effects of a small change in nominal money, $dM$. The intuitive argument is the following.

At the initial nominal prices and wages, the change in nominal money leads to a change in aggregate demand, thus to a change in the demand facing each firm. If demand is satisfied, the change in output implies in turn a change in the derived demand for labor, thus a change in the demand facing each worker. Unless firms operate under constant returns, each firm wants to change its relative price. Unless workers have constant marginal utility of leisure, each worker wants to change his relative wage. The loss in value to a firm which does not adjust its relative price is, however, of second order; the same is true of the utility of a worker who does not adjust his relative wage. Thus second-order menu costs may prevent firms and workers from adjusting relative prices and wages. The implication is that nominal prices and nominal wages do not adjust to the change in nominal money. The second part of the argument is to show that the change in real money balances has first-order effects on welfare; we show that it is indeed first order, and of the same sign as the change in money. The argument has very much the same structure as the aggregate demand externality argument of the previous section. This coincidence is not accidental, and we return to it below.

The first part is a direct application of the envelope theorem. Consider firms first. Let $V_i$ be the value of firm $i$. $V_i$ is a function of $P_i$ as well as of $P$, $W$, and $M (V_i = V_i(P_i, P, W, M))$. Let $V_i^*$ be the maximized value of firm $i$ after maximization over $P_i$; $V_i^* = V_i^*(P, W, M)$. The envelope theorem then says that

$$dV_i^*/dM = \partial V_i/\partial M + (\partial V_i/\partial P_i)(dP_i/dM)$$

$$= \partial V_i/\partial M.$$

To a first order, the effect of a change in $M$ on the value of the firm is the same whether or not it adjusts its price optimally in response to the change in $M$. Exactly the same argument applies to the utility of the household. Thus, second-order menu costs (larger than the second-order loss in utility or in value) will prevent each firm from changing its price given other prices and wages and each worker from changing its wage given other prices and wages. The implication is that all nominal prices and wages remain unchanged and that the increase in nominal money implies a proportional increase in real money balances.

What remains to be shown is that the increase in real money balances has positive first-order effects on welfare. However, we have already shown in the previous section that the increase in real money balances associated with the increase in aggregate demand and employment raises firms' profits and the households' surpluses from supplying labor. Thus it increases welfare in the neighborhood of the monopolistically competitive equilibrium.

There is clearly a close relation between the *aggregate demand externality and the menu-cost argument* of this section. This relation is most simply shown in the special case where the marginal utility of leisure is constant, where there are no menu costs in wage setting, and where we can concentrate on the interactions between price setters only. Equation (14), which gives the individual price rules in the absence of menu costs, can be rewritten as

$$P_i/M = k(P/M)^{[1+(\theta-1)(\alpha-1)]/(1+\theta(\alpha-1))}. \tag{15}$$

Figure 3 plots the price chosen by firm $i$ as a function of the price level, both as ratios to nominal money. In the presence of monopoly power, the price rule has a slope smaller than one. We also draw iso-profit loci, giving combinations of $(P_i/M)$ and $(P/M)$ that yield the same level of real profit for the firm.[13] The symmetric monopolistically competitive equilibrium is

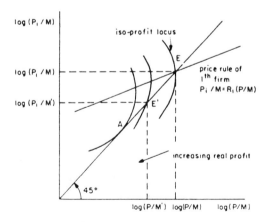

**Figure 3**
Aggregate-demand externalities and menu costs

given by the intersection of the price rule and the 45° line, point $E$. Point $A$ gives the highest real profit point on the 45° line.

The aggregate demand externality argument can then be stated as follows. Consider a *small proportional decrease of prices* keeping nominal money constant. The equilibrium moves from point $E$ to a point like $E'$ along the 45° line. The profit of each firm rises with the increase in aggregate demand. However, in the absence of coordination, no firm has an incentive to reduce prices away from the equilibrium point $E$.

The menu-cost argument considers instead a *small increase in nominal money*. At the initial set of prices, real money balances would increase and the economy would move from point $E$ to a point like $E'$. But, absent menu costs, each firm would find it in its interest to increase its price until the economy had returned to point $E$. In the presence of menu costs, however, these menu cost, if large enough, can prevent this movement back to $E$, so that the economy remains at $E'$ and all firms end up with higher real profits. (A similar argument, although slightly more complicated, holds for the general model. We will not present it here.)

It is also important to note the *specific role played by money* in this section. The presence of an aggregate demand externality does not depend on the nature of the nonproduced good, or on the nature of the numeraire. The results of this section depend on money being the nonproduced good and the numeraire. That money is the numeraire implies that given menu costs, unchanged prices and wages mean unchanged nominal prices and wages. That money is the nonproduced good implies that as the government can vary the amount of nominal money, it can, if nominal prices and wages do not adjust, change the amount of real money balances, the real quantity of the nonproduced good.

### The effects of larger changes in nominal money

For larger changes in money, the private opportunity costs of not adjusting prices in response to the change in money (private costs, for short) are no longer negligible and depend on the parameters of the model. We now investigate this dependence.

The *private costs* faced by a firm depend on the size of the demand shifts as well as on the two parameters $\alpha$ and $\theta$. As we have seen, these costs are of second order in response to a change in aggregate demand, and roughly proportional to the square of the change in aggregate demand. More precisely, define $L(\Delta; \alpha, \theta)$ to be the private opportunity cost to a firm expressed as a proportion of initial revenues, associated with not adjusting its price in response to a change of $100\Delta\%$ in aggregate demand, when all other firms and households keep their prices and wages unchanged. Then, by simple computation, we get

$$L(\Delta; \alpha, \theta) = \frac{[(\alpha - 1)^2(\theta - 1)]}{[2(1 + \theta(\alpha - 1))]} \Delta^2 + 0(\Delta^2),$$

where $0(\Delta^2)$ is of third order.

The closer $\alpha$ is to one, that is, the closer to constant returns to scale, the smaller the private cost. In the limit, if $\alpha$ is equal to one, then private costs of not adjusting prices are equal to zero, as the optimal response of a monopolist to a multiplicative shift in iso-elastic demand under constant marginal cost is to leave the price unchanged. Thus private costs are an increasing function of $\alpha$. They are also an increasing function of $\theta$; the higher the elasticity of demand with respect to price, the higher the private costs of not adjusting prices.

Exactly the same analysis applies to workers. The two important parameters for them are $\beta$ and $\sigma$. If we define the function $L$ in the same way as above, the private opportunity cost to a worker (measured in terms of consumption and expressed as a proportion of initial consumption) associated with not adjusting the wage in response to a change of $100\Delta\%$ in aggregate demand when all other firms and households keep their prices and wages unchanged, is given by $[(\theta - 1)/\theta\alpha]L((1 + \Delta)^\alpha - 1; \beta, \sigma)$, where $(\theta - 1)/\theta\alpha$ is the initial share of wage income in GNP.

If $\beta$ is close to unity, that is, if the elasticity of the marginal disutility of labor is close to unity, private costs of not adjusting wages are small. In the limit, if marginal disutility of labor is constant, private costs are equal to zero. If $\sigma$ is very large, if different types of labor are close substitutes, private costs of not adjusting wages are high.

Table 1, part a, gives the size of menu costs as a proportion of the firm's revenues (GNP produced by the firm) that are just sufficient to prevent a firm from adjusting its price in response to a change in demand. Table 1, part b, gives the size of menu costs as a proportion of initial consumption (GNP consumed by the worker) that are just sufficient to prevent a worker from adjusting his (her) wage.

Thus, given the unit elasticity of aggregate demand with respect to real money balances and the assumption that all other prices have not changed, part a of table 1 gives the private costs to the firm associated with not

**Table 1**
Changes in aggregate demand and menu costs

| (a) Loss in value to a firm from not adjusting prices (as a proportion of initial revenues) (%) | | | | (b) Loss in utility (in terms of consumption) to a worker from not adjusting wages (as a proportion of initial consumption) (%)[a] | | | |
| --- | --- | --- | --- | --- | --- | --- | --- |
| | | $M_1/M_0 =$ | | | | $M_1/M_0 =$ | |
| $\alpha$ | $\theta$ | 1.05 | 1.10 | $\beta$ | $\sigma$ | 1.05 | 1.10 |
| 1.0 | 5 | .000 | .000 | 1.2 | 5 | .025 | .100 |
| 1.1 | 5 | .003 | .013 | 1.4 | 5 | .066 | .265 |
| 1.1 | 2 | .001 | .004 | 1.4 | 2 | .027 | .111 |
| | 20 | .008 | .031 | | 20 | .105 | .418 |
| 1.3 | 5 | .018 | .071 | 1.6 | 5 | .112 | .451 |

Notes: $M_0$ is the initial level of nominal money; $M_1$ the level after the change.
a. $\theta = 5$; $\alpha = 1.1$.

changing prices in the face of 5 and 10 percent changes in demand to the firm. The main conclusion is that very small menu costs, say less than .08 percent of revenues, may be sufficient to prevent adjustment of prices. Results are qualitatively similar for workers. Part b of table 1 gives the private costs of not changing wages in response to changes of + 5 and + 10 percent in the demand for goods. It assumes that $\alpha$ is equal to 1.1, so that changes in the derived demand for labor are 5.5 and 11 percent approximately. We expect $\beta$ to be higher than $\alpha$, so part b of table 1 looks at values of $\beta$ between 1.2 and 1.6. For values of $\beta$ close to unity, required menu costs are again very small. As $\beta$ increases however, required menu costs become non-negligible: for $\beta = 1.6$ and an 11 percent change in demand, they reach .45 percent of initial consumption, a number which is no longer negligible.

The more relevant comparison, however, at least from the point of view of welfare, is between private costs and *welfare effects*, that is, the change in utility resulting from the changes in output, employment, and real money that are implied by a change in nominal money at given prices and wages. Welfare effects depend on the size of the change in nominal money as well as on the parameters $\alpha$, $\beta$, $\theta$, and $\sigma$; the dependence is a complex one and we shall not analyze it here in detail. Table 2 gives numerical examples. It gives the required menu costs and welfare effects associated with two different changes in nominal money (5 and 10 percent), and different values of the structural parameters.

**Table 2**
Menu costs and welfare effects

| | | $M_1/M_0 = 1.05$ | | | $M_1/M_0 = 1.10$ | | |
|---|---|---|---|---|---|---|---|
| $\alpha$ | $\beta$ | Menu costs (%) | Welfare effects (%) | Ratio | Menu costs (%) | Welfare effects (%) | Ratio |
| $(\theta = \sigma = 5)$ | | | | | | | |
| 1.1 | 1.2 | .03 | 1.79 | 60 | .11 | 3.54 | 32 |
| | 1.4 | .07 | 1.83 | 26 | .28 | 3.60 | 13 |
| | 1.6 | .11 | 1.91 | 17 | .46 | 3.72 | 8 |
| 1.2 | 1.2 | .04 | 1.82 | 45 | .15 | 3.57 | 24 |
| | 1.4 | .08 | 1.87 | 24 | .33 | 3.67 | 11 |
| | 1.6 | .13 | 1.98 | 15 | .53 | 3.85 | 7 |
| $(\theta = \sigma = 10)$ | | | | | | | |
| 1.1 | 1.2 | .03 | .94 | 31 | .11 | 1.86 | 17 |
| | 1.4 | .06 | 1.02 | 17 | .23 | 1.93 | 8 |
| | 1.6 | .09 | 1.11 | 12 | .36 | 2.05 | 6 |
| 1.2 | 1.2 | .04 | .99 | 25 | .16 | 1.87 | 12 |
| | 1.4 | .07 | 1.07 | 16 | .29 | 2.01 | 7 |
| | 1.6 | .11 | 1.27 | 12 | .44 | 2.24 | 5 |

For each of the two changes in money, the first column gives the minimum value of menu costs, expressed as a proportion of GNP, that prevents adjustment of nominal prices and wages. This value is the sum of menu costs required to prevent firms from adjusting their prices and workers from adjusting their wages given other wages and prices. The second column gives the welfare effects of an increase in nominal money at unchanged prices and wages, expressed in terms of consumption, again as a proportion of GNP. The third gives the ratio of welfare effects to menu costs.

Welfare effects turn out to be not much affected by the specific values of the parameters, at least for the range of values we consider in the table. Thus the ratio of welfare effects to menu cost has the same qualitative behavior as that of the ratio of output movement to menu costs. It is largest for values of $\alpha$, $\beta$, $\theta$, and $\sigma$ close to unity and decreases as these parameters increase. In the table it varies from 60 for low values of $\alpha$, $\beta$, $\theta$, and $\sigma$ to 5 for high values of these parameters.

**Strategic complementarities and multiple equilibria**

We have shown that if menu costs are sufficiently large, there is an equilibrium where, in response to an increase in nominal money, nominal prices and wages remain unchanged and nominal money has real effects. What we have not shown, however, is that this was the only equilibrium. It turns out that, if the condition that Cooper and John have called "strategic complementarity" is satisfied, there exists a range of menu costs for which the equilibrium is not unique. This has been shown by Julio Rotemberg and Garth Saloner (1986a, 1986b) and, in the context of this model, by Laurence Ball and David Romer (1987). We give a brief sketch of their argument but refer the reader to those papers for details.

To discuss the existence and the role of strategic complementarity in this context, it is again easiest to study the special case where the marginal utility of leisure is constant and where there are no menu costs in nominal wage setting, so that real wage is constant and we can concentrate on the interactions between price setters. Following Cooper and John's definition, strategic complementarity corresponds, then, to the case where an increase in the price level leads a firm, absent menu costs, to increase its own nominal price. Strategic substitutability corresponds to the case where an increase in the price level leads the firm instead to decrease its nominal price.

In the special case we are considering, the price that each firm would choose, absent menu costs, is given by equation (14). An increase in $P$ has two effects on $P_i$. At a given level of aggregate demand, the firm wants to keep the same relative price, and increase $P_i$ in proportion to $P$. But an increase in the price level also decreases real money balances and aggregate demand, leading the firm to want a decrease in its relative price. The net effect is, in our context, unambiguous: the relative-price effect dominates the aggregate-demand effect, so that an increase in $P$ leads to an increase in $P_i$, although less than one for one. Thus, the model exhibits strategic complementarity. This is not, however, a robust feature of the model: if the elasticity of aggregate demand with respect to real money balances exceeded one, the aggregate demand effect could dominate the relative price effect; an increase in $P$ could lead the firm to decrease rather than increase $P_i$, and the model would exhibit instead strategic substitutability. It is clear that the results derived above on the inefficiency of the monopolistically competitive equilibrium, the existence of an aggregate demand externality, and the role of menu costs do not depend on whether the model exhibits strategic complementarity or substitutability. But, if the model exhibits strategic complementarity, however, the equilibrium with menu costs may not be unique.

Consider what a particular firm should do after an increase in nominal money. If other firms do adjust their prices, and if prices are strategic complements, the firm's optimal price, $P_i$, increases because of both the increase in $M$ and the increase in $P$. If, instead, other firms do not adjust their prices, so that the price level does not change, the optimal price $P_i$ increases, but by less. Put another way, the larger the proportion of firms which do not adjust their prices, the lower the opportunity cost to a firm of not adjusting its price. Thus, for some values of the menu costs, there will be two equilibria, one in which all firms adjust, making it costly for a given firm not to adjust, and the other in which no firm adjusts, making it less costly for a given firm not to adjust.

Strategic complementarity can therefore lead to multiple equilibria in the context of monopolistic competition with menu costs.[14] These equilibria are associated with different levels of welfare, and to the extent that the economy ends at a low welfare equilibrium, this can be seen as a "coordination failure," the term used by Cooper and John.

**Demand determination of output**

We have until now assumed that increases in real money balances at constant prices and wages led to increases in output and employment. When analyzing the effects of small changes in money, this assumption was clearly warranted; in the initial equilibrium, as price exceeds marginal cost, firms will always be willing to satisfy a small increase in demand at the existing price. The same is true of workers: as the real wage initially exceeds the marginal disutility of labor, workers will willingly accommodate a small increase in demand for their type of labor. When we consider larger changes in money, this may no longer be the case. Even if firms do not adjust their price, they have the option of either accommodating or rationing demand; they will resort to the second option if marginal cost exceeds price. The same analysis applies to workers. From standard monopoly theory, we know that firms and workers will accommodate relative increases in demand, respectively, of $(\theta/(\theta-1))^{1/(\alpha-1)}$ and $(\sigma/(\sigma-1))^{1/(\beta-1)}$.

This raises the question of whether, assuming menu costs to be large enough, an increase in demand can increase output all the way to its competitive level. The answer is provided in figure 4. This figure replicates figure 2 and draws the aggregate price and wage rules under competitive and monopolistically competitive conditions. Point A is the monopolistic competitive, and $A'$ the competitive one. Along the monopolistically competitive price rule, price exceeds marginal cost; thus firms will satisfy demand, at a given price-wage ratio until marginal cost equals price,

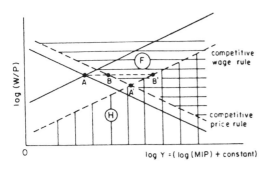

**Figure 4**
Demand determination of output

that is, until they reach the competitive locus. In our case, firms will supply up to point $B$. The shaded area $F$ is the set of outputs and real wages at which firms will ration rather than supply. By a similar argument, workers will supply up to point $B'$. The shaded area $H$ is the set of real-wage combinations where workers do not satisfy labor demand. The figure makes it clear that an increase in nominal money will increase output and employment. It also makes clear that, no matter how large menu costs are, it is impossible, unless the competitive and monopolistically competitive real wages are equal, to attain the competitive equilibrium through an increase in nominal money.

What happens as demand increases, therefore, depends on both menu costs and supply constraints. If menu costs are large, supply constraints will come into effect first. If menu costs are small, a more likely case, prices and wages adjust before supply constraints come into effect.

## 4 Fixed Costs and Aggregate Demand Movements

Until now, we have taken the number of firms as given and fixed costs have played no role in our analysis. Both the aggregate demand externality and the menu costs arguments hold, irrespective of the presence of fixed costs.

In this section, we want to study further the effects of aggregate demand on activity, taking as given that, because of menu costs, such movements in aggregate demand affect output. It is then essential to introduce fixed costs, as they have important implications for productivity, profitability, and the potential for entry by new firms in response to movements in output induced by aggregate demand.

**Fixed costs and the general equilibrium**

To introduce fixed costs, we change the specification of the production function to

$$Y_i + F = \left( \sum_{j=1}^{n} N_{ij}^{(\sigma-1)/\sigma} \right)^{\sigma/(\sigma-1)}, \tag{1'}$$

where $F$ can be interpreted as being in terms of the firm's own output, or as overhead labor requiring all types of labor in the same proportions as regular production.[15] For convenience we also assume that, apart from the fixed cost, firms operate under constant returns to scale, so that $\alpha = 1$.

Given this specification of fixed costs, equations characterizing equilibrium are very similar to equations (5) to (13). The relation between real money balances and aggregate demand is unchanged. The demand functions for goods are still given by equation (7), while in the demand functions for labor, equation (8), $Y$ is replaced by $(Y + mF)$. The price rules are still given by equation (10), which becomes under the assumption that $\alpha$ is equal to unity

$$(P_i/P) = (\theta/(\theta - 1))K_p(W/P), \qquad i = 1, \ldots, m. \tag{10'}$$

The wage rules are given by equation (11), where $Y$ is replaced by $(Y + mF)$.

Equations (12) and (13), which give the aggregate price and wage rules, become

$$(P/W) = (\theta/(\theta - 1))K_p \tag{12'}$$

$$(W/P) = (\sigma/(\sigma - 1))K_w(Y + mF)^{\beta-1}. \tag{13'}$$

Together they determine, as before, equilibrium aggregate output and real wages. From the assumption of constant returns in this section, the markup and its inverse the real wage are independent of the level of demand and are determined by (12'). Given the real wage, (13') determines the level of output.

We can now go further and determine the equilibrium number of firms. For a given number of firms, $m$, the real profit of each firm after profit maximization is given by

$$V_i/P = K_v(1/m)(W/P)^{1-\theta}Y - K_p(W/P)F, \tag{16}$$

where $K_v$ and $K_p$ depend on the structural parameters but not on the number of firms. An increase in $m$ has two effects on the profit of each firm. Given $Y$ and $(W/P)$, it decreases the sales of each firm and decreases profit: this effect is captured by the term $(1/m)$ in (16). But it also affects the equilibrium value of $Y$; while the constants $K_p$ and $K_w$ in (12') and (13') do not depend on $m$, the level of employment associated with a given level of output increases with aggregate fixed costs and therefore with $m$. This leads to a lower equilibrium value of $Y$; given the assumption of constant returns, and given that $K_p$ is independent of $m$, the value of $(W/P)$ is unaffected by $m$; lower aggregate output in turn decreases profit.

If we assume that entry takes place until profit is equal to zero, equations (12') to (16) and the zero-profit condition determine the equilibrium number of firms. We shall assume in what follows that the number of firms is initially given by zero-profit conditions but is going to be fixed in the short run.

### Movements in aggregate demand, profit, and entry

Aggregate demand depends on real money balances, the ratio of nominal money to the price level. Under constant returns with a fixed markup of prices on wages, aggregate demand is therefore a function of the ratio of nominal money to the nominal wage, money in wage units. We now consider the effects of movements in $(M/W)$. This may be due to a movement in nominal money, with no adjustment in nominal wages because of menu costs as in the previous section. Or it may be due to a change in the nominal wage given nominal money, the reason need not concern us in this section. Movements in $(M/W)$ lead to one-for-one movements in aggregate demand and employment.

The first obvious implication of fixed costs is that productivity, given by $(Y/(Y + mF))$, varies procyclically. We focus on a related implication, the procyclical behavior of profit. From equation (16), given nominal wages and prices are fixed, profit is an increasing function of output. If profit was initially equal to zero, it becomes negative with a decrease in $(M/W)$, positive with an increase in $(M/W)$. Both procyclical productivity and profitability seem to be in accordance with the facts.

Procyclical profitability has interesting implications for entry. Keeping the number of firms constant, we examine the return to entry as a function of aggregate demand.[16] Consider the effects of a decrease in nominal money in wage units and the associated reduction in output. Existing firms make negative profits and thus if a potential entrant has to pay the prevailing wage, it will not want to enter. We can go further and derive the shadow wage, say $W^*$, which would make a potential entrant indifferent to entry, as a function of $(M/W)$. Going back to equation (5), (12′), and (16), given $M$ and the aggregate nominal wage $W$, if a firm can pay its workers $W^*$, it will make profits of

$$[K(K_v/m)((\theta - 1)/\theta K_p)^{\theta-2}](W^*/W)^{1-\theta}(M/W)$$
$$- [(\theta - 1)/\theta](W^*/W)F].$$

For a potential entrant to be indifferent to entry, this expression has to be equal to zero. Assuming zero profit for the potential entrant, we can derive the elasticity of the relative wage $(W^*/W)$ to the money stock in wage units $(M/W)$. Denoting it by $\eta$, we have $\eta = (1/\theta)$.

Equivalently the elasticity of the shadow nominal wage to the aggregate nominal wage is given by $1 - (1/\theta)$.[17] Thus the higher are aggregate nominal wages, the more difficult is entry, the lower the relative wage a new entrant can offer to its workers. This result depends on both the presence of monopolistic competition and fixed costs. Fixed costs imply that when higher nominal wages decrease aggregate demand, the profit of all firms can be negative; the fact that products are imperfect substitutes implies that new entrants face downward-sloping demands and cannot capture all of demand by simply undercutting the prices of existing firms.

This result has two implications. In the previous section we showed that if the number of firms was given, menu costs could lead firms not to change prices in response to changes in nominal money. We see that, with respect to decreases in money, allowing for entry will not change the result. More generally (and outside our model), this result implies that if nominal wages are too high, perhaps because of union push, and lead to unemployment, new firms will not want to enter, even if they can pay wages to the unemployed that are far below those paid to the employed[18] Absent fixed costs, entry would occur and unemployment would subside.[19]

## 5  Conclusion

The results of this paper are tantalizingly close to those of traditional Keynesian models: under monopolistic competition, output is too low because of an aggregate demand externality. This externality, together with small menu costs, implies that movements in demand can affect output and welfare. In particular, increases in nominal money can increase both output and welfare. In the presence of fixed costs, output, productivity, and profitability move in the same direction.

We believe these results to be important to the understanding of macroeconomic fluctuations, but we want to point out the obvious limitations of the analysis as it stands.

The scope for small menu costs to lead to large output effects in our model depends critically on the elasticity of labor supply with respect to the real wage being large enough (on $(\beta - 1)$ being small). Evidence on individual labor supply suggests, however, a small elasticity. Thus the "menu cost" approach runs into the same problem as the imperfect-information approach to output fluctuations: neither can easily generate large fluctuations in output in response to demand if the real-wage elasticity of labor supply is low. As in the imperfect-information case, the theory may be rescued by the distinction between temporary and permanent changes in demand. Another possibility is that unions have a flatter labor supply than individuals or do not represent the whole labor force. More likely, the assumption that labor markets operate as spot markets (competitive or monopolistically competitive) will have to be abandoned.[20]

The analysis of this paper is purely static. There are two main issues involved in extending the model to look at the dynamic effects of aggregate demand on output in the presence of menu costs.

The first is that we have assumed all prices to be initially equal and set optimally. In a dynamic economy and in the presence of menu costs, such a degenerate price distribution is unlikely. But, if prices are initially not all equal or optimal, it is no longer obvious that even a small change in nominal money will leave all prices unaffected. It is no longer obvious that money, or aggregate demand in general, will have large effects on output.

The second is that, even if nominal money has large effects on output, it must be the case that money is sometimes unanticipatedly high, sometimes unanticipatedly low. When money is high, output increases, and so does welfare to a first order. When money is low, output decreases, and so does welfare, again to a first order. These welfare effects would appear to cancel out to a first order. It is therefore no longer obvious that even if menu costs lead to large output fluctuations, the welfare loss of those fluctuations exceeds the menu costs which generate them.

Fortunately, all these issues are the subject of active research. Recent developments are reviewed in Blanchard (1987) and Rotemberg (1987).

## Appendix

This appendix derives the market-equilibrium conditions (5) to (11) given in the text. It proceeds in three steps. The first derives the demand functions of each type of labor and each type of product by solving part of the maximization problems of firms and households. These functions hold whether or not prices and wages are set by workers and firms at their profit- or utility-maximizing level. The second derives price rules from firms' profit maximization, and wage rules from workers' utility maximization. The third characterizes market equilibrium.

### Demands for product and labor types

**Demand for product of type $i$.** In order to maximize utility, each household chooses the optimal composition of consumption and money holdings for a given level of total wealth $I$ and product prices:

$$\max_{c_{ij}, M'_j} \Lambda_j = \left( \sum_{i=1}^{m} C_{ij}^{(\theta-1)/\theta} \right)^{\theta\gamma/(\theta-1)} m^{\gamma/(1-\theta)} (M'_j/P)^{1-\gamma}$$

subject to $\sum_{i=1}^{m} P_i C_{ij} + M'_j = I_j.$

Solving this maximization problem gives

$$C_{ij} = (P_i/P)^{-\theta}(\gamma I_j/mP) \tag{A1}$$

$$M'_j = (1 - \gamma)I_j \tag{A2}$$

$$\Lambda_j = \mu I_j/P \tag{A3}$$

where

$$P = \left( (1/m) \sum_{i=1}^{m} P_i^{1-\theta} \right)^{1/(1-\theta)} \quad \text{and} \quad \mu = \gamma^\gamma(1 - \gamma)^{1-\gamma}. \tag{A4}$$

The parameter $\mu$ can be interpreted as the marginal utility of real wealth.

The demand for product of type $i$ is therefore given by

$$Y_i = \sum_{j=1}^{n} C_{ij} = (P_i/P)^{-\theta}(Y/m), \tag{A5}$$

where

$$Y = \left( \sum_{j}^{n} \sum_{i}^{m} P_i C_{ij} \right) \Big/ P = (\gamma/P) \sum_{j=1}^{n} I_j. \tag{A6}$$

$Y$ denotes real aggregate consumption expenditures of households and will be referred to as "aggregate demand." Equation (A5) is equation (7) in the text. Note also that equations (A1), (A2), (A5), and (A6) imply the following relation between aggregate demand and aggregate desired real money balances:

$$Y = (\gamma/(1 - \gamma))M'/P, \tag{A7}$$

where    $M' = \sum_{j=1}^{n} M_j'$.

**Demand for labor of type $j$.**   In order to maximize profit, each firms minimizes its production cost for a given level of output and wages:

$$\min_{N_{ij}} \sum_{j=1}^{n} W_j N_{ij}$$

subject to    $\left( \sum_{j=1}^{n} N_{ij}^{(\sigma-1)/\sigma} \right)^{(\sigma/\sigma-1))1/\alpha} = Y_i.$

Solving this minimization problem gives

$$N_{ij} = (n^{\sigma/(1-\sigma)})(W_j/W)^{-\sigma} Y_i^{\alpha}$$

and

$$\sum_{j=1}^{n} W_j N_{ij} = n^{\sigma/(1-\sigma)} W Y_i^{\alpha} \tag{A8}$$

where

$$W = \left( \frac{1}{n} \sum_{j=1}^{n} W_j^{1-\sigma} \right)^{1/(1-\sigma)}. \tag{A9}$$

The demand for labor of type $j$ is therefore given by

$$N_j = \sum_{i=1}^{m} N_{ij} = (W_j/W)^{-\sigma} N/n, \tag{A10}$$

where

$$N \equiv \left( \sum_i^m \sum_j^n W_j N_{ij} \right) \bigg/ W = n^{1/(1-\sigma)} \sum_{i=1}^m Y_i^{\alpha}. \tag{A11}$$

$N$ can be interpreted as the aggregate labor demand index.

**Price and wage rules**

(a) Taking as given wages and the price level, each firm chooses its price and output so as to maximize profit:

$$V_i = P_i Y_i - \sum_{j=1}^n W_j N_{ij}, \tag{A12}$$

subject to the cost function (A8) and the demand function for its product (A5). Solving the above maximization problem gives

$$P_i/P = [((\theta/(\theta - 1))n^{1/(1-\sigma)}\alpha m^{1-\alpha})(W/P) Y^{\alpha-1}]^{1/(1+\theta(\alpha-1))}. \tag{A13}$$

Equation (A13) implies that the price is equal to $\theta/(\theta - 1)$ times the marginal cost. Equation (A13) is equation (10) in the text.

(b) Taking as given prices and other wages, each household chooses its wage and labor supply so as to maximize utility. Using (A3),

$$U_j = \mu I_j/P - N_j^{\beta}, \tag{A14}$$

subject to the demand for its type of labor (A10) and the budget constraint:

$$I_j = W_j N_j + \sum_{i=1}^m V_{ij} + M_j. \tag{A15}$$

Solving this maximization problem gives

$$W_j/W = [((\sigma/(\sigma - 1))(\beta/\mu)n^{1-\beta})(P/W)N^{\beta-1}]^{1/(1+\sigma(\beta-1))}. \tag{A16}$$

Equation (A16) implies that the real wage, in terms of utility, is equal to $\sigma/(\sigma - 1)$ times the marginal disutility of labor.

**Market equilibrium**

In equilibrium, desired real money balances must be equal to actual balances. Thus $M = M'$. Replacing in (A7) gives

$$Y = (\gamma/(1 - \gamma))M/P. \tag{A17}$$

This gives equation (5) in the text.

Replacing the $Y_i$s in (A11) by their value from (A5) gives

$$N = [n^{(1/(1-\sigma))}m^{-\alpha}]\left(\sum_{i=1}^{m} (P_i/P)^{-\alpha\theta}\right) Y^\alpha. \tag{A18}$$

If all firms choose the same (not necessarily optimal) price, this reduces to

$$N = [n^{1/(1-\sigma)}m^{1-\alpha}] Y^\alpha. \tag{A19}$$

Substituting $N$ from equation (A19) into (A10) gives the demand function for labor $j$, equation (8) in the text. Note that the demand functions for goods and labor, and the relation between aggregate demand and real money balances, have been derived without use of the price and wage rules and therefore hold whether or not wages and prices are set optimally.

Substituting $N$ from equation (A19) into equation (A16) gives the wage rule, equation (11) in the text. This completes the derivation.

## Acknowledgments

We thank Andrew Abel, Laurence Ball, Russell Cooper, Rudiger Dornbusch, Stanley Fischer, Mark Gertler, Robert Hall, Andrew John, Kenneth Rogoff, Jeffrey Sachs, Lawrence Summers, Martin Weitzman, and two referees for discussions and suggestions. We thank the National Science Foundation and the Sloan Foundation for financial support.

## Notes

1. A Clower Constraint would lead to similar results. Developing an explicitly intertemporal model to justify why money is positively valued did not seem worth the additional complexity in this context.

There are, however, differences between money and a standard nonproduced good that arise from the fact that real, not nominal, money balances enter utility; we shall point out these differences as we go along.

2. The main alternative to product diversification à la Dixit-Stiglitz, is geographic dispersion. This is the approach followed by Weitzman.

3. Our assumptions imply a constant elasticity of demand, and a constant markup of price over marginal cost. Some recent work on the implications of imperfect competition for macroeconomics has precisely focused on why markups may not be constant, either because of changes in elasticity of demand, or of changes in the degree of collusion between firms. See, for example, Stiglitz (1984), Rotemberg and Saloner (1986), and Bils (1985).

4. Kiyotaki (1985b) studies the implications of monopolistic competition for investment and the likelihood of multiple equilibria.

5. Since in equilibrium each labor supplier sells some of his (her) labor to all firms, it is more appropriate to think of labor suppliers as craft unions or syndicates, as in Hart, rather than individual workers. However, since we want to analyze labor supply and consumption decisions simultaneously, we shall continue to refer to labor suppliers as "consumer-workers" or "households."

6. The assumption that utility is homogeneous of degree one in consumption and real money balances, as well as additively separable in consumption and real money balances, on the one hand, and leisure, on the other, eliminates income effects on labor supply. Under these assumptions, competitive labor supply would just be a function of the real wage using the price index defined in the text. It also implies that utility is linear in income, and this facilitates welfare evaluations.

For reasons that will be clear below, we exclude the case where both $\alpha$ and $\beta$ are equal to unity.

7. Laurence Ball and David Romer (1987) derive the equilibrium for such an economy.

8. Note that, as there are distortions in two sets of interrelated markets, the economy is operating inside its production frontier. This point is developed by Rotemberg (1982).

9. An alternative way of stating the argument is as follows: If starting from the monopolistically competitive equilibrium, a firm decreased its price, this would lead to a small decrease in the price level and thus to a small increase in aggregate demand. While the other firms and households would benefit from this increase in aggregate demand, the original firm cannot capture all of these benefits and thus has no incentive to decrease its price. We have chosen to present the argument in the text to facilitate comparison with the argument of section 3.

10. What happens to the real value of firms is obviously of no direct relevance for welfare. This step is required, however, to characterize what happens to the utility of households below.

11. Note that, if we were performing the same experiment in the neighborhood not of the monopolistically competitive equilibrium but of the competitive equilibrium, the first two terms would be equal to zero. The third, however, would still be present. This is one of the implications of our use of real money as the nonproduced good. If real money enters utility, then the competitive equilibrium is not Pareto optimal, as a small decrease in the price level increases welfare. This inefficiency of the competitive equilibrium disappears if money is replaced by a nonproduced good, while the aggregate demand externality under monopolistic competition remains (see Kiyotaki 1985a).

12. Akerlof and Yellen assume "near rationality" that is equivalent to rationality subject to second-order costs of taking decisions.

13. The figure assumes decreasing returns to scale. Note also that as firms take the price level as given when choosing their own price, iso-profit loci are vertical along the price rule.

14. Strategic complementarity turns out to play an important role in dynamic models with menu costs. See the surveys by Blanchard (1987) and Rotemberg (1987).

15. An alternative is to assume that fixed costs for a given firm are in the form of other goods. A convenient assumption is to assume that the fixed cost is a CES function of all goods, with elasticity of substitution $\theta$. This assumption insures that the demand functions for goods still have elasticity $\theta$.

16. An alternative would be to determine the equilibrium number of firms as a function of the level of aggregate demand. This is the route pursued by Robert Solow (1984).

17. As $\theta$ is greater than unity, the elasticity of the shadow wage with respect to the aggregate wage is positive. If we had formalized fixed costs in terms of a basket of goods, however, the sign of the elasticity would depend on whether $\theta$ is greater or smaller than 2. The difference comes from the fact that, in our case, a decrease in the shadow wage decreases the fixed cost whereas under this alternative assumption it does not.

18. We are indebted to Larry Summers for suggesting this argument.

19. This is our interpretation of Weitzman's argument that increasing returns are a necessary condition for unemployment to persist.

20. This is indeed the direction taken by Akerlof and Yellen (1985b) who formalize the goods market as monopolistically competitive and the labor market using the "efficiency wage" hypothesis.

# References

Akerlof, George, and Yellen, Janet, "Can Small Deviations from Rationality Make Significant Differences to Economic Equilibria?" *American Economic Review*, September 1985a, 75, 708–721.

Akerlof, George, and Yellen, Janet, "A Near-Rational Model of the Business Cycle, with Wage and Price Inertia," *Quarterly Journal of Economics*, 1985, suppl., 100, 823–838.

Ball, Laurence, and Romer, David, "Sticky Prices as Coordination Failure," mimeo., Princeton University, March 1987.

Bils, Mark, "Essays on the Cyclical Behavior of Price and Marginal Cost," unpublished doctoral dissertation, MIT, 1985.

Blanchard, Olivier, "Why Does Money Affect Output?" in Benjamin Friedman and Frank Hahn, eds., *Handbook of Monetary Economics*, Amsterdam: North-Holland, 1987.

Cooper, Russell, and John, Andrew, "Coordinating Coordination Failures in Keynesian Models," mimeo., Yale University, July 1985.

Dixit, Avinash, and Stiglitz, Joseph, "Monopolistic Competition and Optimum Product Diversity," *American Economic Review*, June 1977, 67, 297–308.

Hart, Oliver, "A Model of Imperfect Competition with Keynesian Features," *Quarterly Journal of Economics*, February 1982, 97, 109–138.

Kiyotaki, Nobuhiro, "Macroeconomics of Monopolistic Competition," unpublished doctoral dissertation, Harvard University, May 1985a.

Kiyotaki, Nobuhiro, "Implications of Multiple Equilibria under Monopolistic Competition," mimeo., Harvard University, 1985b.

Mankiw, N. Gregory, "Small Menu Costs and Large Business Cycles: A Macroeconomic Model of Monopoly," *Quarterly Journal of Economics*, May 1985, 100, 529–539.

Rotemberg, Julio, "Monopolistic Price Adjustment and Aggregate Output," *Review of Economic Studies*, October 1982, 44, 517–531.

Rotemberg, Julio, "The New Keynesian Microfoundations," NBER *Macroeconomics Annual*, Cambridge: MIT Press, Vol. 2, forthcoming 1987.

Rotemberg, Julio, and Saloner, Garth, "A Supergame-Theoretic Model of Price Wars during Booms," *American Economic Review*, June 1986a, 76, 390–407.

Rotemberg, Julio, and Saloner, Garth," The Relative Rigidity of Monopoly Pricing," NBER, working paper no. 1943, June 1986b.

Solow, Robert, "Monopolistic Competition and the Multiplier," mimeo., MIT, 1984.

Stiglitz, Joseph, "Price Rigidities and Market Structure," *American Economic Review Proceedings*, May 1984, 74, 350–355.

Weitzman, Martin, "Increasing Returns and the Foundations of Unemployment Theory," *Economic Journal*, December 1982, 92, 787–804.

# 14 Imperfect Competition and the Keynesian Cross

N. Gregory Mankiw

## 1 Introduction

Fiscal policy multipliers are central to Keynesian macroeconomics. In this paper I explore a possible microeconomic foundation for one fundamental theory of income determination, the "Keynesian cross." My model deviates from a Walrasian equilibrium model only by the assumption of imperfect competition in the goods market. I show that textbook fiscal policy multipliers arise as a limiting case.[1]

Under imperfect competition, firms are always eager to sell an additional unit of output, since price exceeds marginal cost. This profit margin creates the potential for the multiplier. An expansionary change in fiscal policy increases aggregate expenditure, which increases profits, which in turn increases expenditure, and so on.

The theme that imperfect competition may be crucial to macroeconomic issues is increasingly prevalent. See, for example, the work of Weitzman (1982), Hart (1982), Solow (1984), Blanchard and Kiyotaki (1985), and Startz (1986). The purpose of the model presented here is partly peda-gogical. I therefore do not hesitate making strong (yet not implausible) assumptions about the economic structure: Cobb-Douglas utility, constant marginal cost, and constant mark-up pricing. There is no reason to suppose, however, that the sorts of effects highlighted here are specific to these assumptions.

While the model is in some ways surprisingly similar to the standard Keynesian model, in other ways it differs greatly. In particular, it in-corporates both an equilibrium labor market and a static environment. These features are chosen for simplicity rather than realism. The goal is not to provide a complete reformulation of Keynesian economics, but only to illustrate what sort of Keynesian results one can obtain with a small movement away from Walrasian equilibrium in the direction of imperfect competition.

*Economics Letters* 26 (1988): 7–14. Copyright © by Elsevier Science Publishers B.V. (North-Holland). Reprinted with permission.

## 2   The Economy

This section describes the economy. The following section discusses the
response of the economy to changes in fiscal policy.

### People

All people are the same. The representative person maximizes a Cobb-
Douglas utility function over consumption of the single produced good $(C)$
and leisure $(L)$:

$$U = \alpha \log C + (1 - \alpha) \log L. \tag{1}$$

Leisure is the numeraire. If $\omega$ is the endowment of time, then $\omega - L$ is labor
income. Total after-tax income is $(\omega - L) + \Pi - T$, where $\Pi$ is profits and
$T$ is the lump-sum tax levied by the government. The individual's budget
constraint is therefore

$$PC = (\omega - L) + \Pi - T, \qquad PC + L = \omega + \Pi - T, \tag{2}$$

where $P$ is the price of the consumption good.

The Cobb-Douglas utility function implies a constant share $\alpha$ of "full
income" is devoted to consumption. That is,

$$PC = \alpha(\omega + \Pi - T). \tag{3}$$

Equation (3) is the consumption function, and $\alpha$ is the marginal propensity
to consume.

### Government

The revenue raised by the government is used for two purposes. An amount
$G$ is used to purchase the produced good, and $W$ government workers are
hired. The government budget constraint requires that government spending equals revenue. That is,

$$T = G + W. \tag{4}$$

Total expenditure on the produced good is

$$Y = PC + G. \tag{5}$$

Using equation (3) to substitute into equation (5), we find

$$Y = \alpha(\omega + \Pi - T) + G. \tag{6}$$

Expenditure therefore depends positively on profits and government purchases and negatively on taxes.

**Firms**

There are $N$ firms producing the single good. The industry takes expenditure in the economy as given.[2] That is, the industry demand function is unit elastic:

$$Q = Y/P. \tag{7}$$

where $Q$ is total output.

The $N$ firms have the same increasing returns to scale technology. The technology requires $F$ units of overhead labor. After the plant is set up, one unit of output requires $c$ units of labor. The cost function of each firm is therefore

$$TC(q) = F + cq, \tag{8}$$

where costs are measured in terms of the numeraire, leisure.

The $N$ firms play some oligopoly game, the details of which I do not need to specify. This game determines the profit margin

$$\mu = (P - c)/P. \tag{9}$$

As an example, if the firms act as Cournot oligopolists, then $\mu = 1/N$. More generally, a conjectural variation equilibrium allows all possibilities between Bertrand competition ($\mu = 0$) and perfect collusion ($\mu \to 1$); in each case $\mu$ depends only on $N$ and the conjectural variation. I therefore take the profit margin $\mu$ as given for any fixed number of firms $N$.[3]

Note the relation between output and expenditure:

$$Q = [(1 - \mu)/c]\, Y. \tag{10}$$

For given values of the profit margin $\mu$ and marginal cost $c,$ expenditure on the produced good and output are proportional. Government workers $W$ are not included in expenditure $Y$ or output $Q$; hence, these measures are analogous to industrial production rather than GNP.

Total profits are revenue less costs:

$$\Pi = PQ - NF - cQ. \tag{11}$$

Using equations (7) and (9), aggregate profits can be expressed in terms of expenditure $Y$ and the profit margin $\mu$:

$$\Pi = \mu Y - NF. \tag{12}$$

Hence, higher aggregate expenditure implies higher aggregate profits.

**The labor market**

The above discussion centers on the goods market. Walras' law ensures that the labor market clears if the above relations are satisfied. To see that this is true, note that labor supply is the time endowment less the demand for leisure:

$$\text{labor supply} = \omega - (1 - \alpha)(\omega + \Pi - T),$$

$$= \alpha\omega - (1 - \alpha)(\Pi - T); \tag{13}$$

labor demand is the sum of firms' demand, $NF + cQ$, and government demand, $W$. Thus,

$$\text{labor demand} = (NF + cQ) + W,$$

$$= (Y - \Pi) + (T - G),$$

$$= (\alpha(\omega + \Pi - T) + G - \Pi) + (T - G),$$

$$= \alpha\omega - (1 - \alpha)(\Pi - T).$$

Hence, goods-market equilibrium (including the government budget constraint) implies that supply equals demand in the labor market as well.

**Summary**

The two key equations are (6) and (12):

$$Y = \alpha(\omega + \Pi - T) + G \tag{6}$$

$$\Pi = \mu Y - NF \tag{12}$$

Expenditure depends on profits and the fiscal policy variables, while profits depend on expenditure.

## 3   Fiscal Policy

This section addresses the impact of fiscal policy. The analysis is short-run in that the number of firms $N$ and thus the profit margin $\mu$ are held fixed.

## The balanced budget multiplier

Consider first an equal increase in government purchases $G$ and taxes $T$. Equations (6) and (12) imply that

$$\frac{dY}{dG}\bigg|_{dT=dG} = \frac{1-\alpha}{1-\alpha\mu}. \tag{15}$$

The multiplier thus depends on both the marginal propensity to consume $\alpha$ and the profit margin $\mu$. Under perfect competition ($\mu = 0$), the balanced budget multiplier is $1 - \alpha$. In the limiting case in which the revenue from the marginal unit goes entirely to profit ($\mu = 1$), the balanced budget multipler is unity.

The story that accompanies this multiplier is in many ways standard. Initially the increase in government purchases of $\Delta G$ raises expenditure by $\Delta G$, while the equal tax increase lowers private expenditure by $\alpha\Delta G$. The net increase in expenditure is thus $(1 - \alpha)\Delta G$, which raises profits by $\mu(1 - \alpha)\Delta G$. The increase in profits in turn raises expenditure by $\alpha\mu(1 - \alpha) \Delta G$, which again raises profits, and so on. This multiplier process yields the infinite series, $(1 - \alpha) + \alpha\mu(1 - \alpha) + \alpha^2\mu^2(1 - \alpha) + \alpha^3\mu^3(1 - \alpha) + \ldots$, which equals the balanced budget multiplier in equation (15). Imperfect competition plays a key role here, for if the profit margin were zero, the process would end after the initial increase in expenditure.

## The tax multiplier

Consider now an increase in taxes $T$, holding constant the level of government purchases $G$. The government budget constraint (4) implies that the amount of labor purchased by the government $W$ must increase by $\Delta T$. The extra labor income received by government employees exactly equals the extra taxes paid; on net, individuals give up their time but receive no additional income. This policy intervention is thus equivalent to a reduction in the endowment $\omega$ of $\Delta T$.

In standard analysis, tax increases are coupled with reductions in government debt. Government debt serves the function of transferring resources from future generations to the current generation. Hence, a tax increase is an endowment reduction to the current generation. In this sense, a tax increase in the static model of this paper is analogous to a debt-financed tax increase in intertemporal (finite horizon) models.

Equations (6) and (12) imply that the tax multiplier is

$$\frac{dY}{dT} = \frac{-\alpha}{1 - \alpha\mu}.$$ (16)

Under perfect competition ($\mu = 0$), the tax multiplier is $-\alpha$. As competition becomes less perfect ($\mu \to 1$), the tax multiplier approaches $-\alpha/(1 - \alpha)$. Again, the multiplier process works through profits. The tax increase lowers expenditure, which lowers profits, which lowers expenditure, and so on.

**The government purchases multiplier**

Consider now an increase in government purchases $G$ where the level of taxes $T$ are held constant. In standard analysis, future generations pay for a debt-financed increase in purchases. Here, the increase in purchases is financed by a reduction in $W$. In both cases, there is no immediate impact on the current individuals' budget constraint (2).

Equations (6) and (12) imply that the government purchases multiplier is

$$\frac{dY}{dG} = \frac{1}{1 - \alpha\mu}.$$ (17)

Under perfect competition, $dY/dG$ is unity. As the profit margin approaches one, $dY/dG$ approaches the standard Keynesian value of $1/(1 - \alpha)$.

Figure 1 shows how to demonstrate the multiplier graphically. Expenditure $Y$ is a linear function of profits $\Pi$, with a slope of the marginal propensity to consume $\alpha$. Profits are also a linear function of expenditure;

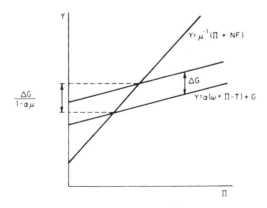

**Figure 1**
A new Keynesian cross

the slope of this line is $1/\mu$.[4] In the limiting case in which $\mu = 1$, this locus become the $45°$ line of the Keynesian cross. An increase in government purchases shifts the expenditure function upward by $\Delta G$, which causes a multiplied increase in total expenditure.

**Welfare analysis**

Here I examine the effect of fiscal policy on the welfare of the representative person, as judged by his utility function (1). Government purchases are assumed not to affect utility directly. A complete evaluation of fiscal policy would also take account of the benefit received from public expenditure. The analysis here is thus limited in scope.

An individual's utility increases only if his budget set, as defined by equation (2), is expanded. Since relative prices are constant, profits less taxes, $\Pi - T$, are sufficient for utility. The impacts of the fiscal policy changes on $\Pi - T$ are

$$\frac{d(\Pi - T)}{dG}\bigg|_{dT=dG} = \frac{-(1 - \mu)}{1 - \alpha\mu}, \tag{18}$$

$$\frac{d(\Pi - T)}{dT} = \frac{-1}{1 - \alpha\mu}, \tag{19}$$

$$\frac{d(\Pi - T)}{dG} = \frac{\mu}{1 - \alpha\mu}. \tag{20}$$

A balanced budget fiscal stimulus in general reduces welfare. In the limiting case in which $\mu = 1$, however, a balanced-budget increase has no impact on welfare. As the textbook Keynesian cross suggests, the increase in government purchases has no social cost. The increase in income (here, profits) exactly offsets the higher tax bill.

Both increases in government purchases and reductions in taxes increase welfare. In standard analysis, increases in $G$ or reductions in $T$ are financed by future generations. Here these changes are financed by reductions in government workers $W$. In neither case is it surprising that the welfare of current individuals increases.

## 4  Conclusion

The model examined here is surprisingly similar to both Walrasian models of general equilibrium and Keynesian models of income determination. It deviates from a standard general equilibrium model only by the assumption of imperfect competition in the goods market. As competition in the goods market becomes less perfect, the fiscal-policy multipliers approach the values implied by the Keynesian cross.

The model could be usefully extended in several directions. First, the labor market might be made less classical. One could posit imperfect competition among workers, for example. Some of the rents generated by expansionary fiscal policy would therefore accrue as labor income. The multiplier would thus work through both labor income and firm profits.[5]

Second, the model could be made intertemporal. The impact of debt-financed fiscal policy obviously cannot be studied in a static model. That saving and investment play an important role in standard Keynesian analysis also suggests extending this model to a dynamic setting.

## Acknowledgments

I am grateful to David Romer and the participants in the NBER Summer Institute on Industrial Organization and Macroeconomics for helpful comments, and to the National Science Foundation for financial support.

## Notes

1. For an exposition of the Keynesian cross, see Samuelson (1948) or almost any introductory text.

2. One might object that this assumption is not reasonable because expenditure depends on industry profits. The model could easily be amended, however, to include a continuum of industries; the demand curve of each industry would depend on aggregate profits.

3. One could also imagine that each firm produces a differentiated product. In this case, the profit margin $\mu$ depends on each firm's elasticity of demand, which could plausibly be assumed to be constant.

4. Note that the second line is always steeper than the first, since $\alpha < 1 < 1/\mu$.

5. Alternatively, the labor market could be characterized by efficiency wages.

## References

Blanchard, Olivier J., and Nobuhiro Kiyotaki, 1985, "Monopolistic Competition, Aggregate Demand Externalities, and the Real Effects of Nominal Money," NBER working paper no. 1770.

Hart, Oliver, 1982, "A Model of Imperfect Competition with Keynesian Features," *Quarterly Journal of Economics* 87, 109–138.

Samuelson, Paul A., 1948, "The Simple Mathematics of Income Determination," in *Income, Employment and Policy* (Norton, New York). Reprinted in *The Collected Scientific Papers of Paul A. Samuelson*.

Solow, Robert M., 1984, "Monopolistic Competition and the Multiplier" (MIT, Cambridge).

Startz, Richard, 1986, "Monopolistic Competition as a Foundation for Keynesian Macroeconomic Models" (University of Washington, Seattle, Washington).

Weitzman, Martin L., 1982, "Increasing Returns and the Foundations of Unemployment Theory," *Economic Journal* 92, 787–804.

# 15 Market Structure and Macroeconomic Fluctuations

## Robert E. Hall

Market structure and macroeconomic fluctuations are related to each other in two different ways. First, macroeconomic fluctuations reveal a good deal about market structure. Students of industrial organization have not generally exploited cyclical movements in their research; they have concentrated almost entirely on cross sectional analysis. One of my goals in this paper is to look at some standard issues in industrial organization through time series variation in individual industries as it is associated with the aggregate business cycle. Second, market structure has an important role in the propagation of macroeconomic shocks. In competitive industries, there are strong forces pushing toward equilibrium. Hence, competitive market structure seems to require an equilibrium interpretation of fluctuations. Where sellers have market power, on the other hand, there is no presumption of full, efficient resource utilization. Fluctuations may be the perverse consequence of noncompetitive conditions.

The first part of the paper looks at the experience of some fifty industries at the two-digit standard-industrial-classification (SIC) code level, covering all sectors of the U.S. economy. It reaches two basic conclusions about the market structure of American industry. The first is that the majority of the industries are noncompetitive in an important way. Specifically, they choose to operate at a point where marginal cost is well below price, a policy that makes sense only if firms influence prices through their volumes of production, that is, if they are noncompetitive. I measure marginal cost in a straightforward way. Each boom or recession in the national economy causes increases or decreases in output and cost in an industry. Of course, changes in the prices of inputs also cause changes in cost, but such changes can be measured and eliminated. The ratio of the change in cost, adjusted for input price changes, to the change in output is marginal cost. Comparison of marginal cost to price, observed directly, completes the analysis. I estimate the markup ratio, the ratio of price to marginal cost. In competition, the markup ratio is 1, whereas with market power it exceeds 1. In most industries in my sample, the hypothesis of unit markup is rejected in favor of higher values. In many industries the markup ratio is above 1.5 and in a few it exceeds 3.

*Brookings Papers on Economic Activity* 1986, no. 2: 285–322. Copyright © 1986 by the Brookings Institution. Reprinted with permission.

My second conclusion about market structure turns on the question of whether market power necessarily translates into excess profit. At a minimum, this investigation is needed in order to make my findings of significant market power credible in view of the fact that the total profitability of U.S. business is not far above the level that represents a reasonable return to capital. Some explanation is needed for market power's failure, to bring much profit. My work asks whether firms minimize cost with respect to a constant-returns technology, or whether, on the contrary, they incur fixed costs or other types of costs in excess of that benchmark. The conclusion favors the second case: many industries have costs above the level implied by minimizing cost with respect to a constant-returns technology. The typical firm in these industries is operating on a decreasing portion of its average cost curve. Again, fluctuations in the overall economy are used to measure marginal cost. A firm that minimizes cost with constant returns will earn the market return on its capital when the return is calculated as profit using marginal cost in place of price to value output. In most industries in the sample, the return to capital calculated in this way is negative, indicating that they cannot be minimizing cost with respect to a constant-returns technology. They hold chronic excess capacity because of a minimum practical scale of operation or they have true fixed costs.

These findings support a view of the typical industry originally proposed by Edward Chamberlin.[1] Through product differentiation or geographical separation, firms have power in their own markets. However, there are no barriers to market entry, so firms enter each niche until profit is driven to zero. Because of a minimum practical scale of operation, the typical production unit has excess capacity in the zero-profit equilibrium.

The second part of the paper examines the implications of these findings for macroeconomics. The most straightforward implication is a simple explanation for the well-documented phenomenon of procyclical productivity. In the type of equilibrium consistent with my empirical findings, marginal cost falls considerable short of price. Hence, the calculation of total-factor productivity through the method developed by Robert Solow, which assumes the equality of price and marginal cost, involves a bias. I show that this bias has the right sign and magnitude to explain the observed procyclical behavior of productivity.

The findings about industry structure also have important implications for macroeconomic fluctuations. It is now well understood that a noncompetitive economy does not have the automatic full-employment tendency of the competitive economy. Recent authors have built theoretical models in which market power implies that the equilibrium of the economy occurs at a point with unused labor. Some of these models have multiple equilibria. However, there is still a large gap between the theoretical models and empirical work.

The ultimate goal of research in this area is to build and estimate a model in which the economy moves from one equilibrium to another, each involving different levels of resource utilization. A recession and succeeding recovery would be explained as an episode during which output and employment as determined by the equilibrium of the model first shrank and later expanded. However, work has not yet reached this point. Therefore, I will limit my own consideration to the question of how market power and excess capacity diminish the strength of the economy's drive to full employment.

Consider a competitive firm with a well-defined level of capacity (capacity is the level of output where the marginal cost curve turns upward and becomes nearly vertical). Such a firm is unlikely to be satisfied with producing less than its capacity output. As the empirical work in the first part of the paper shows, marginal cost is low when output is below capacity. Unless price falls all the way to the low level of marginal cost along the flat part of the marginal cost schedule, there is substantial incremental profit to be made by putting more output on the market. The competitor never fears that added output will spoil the market, for the absence of that concern is the definition of competition. Hence, output rises to capacity. The only other possibility is for price to fall to a low level.

In the world described by my empirical findings, the incentive to keep output at capacity is nowhere near as strong. A business faced with disappointing sales in a recession hesitates to push more output on the market, because the market will absorb it only at a lower price. Profit will hardly rise. Indeed, profit may not rise at all—the decline in price may exactly offset the increase in sales volume.

For a business in a Chamberlinian equilibrium, the trade-off between sales volume and product price is a matter of low priority because it has only small implications for profit. Product design, cost control, and marketing are the important business decisions. It is true, of course, that recessions bring large reductions in profit for most businesses. However, they cannot recover profit by cutting price and raising volume. A minimum conclusion from my research, then, is that the incentives are weak for those business actions that would restore full employment.

## Macroeconomic Fluctuations and Market Structure

Macroeconomic fluctuations continuously bring about natural experiments that reveal marginal cost. When a boom causes a firm to raise its output, the firm incurs extra cost to produce that output. The ratio of the cost increase to the output increase is marginal cost. The empirical work described in this section is no more than a refinement of this simple idea. A much more complete exposition of the technique is available in an earlier paper of mine.[2]

Some economists make a distinction between short-run and long-run marginal cost. For my purposes, that distinction is somewhat off the point. I define marginal cost as the derivative of the cost function with respect to output, holding the capital stock constant. In the out years of a firm's plan, my measure of marginal cost will equal long-run marginal cost, because the firm will plan a cost-minimizing capital stock. In competition, the firm will equate its marginal cost to the market price of its product, where marginal cost is defined as I have indicated. The equality will hold whether or not the firm is capable of adjusting its capital stock to the current market price. If the firm cannot adjust its capital stock in the short run, then my definition corresponds to the usual concept of short-run marginal cost.

### Comparing marginal cost and price

The simplest version of my method applies when output and employment change from one year to the next, but the capital stock remains constant. I will also assume that the firm does not use any materials as inputs; labor is the only variable input. Then I measure marginal cost, $x$, as

$$x = w \frac{\Delta N}{\Delta Q - \theta Q},$$

where $w$ is the hourly wage, $N$ is hours of work, $Q$ is the quantity of output, and $\theta$ is the rate of technical progress. Note that the change in output, $\Delta Q$, must be adjusted for the amount by which output would have risen, $\theta Q$, had there been no increase in labor input.

All the variables in the marginal cost formula are observed directly except for marginal cost and the rate of technical progress. Robert Solow exploited that fact in his famous paper on productivity measurement in which he assumed that marginal cost was equal to price and solved the equation for the rate of technical progress.[3] Not surprisingly, all of the calculations in Solow's paper are closely related to productivity measurement, and the results are intimately related to the cyclical behavior of productivity.

I will proceed in a somewhat different way from Solow. Instead of making the assumption that marginal cost equals price, I will make assumptions about technical progress and derive conclusions about the relation between marginal cost and price. The assumption is that technical progress can be viewed as random deviations from an underlying constant rate: $\theta_t = \theta + \mu_t$. The randomness of the deviation is expressed in a particular way, which is absolutely central to all of the empirical work in this paper: $\mu_t$ is uncorrelated with the business cycle. That assumption is based on two hypotheses of this work. First, the ups and downs of the economy, from whatever source, do not cause year-to-year changes in productivity. On-the-job learning by doing or research and development stimulated by a vibrant economy does not yield immediate improvements in productivity. The effects are spread over sufficiently many years that the correlation of $\mu_t$ with the business cycle is negligible. Second, fluctuations in productivity growth do not themselves cause the business cycle. That is, I assume that recessions are not the result of a sudden reduced effectiveness of technology, nor are booms episodes in which output rises more than usual because production functions have shifted favorably. In this respect, my assumption conflicts squarely with the "real business cycle" school, which views variations in the rate of technical progress as one of the main driving forces of the business cycle.

Another assumption I make is that a firm's markup ratio—the ratio of price to marginal cost—can reasonably be approximated as a constant over time. The assumption does not commit me to a "markup" theory of pricing. Rather, it says only that the outcome of the decision process by which a firm chooses its marginal cost and, possibly, its price is such that the ratio of the two is approximately a constant. The assumption is completely compatible with competition, where the markup ratio must be 1. I denote the markup ratio as $\mu$.

Inserting the assumptions about productivity growth and the markup ratio into the formula for marginal cost gives

$$\frac{p}{\mu} = \frac{w\Delta N}{\Delta Q - (\theta + u)Q}.$$

Solving for the change in output yields

$$\Delta Q = \mu \frac{w}{p}\Delta N + (\theta + u)Q.$$

In rates of change, this is

$$\frac{\Delta Q}{Q} = \mu \frac{wN}{pQ}\frac{\Delta N}{N} + \theta + u.$$

Letting $\Delta q$ and $\Delta n$ be the rates of change, and letting $\alpha$ be the revenue share of labor, $wN/pQ$, I get finally

$$\Delta q = \mu\alpha\Delta n + \theta + u.$$

To see what this formula means, consider first the case of competition, where $\mu$ is 1. In this case, the formula says that the rate of change of output is equal to the rate of change of labor input weighted by labor's share in revenue, $\alpha$, plus the constant and random elements of productivity growth. Note that, under competition, the revenue share is a measure of the elasticity of the production function with respect to labor input.

Solow's method for measuring productivity growth is simply to move $\theta$ to the left-hand side of the equation and output growth to the right-hand side. The "Solow residual" is just $\Delta q - \alpha\Delta n$, the part of output growth not explained by growth in labor input.

As stated, my assumption is that $u$ is uncorrelated with the business cycle. As is well known and amply confirmed by the results of this paper, the Solow residual is quite procyclical. Recall that Solow's approach assumes competition, that is, $\mu = 1$. The finding of a procyclical Solow residual leads to one of two conclusions: either my assumption of zero correlation is incorrect, or the firm is not competitive. My work follows the path of the second conclusion. A value of $\mu$ in excess of 1 will lower the correlation of the residual, $u$, and the business cycle. My approach, stripped to its absolute basics, is to choose as the estimate of $\mu$ the value that is just high enough to leave the residual uncorrelated with the business cycle. Plainly, the truth lies somewhere between the polar cases. Not every industry is perfectly competitive even in the most optimistic view, and some degree of correlation between productivity shifts and the business cycle would be conceded by any reasonable observer. However, my work proceeds on the assumption that the correlation is small enough to be ignored.

But, a chorus of readers will object, there are numerous sound economic reasons why productivity should be procyclical. All of those sound economic reasons, however, turn out to involve noncompetitive behavior. Consider the explanation based on labor hoarding. Productivity declines in a temporary slump because idle workers are kept at the firm in anticipation that their future employment will be profitable. However, in a competitive industry one of two things will happen in a slump. If workers are idle, marginal cost is at a low level because additional hours of labor are available for free. The industry price must fall to this low level of marginal cost, or it must fall far enough to stimulate demand to the point of eliminating all hoarded workers. In the latter case, neither output nor employment falls in the slump, so nothing happens to productivity. In the former case, the decline in the price has to be considered in the productivity calculation. The price decline makes the revenue share of labor, $\alpha = wN/pQ$, rise dramatically. The residual gives a much higher than normal weight to whatever employment decline occurs, enough so that measured productivity is unchanged.[4]

Other explanations of procyclical productivity either are also founded on assumptions of noncompetitive firms or fail to explain why Solow's method for measuring productivity has a procyclical bias. For example, it is true that productivity will be found to be procyclical in an industry where all firms operate chronically on the declining portion of their average cost curves. However, such industries cannot be competitive, because when price and marginal cost are equal and marginal cost is below average cost, firms would have losses at all times. Or, if firms have overhead labor but 'are competitive, then Solow's calculation will not give procyclical productivity. The reason is that Solow uses the observed real wage to adjust for the impact of those changes in employment that actually occur over the cycle. Under competition, where the real wage correctly measures the marginal product, his adjustment will operate exactly to offset the changes in output in the productivity calculation. It is true that overhead labor makes output per employee-hour procyclical, but it does not make Solow's productivity measure procyclical.

My argument that competition rules out procyclical productivity applies only to Solow's type of calculation, not to measures such as output per employee-hour. Other measures could easily be procyclical. But my work rests on Solow's measure, in which the response of price rules out procyclical productivity under competition.

Of course, in the real world, firms hoarding labor do not cut their prices to the level of marginal cost with free labor. Price remains high even when marginal cost falls. But this only confirms my point that procyclical productivity involves noncompetitive behavior.

**Changes in the capital stock**   My derivation so far has assumed that the capital stock does not change from one observation to the next. The computations are easily modified to handle the case where capital does change. In fact, all that is involved is redefinition of $\Delta q$ as the proportional change in the output-capital ratio and of $\Delta n$ as the proportional change in the labor-capital ratio.

Errors in measuring capital are a potential source of bias in my method for estimating the markup ratio. A bias in the estimate of $\mu$ will occur if the measurement error is correlated with the business cycle. The most likely source of bias is that the capital stock will be measured as the amount of capital available to the firm, whereas the calculations should use the amount of capital actually in use. Such an error would certainly be correlated with the business cycle, since capital utilization falls in a slump. However, the bias from this source depends on the pure user cost of capital. If the firm perceives the cost of higher capital utilization to be zero, because there is no pure user cost of capital, then the bias is zero. If the pure user cost is positive, the bias in the estimate of the markup ratio, $\mu$, is positive.

**Materials**   Generalization of Solow's method for productivity measurement to include inputs of materials is straightforward. Each input appears on the right-hand side of the equation as the product of its revenue share and its rate of growth. Practitioners of total factor productivity have made calculations with dozens of different factors treated in this way. However, the data available for my work do not include explicit measures of materials. Instead, materials have been subtracted from output in order to arrive at value added. I have carried out a full analysis of the implications of applying my version of Solow's method to data on value added.[5] In general, the estimate of the markup coefficient, $\mu$, obtained from the relation between labor input and real value added is an overstatement of the markup of the full price of output over marginal cost. The magnitude of the overstatement depends on the correlation of materials and output. In the unlikely case where the growth of materials input is uncorrelated with the growth of output, there would be no overstatement of $\mu$. At the opposite pole, which is more realistic, when materials grow in strict proportion to output, the overstatement is governed by a simple formula. The estimated markup coefficient, $\mu$, is then interpreted as the ratio of the price deflator to marginal labor cost. Because the price deflator is the price less unit materials cost, and marginal labor cost is marginal cost less the same unit materials cost, the value added markup, $\mu$, necessarily overstates the gross output markup, say $\mu^*$. The formula governing their relation is

$$\mu^* = \frac{\mu}{1 + (\mu - 1)m},$$

where $m$ is the ratio of materials cost to total revenue. The ratio $m$ is available only in those years when the Commerce Department has compiled input-output tables, not on an annual basis.

The gross output markup coefficient, $\mu^*$, measures the markup of the actual price of a product over its marginal cost of production, under the assumption that the firm is a price-taker in its materials markets. But $\mu^*$ understates the departure of any given price from its competitive level, because the materials suppliers are unlikely to be competitive. In principle, in order to find the degree of departure of a given price from its competitive level, one would have to carry out a full analysis of the upstream suppliers, using input-output data. I have not yet tried to do that. However, there is one simple case where the answer is obvious. Suppose the upstream suppliers are similar to the industry under examination—specifically, they have the same markups and the same materials shares. Then the value-added markup for the industry is also the markup of price over full marginal cost, counting the upstream markups. The exercise just considered is made even more relevant by the fact that many of the firms studied here are vertically integrated into their upstream supply industries. Working with input-output data would involve the arbitrary transfer prices used by such firms for their reports to the Commerce Department. In a firm that used its upstream unit's actual marginal cost as the transfer price, all of its market power would be assigned to its downstream unit with my method. On the other hand, if the transfer price includes some monopoly profit, then the analysis of the downstream unit would understate the monopoly power of the integrated operation.

**The econometric method**  The equation of be estimated is

$$\Delta q = \mu \alpha \Delta n + \theta + u.$$

The slope, $\mu$, is the markup ratio and the constant, $\theta$, is the average rate of technical progress. The general principle of estimation is to find the value of $\mu$ such that the residual, $u$, is uncorrelated with the business cycle. More specifically, I use an instrumental variable estimator with the rate of growth of real gross national product, $\Delta y$, as the instrument.

As indicated earlier, the assumption that $u$ is uncorrelated with the change in real GNP derives from two basic hypotheses of this work. First, fluctuations in productivity growth in any given industry are not causes of fluctuations in total real GNP. That is, genuine productivity growth is not a driving force in the business cycle. Shifts in production functions do not occur quickly enough and do not have sufficiently widespread effects to make an important contribution to year-to-year changes in real GNP. Second, the aggregate business cycle does not itself cause fluctuations in productivity. The production function of a given industry does not shift when national output rises or falls. The actual fluctuations in productivity observed over the cycle are either the result of using a method of productivity measurement other than Solow's total factor productivity or the consequence of market power.

Many other instrumental variables could be considered in addition to the change in real GNP. I have experimented with real military spending, but it is inadequate by itself and has little incremental power when the change in real GNP is already used. In future research, I plan to explore the use of industry-specific instruments such as federal purchases of the output of the industry. Better instruments could improve the results in two ways. First, under the hypotheses that justify the use of real GNP as an instrument, additional instruments could reduce the standard error of the estimate of the markup ratio. In industries whose output is hardly correlated with GNP, the improvement could be substantial. Second, alternative instruments might enable me to test the assumption that the productivity disturbance in each industry is uncorrelated with the national business cycle.

**Data**  I have assembled data for forty-eight industries covering all sectors of the U.S. economy and for durables and nondurables within manufacturing.[6] From the national income and product accounts, I have taken real and nominal value-added, indirect business taxes, hours of work of all employees, total compensation for each industry, and aggregate real GNP. In addition, I have used Bureau of Economic Analysis data on the net real capital stock for each industry. From the data, I have computed the price net of indirect business taxes as the ratio of nominal value added less indirect business taxes to real value added. Because compensation includes social security contributions and other fringe benefits, and the concept of price excludes sales taxes and other indirect taxes, the price and labor cost data are on a comparable basis. That is, a competitive industry would equate marginal cost based on this concept of labor cost to this concept of the price of output.

Because the national income and product accounts discontinued the compilation of the comprehensive measure of labor input after 1978, the sample period is 1949 through 1978. The data are annual.

I have used data for all of the two-digit industries included in the national income and product accounts except for the following, where problems in measuring output are so severe as to make the results questionable no matter how they come out: petroleum refining, banking, insurance carriers, real estate, holding companies, health services, and educational services. For petroleum refining, the calculation of value added seems to be severely distorted by the treatment of foreign income taxes. For banking, insurance, and holding companies, there are severe problems in adding back to purchases of services the value of the financial return paid to customers for their financial investments. For health and educational services, many transactions are outside the market. There remain forty-eight two-digit industries after these deletions.

**Results**   Table 1 shows the results of estimation for the forty-eight industries, which are divided into two groups: those in which cyclical fluctuations have enough impact on employment and output to shed some light on the value of the markup ratio and those in which cyclical fluctuations are weak or absent and are thus uninformative. The criterion for choosing the informative cases is that the standard error of the estimate of $\mu$ be 1.0 or smaller. The criterion is loose and merely excludes the cases of completely useless results.

Only three of the forty-eight industries had inadmissible estimates of $\mu$, below 1: other transportation equipment, security and commodity brokers, and agricultural services. All of them are within 1 standard error of the

**Table 1**
Estimates of markup ratios by industry, 1949–1978

| Standard industrial classification (SIC) code | Industry | Markup ratio | Summary statistic | |
|---|---|---|---|---|
| | | | Standard error | Durbin-Watson |
| Meaningful estimates[a] | | | | |
| Substantial market power | | | | |
| 28 | Chemicals | 3.39 | 0.78 | 1.99 |
| 26 | Paper | 2.68 | 0.33 | 1.45 |
| 40 | Railroad transportation | 2.38 | 0.35 | 1.64 |
| 44 | Water transportation | 2.16 | 0.65 | 1.44 |
| 371 | Motor vehicles | 2.07 | 0.22 | 2.42 |
| 33 | Primary metals | 2.06 | 0.15 | 2.36 |
| 42 | Trucking and warehousing | 2.06 | 0.48 | 2.28 |
| Some market power | | | | |
| 32 | Stone, clay, and glass | 1.81 | 0.22 | 2.21 |
| 11 | Coal mining | 1.68 | 0.51 | 0.71 |
| 27 | Printing and publishing | 1.61 | 0.66 | 1.74 |
| 76 | Repair | 1.60 | 0.23 | 2.39 |
| 31 | Leather | 1.59 | 0.33 | 2.66 |
| 70 | Hotels and lodging | 1.59 | 0.88 | 2.76 |
| 39 | Miscellaneous | 1.52 | 0.55 | 2.70 |
| 36 | Electrical machinery | 1.43 | 0.15 | 2.35 |
| 48 | Communications | 1.43 | 0.64 | 1.92 |
| 30 | Rubber | 1.41 | 0.20 | 2.41 |
| 35 | Nonelectrical machinery | 1.39 | 0.10 | 2.23 |
| 34 | Fabricated metals | 1.39 | 0.13 | 1.42 |
| 25 | Furniture | 1.38 | 0.17 | 2.19 |
| 23 | Apparel | 1.30 | 0.24 | 2.04 |
| 38 | Instruments | 1.29 | 0.15 | 2.38 |
| 95 | Total nondurables | 1.61 | 0.19 | 1.81 |
| 96 | Total durables | 1.62 | 0.09 | 1.87 |
| Little market power | | | | |
| 15 | Construction | 1.11 | 0.34 | 1.43 |
| 22 | Textiles | 1.05 | 0.27 | 1.88 |
| 24 | Lumber | 1.00 | 0.21 | 1.87 |
| 7 | Agricultural services | 0.92 | 0.74 | 2.29 |
| 372 | Other transportation equipment | 0.91 | 0.18 | 1.65 |
| 62 | Security and commodity brokers | 0.56 | 0.92 | 2.02 |
| Unreliable estimates[b] | | | | |
| 10 | Metal mining | 2.80 | 1.23 | 2.16 |
| 45 | Air transportation | 3.28 | 1.33 | 1.40 |
| 483 | Radio and TV broadcasting | 2.00 | 1.40 | 2.08 |
| 78 | Motion pictures | 2.87 | 1.63 | 2.46 |
| 20 | Food and beverages | 3.09 | 1.64 | 1.55 |
| 21 | Tobacco | 1.28 | 2.14 | 2.26 |

**Table 1** (continued)

| Standard industrial classification (SIC) code | Industry | Markup ratio | Summary statistic | |
|---|---|---|---|---|
| | | | Standard error | Durbin-Watson |
| 52 | Retail trade | 3.63 | 2.19 | 2.04 |
| 50 | Wholesale trade | 3.67 | 2.67 | 1.35 |
| 81 | Legal services | 4.09 | 2.75 | 1.78 |
| 75 | Auto repair | −1.46 | 4.74 | 0.37 |
| 41 | Local and interurban transit | −1.61 | 7.00 | 1.83 |
| 79 | Amusement | 0.35 | 7.97 | 1.78 |
| 61 | Credit agencies | −0.81 | 8.10 | 0.93 |
| 49 | Utilities | 10.18 | 9.09 | 0.42 |
| 13 | Oil and gas extraction | 11.30 | 13.20 | 0.62 |
| 64 | Insurance agents | −4.14 | 28.10 | 2.32 |
| 1 | Farms | 17.20 | 28.90 | 1.13 |
| 14 | Nonmetallic minerals | 20.30 | 104.00 | 1.61 |
| 46 | Pipelines | 50.50 | 182.00 | 1.94 |
| 73 | Business services | −10.40 | 432.00 | 0.85 |

Sources: Author's estimates as described in text. The data used in the calculations are from the national-income and national-product accounts.

Notes: The markup ratio, $\mu$, is estimated from the equation $\Delta q = \mu \alpha \Delta n + \theta + \mu$ with the rate of growth of GNP, $\Delta y$, as an instrumental variable. The dependent variable, $\Delta q$, is the change in output; $\alpha$ is the revenue share of labor, $\Delta n$ is the change in hours of labor; and $\theta$ is a constant measuring the mean rate of technical progress.

a. Standard error of the estimate of the markup ratio, $\mu$, is 1.0 or smaller.

b. Industries with too little cyclical variation to measure the markup ratio.

competitive value of 1. In thirteen industries, the hypothesis of competition is decisively rejected in favor of market power; the estimate of $\mu - 1$ is more than double its standard error. In most of these instances, the estimated value of $\mu$ indicates economically substantial market power. In six industries—paper, chemicals, primary metals, motor vehicles, railroad transportation, and trucking and warehousing—the value of $\mu$ exceeded 2 and departed from competition by at least 2 standard errors as well. Two of these industries—railroads and trucking—were regulated throughout the sample period. In a decade or so, it should be possible to determine whether deregulation has made them more competitive.

A few industries—textiles, lumber, and other transportation equipment —are shown to be reasonably close to competitive, in that the estimate of the markup ratio is at least 1 standard error below 1.4. In these industries, the data say that the chances are at least five out of six that the markup is 40 percent or less.

Table 1 also shows results for two aggregates within manufacturing—nondurables and durables. The markup ratios are estimated to be 1.61 and 1.62, respectively, with very small standard errors. The hypothesis of competition is decisively rejected for the aggregates as well.

In summary, most two-digit industries show signs of market power, and in a significant part of the economy, market power is substantial. The evidence is based on the finding that increases in output are achieved with increases in labor input that cost relatively little in comparison with the price charged for the output.

**Excess capacity**

With all this market power, shouldn't American industry be inordinately profitable? But if it were, then a new puzzle would result: why wouldn't new firms enter the market and compete away the profit? One powerful body of thought holds that competition is the only possible outcome in the long run in an industry without barriers to entry. According to that view, market power creates profit opportunities, so entry will occur up to the point that market power is fully dissipated by the multiplicity of sellers. Even more optimistically, the "contestable markets" school argues that the mere possibility of entry will enforce competition in a market with few sellers.[7]

The model of the coexistence of market power and free entry, first articulated by Edward Chamberlin and put on a more formal footing by Michael Spence, Avinash Dixit, and Joseph Stiglitz, has two essential ingredients.[8] First, there must be some separation between the markets of rivals. The formal treatments usually consider product differentiation, but geographic dispersion of markets will have the same effect. Second, there must be fixed costs of some kind associated with each distinct market. Absent market differentiation, a single seller could supply multiple markets from a single production unit. As many sellers came to do this, competition would be the result. Absent fixed costs, each market could be served by a great many sellers operating at a small scale, and competition would again be the result.

With differentiated markets and fixed costs, a zero-profit equilibrium with market power will emerge. The smallest markets will be served by a single seller. Although that seller may make some profit, each potential entrant foresees that it cannot cover its fixed costs at the price that would result from the competition between the two were the new seller to enter the market. Hence, the market is in equilibrium with monopoly. Larger markets may be able to sustain more than one seller, but still there will be some market power in equilibrium. The details of the equilibrium with more than one seller depend on what theory of oligopoly governs their interaction. If the sellers reach the monopoly price by collusion or otherwise, then market power will remain strong. If the equilibrium is the type described by Cournot, the price will approach the competitive level as the number of sellers grows. In the version of the story with product differentiation, it generally pays for the entrant to adopt a differentiated product, so there is always just one seller in each market.

The empirical work in this paper does not attempt to test Chamberlin's model specifically, but instead examines the profit earned by various industries and compares it with the profit that would be earned by an industry with the degree of monopoly power found in the results of the previous section. The calculation of latent monopoly profit assumes that the technology has constant returns to scale. In particular, the calculation excludes the possibility of increasing returns in general or fixed costs of any kind; that is, it excludes the possibility that the firm operates most of the time on a decreasing portion of its average cost curve.

The basic finding is that profit is nowhere near as high as it would be under full exploitation of market power with constant returns. My interpretation is that firms face setup costs, advertising costs, or fixed costs that absorb a good part of the latent monopoly profit. In this interpretation, firms frequently operate on the decreasing portions of their average cost curves. Marginal cost is consequently well below average cost, and zero or low levels of actual pure profit are the result.

I retain the approach to the measurement of market power set forth in the previous section. It has the convenient property that market power is expressed as the ratio of price to marginal cost. Once marginal cost is known, then the profit-maximizing price is known directly; my analysis does not need to go through the steps of profit maximization. Similarly, the optimal level of employment is already implicit in the analysis. However, the third dimension of optimization, the choice of the capital stock, now has to be considered explicitly.

Let $\pi$ be the actual rate of pure profit relative to sales:

$$\pi = \frac{pQ - wN - rK}{pQ},$$

where $rK$ is the annual service cost of the capital stock. Under the hypothesis of zero expected pure profit, $\pi$ would be a purely random element, sometimes positive and sometimes negative. On the other hand, if a firm could exercise its full monopoly power and choose its capital stock subject to a constant-returns-to-scale technology, then $\pi$ would be substantially positive, on the average. To see how big it would be, we must consider the firm's optimal choice of capital.

The characterization of the cost-minimizing choice of capital under constant returns is remarkably simple. Think of the firm as divided into a marketing department and a production department. Marketing takes no inputs. Production sells to marketing at a transfer price equal to marginal cost. If production has chosen its capital stock optimally, the pure profit of the production department will be zero on the average. That is, the quantity

$$\pi_p = \frac{xQ - wN - rK}{pQ}$$

should be a purely random element with zero mean. I call $\pi_p$ the firm's "production profit." The other part of the firm's total profit is

$$\pi_M = \pi - \pi_p = (p - x)/p = 1 - 1/\mu,$$

which I call "marketing profit." A properly run firm producing with constant returns to scale has production profit that averages zero over the cycle—production just covers the annual carrying cost of its capital stock. Its marketing department generates all of its pure profit, as measured by $\pi_M$. By contrast, a firm in the situation described by Chamberlin, with zero pure profit, will generate a substantial amount of marketing profit but will lose the corresponding amount in its production department. That is, $\pi_p$ will be sufficiently negative to offset the profit generated by marketing. A competitive firm will have no pure profit in either the marketing or the production departments.

In this section, I will simply compute total profit and its two components based on the estimates of market power from the previous section. That is, I will compute total profit directly from the data, impute marketing profit by inserting the earlier estimates of the markup ratio, $\mu$, into the formula for $\pi_M$ just derived, and then calculate the profit of the production department as the difference between total profit and marketing profit. This procedure does not try to deal fully with the statistical reliability of the decomposition, but other work of mine shows that the estimates of production profit are quite reliable.[9]

Because the imputation of marketing profit is entirely dependent on the earlier estimation of the markup coeffcient, $\mu$, there is no point in trying to make the calculations for this section except for those industries in which there is enough cyclical movement in employment and output to identify the markup. Hence, the results in this section are confined to those industries in the top part of table 1 for which the standard error of the estimate of $\mu$ was 1.0 or smaller.

**Data** All the data for these calculations are the same as in the previous section except for one added series, the rental price of capital ($r$ in the formulas above). Briefly, I computed the rental price according to the Hall-Jorgenson formula, using the dividend yield of the Standard and Poor's 500 as the real interest rate. I obtained values for the depreciation rate, the effective investment tax credit rate, and present discounted value of depreciation deductions from Jorgenson and Sullivan, and the value for the deflator for business fixed investment from the national income and product accounts.[10]

**Results** Table 2 shows the decomposition of pure profit per dollar of sales for the 28 relevant industries. The first column shows total profit on the average over the period, together with the standard error of the estimate of the average. In all but the regulated industries, total pure profit per dollar of sales is positive and usually exceeds zero by many standard errors. A number of industries earn 20 cents or more in pure profit for each dollar of sales. The hypothesis of strict zero profit is rejected by the data. However, this rejection is subject to a number of qualifications. All earnings of the firms not paid out as compensation are treated as profit or the return to capital. The returns to the firm's investments in human capital, research and development, and advertising are included in profit. However, another accounting convention goes in the opposite direction—the costs of these investments are deducted from profit in the year the investments are made. Profit is overstated for slowly growing firms whose current investment falls short of the return earned from past investment and understated for quickly growing ones.

The profit calculations also overstate profit slightly because of the omission of inventories from the capital stock. I have been able to calculate the current market value of inventories for about half of the industries covered

**Table 2**
Decomposition of profit per dollar of value added, 1949–1978

| SIC code | Industry | Profit per dollar | | Marketing[a] | Production[b] | Markup ratio |
|---|---|---|---|---|---|---|
| | | Total | Standard error | | | |
| Substantial market power | | | | | | |
| 28 | Chemicals | 0.22 | 0.013 | 0.71 | −0.49 | 3.39 |
| 26 | Paper | 0.14 | 0.009 | 0.63 | −0.49 | 2.68 |
| 40 | Railroad transportation | −0.30 | 0.011 | 0.58 | −0.88 | 2.38 |
| 44 | Water transportation | −0.36 | 0.018 | 0.54 | −0.90 | 2.16 |
| 371 | Motor vehicles | 0.33 | 0.023 | 0.52 | −0.19 | 2.07 |
| 33 | Primary metals | 0.07 | 0.016 | 0.51 | −0.45 | 2.06 |
| 42 | Trucking and warehousing | 0.20 | 0.005 | 0.51 | −0.31 | 2.06 |
| Some market power | | | | | | |
| 32 | Stone, clay, and glass | 0.12 | 0.011 | 0.45 | −0.32 | 1.81 |
| 11 | Coal mining | 0.17 | 0.018 | 0.40 | −0.24 | 1.68 |
| 27 | Printing and publishing | 0.15 | 0.004 | 0.38 | −0.23 | 1.61 |
| 76 | Repair | 0.31 | 0.230 | 0.38 | −0.07 | 1.60 |
| 31 | Leather | 0.09 | 0.006 | 0.37 | −0.28 | 1.59 |
| 70 | Hotels and lodging | 0.09 | 0.013 | 0.37 | −0.28 | 1.59 |
| 39 | Miscellaneous | 0.16 | 0.006 | 0.34 | −0.19 | 1.52 |
| 36 | Electrical machinery | 0.15 | 0.010 | 0.30 | −0.15 | 1.43 |
| 48 | Communications | −0.01 | 0.015 | 0.30 | −0.31 | 1.43 |
| 30 | Rubber | 0.16 | 0.010 | 0.29 | −0.13 | 1.41 |
| 35 | Nonelectrical machinery | 0.15 | 0.007 | 0.28 | −0.13 | 1.39 |
| 34 | Fabricated metals | 0.10 | 0.006 | 0.28 | −0.18 | 1.39 |
| 25 | Furniture | 0.12 | 0.007 | 0.28 | −0.15 | 1.38 |
| 23 | Apparel | 0.11 | 0.003 | 0.23 | −0.13 | 1.30 |
| 38 | Instruments | 0.15 | 0.010 | 0.22 | −0.07 | 1.29 |
| 95 | Total nondurables | 0.21 | 0.006 | 0.38 | −0.17 | 1.61 |
| 96 | Total durables | 0.15 | 0.009 | 0.38 | −0.23 | 1.62 |

**Table 2** (continued)

| | | Profit per dollar | | | | Markup |
| SIC code | Industry | Total | Standard error | Marketing[a] | Production[b] | ratio |
| --- | --- | --- | --- | --- | --- | --- |
| Little market power | | | | | | |
| 15 | Construction | 0.24 | 0.003 | 0.10 | 0.14 | 1.11 |
| 22 | Textiles | 0.07 | 0.009 | 0.05 | 0.02 | 1.05 |
| 24 | Lumber | 0.21 | 0.007 | 0.00 | 0.21 | 1.00 |
| 7 | Agricultural services | −2.90 | 0.198 | −0.09 | −2.81 | 0.92 |
| 372 | Other transportation equipment | 0.01 | 0.015 | −0.10 | 0.11 | 0.91 |
| 62 | Security and commodity brokers | 0.30 | 0.019 | −0.79 | 1.09 | 0.56 |

Source: Author's estimates as described in text.
Notes: This table includes only those industries in the top part of table 1, where the standard error of the estimated markup was 1.0 or smaller.
a. Calculated as an increasing function of the markup coefficient, $\pi_M = 1 - 1/\mu$.
b. Residual of total profit per dollar and marketing profit per dollar. Figures are rounded.

in table 2. Profit per dollar of value added is generally about 4 cents less than the numbers in table 2 when the service cost of inventories is subtracted from revenue.

The third column shows the marketing profit per dollar of sales. Marketing profit is a simple increasing function of the markup coefficient, $\pi_M = 1 - 1/\mu$. The fourth column then computes production profit as the residual. Production profit is invariably negative for firms with market power, sometimes substantially negative. Not surprisingly, the biggest production losses occur in regulated industries. But chemicals, paper, primary metals, trucking, and stone, clay, and glass all have production losses in excess of 30 cents per dollar of value added.

Production profits are negative because firms are unable to minimize costs by making a free choice of the scale of their productive units. Instead, many of their units are "too big" because they are at the minimum practical scale. Together with their associated marketing departments, they cover their costs, so they are reasonable investments. However, they do not typically operate anywhere near their physical capacities.

**Qualifications and potential sources of bias**

The fact that drives all of my results is well known and uncontroversial: for many industries and all broad aggregates, output can rise substantially with only a modest increase in measured labor input. All measures of productivity, from the simplest measure of output per employee-hour to the most sophisticated computation of total factor productivity, show a pronounced cycle that tracks the movements in employment and output. My work amounts to a new interpretation of this established fact; it attributes procyclical productivity to the existence of market power. As I have already noted, existing explanations of the procyclicality of productivity, such as the hypotheses of labor hoarding and overhead labor, also presuppose noncompetitive behavior and so are harmonious with my explanation.

There is not much doubt, as a matter of economic analysis, that market power distorts the total factor productivity calculations recommended by Solow. Solow's basic idea was to subtract from the growth of output the part that could be explained by the growth of labor input. He used a market measure of the marginal product of labor, the real wage, to provide the coefficient to put in front of labor growth in that calculation. Under competition, the real wage is a proper measure of the marginal product. But with market power, the real wage understates the marginal product of labor. Hence, Solow's calculation makes too small an adjustment for changing labor input in the presence of market power. In an expansion, output rises by more than can be explained by the increase in labor input. Measured productivity rises in the expansion.

The strong assumption that I make is that all of the cyclical behavior of total factor productivity is the result of the understatement of the marginal product of labor on account of market power. I exclude any other factor that does not operate through market power. Here I list and discuss other explanations that I reject by assumption.

**Productivity fluctuations as a driving force in the business cycle**  Fluctuations in productivity have been central to the effort of the real business cycle school to find an explanation for aggregate fluctuations that does not rest on price-wage rigidity, market imperfections, or misperceptions about the state of the economy. The real business cycle school tries to use the same basic microeconomic principles that an economist would normally invoke to explain the ups and downs of, say, onion production. Aggregate output is set by the intersection of a supply function and a demand function; the prices mediating the two are the real interest rate and the real wage.[11] A favorable productivity shift makes output rise; the public perceives a boom. In some other year when productivity was unusually low, the opposite would happen and people would complain of a recession.

In an economy with numerous industries, the productivity shocks would have to be economywide to create meaningful aggregate fluctuations. Were that not so and each of fifty industries had its own independent shock, the law of large numbers would make aggregate GNP almost immune from fluctuations driven by those shocks. In considering what types of productivity shocks might provide a competitive explanation for the findings of this paper, it is essential to restrict consideration to those shocks that operate in tandem across industries and to rule out innovations whose contributions are limited to particular industries.

One obvious common influence is the weather. However, the industry most affected by weather, agriculture, is almost unique in having output fluctuations that are completely uncorrelated with total GNP (see table 3 and the discussion that follows). The hypothesis that weather is an important driving force for total GNP surely faces an uphill battle with the data.[12]

I am also skeptical that process innovation has an important role in aggregate fluctuations. Even if an episode of rapid growth could be traced to the sudden adoption of improved technology, what about contractions in output? Are they periods when businesses throughout the economy choose simultaneously to abandon the most efficient methods?

The only problem with dismissing technology shocks as a driving force for aggregate output is that there must be some driving force—the economy does have important fluctuations. If the driving force is not technology, it must be shifts in preferences, government policies, terms of trade, and other determinants of economic activity. One could be just as scornful about the idea that there are spontaneous shifts in consumption or that investment is driven in part by animal spirits. But some of these forces must drive the cycle, or there would be no recessions and no booms.

**The wage does not control the allocation of labor**   A fundamental hypothesis of my work is that the reported wage governs the firm's choice of labor input. The firm is seen as a price-taker in the labor market. One alternative interpretation of my results is that firms have extensive monopsony power: they hire workers up to the point that the marginal compensation cost equals the marginal revenue product of labor. Under monopsony, marginal compensation cost will exceed the wage. Solow's productivity calculation will go off track because it uses the reported wage, not the higher level of marginal compensation cost, to infer the marginal product of labor. On this interpretation, my results show that the labor market is imperfect, not that the product market is imperfect.

In an economy where the majority of people work in labor markets with thousands of employers, and few workers are highly specialized in the type of work uniquely available from their employer, it seems implausible that monopsony power in its standard sense has much to do with my findings. Of more concern is the monopsony power that arises in the dealings of a firm with its established, long-term employees. That topic has been studied at length in the literature on employment contracts.

Under a long-term contract, it cannot be taken for granted that the wage set by the contract has anything to do with the cost of increasing labor input. The majority of American workers are paid by salary, and it is virtually the definition of a salary that compensation is the same amount each pay period independent of the actual amount of work. Salaried workers are expected to work harder and longer when there is more work to do. Of course, there must be some implicit cost of asking the existing work force to put in more hours, or management would ask them to work harder all the time. The typical salaried job involves an implicit or explicit arrangement whereby weeks with extra hours are balanced by short weeks or time off. In addition, those who put in extraordinary hours are more likely to earn raises.

As it happens, uncompensated fluctuations in work effort are not an important problem for my calculations, provided that the average amount of compensation correctly measures the implicit wage. Contract theory suggests that on the average the two should be equal. The firm should be indifferent whether to ask for more effort from its existing staff or to add new staff. The latter cost is just the average amount of compensation.

Average hourly compensation probably differs from the true implicit cost of labor over the cycle, understating the true cost in good years and overstating it in poor years. However, a cyclical bias has no impact on my calculations.[13] Although the first differences of output and labor input are the essential input to the calculations, it is only the level of the wage, as it appears in labor's share, $\alpha$, that matters. A cyclical error in $\alpha$ is unimportant. Suppose that the error is procyclical, as suggested above. In strong years, employment growth is positive, the growth of real GNP is positive, and the error is positive. Their product is positive. In weak years, all three components are negative, and the product is negative. The net contribution of the error to my calculations is zero, because the weak years offset the strong years.

**Other cyclical errors** The same argument applies to any error whose influence on my calculations is only to introduce a cyclical error in labor's share. Adjustment costs for labor are a good example. With adjustment costs, half the time the firm sees the marginal cost of increasing labor input as above the wage (when growth is high) and the other half of the time it sees the marginal cost of increasing labor input as less than the wage, because of the saving in downward adjustment costs. Another example of a benign cyclical error is price rigidity that is not associated with market power. If the price is less flexible than the competitive price, but the two are equal on the average, then the only result is a cyclical error in labor's share, and that has no impact on my conclusions about market power.

**Errors in measuring labor input** The same argument that shows the irrelevance of cyclical errors in labor's share also demonstrates the sensitivity of my calculations to cyclical errors in measuring labor input. Suppose that the error in measuring hours is negative in strong years and positive in weak years. Then its product with the growth of GNP will be negative in strong years (when the error is negative and the change in GNP is positive) and negative in weak years as well (when the error is positive and the change in GNP is negative). The strength of the association of the change in labor input with the change in GNP will be understated. My estimate of the markup ratio, $\mu$, is the ratio of the covariance of output and GNP changes to the covariance of labor input and GNP changes. That ratio will be overstated in the presence of cyclical errors in measuring labor input.

Two types of cyclical errors in measuring labor input are possible; they both create the same bias. First, fluctuations in reported hours of work may understate actual fluctuations in hours, because firms and workers report a standard forty-hour week and not their actual, more variable work week. My data on hours of work use all available sources to measure actual hours. In particular, the national income and product accounts use the Bureau of Labor Statistics' household survey to measure the hours of nonproduction workers. However, it is likely that there is some element of cyclical understatement of fluctuations in hours.

The second type of cyclical error escapes measurement altogether—fluctuations in the intensity of work effort. One dimension of the proposition that people work harder when there is more work to do is that they get more done per hour of work in the peak than in the trough. It should not be taken for granted, however, that this phenomenon is quantitatively large. It is less persuasive on the downside: in a slump, why would people want to keep coming to work for their usual hours and accomplish less per hour, when they could enjoy more time at home by working as hard as usual, but spending fewer hours at work? Even in normal times, they face the same opportunity to work closer to capacity and spend fewer hours at work, or, for that matter, to work normal hours and earn more.

The only study I know that has examined work effort over the business cycle finds a small increase, not a decrease, during a slump. Jon Fay and James Medoff surveyed almost 200 managers of manufacturing plants and asked whether the work effort of blue-collar workers changed during a large cyclical contraction. A slight majority said effort increased.[14]

## Lessons for Macroeconomics

The results developed here have implications for several important issues in macroeconomics: They add to our understanding of why measured productivity varies cyclically, they demonstrate that economic supply or capacity can be highly elastic, and they explain why market forces provide no strong tendency to move the economy to high-employment levels of operation.

**Cyclical productivity**

At a minimum, macroeconomists should be aware that market power may have an important role in explaining cyclical fluctuations in measured productivity. None of my work tests the alternative hypothesis that cyclical fluctuations in productivity are an exogenous driving force in a competitive model. Rather, I assume that there is no important pattern of true productivity shifts common across industries that create recessions and booms. Those macroeconomists who believe, as I do, that productivity changes do not drive the business cycle should be at least partly convinced that noncompetitive conditions explain cyclical fluctuations in measured productivity as a response to changes in the forces that cause recessions and booms.

Labor hoarding is an important ingredient in the explanation of why small fluctuations in employment accompany large fluctuations in output. A competitive firm is unlikely to let its work force remain idle. It can sell added output without depressing the price. Unless the price is so low that it cannot cover the cost of materials, the firm can make added profit by putting all of its workers to work. But a firm with market power may well hoard workers during a temporary downturn, because the alternative of dumping output on the market is unattractive on account of its depressing effect on price.

**Capacity constraints**

Another important implication of my findings is that it is physically possible for aggregate supply to be highly elastic. In the equilibrium I described in the first part of the paper, numerous firms inhabit market niches with surplus capacity because the constraint of minimum scale is binding. Each is capable of increasing output above its normal level by hiring only a little new labor. Because price far exceeds marginal cost, the increment to GNP from the added output will be worth more than the added wage cost. The output of the economy is constrained by demand in this type of equilibrium. An episode such as a major war or a dramatic, prolonged monetary stimulus can draw forth huge increases in GNP.

If some stimulus—fiscal, monetary, or other—raises demand in a way that is expected to be long-lasting, even more capacity will be created. Higher demand will raise profit in existing niches, stimulating the entry of new capacity in them, and will also make new niches sufficiently profitable for exploitation. In the new equilibrium, expected profit will be zero once again, but at a higher level of total capacity.

**Incentives to expand to full employment**

Perhaps the most important implication of excess capacity and market power in many industries is that businesses have little or no incentive to expand to full capacity. A number of theoretical models have made this point recently. Oliver Hart's model of general equilibrium with market power posits market power in both product markets and labor markets and a single equilibrium in which output and employment are below their competitive levels.[15] In Hart's model, economic activity is sensitive to government interventions that would have little impact in a competitive economy. Procompetitive government policies that would increase the number of sellers in each product market would increase output and welfare. Hart's work offsets earlier partial-equilibrium analysis that concluded that the welfare costs of market power were only small Harberger triangles summing to a fraction of a percent of GNP.

Walter P. Heller's more recent work considers a related model with a multiplicity of equilibria.[16] One of the equilibria is similar to Hart's. Others involve even lower output. There is no obvious economic force that will take the economy from its poorer equilibria to the best one. And even the best one has lower output than does competition.

There is a tremendous gap between the theoretical models just described and the actual U.S. economy. Rather than discuss any more elaborate general equilibrium models, I want to consider some features of partial equilibrium with excess capacity and market power at a somewhat more practical level. In particular, I will examine the issue of the incentives that a firm perceives to expand output when it is below its equilibrium output. I will enlarge upon an idea first advanced in the "small menu costs" literature, which has argued that prices are rigid in response to small changes in market conditions.[17] When a firm with market power sets a price to maximize profit, it picks the price where profit is locally unaffected by small changes in the price—the curve showing profit as a function of price is flat at its maximum. Consequently, within some region, the firm cannot improve its profit by enough to justify even small costs of changing its price. It keeps its price at its previous level even though new conditions would justify a different price if the change were costless.

The literature on small menu costs has considered the relation between price and profit, because the firm with market power is normally considered as setting a price and meeting the demand forthcoming at that price. However, the principal task of macroeconomics, in my view, is to explain the behavior of output, not prices. Price rigidity is significant to the extent that it brings about excessive fluctuations in output, not because prices are intrinsically important. Hence, it is important to look at the relation between profit and output. In doing so, I am not suggesting that firms consider output to be their control variable. Rather, I continue to assume that firms set prices and let their customers choose the quantity sold, but I look at the implications in terms of the resulting relation between output and profit. It turns out that for a broad class of circumstances, that relation is extremely flat.

When a firm finds itself out of equilibrium, with a level of output different from the profit-maximizing one, the incentive to make an adjustment depends on the flatness of the output-profit curve. The flatness depends, in turn, on the degree of market power—that is, on the elasticity of demand facing the seller, on the way that elasticity changes with output, and on the shape of the marginal cost curve.

**Constancy of marginal cost**   Here I will demonstrate a proposition that is central to the view put forth in this paper: an industry that achieves its equilibrium along a flat portion of the marginal cost curves of its firms is more likely to have a nearly indeterminate equilibrium than is an industry at equilibrium along a rising portion of the marginal cost curve. Consider a firm facing given factor prices and stable behavior on the part of its rivals. The firm is thinking about alternative levels of its own output, achieved by setting different prices. If the firm's marginal cost schedule is steep, an increase in output moves the firm into a region where cost rises more steeply with output and hence profit falls rapidly. The maximum of profit is well defined. On the other hand, with flat marginal cost, only the decline in marginal revenue makes profit begin to decline as output rises above the point where profit is maximized.

What type of industry achieves equilibrium with its firms operating along flat parts of their marginal cost schedules? I will argue that this outcome is much more likely in Chamberlinian equilibrium than in competition, though it is not inevitably a feature of the Chamberlinian equilibrium. A competitive industry generates an expected return high enough to attract capital by having a level of capacity small enough, in equilibrium, so that demand occasionally presses against capacity and high prices are the result. Absent these periods of scarcity pricing, revenue would cover only variable costs, and capital would earn an inadequate return. On the other hand, when firms have market power in equilibrium, the profit derived from that power is itself an attractor of capital. Periods of scarcity pricing only add to the attraction of investment in the industry. It is perfectly possible for equilibrium to occur with sufficient underutilized capital that output never enters a region of rising marginal cost. To summarize, constant marginal cost is an impossibility under competition, because it cannot generate the revenue to pay for the capital stock, but constant marginal cost is completely consistent with an equilibrium with market power. Hence a finding of market power points in the direction of constant marginal cost.

In my findings in the first part of this paper, competition is ruled out for industries with markup ratios substantially above 1. While the results are consistent with the explanation I have just given for flat marginal cost, the argument is not conclusive. There are alternative explanations for the findings of market power with little profit, and not all of them require that marginal cost be flat. For example, suppose that an advertising campaign is needed to establish brand-name recognition in order to enter the industry. The technology has constant returns to scale and there is no minimum practical scale. The equilibrium will not involve excess capacity and a level of output on a flat part of the marginal cost schedule. Instead, all of the latent profit from market power will be dissipated by advertising a sufficiently large number of products.

My results to date support the hypothesis that the marginal cost curve is flat but are also consistent with noncompetitive alternatives. Unfortunately, a direct empirical attack on the problem is difficult because of the cyclical measurement errors that are likely to pervade the data. These errors have a benign effect on my measures of market power and profitability but stand in the way of measuring the slope of the marginal cost schedule.

**Implications of constant marginal cost**   The findings of the first part of this paper are consistent with an industry equilibrium along a flat part of the marginal cost schedule of each firm. In order to draw out the implications

*Lost profit as percent of value added*

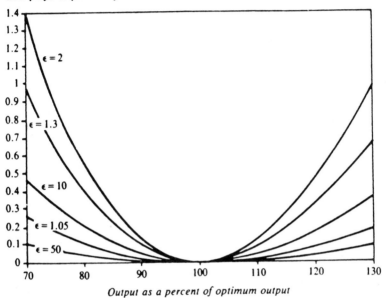

*Output as a percent of optimum output*

**Figure 1**
Profits and output with constant marginal cost. The source is the author's calculations as described in the text. These calculations assume that firms face constant marginal cost and constant elasticity of demand. Each profit-output curve is labeled with its demand elasticity, $\epsilon$.

of constant marginal cost, I will make the additonal assumption that the demand schedule perceived by each firm has constant elasticity. Figure 1 shows various output-profit curves for different elasticities. Each curve is labeled with its elasticity, $\epsilon$; the corresponding markup, $\mu$, is related by $\mu = 1/(1 - 1/\epsilon)$. Profit is most sensitive to output when the elasticity of demand is around 2. The curve for $\epsilon = 2$ shows that profit falls short of its maximum by about 0.6 percent of value added when output is 20 percent below its optimum and by about 0.5 percent when output is 20 percent too high. Even in this worst case, profit is hardly sensitive to output deviations of 20 percent. And when market power is either greater ($\epsilon = 1.3$ or 1.05) or smaller ($\epsilon = 10$ or 50), profit falls short of its maximum by only one or two tenths of a percent of value added for output deviations of 20 percent.

Figure 1 measures lost profit in relation to value added. Other normalizations might generate larger percentages, but it is important to understand how the normalizations differ. In particular, normalization by the value of profit itself is problematical. Profit is zero on the average in competitive industries and I have argued that it is fairly close to zero even with market power because of the process of entry. Hence a normalization by pure profit would not make sense. Normalization by the total earnings of capital, which are between a quarter and a third of value added, would triple or quadruple the percentages shown in figure 1, but they would still be very small.

The case of constant elasticity of demand is no more than illustrative. The elasticity of demand can decrease with output, or it can increase. The linear demand curve is an example in which the elasticity of demand is higher at point of high price and low quantity. And any demand curve that intersects the vertical axis has at least a region where elasticity decreases with output. When elasticity increases mildly with output, profit is even less sensitive to output than it is in the case of a constant elasticity. There are good reasons to think that elasticity may increase with output for many products. Suppose that a product is sold to a number of groups of customers and the groups have different, but constant, elasticities. Then the total demand for the product must exhibit increasing elasticity. As price falls, the demands of the more elastic groups increase as a fraction of total demand. The elasticity of total demand is the weighted average of the elasticities of the groups, so it must rise when the more elastic groups are a larger part of the total. When elasticity increases with output at just the right rate, profit will be perfectly flat for a range of levels of output. That is, it is possible for marginal revenue to be a constant corresponding with marginal cost.

The upshot of this investigation of the implications of constant marginal cost is that the incentive to set exactly the profit-maximizing price and produce exactly the corresponding quantity is weak and may even be absent when the elasticity of demand is constant or increases with output. Output can be nearly indeterminate over a wide range with the right curvature of the demand schedule.

With indeterminacy, a firm perceives itself as capturing a fixed amount of profit no matter what its price and output are. Even if indeterminacy does not hold, the incremental profit from adjusting output by, say, 10 percent, is tiny. In businesses with the flat marginal cost curves suggested by my results, fine-tuning output and price is not a matter of priority for management. Managers perceive that lowering a price will raise volume, but they also know that the volume and price effects will cancel each other to a first approximation. Other areas of management, such as better products, more effective promotion, and reduction in overhead and production costs, receive higher priority because there is no automatic offset to their benefits.

Everyday economic life is full of examples of near-indeterminacy at work. In most communities today, the prices of essentially identical gasoline at neighboring stations can differ by several cents a gallon. Dispersion in prices persists for months, but the pattern is not permanent. Chevron was once at the top of the distribution, but is now near the bottom. Stations with low prices do vastly more business, but their profit per gallon is enough less that they are no more profitable than the high-priced ones. Indeterminacy of quantity seems the only reasonable explanation. A condominium in Maui has raised its daily rate 10 dollars each year for the past seven years, quite heedless of what has happened to other rates or to the general state of the market. The occupancy rate is down considerably, but the owners are satisfied that they could not earn more (or less) by bringing their rate back to its historical relation to other rates. During the Great Depression, International Nickel, then a monopoly, did not bother to change the dollar price of nickel for eight full years, in spite of large reductions in costs and output.

**Time series implications**    This line of thought implies that output in sectors with constant marginal cost is close to indeterminate. If a shock depresses the output of a firm governed by the constant marginal cost hypothesis, there is no strong force tending to restore output to its previous level. The shock may depress profit, but the firm cannot raise profit by adjusting its price so as to raise its output. However, indeterminacy does not imply any particular time series behavior for output. A firm could choose to stabilize its output and let price absorb all shocks. Or, if it had market power, it could stabilize price and let quantity track shifts in demand. Both strategies would yield the same stream of profits. It is tempting to jump to the conclusion that price stabilization is the prevailing mode in industries with market power. The industries shown in table 1 to have market power seem to be ones where management sets a price and customers choose the quantity. However, the data on the time series properties of output by industry do not give strong support to that proposition. Table 3 shows the standard deviation and the serial correlation of the rate of growth of output of the industries in table 1.

Table 3
Statistics on the rate of change of output by industry, 1949–1978

| SIC code | Industry | Standard deviation | Serial correlation | Correlation with cylical industries |
|---|---|---|---|---|
| Meaningful estimates[a] | | | | |
| Substantial market power | | | | |
| 28 | Chemicals | 0.053 | −0.318 | 0.795 |
| 26 | Paper | 0.082 | −0.177 | 0.701 |
| 40 | Railroad transportation | 0.074 | −0.074 | 0.788 |
| 44 | Water transportation | 0.110 | −0.193 | 0.459 |
| 371 | Motor vehicles | 0.195 | −0.381 | 0.743 |
| 33 | Primary metals | 0.126 | −0.284 | 0.871 |
| 42 | Trucking and warehousing | 0.057 | −0.143 | 0.764 |
| Some market power | | | | |
| 32 | Stone, clay, and glass | 0.067 | −0.243 | 0.847 |
| 11 | Coal mining | 0.095 | −0.166 | 0.463 |
| 27 | Printing and publishing | 0.034 | 0.067 | 0.533 |
| 76 | Repair | 0.039 | 0.122 | 0.216 |
| 31 | Leather | 0.077 | −0.425 | 0.686 |
| 70 | Hotels and lodging | 0.038 | −0.072 | 0.365 |
| 39 | Miscellaneous | 0.052 | −0.400 | 0.765 |
| 36 | Electrical machinery | 0.089 | 0.119 | 0.881 |
| 48 | Communications | 0.020 | −0.250 | 0.426 |
| 30 | Rubber | 0.092 | −0.044 | 0.861 |
| 35 | Nonelectrical machinery | 0.092 | 0.057 | 0.766 |
| 34 | Fabricated metals | 0.077 | −0.090 | 0.945 |
| 25 | Furniture | 0.090 | −0.222 | 0.799 |
| 23 | Apparel | 0.053 | 0.061 | 0.759 |
| 38 | Instruments | 0.073 | 0.127 | 0.804 |
| 95 | Total nondurables | 0.038 | −0.111 | 0.888 |
| 96 | Total durables | 0.083 | −0.102 | 0.987 |
| Little market power | | | | |
| 15 | Construction | 0.051 | 0.211 | 0.709 |
| 22 | Textiles | 0.074 | 0.126 | 0.640 |
| 24 | Lumber | 0.085 | 0.103 | 0.622 |
| 7 | Agricultural services | 0.052 | −0.281 | 0.313 |
| 372 | Other transportation equipment | 0.125 | 0.590 | 0.417 |
| 62 | Security and commodity brokers | 0.067 | 0.334 | 0.273 |
| Unreliable estimates[b] | | | | |
| 10 | Metal mining | 0.108 | −0.370 | 0.443 |
| 45 | Air transportation | 0.065 | 0.445 | 0.613 |
| 483 | Radio and TV broadcasting | 0.065 | 0.116 | 0.127 |
| 78 | Motion pictures | 0.068 | 0.232 | 0.270 |
| 20 | Food and beverages | 0.033 | −0.212 | 0.554 |
| 21 | Tobacco | 0.051 | −0.087 | −0.028 |
| 52 | Retail trade | 0.028 | −0.140 | 0.734 |

Table 3 (continued)

| SIC code | Industry | Standard deviation | Serial correlation | Correlation with cylical industries |
|---|---|---|---|---|
| 50 | Wholesale trade | 0.030 | −0.145 | 0.726 |
| 81 | Legal services | 0.042 | 0.113 | −0.033 |
| 75 | Auto repair | 0.048 | 0.122 | 0.547 |
| 41 | Local and interurban transit | 0.048 | 0.213 | 0.246 |
| 79 | Amusement | 0.031 | 0.301 | 0.160 |
| 61 | Credit agencies | 0.030 | 0.487 | 0.496 |
| 49 | Utilities | 0.032 | 0.145 | 0.169 |
| 13 | Oil and gas extraction | 0.039 | 0.090 | 0.661 |
| 64 | Insurance agents | 0.029 | 0.041 | 0.559 |
| 1 | Farms | 0.034 | −0.503 | −0.380 |
| 14 | Nonmetallic minerals | 0.051 | −0.126 | 0.777 |
| 46 | Pipelines | 0.051 | 0.210 | 0.651 |
| 73 | Business services | 0.035 | 0.059 | 0.519 |

Source: Author's estimates as described in text.
a. Standard error of the estimate of the markup ratio, $\mu$, is 1.0 or small.
b. Industries with too little cyclical variation to measure the markup ratio.

The standard deviation of the rate of change of output is a summary measure of the variability of output in an industry. Under competition, the equilibrium profit-maximizing level of output should rise along with capacity. This proposition would remain true even if there were shifts in demand, because the competitive industry operates at capacity and absorbs demand shifts through price variations. Only shifts in the capacity level of output could explain significant random variation in output growth in the competitive industry.[18] Table 3 does show a slight positive relation between market power and output instability, but plainly market power is not the prime determinant of instability. For example, output growth in durables has a standard deviation of 8.3 percent as against 3.8 percent in nondurables, even though measured market power is identical and substantial in both. Textiles is found to be a competitive industry, but its standard deviation is 7.4 percent. In fact, none of the industries found to be approximately competitive has smooth output growth. But those industries with the most market power do tend to have the most unstable output.

Another dimension of the time series behavior of output is the duration of departures from equilibrium. The second column of table 3 shows a simple measure of persistence, the serial correlation of the rate of change of output. A serial correlation of zero means that output is a trended random walk. Shocks are infinitely persistent; there is no tendency for an increase in one year to be followed by a decrease in the following year as output returns to its equilibrium level. Negative serial correlation means that shocks are temporary. The recent literature on random-walk components of macroeconomic variables has called attention to the importance of the serial correlation of the first difference of output.[19] For total real GNP the serial correlation is roughly zero. The market power—excess capacity hypothesis is consistent with random-walk behavior of output but does not mandate it. Table 3 shows quite clearly that output is more like a random walk in competitive industries than in those with market power. All of the industries found to have substantial market power have negative serial correlations of output changes. Only one of the competitive industries shows a negative serial correlation. A glance at the data for the industries with substantial market power shows why the serial correlation is negative. Each recession brings a large reduction in output. In the succeeding year, part, but not all, of that decline is usually reversed. These observations dominate the calculation of the serial correlation.

The fundamental identifying hypothesis of this line of research holds that productivity fluctuations are not a driving force in the business cycle. This hypothesis enables me to interpret the empirical findings of the paper as revealing that market power is extensive. Under the alternative hypothesis— that productivity shifts are the driving force of macroeconomic fluctuations —the results have just the opposite interpretation. To the extent that it is hypothesized that productivity is procyclical, there is less room for market power to explain the same facts. At the polar extreme, if all observed productivity fluctuations are taken to be exogenous driving forces, then there is an implicit assumption of pure competition.

The third column of table 3 presents a rough test of the hypothesis that productivity shifts are not a driving force in aggregate fluctuations, based on the following logic: suppose the hypothesis is wrong. The origin of what we observe as the cycle is basically durables and construction. The cycle must be driven by productivity shifts in those industries. In years when productivity is low and the economy is in recession, labor should move out of those industries and into unrelated industries. Output in those industries should rise as a result. The competitive real business cycle model seems to require that at least some industries should be countercyclical. Column 3 shows that essentially every industry is procylical. The only industry with a meaningfully negative correlation with the cyclical industries is farming.

The only way to save the real business cycle view is to appeal to a systematic tendency for productivity shifts to occur simultaneously in the same direction in most sectors. The data are inconsistent with the notion that the cycle has its origin in productivity shifts in the most cyclical industries and that other sectors merely respond to those shifts.

The negative correlation for farming has another implication, unfavorable to the real business cycle view as well: the one common influence on productivity on which we can all agree is the weather. Probably the bulk of the fluctuations in real output in farming are the result of changes in the weather. Hence, farming serves as a proxy for the influence of weather on all industries. But the negative cyclical correlation of farm output casts doubt on the one reasonable influence that operates across all industries.

## Conclusions

The findings of this paper support a view about the operation of product markets in the U.S. economy that is consistent with the observed pattern of large, persistent movements in aggregate real output. However, the view is anything but firmly established. In essence, the view is that many industries are in equilibrium along a flat part of each firm's marginal cost schedule. The rents associated with efficient use of resources, with equilibrium on a steeper part of marginal cost, would attract additional entry. A firm with constant marginal cost is virtually indifferent to alternative levels of output. When output is 10 or 20 percent below the profit-maximizing point, profit is only a few tenths of a percent below its maximum, as a proportion of sales.

With extremely weak incentives to restore previous levels of output, it is no mystery that industries and the entire economy can undergo large and persistent fluctuations in output. This insight does not lead to accurate predictions about movements in output and the corresponding movements in prices. Rather, it supplies the answer to the question that has acutely troubled disequilibrium business cycle theorists for the past two decades: how are sluggish price adjustment and large output fluctuations consistent with rational economic behavior?

All of the conclusions of this paper follow from the fact that total factor productivity is procyclical. The measures of the markup coefficient are no more than an interpretation of that fact. And the conclusions about excess costs are based entirely on the interpretation that procyclical productivity reveals market power.

The competing explanation for procyclical productivity appears in the active and growing literature on real business cycles. According to this view, exogenous productivity shifts, positively correlated across industries, are a prime moving force in the business cycle. Consequently, productivity growth and output growth are positively correlated in each industry. Real business cycle theorists tend to assume competition, and this assumption is consistent with my results: if cyclical shifts in productivity are an important reason for the procyclical behavior of productivity, market power must be correspondingly less important.

As the evidence now stands, one has a choice between these two very different views, both consistent with the principal evidence. Prior beliefs about the plausibility of large exogenous shocks in productivity are the primary basis upon which the choice has to be made. My own view is that productivity shocks, in the narrow sense of shifts of production functions, are not an important source of aggregate fluctuations. Hence, I believe that the observed procyclical behavior of measured productivity is in some considerable part the result of market power. Moreover, I think that the finding of market power in many industries opens up avenues of explanation of the vulnerability of total output to many other types of shocks, including shifts in the terms of trade, spontaneous shifts in consumption and investment, and changes in government policy.

## Acknowledgments

This research is part of the National Bureau of Economic Research's program on economic fluctuations. I am grateful to Michael Knetter and David Bizer for outstanding assistance. The National Science Foundation supported this work. Data for this study are available from the author.

## Notes

1. Edward Hastings Chamberlin, *The Theory of Monopolistic Competition* (Harvard University Press, 1933).

2. Robert Hall, "The Relation between Price and Marginal Cost in U.S. Industry" (working paper E-86-24, Hoover Institution, Stanford University, June 1986). An earlier version appeared as working paper 1785 (National Bureau of Economic Research, January 1986).

3. Robert M. Solow, "Technical Change and the Aggregate Production Function," *Review of Economics and Statistics*, vol. 39 (August 1957), pp. 312–320.

4. See Hall, "Relation between Price and Marginal Cost," pp. 7–9, for the details.

5. Hall, "Relation between Price and Marginal Cost," pp. 10–13.

6. Most of the industries are at the two-digit SIC level; some are groups of two-digit industries and some are three-digit or groups of three-digit industries. The grouped industries are coal mining (code 11 in tables, SIC codes 11 and 12), other transportation equipment (372 in tables, SIC codes 372–379), farms (1 in tables; SIC codes 1 and 2), agricultural services (7 in tables, SIC codes 7, 8, and 9), construction (15 in tables, SIC codes 15, 16, and 17), wholesale trade (50 in tables, SIC codes 50 and 51), and retail trade (52 in tables, SIC codes 52–57).

7. And the school is based far to the east of Chicago. See William J. Baumol, John C. Panzar, and Robert D. Willig, *Contestable Markets and the Theory of Industry Structure* (Harcourt, Brace, Jovanovich, 1982).

8. Chamberlin, *The Theory of Monopolistic Competition*; Michael Spence, "Product Selection, Fixed Costs, and Monopolistic Competition," *Review of Economic Studies*, vol. 43 (June 1976), pp. 217–235; and Avinash K. Dixit and Joseph E. Stiglitz, "Monopolistic Competition and Optimum Product Diversity," *American Economic Review*, vol. 67 (June 1977), pp. 297–308.

9. Robert E. Hall, "Chronic Excess Capacity in U.S. Industry" (working paper 1973, National Bureau of Economic Research, July 1986).

10. Robert E. Hall and Dale W. Jorgenson, "Tax Policy and Investment Behavior," *American Economic Review*, vol. 57 (June 1967), pp. 391–414; Dale W. Jorgenson and Martin A. Sullivan, "Inflation and Corporate Capital Recovery," in Charles R. Hulten, ed., *Depreciation, Inflation, and the Taxation of Income from Capital* (Washington, D. C.: Urban Institute, 1981), pp. 171–237.

11. See Martin Eichenbaum and Kenneth J. Singleton, "Do Equilibrium Real Business Cycle Theories Explain Postwar U.S. Business Cycles?" in Stanley Fischer, ed., *NBER Macroeconomics Annual 1986*, pp. 91–135.

12. Research in progress by Jeffrey Miron has shown directly that fluctuations in temperature and precipitation have almost no relation to output by state and industry.

13. See Hall, "Relation between Price and Marginal Cost," pp. 36–41, for a formal demonstration of this point.

14. Jon A. Fay and James L. Medoff, "Labor and Output over the Business Cycle: Some Direct Evidence," *American Economic Review*, vol. 75 (September 1985), pp. 638–655.

15. Oliver Hart, "A Model of Imperfect Competition with Keynesian Features," *Quarterly Journal of Economics*, vol. 97 (February 1982), pp. 109–138. Another important paper is Martin L. Weitzman, "Increasing Returns and the Foundations of Unemployment Theory," *Economic Journal*, vol. 92 (December 1982), pp. 787–804.

16. Walter P. Heller, "Coordination Failure under Complete Markets with Applications to Effective Demand" (University of California, San Diego, August 1985).

17. George A. Akerlof and Janet L. Yellen, "A Near-Rational Model of the Business Cycle, with Wage and Price Inertia," *Quarterly Journal of Economics*, vol. 100 supplement (1985), pp. 823–838; Olivier J. Blanchard and Nobuhiro Kiyotaki, "Monopolistic Competition, Aggregate Demand Externalities, and Real Effects of Nominal Money" (working paper 1770, National Bureau of Economic Research, December 1985); N. Gregory Mankiw, "Small Menu Costs and Large Business Cycles: A Macroeconomic Model of Monopoly," *Quarterly Journal of Economics*, vol. 100 (May 1985), pp. 529–539; and Julio J. Rotemberg and Garth Saloner, "The Relative Rigidity of Monopoly Pricing" (working paper 1943, National Bureau of Economic Research, June 1986).

18. If capacity changes abruptly from year to year, a competitive industry could show considerable fluctuations in the rate of growth of output. To check this point, I calculated the standard deviation of the rate of growth of the output-capital ratio for each of the industries. In competition, this ratio would remain nearly stable over time. In fact, the standard deviations of the rates of growth of output and the output-capital ratio are almost the same in each industry. Irregular capacity growth is not the explanation of irregular output growth.

19. Charles R. Nelson and Charles I. Plosser, "Trends and Random Walks in Macroeconomic Time Series: Some Evidence and Implications," *Journal of Monetary Economics*, vol. 10 (September 1982), pp. 139–162; John Y. Campbell and N. Gregory Mankiw, "Are Output Fluctuations Transitory?" (working paper 1916, National Bureau of Economic Research, May 1986).

# Contributors to Volume 1

George A. Akerlof, University of California at Berkeley
Laurence Ball, Princeton University
Olivier J. Blanchard, Massachusetts, Institute of Technology
Andrew S. Caplin, Columbia University
Dennis W. Carlton, University of Chicago, Business School
Stephen G. Cecchetti, Ohio State University
Gary Fethke, University of Iowa
Stanley Fischer, Massachusetts Institute of Technology
Robert E. Hall, Stanford University
Oliver Hart, Massachusetts Institute of Technology
Nobuhiro Kiyotaki, University of Wisconsin
N. Gregory Mankiw, Harvard University
David Romer, University of California at Berkeley
Andrew Policano, State University of New York at Stony Brook
Daniel F. Spulber, University of Southern California
John Taylor, Stanford University
Janet L. Yellen, University of California at Berkeley

# Name Index